LABOR AND COMMUNISM

*The Conflict that Shaped
American Unions*

This book was published for the Research Institute on International Change, Columbia University, by Princeton University Press.

A list of other Institute publications appears at the back of this book.

LABOR AND COMMUNISM

*The Conflict that Shaped
American Unions*

BY BERT COCHRAN

PRINCETON UNIVERSITY PRESS
PRINCETON, NEW JERSEY

Copyright © 1977 by Princeton University Press
Published by Princeton University Press, Princeton, New Jersey
In the United Kingdom: Princeton University Press, Guildford, Surrey

All Rights Reserved

Library of Congress Cataloging in Publication Data will
be found on the last printed page of this book

This book has been composed in VIP Caledonia

Printed in the United States of America
by Princeton University Press, Princeton, New Jersey

Contents

LIST OF ILLUSTRATIONS AND TABLES   vii

PREFACE   ix

ABBREVIATIONS   xiii

ONE · *The Communist Party—Structure and Evolution*   3

TWO · *Decade of Failure*   20

THREE · *Red Unionism*   43

FOUR · *Who Gets the Bird?*   82

FIVE · *From Akron to Flint*   103

SIX · *Factionalism and Anti-Communism*   127

SEVEN · *Political Strikes in Defense Period*   156

EIGHT · *War Years—I*   196

NINE · *War Years—II*   229

TEN · *Communists vs. CIO, 1946-1947*   248

ELEVEN · *Showdown in Auto and Electrical Unions*   272

TWELVE · *CIO Purge and Aftermath*   297

THIRTEEN · *Postscript: Concepts of Labor Development*   332

APPENDIXES   345

NOTES   351

INDEX   387

Illustrations, following pages 102 and 228

1. Girl textile workers, Gastonia, N. C., attempt to disarm National Guardsman during 1929 strike. *Wayne State Labor Archives*

2. In 1934 textile general strike, pickets at Macon, Ga., overturn car in which three company officials sought to enter plant. *Wayne State Labor Archives*

3. Strikers, enveloped by tear gas, use paving stones to combat state troopers at Auto-Lite in Toledo. *Wayne State Labor Archives*

4. A section of the mile-long demonstration during the breakthrough Goodyear strike in Akron. *Wayne State Labor Archives*

5. In support of General Motors strikers, sit-downers settle in for the night at company supplying cotton stuffing for Chevrolet and Buick cars. *UPI*

6. Ford Company service men beat up Richard Frankensteen at River Rouge, May 1937, after union representatives tried to distribute literature. *Wayne State Labor Archives*

7. Reuther and Frankensteen console each other after beating. *International News*

8. Lewis, flanked by Murray and Hillman, founding CIO convention, Pittsburgh, November 14-18, 1938. *Wayne State Labor Archives*

9. Automobile tie-up employed to block access to Ford River Rouge plant, April 1941. *Wayne State Labor Archives*

10. Sixteen thousand UE members walk out at Westinghouse plant in East Pittsburgh, April 1951, to protest suspension of a shop steward. *Pittsburgh Sun-Telegraph*

11. Communist-led group demonstrates against Curran administration of National Maritime Union, 1948. *Federated Press*

12. Police intervene in battle between AFL Seamen and CIO Marine Cooks and Stewards at a San Francisco pier in 1953. *San Francisco Call Bulletin*

13. Harry Bridges (right), International Longshoremen's president, before a House Labor subcommittee in connection with a West Coast dock strike. *UPI*

14. John Bugas, for Ford Motor Company, and Walter Reuther, for UAW, at contract-signing, June 1955, that first established the Supplemental Unemployment Benefit Plan. *Wayne State Labor Archives*

TABLES, pages 165 and 166

1. Communist-Led-Strike Disputes Certified to National Defense Mediation Board, March-November 1941.

2. Communist-Threatened-Strike Disputes Certified to National Defense Mediation Board, March-November 1941.

Preface

THERE is a marked discontinuity in the history of American radicalism because radicalism has never established itself at the center of the country's politics, and its organizations peter out in the dry seasons. When this is coupled with the Americans' cultural trait of a short memory span, it is little wonder that the present generation of students has difficulty in grasping the special position occupied by Communists in a previous period. There exists some vague perception of a 1930s phenomenon of an important Communist movement, but it is like a ghost out of a world that is no more. Yet a mere twenty-five and thirty years ago, American Communism was on the priority list of concerns of government officials and newspaper editors, and the topic of endless discussions at both workingmen's bars and middle-class cocktail parties. When we consider that the influence of Communists, and of liberal tolerance of Communists, were expunged in a major convulsion that shook up American institutions and attitudes—the aftereffects of which have still not died out—and that the labor movement was probably the single most important battleground of that internal cold war, the significance of a study on this subject falls into proper place.

I have thought for some time that there was strong need for a book on American Communism and the unions, that a crucial piece of recent history had been unjustifiably left to the propagandists, that this was a gap in the literature that should be filled. The project set up by the Fund for the Republic in the mid-fifties under the editorship of Clinton Rossiter to assess the influence of Communism in American life led to the publication of several excellent volumes, but although the labor topic was included and assigned to two scholars, for one or another reason, that study was never written. All this time, in a desultory way, I have been gathering materials on these matters, thinking of writing at some indefinite point an article or several articles, not a full-scale study. It was only when, by a turn of circumstances, I was granted recently both the time and backing that I marshaled my researches and materials and set to work to write this book.

I held a number of offices in the auto union as a younger man and participated in some of the events covered here. Although my opinions have inevitably been affected by these experiences, and have taken their present shape in later cogitations, reconsiderations, reevaluations of them, this is in no sense a memoir. I have written a work of general analysis that depends only incidentally on personal encounters. It rests rather on the kind of sources, printed and in manuscript, to which a historian customarily refers. Of course, I had many discussions in the fifties with different union officials, shop committeemen, stewards, on many of the themes covered in the book, and kept memos on a number of these discussions. I was able to review this history in the light of the present with a dozen of these same officials when pursuing my recent researches. But in no case have I used information—even where it rang absolutely true to me—that could not be substantiated by some documentary material or trustworthy independent corroboration. These discussions, past and present, gave me a stock of colorful incidents (unfortunately, I could not use many of them), a more sensitive reading of the changing temper of unions, an authoritative statement of how union officials view the postwar struggles that brought most of them to prominence. In all candor, however, I doubt that the text would have been substantially different than it is had I relied exclusively on documentation.

I have tried to follow conscientiously the traditional rules of investigation: to keep burrowing for the relevant facts whether they support or contradict one's own preconceptions and to follow the facts where they appear to lead; to try to get the sense of an epoch as the data unfolds that epoch's contours. I am well aware that as soon as an investigator goes beyond a simple stringing together of elementary facts to bring out causalities and inner relationships, his own judgments determine the selection and ordering of the material and the criteria of relevance and emphasis. I make no secret of this; I have candidly acknowledged my interpretations and supplied the basis for them. I proceed nonetheless from the belief that history can be written within conventionally conceived norms of accuracy, balance, and professional conscientiousness. There is a difference between evaluations that flow from the data, and whose justification is in evidence that can be checked, and pronouncements that are imposed by main force on the events.

I was faced with a decision on structure before putting pen to paper. There could be a methodical exploration of the main subdivisions bearing on the subject, e.g., ideologies and ideological conflicts in early labor history, industry-by-industry consideration of Communist boring-from-within and of red unionism, chronological accounts of Communist strategies and institutional progress in most of the sixteen to eighteen unions in which they had significant influence after the formation of the CIO, etc. Such a study would necessarily take on encyclopedic dimensions and was ruled out on grounds of practicality: no publisher would consent to print it (and very few readers would have the temerity to wade into it). If the study was kept to a reasonable length under the same schema, it would perforce take on the character of an inventory, not an analysis. Since what was contemplated was an interpretative history that made manifest the dynamics of the conflict and the inner character of the principals in a changing political environment, the decision went in favor of a text in which attention was centered on key situations in the national CIO and several of the more important industrial unions. Data from other unions was introduced on selective principles to delineate major tendencies or problems in the sequential series of struggles and alliances that went on over a period of three decades. The gain in depth and perspective more than made up for the loss in extensity of detail.

It is a pleasure to acknowledge the assistance that I received in writing this book. My thanks go to Zbigniew Brzezinski, director of the Research Institute on International Change at Columbia University for the senior fellowship that he and his colleagues on the administrative board awarded me beginning with the fall semester of 1973, and for his unfailing consideration during the period of my residence. I am indebted to Sophia Sluzar, the administrative assistant director, for providing services beyond the call of duty. A salute is due to the graduate students attached to the institute during my stay who tracked down all sorts of information for me, and to Susan Gewirth and Reet Varnick for their care in typing the manuscript and in providing secretarial help.

I am not listing the names of the union officials, including several ex-Communist union officials, who gave so generously of their time and knowledge, because I pledged to several of them when interviews were first arranged that the conversations would be for background only. I have concluded that to name some and not others might lead to misunderstanding; so I have sent all of them my thanks privately and explained the reasons for my reticence.

I am under obligation to John Gates, Joseph R. Starobin, George Blake Charney, Al Richmond, and Dorothy Healy for giving me their impressions of aspects of the Communist movement; to Philip J. Jaffe for making some documentation available to me from his extensive private library; to Theodore Draper for permission to examine his collection at the Hoover Institution on War, Revolution, and Peace; to B. J. Widick for details on the rubber union in the forties; to William Browder for permission to read Earl Browder's transcript at the Columbia University oral history division; to the late Russell Nixon, former legislative director of the electrical union, and when I talked to him, professor of social work at Columbia University, for information on the union's inside workings; and to Sol Dollinger for interviewing a number of people on my behalf.

Irving Bernstein of the University of California at Los Angeles, Albert A. Blum of the University of Texas at Austin, Sidney Fine of the University of Michigan, and Walter Galenson of Cornell University, read part or all of the manuscript. I appreciate their comments and criticisms, very helpful in preparing the final draft of the manuscript—for which, naturally, I assume sole responsibility.

Abbreviations

ACTU	Association of Catholic Trade Unionists
ACW	Amalgamated Clothing Workers of America
ADA	Americans for Democratic Action
AFL	American Federation of Labor
ALP	American Labor Party
BLS	Bureau of Labor Statistics
CGT	Confédération Générale du Travail
CGTU	Confédération Générale du Travail Unitaire
CIO	Committee for Industrial Organization
	Congress of Industrial Organizations
Citizens	National Citizens Political Action Committee
COPE	Committee on Political Education
CP	Communist Party of the United States
ECA	European Cooperation Administration
ECCI	Executive Committee, Communist International
Electrical union (AFL)	International Brotherhood of Electrical Workers
FE	United Farm Equipment and Metal Workers Union
FEPC	Fair Employment Practices Committee
Food and Tobacco	Food, Tobacco, Agricultural and Allied Workers Union
FWIU	Food Workers Industrial Union
Fur	International Fur and Leather Workers Union
GM	General Motors Corporation
GPU	Gosudarstvennoe Politicheskoe Upravlenie (Soviet political police agency)
Hotel and Restaurant (AFL)	Hotel and Restaurant Employees and Bartenders International Union
IAM	International Association of Machinists and Aerospace Workers
ICC-ASP	Independent Citizens Committee of the Arts, Sciences, and Professions

Abbreviations

ILD	International Labor Defense
ILG	International Ladies Garment Workers' Union
ISU	International Seamen's Union
IUE	International Union of Electrical, Radio and Machine Workers
IWA	International Woodworkers of America
IWO	International Workers Order
IWW	Industrial Workers of the World
Longshore union	International Longshoremen's and Warehousemen's Union
MESA	Mechanics Educational Society of America
Mine Mill	Mine, Mill and Smelter Workers Union
MWIU	Marine Workers Industrial Union
NAACP	National Association for the Advancement of Colored People
NAM	National Association of Manufacturers
NLRB	National Labor Relations Board
NMU	National Maritime Union
NRA	(shortened form for NIRA) National Industrial Recovery Act
NTW	National Textile Workers Union
Office union	United Office and Professional Workers Union
OIAA	Office of Inter-American Affairs
OPA	Office of Price Administration
OPM	Office of Production Management
PAC	Political Action Committee (CIO)
PCA	Progressive Citizens of America
Profintern	Russian acronym for Red trade union international
Rubber union	United Rubber, Cork, Linoleum and Plastic Workers of America
SMWIU	Steel and Metal Workers Industrial Union
Steel union	United Steelworkers of America
SWOC	Steel Workers Organizing Committee
TUEL	Trade Union Educational League
TUUL	Trade Union Unity League
UAW	International Union, United Automobile, Aerospace and Agricultural Implement Workers of America
UE	United Electrical, Radio and Machine Workers of America
UMW	United Mine Workers of America
WLB	War Labor Board

LABOR AND COMMUNISM

*The Conflict that Shaped
American Unions*

ONE · *The Communist Party—Structure and Evolution*

WHEN the conflict between the United States and Soviet Russia grew into a cold war in the late 1940s, the American Communist party found itself inevitably in the eye of the storm. Within a few years, the cumulative effect of denunciations, proscriptions, administrative sanctions, and judicial convictions, was the quasi-illegalization of the Party, and the removal of all but a handful of its effectives from leading positions in the labor movement. It is outside the scope of this study to catalog the major episodes of a campaign that, as it intensified, became a witch hunt and, in its McCarthyite phase, sought to engulf liberalism and the Democratic party itself.[1] What is relevant for understanding the effects of such a campaign on the labor movement is the rationale with which liberals and unionists sought to justify inquisitional pursuits that reversed or drastically revised their traditional libertarian concerns, particularly since it was this rationale that animated the "vital center" of American politics for two decades, and set the labor movement in the mold of the conservative fifties.

An authoritative statement of the liberal position was drawn up by Justice Robert H. Jackson when the United States Supreme Court ruled favorably on the constitutionality of the non-Communist affidavit clause of the Taft-Hartley Act.[2] Sidney Hook, a leading cold war ideologist, codified and widened the application of these and related appreciations in a vigorous polemic, *Heresy, Yes; Conspiracy, No*, which became something of a credo of anti-Communist intellectuals.[3] (The different nuances in the two do not affect the basics.) The Jackson-Hook thesis—if a thesis that was fathered and nurtured by dozens of authors from Reinhold Niebuhr on down can be so designated—had the simplicity and force of a Euclidian axiom, and its validity seemed as self-evident at the time to the liberal public. Its main propositions, in bare outline, sought to establish the following: (1) The Communist party is not an authentic party, not a legitimate association of heretics, not like past extremist oppositions to the established order. It is, in fact, "a conspiratorial and revolutionary junta," and seeks by means of duplicity, chicanery, false

3

fronts, and underhanded strategems to subvert the democratic order. Through systematic infiltration it captures a wide variety of private organizations—notably the labor unions—in order to impose policies alien to their purposes. This is a conspiracy that cannot be tolerated without its leading to the stultification of liberal society. (2) The Communist party alone among American parties past or present is controlled by and subservient to a foreign government. The Party "is not native to this country and its beginnings here were not an effort of Americans to answer American problems." The Party adopts the terroristic and undemocratic techniques of a cabal since it has no hope of winning over the American people through persuasion. It fears open and honest confrontation of ideas. Wherever Communists seize control of government, they convert the country into a satellite and vassal of the Soviet Union. A Communist victory spells the end of liberal civilization and with it the right to heresy and dissent. (3) Every member of the Communist party is an agent of its purposes. Every member works under an "ironclad discipline" to carry out the Party's dictates and directions. Members are admitted only after they are effectively indoctrinated, tested for reliability, and totally committed. For any deviation or refusal to carry out orders they are summarily purged. Since membership excludes those who are inactive or in disagreement with the line or directives of the party on any question, there are no noncombatants or innocents.[4]

This was the thesis, and like so many ideological pronouncements, it combined the true and false, and was shaped decidedly by the social and political imperatives of the period. Some liberals who had made fools of themselves in the popular-front decade by denying that Communists were manipulated by the Kremlin, or by offering solemn assurances that Stalin's Russia was a special form of populist democracy, now swung to the other extreme in tropistic response to changed stimuli, to describe the Communist movement as essentially a ring of foreign agents. Others concluded that since our society was engaged in a kind of war, then the rules of war must apply; that the need of the hour was for unabashed advocates, not fussy pedants. Whether they subscribed to the more extreme dictums that in the new era of psychological warfare the Holmes-Brandeis test of "clear and present danger" had to be discarded in favor of a more dynamic doctrine enabling a free society to stop a foreign subversive agency before it showed up as a palpable danger (by which time it would probably be too late for the free society to

4

save itself); or whether they maintained that while there must be swift punishment of all who disobeyed the statutes, the free society could adequately protect itself within the framework of its traditional laws and customs—they were all part of the consensus in the anti-Communist camp that viewed the Communist movement as a fifth column. Thus, their attention shifted imperceptibly away from illegal activities and acts toward dangerous thoughts and unpopular associations. Due process and the Holmes-Brandeis maxims bent perforce before the storms of anti-Communism.[5]

2

A quarter century has elapsed since the issuance of these papers and pronouncements, the anxieties of the cold war have declined, passions have cooled, and some of the intellectual constructs that then seemed so solid and impregnable have succumbed to the corrosions of time and tide. Who talks about monolithic international Communism today? Tito struck the first crack in the structure—on the issue of national independence—at the very time that Jackson and Hook were writing their briefs.[6] A decade later came Communist China's breakaway destroying Moscow's hegemony of four decades; with that, beatitude and authority, as from Christianity in the ancient world, radiated from Sino-Byzantium as well as from Muscovite Rome. How many students of Communist movements would argue today that the program of world revolution pursued by Lenin and Trotsky in the first impassioned years of the Russian Revolution continued to determine Kremlin policy under Stalin and his successors? It took new big historical events to disprove or make obsolete parts of the cold war scripture; which is not to deny that much of the original text consisted of a slap-dash, tendentious working up of selected data for propaganda purposes.

At the heart of the analytical problem is whether the Communist party was a conspiracy or an authentic heretical association—and neither of the two embattled principals would or could countenance the third possibility that it might be both. We can now better observe the Hydra in its development, and just as Darwinism opened the door to understanding aberrant species in the study of biological phenomena, so a historical approach may help the investigator to lay bare the sociological character of a decidedly deviant order.

The American Communist party originated in the left wing of the Hillquit-Debs Socialist party, the transformation of the old left faction under the influence of the Bolshevik Revolution, and its sub-

5

sequent split from the parent body in 1919.[7] The founding leaders and members of the Communist movement were neither agents sent over to this country by the Russians, nor a collection of adventurers attracted to occupations associated with espionage, sabotage, industrial violence, or international intrigue; nor did they comprise a militarist or Blanquist camarilla designing plots for a coup d'état. They were, in fact, typical members of a millenarian sect (at first, of two competing millenarian sects), bickering zealots, ideologues, extremists, romantics, firebrand militants and saints, unworldly dreamers and worldly egotists, utopians and would-be world-saviors and men of destiny; in other words, the not uncommon conglomeration of humanity that made up world-sanctifying movements from the 1848 revolutions onwards. What was special about this particular sect was that its inspirers pushed to hitherto unprecedented extremes the rhetorical shrillness, factional contentiousness, and those elements of unreal metapolitics traditional in American left-wing circles, because they were intoxicated by the heady wine that the socialist's dream had at last come true in Russia, and that its realization was inevitable and near even in the forbidding environment of capitalist America. They worshipped at the Russian shrine with the naive adoration of young novices to whom had been revealed the true path of their own destiny.

This should not be taken to mean that the Communists were primarily an assortment of eccentrics and neurotics whose enthusiasm was totally unrelated to anything going on in the larger society. The Russian Revolution whipped up a chiliastic storm throughout war-shattered Europe. In the initial years, a galaxy of intellectuals, including some of the brilliant minds and talents of the day, proclaimed their conversion, while considerable sections of the labor movements of Germany, France, Italy, and the Scandinavian countries, adhered to the Communist camp. To many, Communism was the only firm ground to stand on amidst a dying civilization that had torn itself apart in an insane war of mass carnage; the only beacon of hope in a morally bankrupt order in which even Socialists had abandoned their international professions to side with their own belligerents. Now the star of Bethlehem had risen again in the East. Not since the French Revolution were the golden portals of the New Jerusalem glimpsed so clearly by so many. Even in the faraway United States, where politics meant arid electoral contests between Democrats and Republicans, where a hack politician like Harding, calling for a return to "normalcy," was to be sent to the

6

White House in a landslide vote—enthusiasm for the Bolshevik cause was unbounded at first among politicized intellectuals, dissenting liberals, and left laborites. Eugene Debs, the perennial Socialist presidential standard-bearer, proclaimed, "From the crown of my head to the soles of my feet I am Bolshevik, and proud of it." John Reed's *Ten Days that Shook the World* became an authoritative civics text of the new society; and Lincoln Steffens' catch phrase, "I have been over into the future, and it works," became an aphorism. The early American Communists lived and worked in a sympathetic milieu far larger than their own orbit of influence, even though that milieu was unrepresentative of the country's political environment.[8]

It is true that early Communist membership was overwhelmingly of foreign origin, but given the character of the national population, that did not make the Communist party an alien intrusion. According to the 1920 census the percentage of foreign born in major ethnic groups ranged from over a quarter among Germans, to over a half among Jews, Hungarians, Lithuanians, and Letts, to over 90 percent among Bulgarians. Louis Fraina (who later wrote under the name of Lewis Corey) reported to the Communist International in the same year that foreigners accounted for 60 percent of the American industrial proletariat. The U.S. Immigration Commission used the same figure in its 1911 report for wage earners in 21 principle branches of industry, and reported that another 17 percent were the children of immigrants. Even the IWW (Industrial Workers of the World), described by labor historians as a pure emanation of native radicalism, had a membership that was largely foreign-born.[9]

The proximate cause for this lopsided ethnic composition was the Communist movement's issuing out of the Socialist left wing; by 1919, the Socialist party's foreign-language federations accounted for over half the total members. These federations grew most rapidly in response to the party's opposition to the war, and in the great excitement over the Russian Revolution in left ranks. It might therefore be inferred that the appeal of the revolution was primarily to the foreign-born and not the native American. This argument cuts across other statistics: most leaders of the American Communist movement were native Americans, some with forebears going back many years; and foreign-born Russians, Italians, Jews, etc. who were Communists made up an insignificant percentage of

7

their own ethnic communities. This would suggest that the restricted data supplied by a very small social movement is inadequate for a broad sociological generalization. What is more cogent, at any rate, is that in origin the American Communist party was in the line of the country's historic Left.

Then, for the next half century, even after the Party had become thoroughly Stalinized at the end of the twenties, and its uncritical enthusiasm for the Russians had been transformed into abject slavishness in following Kremlin dictates, the overwhelming mass of the Party's activities consisted of holding meetings, organizing demonstrations and rallies, issuing newspapers and publications, gathering signatures, running candidates and subscription campaigns, raising funds, recruiting new members, and the like. In other words, it was engaged in the usual round of activities associated with Marxian or other left-wing organizations; it was appealing to the public and trying to recruit members to its cause as an American radical organization of a Marxian type. In the four decades from the time of its formation to the time of its disintegration, the violence with which the Communist movement was generally associated was the traditional sort that arose out of bitterly fought industrial strikes, or from public demonstrations and marches, not in plots to seize government installations, blow up arsenals, or assassinate public figures. When Communist leaders were tried for violation of the Smith Act—the Alien Registration Law of 1940—the testimony against them was of advocating violence in study classes and lectures for the organization of a revolution at some indeterminate future date, not of hatching current plots. When, in the sixties, there actually occurred outbreaks of sabotage, shootings, bombing of banks and public buildings, these were practiced by a new generation of insurgents who were unconnected with, and contemptuous of, the Communists, and from whom the Communists kept studiously aloof.

There remains the possibility that the Communists' public activity was a false front to gull the public. They could have been manipulating, by means of secret caucuses and cells, all sorts of front groups and penetrated organizations in order to transform these into conveyors of Stalinist purposes. Did not those operations, of a conspiratorial or semi-conspiratorial type, actually define the inner nature of the Party's activities, regardless of how much time was apportioned between open and covert operations?

We are dealing with a twisted, convoluted organism whose work-

8

ings can be grasped only by understanding the motivations and "false consciousness" of its human components. Communist leaders knowingly accepted every instruction from Russia as Holy Writ, but they thought that the orders of Stalin and the historic interests of the American working class were in mystic harmony; better yet, that solidarity with the Soviet Union—as they defined it—enhanced the position of "progressive forces" everywhere to redound to the benefit and the strengthening of the American constituency. Without a doubt, these Communist leaders, entangled in the Byzantine intrigues of the Comintern and Cominform, housebroken by Stalinist drill masters, were not the same starry-eyed militants who had earlier embraced the Communist faith. The revolutionary zealot had become the revolutionary bureaucrat. But aside from the few who became outright cynics or misanthropes, Communist leaders did not view themselves as members of an antinational column with hostile intentions toward things American. In their own minds, they made up the dedicated general staff of the American working class, indefatigably guarding its true interests—"scientifically" understood.[10] Because they were members of a superior, incorruptible order, they could shrug off the attacks of the infidel world that called them agents and apologists for one of the bloodiest tyrannies of history, attacks that originated from unclean, untrustworthy sources.

For some analysts, the Party's connections with Soviet espionage appeared to clinch the case for considering the Party a conspiracy operating under a false front. The luridly publicized revelations of spy rings in the early fifties fixed in the popular mind the idea that the Communist party and Soviet espionage cells were an interlocking enterprise. Actually, the connection was peripheral, of less importance and consequence than the Communists' overall political subservience to the Moscow regime. The party per se did not engage in espionage. Soviet agents recruited at times among the ranks of members and sympathizers. Once a member was taken in tow he dropped out of the Party and dropped his former associations, as happened to Whittaker Chambers. Soviet espionage crews had to enforce a rigid separation for their own security reasons, even though they had no compunction in subjecting foreign parties to unwarranted risks with such raiding expeditions. Some top Party leaders were aware of these specialized activities; quite a few more probably had some inkling of them; and it is possible that one member of the secretariat had a specific assignment to maintain a liaison with a Soviet representative. Aside from these, neither the party leadership nor the membership knew about the goings-on; they were not a significant part of organization pursuits and preoccupations; even for those who were "witting" or "half-witting," it was a simple matter for people who had thought internationalism meant taking orders from Kremlin bureaucrats, to rationalize the rendering of such occasional "fraternal help" in the common cause.[11] Transposed into the language of political sociology, this is an example of the principle of internationalism colliding with the principle of nationalism—the internationalism, in this case, a make-believe for another, a foreign nationalism.

Does the Communists' self-image matter? We do not usually accept a person, particularly a political personality, at his evaluation of himself. In their case, its significance rested on the fact that it was the open party—led by domesticated bureaucrats, to be sure, but bureaucrats who considered themselves (and tried to act like) popular tribunes—that made its appeal to the interested public and enlisted adherents on the strength of its public claims and activities.[12] Certainly, the vast majority of members, recruited through all sorts of militant appeals for social justice, had to be convinced that the Party was living up to its public professions. One must keep in mind that although it was run on semi-militarist lines so far as determining policy was concerned, the Communist party is utterly unlike the United States Army or other military formations in one crucial respect. In the army, the recruit cannot quit, he cannot resign. If he deserts, he is subject to heavy sanctions. The organization can ordinarily be held together by a purely mechanical discipline.

In contrast, Communist members' adherence had to be ensured by inspirational arts. Of course, even voluntary organizations develop bullying techniques and institutional disciplines to forestall the lukewarm, the inattentive, the restless, from leaving the fold. In the Party, a relatively few depended on Communist support for their positions in unions or in special employments; a somewhat larger number, aware of the Party's vindictiveness toward backsliders, feared losing lifelong friends, undergoing social ostracism, or being villified by erstwhile associates. But these were ancillary measures to shore up the organization. For the general enrollee, there were no penalties for severing relations. When a member became aggrieved, disillusioned, or just bored, he could simply drop away—as over the years several hundred thousand did.[13] To prevent their party from becoming a perfect seive from which everything trickled out, that is, to make their operation possible and feasible, the Communist leaders had to convince their own ranks of the Party's bona fides. (And since they constituted a secular priesthood, it meant that by means of an interoffice theological reasoning, they had to convince themselves, as well.)

The way the Party was finally ripped apart in 1957 similarly shatters the construct of a monolithic, closed-in Communist phalanx hermetically sealed off from American society and its divers influences and lures, fixed exclusively on subverting American institutions for the advantage of its Kremlin superiors. Although the Party lost heavily in the course of the prosecutions and attacks of the cold-war years, its cadre remained substantially intact, and many who dropped away because of fear, retained their beliefs. What produced a disastrous faction fight and split that reduced the Party to another insignificant left sect was the Khrushchev revelations at the Russian Twentieth Party Congress. In other words, the Communists or at least, the majority of them, reacted—though belatedly—like disillusioned leftists, not operatives.

We are not concerned here that membership in the Party fulfilled psychic needs and gave emotional satisfactions; that the Party performed some of the functions of a secular church; that it provided a haven of certainty in an epoch of uncertainty; that it gave a promise of fraternity in a cold, impersonal world; that it infused the mediocre and insignificant personalities, or those deprived of opportunity for utilizing their talents, with the conviction and profound gratification that they were operating the machinery of history. None of this is unique to Communism. Other left-wing factions performed such functions, although in the case of the major ones, not in as caricatured a fashion. What is relevant to emphasize here is the voluntary nature and idealistic attractive power of this organization. In the main, it could not hold itself together and perform by inducements of patronage and material rewards, or by threats of punishment and banishment; it had to rely on the kind of appeals that other left-wing organizations employed.[14]

3

This suggests that he mistakes the nature of the beast who argues that every member of the Party was, or is, a conscious, disciplined agent. Such a conclusion can be drawn only by riveting attention on some of Lenin's essays, or on the rhetoric of party rules and regulations in the more fevered left periods, while ignoring the empirical evidence of the organization's actual behavior. In the Princeton study of Gabriel Almond and his collaborators, the answers to their questionnaire showed that almost three quarters of American respondents looked on the Party at the time of joining as a means of solving nonpolitical problems; that only 28 percent had any exposure to the classical writings of Communism (and this is a generous figure since any reference at all to having read or known about any of the writings put the respondent in this column). Many individuals deliberately avoided the doctrinal complexities. One remarked, "I didn't worry through the thick books on Marx. I joined the party when it moved a widow's evicted furniture back into her house. I thought it was right. That's why I joined."

Almond summarizes that almost all new recruits saw the party at the time of joining in terms of agitational slogans: as a means of fighting fascism or racial, ethnic, and religious discrimination, of gaining labor union objectives, general social improvement, or humanitarian socialist goals. Moreover, there was a deterioration in ideological interest in the popular-front period. Whereas 37 percent of the early recruits had been exposed to what Almond called the "esoteric goals," the figure was only 15 percent with the later joiners. Similarly, where 48 percent of the earlier recruits signed up for personal, nonpolitical reasons, the figure rose to 68 percent later on. Public opinion surveys, taken in 1954 in France and Italy, showed a similar trend "that adherence to, or sympathy for, the party are typically based on the party's agitational themes and not on knowledge of the doctrine of esoteric party practice."

When the individual walks past the portals, however, one might imagine he is then seized by the professional handlers, and subjected to a fierce, unrelenting indoctrination. Not according to Almond. Only 2 percent were sent to the Russian schools; 68 percent—over two thirds—either received no formal training, or described themselves as self-taught. Hence, Almond saw two levels of membership, an inner core of leaders and functionaries who were initiated into the mysteries of doctrine and practice, and the ranks caught up in the party's agitational net. He referred to these two levels as esoteric and exoteric susceptibility to communism, the extremes in the ideological continuum, with most members falling somewhere in between. He concluded that "only a minority of the party membership is fully aware of the integral power orientation of the party and of its relation to the Soviet Union. The rest of the party are dupes or half dupes."[15]

Since the Almond study was based on replies from a small number of ex-Communists, the percentages should be treated as suggestive indicators rather than firm figures. Similarly, one need not concur in the phrasing of Almond's conclusion, with its particular connotations, to be able to reject the model of the Communist party as a cabal of conspirators. Relying on his own observations in earlier years, and many exchanges with others on the Communist phenomenon, this writer would rework the conclusion thus:

Communist party members, including those who joined during the popular front, absorbed Communist exegetics, to one or another extent, through being steeped in the party atmosphere. While small study groups were not unusual, and members read or skimmed a pamphlet occasionally and glanced at the party press irregularly, the act of participating in an exclusive, supercharged society was the decisive education process. It is impossible to talk percentages, but many of the "exoterics" comprehended the exegesis. This was true both of the relatively educated union official who sometimes was of middle class origin and had some college education, and of the ethnic rank-and-filer who had been a factory worker all his life and spoke broken English. The emphasis and explanation may have varied, but adulation of the Soviet Union was a commonplace. For the more seasoned members, it was the socialist leader and model, and Stalin was in the direct line of apostolic succession. For some, it was the only reliable fighter against fascism. During the war, this latter attitude became intertwined with admiration for the Red Army, which was stopping Hitler and making it possible for the democracies to win. Still others were impressed with the Soviet Union's elimination of all racial and ethnic discrimination.[16] (A piece of self-deception resting on ignorance of Soviet nationalities practices—but there it was; and even old-time Jewish Communists successfully suppressed their misgivings during the Stalin-Hitler pact.)[17]

The distinction between "esoteric" and "exoteric" communicants can be accepted provided it is understood that the line of distinction was jagged, blurred, and shifting. The "esoterics" were no less victims of self-deception than the "exoterics," though they could verbalize their rationalizations on a more rarefied plane of sophistication. Almond's proposition that only a minority of the membership

13

was aware of the Party's relation to the Soviet Union should be re-
cast to read: Many or most of the rank and file knew that the Party
revered the Soviet Union and its leaders, that it believed Soviet policy to be a model of Marxism in action—and they accepted, with
varying degrees of interest and thought, the evaluation.

What they did not know was that their top leaders accepted directives from abroad as if they were hired hands; the initiated were
more apt to slither over the possibility that Kremlin-dictated policy
could conflict with American Communists' and American workers'
requirements. On this score, the line of demarcation between ini-
tiates and innocents was indistinct. Many second-line leaders, who
knew more about the workings of the Party and its relation to the
Comintern and Cominform than the innocents, so glued up their
brains with pseudo-Marxist explanations and abstruse formulae that
to all intents and purposes they were gulled no less than the ranks
they were misleading. Al Richmond, a party editor, after a 45-year
sojourn, and on the eve of his resignation, could compare the
American leaders' dependence on Moscow with Morris Hillquit's
reliance on German Socialists. The Khrushchev revelations, which,
aside from some details, told no more than was common knowledge
among the educated since the Moscow Trials, threw a sizable
number of top Communist officials—hardened by years of combat
and intrigue—into a state of shock, followed by breakaways and disillusionment.[18]

4

The Party made its greatest gains in influence and numbers in the
popular-front years, 1935-1939 and 1941-1945. In the latter span, as
soon as it concluded that nothing must stand in the way of uninterrupted production to help our beleaguered Russian ally, then the
Party turned super-patriotic. Exhibiting its customary trait of extremism in whatever cause or direction, and uninhibited by any restraining hand of the membership because of its authoritarian structure, the Party combined with a restricted populism peremptory
calls on working people for war sacrifices that made traditional leaders of moderate socialism appear like flaming Jacobins in comparison. To climax the wartime activities of tossing overboard article
after article of old ideological baggage that was hindering progress
toward complete national unity, the Party concluded that it was itself an impediment. Accordingly, in May 1944, the Party formally
dissolved itself, and the organization was reconstituted as the

14

Communist Political Association, "a non-partisan association of Americans" that "adheres to the principles of scientific socialism, Marxism," and "looks to the family of free nations, led by the great coalition of democratic capitalist and socialist states, to inaugurate an era of world peace, expanding production and economic well-being."[19] At this point, were one to evaluate the American Communist movement by its then current professions and campaigns, one would conclude that it stood to the right of Henry Wallace, Philip Murray, and Walter Reuther. If the Communist organization could have continued along this chosen path for another half-dozen years, it would have congealed into a party of the social-democratic type.

But it was not to be. As we know, the Duclos article appeared in April 1945 in the French Communist monthly magazine; Earl Browder, the national secretary, was castigated for revisionism and liquidationism—either one a mortal sin. The old hands of the Political Bureau grasped very quickly that this was a ukase delivered from the throne. They tumbled all over themselves to shape up for the new line. In the same unanimity with which they had dissolved the Communist party, they now reconstituted it. An emergency convention rewrote the constitution preamble, and adopted resolutions to make it clear that the Party was back on tested Marxist-Leninist-Stalinist rails, pledged to an uncompromising fight against the old familiar devils. How this was to be translated into a concrete platform was left somewhat ambivalent until the comrades could better fathom what the Moscow chancellery had in mind. As summed up by William Z. Foster, who was to inherit the mantle, the new "class struggle" document "outlined a militant win-the-war program; urged the workers to prepare for the difficult struggles of the postwar period; retained the sound Communist policy of building the Roosevelt coalition, and set out to strengthen it in a Leninist sense."[20]

It was this reconversion that was cited by government officials as proof that the Party had abandoned its popular-front program of achieving its objectives peaceably; that it signalized the setting up once again of a tightly disciplined, conspiratorial organization for violent pursuits. But in the many Smith Act trials of Communist national and second-string leaders from 1948 on—in effect, trials to outlaw the Communist party—the prosecution's case, be it noted, rested on the introduction of a number of Marxian classics as evidence of intent to forcibly overthrow the government, buttressed by the testimony of former members and FBI agents who validated that that was the true meaning and purpose of the classes and lectures at which these books were discussed or taught. The Communists were not charged with conspiracy to commit any overt revolutionary act; they were charged with conspiracy to form a party to advocate overthrow of the government. [21]

In 1950, the proverbial visitor from Mars, uninterested in the legal, constitutional, and civil libertarian ramifications, confining himself to an empirical examination of the Communist party, would have been struck by the strange carryings-on, and might have concluded that some revolutionary conspiracy was, in truth, being hatched. That year, the Party broke down its clubs into small units; written communications were reduced to a minimum; instructions were issued to destroy written materials after reading. In July 1951, the Party announced that all members who had not reregistered would be summarily dropped. This deliberate purging of the membership was carried through on the theory that only a battle-worthy outfit of the steeled and dedicated could ride through the stormy period ahead. No one knows how many were removed from the rolls. According to FBI estimates, the membership figure was 43,000 at the beginning of 1950, and 31,600 at the end of 1951. In the later self-criticism, the New York State organization secretary reported that in his state alone, a few thousand members were eliminated for "security reasons." [22]

The die was cast to set up an underground organization when the Supreme Court in June 1951 upheld the jailing of the eleven *Dennis* case Communist leaders. When the time came to surrender themselves, four of them had disappeared. While the Communist party continued as a public political organization, it was now directed by a shadow cabinet consisting of members on the run, or who sent in proposals from jail through intermediaries. Wrote Joseph Starobin, formerly foreign editor of the *Daily Worker*: "Vast sums of money, probably running into millions of dollars, were expended for the lodging, the transportation, and the conclaves of different cadres. Complex systems of couriers were set up. Attempts were made to study the techniques of the several thousand FBI agents who were involved in trying to keep track of this entirely new structure. . . . Conflict broke out in determining the authority of the different echelons; factions quickly formed as the normal restraint on Party behavior disappeared. . . . It quickly became evident that the FBI was well aware of this underground, and was following it closely."

16

This desperate exercise to outwit several thousand FBI agents and informers did not stem from a conspiracy to overthrow, or sabotage, or even disturb the government; it was the product of an egregious misreading of the political chart compounded by an accompanying hysteria brought on by the fear of being wiped out by triumphant reaction. Party leaders, mistrained systematically over the years to justify Stalinist peregrinations with logic-chopping, were not well placed to appraise their own situation and needs in the trying circumstances of the cold war.

From the time of the Duclos pronouncement, the American Communist leaders were living in a neurasthenic atmosphere where they were not sure whether war and fascism were generalized evils that might materialize in the fullness of time because of inherent contradictions of capitalism, or constituted imminent perils that the Party had to prepare for forthwith. Like a fevered patient tossing from side to side, the Party lurched from one position to the other, depending on the headlines of the day, and the signals that emitted from the Kremlin watchtower. Through all the oscillations, the Party fever kept rising progressively, however, under the lash of punitive proceedings from the outside; so that by the latter part of 1950, to quote Starobin, "after the passage of the McCarran Act, which proposed to prosecute the party as a 'foreign agent,' an atmosphere of near-panic had gripped the American communists. Offices had been closed down. Public activity had diminished and in some areas ceased. Important cadres had disappeared." It was the conviction that war and fascism were now on the agenda that led the Communist leaders to their ill-advised plunge to the storm cellar. It was a defensive move to ward off a blow; not a plot to deliver one.[23]

There was precious little antigovernment conspiring going on in the underground. Instead of underground rigors transforming the peacetime party into a paramilitary, battle-ready formation, the party began to devour itself in internal witch hunts against alleged deviationists, paralleling Stalinist purges of alleged Titoists in Eastern Europe. A related campaign to cleanse itself of what was denominated as "white chauvinism" wracked the ranks and spilled over into Communist-led unions and the American Labor party. At the moment of greatest peril from without, they were driven by Stalinist furies to destroy themselves from within.

Clearly, we are confronted with a travesty of a radical party, a contradictory creature with an obsession for caricaturing its own

17

conflicting impulses—structure at war with function, as if its creator, in a fit of absent-mindedness, proceeded to supply a lion with the instincts of a jackal. We have a set of officials ready and eager to defy the American government, with its not inconsiderable arsenal of weapons of repression, all the while poised to jump from one end of the political spectrum to the other at the behest of underlings speaking for the Kremlin. We have functionaries on marches and picket lines, braving death or years of imprisonment, trembling at a word of reproof from Russian-appointed overseers. A hermaphrodite had emerged from the formative years of travail, an organism that was both a Left party of dissent and an apparatus of conspiracy. Not primarily because it served as a sometime recruiting ground for Soviet espionage agents, as it undoubtedly did; nor because a few CP leaders had relations with Soviet espionage agents, as they probably did;[24] but above all, because the entire leadership from top to bottom had been carefully selected by a painstaking process of testing and training for subservience to the demands and designs of the Soviet officialdom. This was not a case of a party, with cold-blooded intent, supporting the position of a faction abroad for its own reasons and purposes. This was a case of a party leadership systematically acting for a faction abroad without reference to its own interests and needs. The 28-year relationship of the Communist parties with the Soviet oligarchs, beginning with Stalin's rule in 1928 until the Khrushchev revelation in 1956, unprecedented in the history of Left or Marxist movements, falls within the definition of a conspiracy in the laymen's understanding of the term; but it was a twisted conspiracy, since most members were unaware of the realities of the Moscow nexus. At the same time, when one appraises the totality of the American Communist operation, the element of conspiracy has to be considered overborne by the special character of this Left party (in fact, the preponderant Left party in America from the Great Depression to the mid-fifties). The subsequent assertions of independence by the Italian, French, and other Communist parties brought this into high relief: that the gyroscope of their selfhood was the mass dissenting party—which eventually led them to wriggle free from their vassalage to Moscow. Just as the Communist party could not be relegated to the customary category of either revolutionary or reformist party, so it could not be fitted into the Procrustean bed of standard criminal jurisprudence. Liberal and labor anti-Communists who propagated a monochromatic conspiracy theory implicitly recognized that they

18

were up against some kind of rebel formation when they admitted that the preferred way to beat Communism was to defeat the Communists democratically. Had the Party consisted of a nest of spies, no one would have thought that town-hall debates were in order.[25] For the same reason, it was impossible to conduct a generalized persecution of Communist activists without diminishing the civil liberties of other dissenters, and undermining society's liberal traditions.

TWO · *Decade of Failure*

IN Marxist doctrine the working class was the repository of revolutionary virtues. According to the sacred writings, this class was the chosen leader to propel the nation along the path of progress, the battering ram for the revolutionary overthrow of capitalism, the host disciplined in the production process, able and ready to battle the enemy in preparation for the great day. It was therefore self-evident that the Party, advance guard of the proletariat, had to be overwhelmingly proletarian in social composition; and since labor unions are the basic organizations of workers, that the Communist party had to have substantial influence, and eventually, the dominant position in these bodies. More time, effort, and attention was paid to workers' doings, labor strikes, trade-union intricacies and tactics, than to any other matters. Lacking representation in government legislatures, unions inevitably became for the Communists the major arena of preoccupation and ambition because of both ideology and circumstances.

Despite this extraordinary concentration of effort, the Communist record in the mid-thirties, before the CIO movement took hold, was abysmal. In the sixteen years since the formation of the Communist party (CP), its leaders had tried every conceivable variant and tactic, only to suffer crushing reverses. Were a labor student to write on Communist activity in the union field up to that time, he could entitle his dissertation, "A History of Failure." While these earlier activities are not the main focus of this study, they have to be considered, even if briefly, because they are crucial for making out the later pattern. Just as in the formative years an American radical movement had been transformed into an appendage of Russian national power, so its trade-union section was transformed from an assemblage of militants in the De Leon-Debs-IWW tradition to a bureaucratized caucus whose oscillations and inconsistencies made no sense in their own terms, but fell into place when viewed as part of a Stalinized supranational operation.

American Communists carried over initially from the Socialist left wing a romantic attachment to the IWW. The IWW was supposed to be the embodiment of revolutionary unionism as against reformist or reactionary unionism represented by the AFL. It was in this spirit that in 1920 one of the Communist factions distributed a handbill to New York subway workers striking for a wage increase to urge on them the need for armed insurrection, soviets, and the proletarian dictatorship.[1] The Communists were weaned by Moscow away from these extravagancies, later. The more realistic policy dated from 1921 when the Profintern—the Red International of Labor Unions, a division of the Communist International charged with carrying out the general line in trade-union matters—discarded the left-wing position that the AFL was a bulwark of capitalism which had to be crushed bodily. It laid down the new policy of revolutionizing AFL unions from within by recognizing William Z. Foster's Trade Union Educational League as its American section.

The deal between Foster and the Communists seemed mutually advantageous. Foster had convinced himself by this time that without significant aid from a new source, his TUEL, which he had formed the year before, would be stillborn; with Profintern backing, it had a future. Better yet, Foster joined with the Communists on what he thought were his own terms. He was to head the Party's trade-union activity, the direction of which was delegated to the TUEL, and was to be at the same time a Communist leader of the first rank (although his membership was not formally acknowledged for two years).[2] As for the American Communist movement, without any influence in the unions in the first two years of its existence, it was assured a tangible base headed by a well-known trade-union figure who, in left-wing circles, still wore the aureole for having been the architect of the great national steel strike. From its absorption in hairsplitting disputations and factional grand strategy over Marxian exegetics conducted in "underground" cells, the Party was thrust into the daylight of actual contact with American workers. Thus, with one stroke, American Communists were saved years of inexpert groping and time-consuming debates, were handed gratis a more effective trade-union strategy under the ready-made leadership of an experienced individual with a reputation and with connections in the field. If some critic were to declare that a decision of this magnitude should be made by the party membership itself, he might be answered in the way James P. Cannon (one of the party leaders fighting for an Americanized party; later, the founder of American Trotskyism) answered a left-wing doubter who feared Moscow's system of dictation: "We who have fought for a realistic

21

party have found our best friend in 'Moscow.' "[3] The more substantial Communist leaders were grateful for dictation from Moscow which furthermore in 1923 forced two squabbling Communist parties to fuse, and to abandon an isolated, underground existence in favor of "mass work."

This surrender of independence to the Moscow center was as fateful a decision for the Party as Faust's bargain with Mephistopheles. The leaders, for all the foxiness they acquired in the course of faction jousting, did not comprehend the nature of the bargain they had struck: (1) In giving up party sovereignty, they made a mockery of the discussion and decision-making apparatus of their organization. The membership could talk and vote—but decisions were made elsewhere. When this system of organization became widely known in later years, it put the Communists in an untenable position. It was not a system that could withstand examination and criticism. (2) In the Bolshevik concept of a tight-knit international organization, whose authority superseded that of all national executive bodies, hegemony was inevitably handed over to the Russian leaders. All other Communist parties were weak, often mere skeleton organizations. Their leaders had no standing with the broad publics of their own countries or with the international left-wing elites. The Moscow leaders, in contrast, were clothed with the authority of the one and only successful proletarian revolution, and could, in addition, provide finances and personnel that State power put at their disposal.

That contentious and headstrong individuals could voluntarily put their heads into the noose of this unequal system—and be cheered on by their fellows to do so—was least of all dependent on Moscow gold, or the vicarious thrill accorded Communist leaders, pariahs in their own countries, by hobnobbing with revolutionary gods abroad (although both the gold and the hobnobbing were more than welcome). It was the way the Marxian movement evolved that made the Leninist pretention persuasive. The theorem went: the Socialist leaders of the Second International had failed, had betrayed the cause. Why? Because they tried to uphold national parties and national loyalties in an era when the national state was anachronistic and reactionary. The Bolsheviks, animated by Leninist internationalism, restored the honor of socialism; they showed how to make a successful revolution—the first step of a Europe-wide, and eventually world-wide, overturn. Ergo, organization has to correspond to the political requirements of the new transnational era of wars and revolutions; world revolution necessitates a general staff that can comprehend the entire field of action, that can subordinate purely parochial, regional, or national considerations in favor of international interests and purposes.[4] When this theorem was backed by the authority of the makers of the Russian Revolution, no Communist could resist it. In the first few years, the gravitational pull on the entire Left was strong enough to force the American Socialist leaders, as others, to engage in protracted negotiations to be permitted to join the Comintern, provided they could secure less onerous terms than those dictated in Lenin's "21 Conditions." Hillquit, Turati, and others were really little interested in tying themselves to the Muscovite Leviathan, but they had to go through the motions to satisfy their ranks that the onus for their not joining was with the other side.

American Communist officials, including the majority who had turned into hard-boiled operators, had as little understanding of the dynamics and direction of the Soviet regime as any dazed true believers. Even in the first few heroic years, when the Russians had high hopes of revolutions in Germany and elsewhere, the Comintern became a hotbed of Byzantine struggle for status and place. The high excitement and glamor connected with the headquarters for remolding the entire planet attracted inevitably, along with idealists, a host of adventurers and outright rascals on the make. "The bazaars of Khiva and Bokhara," was the way one early Communist dissenter described the operation. The Comintern—run in the last analysis by the Russian government heads—perfected a system to boss the foreign parties through plenipotentiary representatives, plenum resolutions, and cablegrammed instructions. Instead of the semimilitary centralization furthering "world revolution" in the lands of the capitalist infidels, the system led to the internationalization of mistaken policies and the organization of catastrophes.[5]

Lenin's death in 1924 precipitated among the Russian leaders a ferocious struggle for the succession that went on until Stalin consolidated his autocratic rule five years later. The foreign Communist leaders were made to line up, like recruits on the drill ground, in support of whatever faction or bloc was in control of the Kremlin. Policy matters affecting the life and future of the foreign parties were decided during the interregnum not so much to suit the needs of the Soviet regime as the needs of the dominant faction leaders. The American party officials quickly learned the lesson that the art of getting one's proposal adopted consisted of getting the ear of the right people in Moscow. From that, they went over to the more advanced position of studying the omens and wind drifts to devise a policy ahead of their faction rivals that would anticipate the wishes of the Moscow overseers, and thereby enhance their own reputations. Individuals who entered the Communist movement as firebrands adapted themselves, step by step, for the professions of courtiers, tricksters, and bureaucrats. Party regularity and unquestioning obedience were the desired traits. By the time Stalin took over as undisputed master, two of the three major leaders of the American Communist party had been expelled, and the third was relegated to the status of an honored supernumerary. With the crushing of the Cannon and Lovestone factions, and the elevation of Browder, a former Foster adherent utterly dependent on Moscow's favor, the American party had become Stalinized. Not that Jay Lovestone or Foster would have been averse to adopting whatever policies headquarters called for. But Stalin had foresight as well as insight. He did not want foreign leaders who had either independent standing or tendencies. The apparatchik had come into his own.

2

The new Communist labor policy recorded some successes at the beginning. Foster had the help of a number of Communist trade unionists in Chicago, and had struck up an important alliance with the leaders of the Chicago Federation of Labor. John Fitzpatrick, the president (a former blacksmith), was a populist radical type who had been against the war, was an admirer of the Russian Revolution, had no qualms about tangling with Gompers, the AFL head, and was all in favor of Foster's progressive unionism. With the Chicago Federation of Labor as his base, Foster started a campaign around the issue of amalgamation of craft unions. Within a year favorable resolutions had been passed by fourteen international unions, numerous state federations and city centrals, and innumerable local unions. Foster implemented the amalgamation campaign by supporting progressive opposition slates. William R. Knudsen, who came out for industrial unionism and a worker's republic, was backed against the incumbent for the presidency of the International Association of Machinists, and received about 30 percent of the vote. In the United Mine Workers, an alliance was forged with Alexander Howat, president of the Kansas district. A railroad conference held at the end of 1922 drew many working delegates from the shop crafts and brotherhoods. TUEL chapters sprang up in many local unions, and TUEL publications were well received by substantial numbers of unionists.[6]

By 1924 all this promising activity was at an end. The TUEL was an ash heap. The devolution began with the break with Fitzpatrick and the Chicago Federation of Labor. The Communists had an agreement with him to participate in a convention set for July 1923 to form a national farmer-labor party. Fitzpatrick wanted their help, but warned them not to get too prominent, not to push. He was up against the innate Communist dynamic to dominate and control. As well try to stop a volcano from erupting. Intoxicated by their seeming opportunity to take over a mass party, the Communists flooded the convention with delegates from paper and concocted organizations.[7] In return for capturing themselves, they lost the ally who gave them the indispensable base for their trade-union enterprise.

At the Portland AFL convention in the fall of that year Gompers and his entourage took full advantage of the Communists' exposed position. They branded the TUEL a dual union, denied William F. Dunne, a regularly elected delegate of the Silver Bow Trades and Labor Council of Butte, Montana, his seat, and declared war to the knife against Communists and their supporters. There followed mass expulsions of all known TUEL adherents. Foster's insurgency was effectively confined to isolated enclaves.[8] To complete the disaster, the Americans' decision to try to salvage a third party movement out of the wreckage by going along with the La Follette candidacy became entangled in the Russian succession struggle. The American delegation, arriving in Moscow for the April-May 1924 plenum, found everything revolving around the contest between the Zinoviev-Kamenev-Stalin triumvirate and Trotsky; and the latter singling out the proposed alliance with La Follette as a horrible example of the other side's opportunism.[9] To take the issue away from Trotsky, Zinoviev demonstratively banned cooperation with liberal or social democratic parties, and the American Communist party was ordered to disassociate itself from La Follette. Foster returned from Moscow on June 1 with the Comintern's secret ukase and read it to an astounded Central Committee. Alexander Bittelman, one of his faction associates, described its effects on the shopworn leadership:

All our tactics, all our literature, all of our slogans formulated during the months of January to May were based on this general

25

idea of the third party alliance and then at a certain moment the Communist International said to our party, you cannot do it. . . . We were confronted with the necessity of completely reorienting ourselves practically within 24 hours . . . a reorientation of a political party on the open political arena, under the very fire of the enemy. . . . To have changed within one day, almost, fundamentally, our main political line . . . without in the least demoralizing our ranks, was proof not only of the political flexibility of the Central Executive Committee, but also of the discipline of the party as a whole.[10]

Bittelman was to learn in later years the fearful cost of a 180-degree turn "under the very fire of the enemy." Despite the public character of these proceedings, and the common knowledge among leftists of the Muscovite decree, the specifics of this domination were not firmly implanted in the public mind.[11] In the Harding-Coolidge era, "agents of Moscow" was a generalized, pejorative appellation that was not taken literally; it was part of an overall repudiation of Communism—as an unpatriotic, undemocratic, unrealistic, foreign-influenced movement. Besides, from the time of the A. Mitchel Palmer raids, the charge of Communism was used so indiscriminately and irresponsibly as to dull its cutting edge. The damage was to Communists' connections: the abrupt change of line lost the Communists their few remaining farmer-labor allies. William Mahoney, editor of the St. Paul central labor body newspaper, who stuck with the Communists through the Fitzpatrick debacle, felt he had been used, and shortly after, was instrumental in having the Communists barred from the Minnesota Farmer-Labor Federation.[12]

When the smoke of electoral battle cleared in November, Coolidge was swept back to the White House with almost twice the vote of his Democratic opponent; La Follette polled less than 5 million votes, which sorely disappointed his followers and finished the Progressive movement; and the Communists, with Foster their banner-bearer, weighed in with 33,000 votes. So ended the grand maneuver to capture a mass movement. The Communists thought to manipulate their allies; instead, they worked themselves back into isolation. The vaunted scientific doctrine, and the unique party mechanism, which were supposed to ensure the Communists' superiority, made them unfit for sustained riding of the turbulent waters of democratic political infighting.

26

3

The TUEL campaigns for industrial unionism and a third party were
the biggest things the Communists had engaged in up to this time.
They should have conducted a post-mortem. Instead, they demonstrated that the Communist party, subjecting all of creation to
analysis, was incapable of analyzing itself. The Communists could
not make their own mistakes; they had to import them. Worse than
that, there could be no candid discussion of what had been done
wrong, and what should have been done instead. Like theologians
caught in a closed system, they had a doctrine that could not be
questioned, and they were under an authority that could not be
criticized. Blame could not be assigned to the authors of a disastrous
policy, but was invariably passed on to those who could not fight
back. The result was the elevation of hypocrisy and charlatanry into
a system, and the debasement of political analysis into a self-serving
mystification. Everything—doctrine, criticism, theory, tactics, administrative proposals—became operational. No wonder the organization men began to lose the ability to distinguish the real from
the unreal. Before many months had passed, the opposing faction
leaders returned from their next Moscow pilgrimage in the spring of
1925, this time with a pro-labor party resolution in their pocket.
(The line had changed again; Stalin, in a bloc with Bukharin, was
executing a qualified "right turn.")[13] In the circumstances, the disoriented leaders and ranks could retain sensibility only by clinging
to stereotyped articles of faith: Marxism-Leninism, international
leadership, the party as a Mother Church abstraction.

The other matter that no one considered, but which should have
induced a lot of soul-searching, was the underlying dynamic that led
to the break with Fitzpatrick. One can say that the Communists
were obsessed with gaining control, they were treacherous, they
did not honor agreements and commitments; those who tried to
work with them in good faith learned that this was impossible unless
they were prepared to surrender to them. In a word, here was a sink
of iniquity in a world otherwise characterized by candor and virtue.
If we probe more deeply into what happened between the Communists and Fitzpatrick, however, we find that the conflict between
the two arose because Fitzpatrick wanted the alliance, but also
wanted the Communists to take a back seat.[14] When, in effect, they
ignored his demand, there came the break. To put it another way,
Fitzpatrick wanted the Communists to use their forces to build up

the farmer-labor movement, but to refrain from trying to become leaders of it. In customary negotiations for alliances, such a proposition would be considered inequitable. Why should one side do the heavy work, and the other side take the credit and the authority? In this case, the proposal had merit because once the word got out that the farmer-labor movement was Communist-controlled, that would have been its finish. (That is exactly what happened when Communists took over the Federated Farmer-Labor Party convention.) But does a party that is in this predicament have any future? It lacks ability to make headway under its own banner and with its own message. It has to camouflage itself and deny its participation when it builds another movement in alliance with non-Communists. How much are alliances of this sort worth to the Communists?

Every disinterested observer could see that the break with Fitzpatrick and the break with La Follette were ruinous. How much profit would there have been for the Communists and their cause had they gone along with Fitzpatrick, denied their existence, and asked for no recognition in return for their exertions? It stands to reason that in time they would have been hurled into a crisis of identity, they would have been hard-pressed to keep their own ranks intact. It is one thing for one party to make an alliance with another party for a specific purpose, e.g., to force out an existing government, or to pass or defeat a piece of legislation. It is one thing for several like-minded groups to form a coalition to set up a new party. It is something else entirely for a revolutionary party to help set up a mildly reformist nonrevolutionary organization that it does not believe in so as to have an arena to proselytize, to place Communists in influential jobs, to manipulate a membership by indirection. The question can be put this way: Can a party that is unable to make headway under its own aegis because it is abhorred—not so much for this or that dereliction, but because communism is unpopular in a conservative country—can such a party solve its problem of growth by disadvantageous liaisons of convenience? Such considerations were never brought up in Party discussions because they called into question not tactics, but the validity of the Communist enterprise itself.

Nevertheless, a society is not cut of one piece, all the more so in a big turbulent country like the United States in which traditional class conflicts are interlaced and often overborne by ethnic, racial, and other animosities and assertions. On the one hand, there has been the strong thrust of conservatism in national politics since Civil

War days, piercing and eventually overwhelming both the Progressive and New Deal insurgencies. On the other hand, this country has had the most violent labor history of any industrial nation in the world. The result has made for a study in ambivalence and dialectical contradiction. The United States is at once a world leader in the stability of its political institutions—and of labor violence; low on the scale of law-abiding nations—but its political system buttressed securely by overwhelming popular legitimacy.[15] Were an observer not aware of this underlying stability, he might have surmised that the country time and again was on the verge of revolution in the many upheavals from the rail strike of 1877 to the sit-down strike at General Motors in 1937, to the demonstrations in black ghettos and on college campuses in the 1960s. Theoretically, such outbursts of violence can be construed as head-on clashes with the political directorate, because they challenge the state's monopoly of violence and shut off parliamentary processes. On an abstract level of analysis the difference between a riot and a revolution is one of degree, not of kind; the riot, given favorable political winds, can spread uncontrollably to accumulate the force for a revolution.[16] The danger has been exclusively theoretical owing to the middle-class modes of thought and aspiration, to the limited reformist aims of all major historical insurgents and their allies, and to the fundamental patriotism of the bulk of the population. Insurgents' ferocity in method—often engendered by desperation, by inability to gain attention for grievances through normal political processes, by the ruthlessness of establishment forces arrayed against them—went hand in hand with moderation in programmatic objectives. America's checkered history suggests nonetheless that all is not Arcadian beneath the solid crust of political conservatism. It was the other America, periodically erupting in violent protests, that nourished radical hopes for deep changes, and was the source for the trickle of recruits which enabled radicals to eke out an existence on the extremity of American politics.

It might be thought logical, considering the middle-class character of the country and the moderation of the trade unions, that reform-minded Socialists and gradualist meliorists would become the leading spokesmen on the Left, and that revolutionists would be in the minority. However, this was not the case in the twenties (as it had not been the case for large sections of the pre-World War I Socialist party or for the New Left of the sixties), owing to the specialized evolution of radicalism in the inhospitable American environment. Over the years, American radical formations never became sizable and durable enough bodies to fall under the country's gravitational influence. In elections, it was true, Socialists received many times more votes than Communists; they were the major beneficiaries, as one would expect them to be, of protest voting.[17] But among left activists, ordinary Newtonian laws did not apply. Radicals dwelt in their own rarefied milieu, subject to influences, and governed by imperatives, derived from their own unique traditions, and here the drawing power of the Russian Revolution was intense. Since the American Communists held the official franchise for the firm, the *élan vital* passed to them.*

4

After the Communist bloc with the Chicago progressives and the farmer-laborites was broken and the AFL chieftains resorted to summary expulsions, the TUEL was reduced, for practical purposes, to another front group (aside from special situations, as in the New York needle trades). The more restricted TUEL got, the more radical it got. The "proletarian dictatorship" was included in its program at the same time that its publication, *The Labor Herald*, had to merge with a Party publication, *The Workers Monthly*. Then Moscow made a quarter turn in 1925 away from the original TUEL concept when it proposed that the Party take the initiative to organize new unions in unorganized shops and industries. The new ap-

* In later years, Browder (Oral History, p. 258) and others of different persuasion (Michael Harrington, *Socialism*, Saturday Review Press, 1972, pp. 260-263) made the point that the Communists gained members and influence in the thirties by making coalitions with liberals, while the Socialists, who under Norman Thomas polled close to a million votes in 1932, disintegrated because they were adhering to a strict socialist line. The explanation is incomplete. It should be taken into account that right-wing Socialists—abler, and more accepted, man for man than the Communists ever were—had alliances with liberals and business unionists before the Communists adopted the popular-front policy; they prospered, however, only as individuals, not as a movement. As a matter of fact, their adherence to the Roosevelt camp led to the atomization of their group. Most of them could see no purpose in perpetuating a small Socialist sect when they could participate in the larger reform enterprise. Communists held hegemony inside the Left in the early united-front period, in the subsequent ultra-revolutionary period, as well as the succeeding popular-front period. They had this unique hold on radicals so that they could harness their energies—in opposition to, or in alliance with, liberals. A chain reaction had been set off: the Russian Revolution ignited militant youth; the militant youth were in the forefront of social battles, which reinforced the conviction in the radical world that only Communists stood ready to fight the system while others merely talked about it.

proach was taken up gleefully by Foster's opponents, the Ruthenberg faction in control of the Party at this time, and given a major tryout in the Communist-led Passaic strike of 1926.[18]

For the next six to seven years, the Communist party resembled the prewar IWW to the extent that it supplied leadership for workers abandoned or ignored by AFL officials. These groups of workers, isolated and without finances, forced into hopeless strikes against superior forces, were not in a position to choose their allies, and because of their desolate state, were impervious to the usual anti-Communist tirades. In Passaic, thousands of immigrant textile workers, earning less than $15 a week, became desperate when Botany Mills and several other companies ordered a 10 percent cut in wages in September 1925. The Communists, who had been making some headway with united-front committees in several textile centers in Massachusetts, proceeded to set up such a committee in Passaic, a concentration point of woolen textiles at this time. Although calling itself a committee, it soon issued its own membership books and conducted itself like a sovereign union. The organization's 25-year-old leader, Albert Weisbord, had been a Phi Beta Kappa student at Harvard Law School and national secretary of the Young People's Socialist League. When he went over to the Communists, he threw up his legal career and spent a year working in textile mills.

Late in January 1926, after many workers were discharged, a strike was called at Botany and spread quickly to other mills in the region. The mill owners refused to have any dealings with Weisbord or the committee; city officials invoked a Riot Act from Civil War days to prohibit all meetings and picketing; strikers were attacked indiscriminately with clubs, fire hoses, and tear gas; mass arrests were resorted to; news photographers had their cameras smashed repeatedly; and Norman Thomas, the Socialist leader, was indicted when he sought to hold a meeting to test the constitutionality of the Riot Act. The attack on the strike became a national scandal, and the brutality of the mill owners and police officials was widely reported. Senator La Follette introduced a resolution to investigate the imbroglio; later, he agreed to act as arbitrator if both sides consented. The governor of the state offered to mediate while proposing that the strikers join the AFL and dump Weisbord. These and many other proposals broke on the obduracy of the employers. The Communists, using tactics perfected earlier by the Wobblies, made the Passaic strike "the outstanding labor conflict of the Coolidge

31

era," and Weisbord, who was a hero to the strikers because of his bold, purposeful behavior, emerged as a national figure.[19]

As one might expect, a *deus ex machina* was soon introduced to unravel the plot. Foster and Ruthenberg, both in Moscow for the Comintern's Sixth Plenum, which opened in the middle of 1926, learned that the line had zig-zagged again. Since Stalin set out to destroy the Zinoviev-Kamenev faction, and to eliminate the allied Fischer-Maslow leadership of the German party, the main danger was now declared to be the "ultra-left"—not just in Germany or Russia, but universally. This meant that Weisbord's strike was in trouble. The new instruction read, "The formation of parallel unions should not be instigated or encouraged in any form." When the leaders returned from Moscow, they overrode Weisbord's demand that the strike be extended to other textile plants; they proposed instead to unload it. In August, Weisbord was forced to step out, and the AFL United Textile Workers, a moribund outfit with less than 3 percent organization in the industry, thereupon agreed to take over the strike, and presumably settle it on more favorable terms than Weisbord could. The mill owners did not act out their part of the projected play. Their attitude was unchanged. Four months later, the strikers trooped disconsolately back to work with no concession except the promise (not kept) to be rehired without discrimination. The strike had already gone on for a year and was not officially called off for another ten weeks.[20]

The Passaic strike highlighted the strengths and weaknesses of the Communist apparatus. The Communists showed that they could conduct a big strike under difficult, virtually hopeless conditions, that they could operate effectively the complicated machinery of mass picket lines, soup kitchens, legal defense, national publicity, strike meetings, and financial solicitation. In the straitened circumstances then prevailing, they were the ones both willing and able to step to the forefront to assume the responsibility and risk, as well as the glory. They were not as imaginative or colorful strike leaders and agitators as the Wobblies. (Weisbord was a find, though somewhat mad. He did not stay with them very long, either.) Because the Party was bureaucracy-ridden, it tended to push to the fore organization men. Because it was doctrinaire-ridden, and obsessed with the need to politicize every conflict, its propaganda ranged far afield, whether it was in a "left" or "right" phase. What in theory was supposed to furnish the Communists with superior guidance, in practice shackled them with a prisoner's chain to a tyrannical and capricious taskmaster. While they were not inhibited by the syndicalist prejudices of the IWW against signed contracts, or opposed to business relations with employers, they were fated by all the circumstances of their possibilities, or lack of them, to repeat in the next several years the Wobbly experience of organizing doomed strikes, not building stable unions. The union membership would spurt up dramatically during an action, and fall just as precipitately when the action was over. Foster was to attack the "tendency to be attracted to the struggle and to make a fight only when the masses are all in motion, but a real union must learn how to conduct the fight in the trough between the waves of the strikes."[21] Just how that was to be effected, he did not volunteer.

Perlman and Taft leveled another accusation after their discussion of the Passaic strike:

> The significance of the Communist campaign to capture the unions lies not so much in that it failed to attain its objective but in that it arrested the natural process of replacement and development of leadership in the American labor movement. In spite of the widespread insurgency in the first half of the twenties, in spite of the elemental militancy and semi-conscious groping for a wider solidarity in nearly all industries and trades, the younger leadership, the less official and more experimental-minded group, had been forced to cease struggling for more progressive policies in the American Federation of Labor. The "progressives" in the American unions who might normally have forced their way to a higher position in the general leadership had instead been driven to come to the old leadership for aid against the undermining tactics of their Communist foes.[22]

This argument can be used in the case of Fitzpatrick of the Chicago Federation of Labor and other individuals here and there. It cannot be sustained as a generalization. The entrenched AFL bureaucrats of this period would not permit "the natural process of replacement" to occur. They threw out TUEL'ers because of congenital opposition to critics as much as doctrinal or ethical opposition to Communists. Gompers' Old Guard did not make finespun distinctions. In the same chapter where Perlman and Taft delivered their Philippic, they described how the AFL in 1928 smeared and proscribed Brookwood Labor College, a center for precisely the kind of progressives who should have been permitted to become more prominent in the unions in the natural course of development. "The

33

[AFL]," justifiably concluded the *Fortune* magazine editors, "has been suffering from pernicious anemia, sociological myopia, and hardening of the arteries."[23] It was because the AFL was hidebound and machine-ridden, its guardians intent on preserving their principalities, that the Communists, despite their handicaps, had the limited attractive power that they did.

5

The Communists went on to lead a number of spectacular, violent, and nationally prominent strikes—all of which were lost. Their big effort in cotton textiles spans the period in which their TUEL policy was abandoned in favor of organizing their own red unions. They had been doing missionary work among immigrant textile workers in Massachusetts before going into Passaic; then in April 1928, a strike exploded in all New Bedford mills when the manufacturers' association posted a notice of a 10 percent cut in wages. Operating through a united-front Textile Mill Committee, the Communists followed procedures they had introduced at Passaic, and the mill owners and police authorities responded with similar bellicosity. The battle was fought out grimly for twenty-three weeks, although the strike petered out in July when United Textile Workers officials acceded to a 5 percent wage cut. Their intransigence won the Communists a following of diehards in the industry, and it was the New Bedford contingent that made up the main worker support of the new red union, National Textile Workers (NTW), set up in September.[24]

The bloody encounter at Gastonia in March 1929 consequently occurred under the aegis of the new trade union policy—although the concrete behavior of the Communists varied little from one strike to the other. The Gastonia strike was one of a series of outbursts that year in the southern textile mills. Textiles had been moving steadily from New England to the South throughout the decade, and the inducement to move was the plentiful supply of cheap, docile labor. It was reported that it generally took three wage earners in a family to piece together a subsistence wage. Despite the southern operators' advantages, the cotton-goods industry was shaky because of overproduction and cutthroat competition, even before the depression struck. Company officials sought to lower production costs by cutting the already meager wages and imposing the stretchout—requiring the worker to operate more machines with little or no increase in pay. The textile workers' revolt was a response of sheer desperation. In the month that the Communist strike was called, spontaneous strikes broke out in Elizabethton, Tennessee and the Piedmont region of South Carolina.

The new-spangled National Textile Workers union determined on a southern campaign, and sent down Fred Beal to lead it. Beal had been a textile worker and a radical all his life, had been in the IWW Lawrence strike of 1912, and joined with the Communists at the time of the New Bedford strike. He arrived in January, worked for two months in the Charlotte, North Carolina area to familiarize himself with conditions, then in March he moved over to Gastonia, which at the time was the leading southern textile center. He rapidly built up an underground organization at the Loray mill, the largest plant in the area employing 3,500 workers. A company spy reported to management that the union was making rapid progress, and when five unionists were fired, Beal was unable to restrain the ranks; on April 1 both shifts walked out. The main demands submitted to the company were elimination of piecework, $20 minimum wage, 40-hour week, abolition of the stretchout, and union recognition.

The Communists now met the full fury of a semi-police state. The National Guard, which was ordered into the town, stopped mass picketing; and the local powers started a systematic incitation to violence against the unwelcome intruders. The *Gastonia Daily Gazette* ran a picture on the front page of an American flag, a snake coiled at its base, with the inscription. "Communism in the South. Kill it!" Handbills containing inflammatory messages were distributed far and wide. One read, "Would you belong to a union which opposes White Supremacy?" An armed mob descended on the strike headquarters, smashed it, and burned the relief groceries in the commissary. A National Guard troop duly arrived on the scene only after the last of the vandals had left, then turned over to the police a number of the strikers for destroying their own property. In June when the strike was already defeated, and the Communists were conducting rearguard skirmishes, Police Chief O. F. Aderholt and several of his deputies pushed their way without a warrant into the tent colony that the union had set up on the city's outskirts. There was an exchange of gunfire, at the conclusion of which Aderholt, the deputies, and one striker were on the ground wounded, Aderholt mortally.

With that, a reign of terror was on against the union. A mob led by the local attorney for the mill demolished the tent colony; 71

35

unionists were arrested, and 16 were indicted for murder. There was another outbreak of mob violence after the judge declared a mistrial because one of the jurors went insane in the course of the proceedings. That night hundreds of vigilantes in automobiles roamed through Gaston and adjoining counties whipping and otherwise terrorizing union supporters and destroying union properties. Ella May Wiggins, the union songwriter, a 29-year-old mother of five, was murdered when the vigilantes shot up a truck carrying unionists to a meeting. At the second trial the jury returned a verdict of guilty; the four northerners received sentences of 17 to 20 years, two others of 12 to 14 years, the rest of 5 to 7 years.[25]

To what extent did the Communists bring on the calamity by their own brashness? It goes without saying that with the calling of the strike there arrived on the scene the traveling brigade of the Communist union operation, organizers of Workers International Relief, International Labor Defense, the Young Communist League, the *Daily Worker*, and that opportunities—real or imaginary—to politicize the strike were not overlooked. To the Gastonia elite, however, the prime provocation was not the incidental revolutionary mouthings of Communist hotheads, but their presence and intention to set up a union of textile workers. The most provocative part of the NTW program for the community was not the proletarian dictatorship, but equality of blacks and whites—a slogan that the Communists introduced as a matter of overriding principle. (There were only a few blacks employed at the Loray mill.) It can be assumed that Communist sloganeering added to Establishment fury, but Paul Blanshard, who reported the strike for the *Nation*, was skeptical that the reception would have been any different had the strike been led by conservative AFL officials.[26] This can be checked, since concomitant with the Gastonia fray other textile strikes were led in southern mills by the AFL United Textile Workers union.

A year and a half earlier, Alfred Hoffman had been sent down by the AFL union to set up a local in Henderson, North Carolina, where workers were on strike. Hoffman, a product of Brookwood Labor College, was at this time in his early twenties and had little experience, but he was dedicated and capable. In the middle of March 1929, two weeks before the Gastonia eruption, the work forces of two plants owned by the American Glanzstoff Corporation at Elizabethton, Tennessee, walked out demanding an increase in wages (they were earning $10 to $12 per week) and they called on Hoffman to organize them. When the owner repudiated an existing agreement to raise wages and meet with shop grievance committees, and discharged several hundred unionists, AFL president William Green sent his troubleshooter, Edward F. McGrady (later assistant secretary of labor) to Elizabethton to try to renegotiate an agreement. Others had different ideas. At midnight of April 4, Hoffman was seized by a mob, blindfolded, driven over the North Carolina line, and ordered not to return "under pain of death." At 2 a.m., another armed mob led by the local president of the First National Bank, and consisting of the town's "best elements," seized McGrady and dumped him in Virginia. A revolver was pointed at him, and he was similarly warned that he would be a dead man if he returned.

Hoffman and McGrady were back the next day; the union called a second strike on April 15. This time it was met by military force: 800 state police and deputy sheriffs (paid directly $1,000 a day by the Glanzstoff management), enforced an injunction against the strikers, and carried through mass arrests. Under strong AFL urging, the strikers on May 25 called off the strike upon the granting of a "compromise" agreement that gave them no concessions. Unionists were thereafter blackballed, a company union was promoted, and the AFL local disappeared.

While Beal and others were sitting in jail awaiting trial, another great strike exploded at the Baldwin and Clinchfield mills in Marion, North Carolina. Here, too, conditions were atrocious: female employees worked their first thirty days without pay, followed by four months at 5 cents an hour. The shift was 12 hours, the work week 60 hours, wages of $8 to $10 a week were usual, and the stretchout was enforced. Two employees visited Hoffman, who promised help. Management answered the calling of a union meeting by discharging 22 employees. Hoffman rushed to Marion on July 10, and pleaded with the local people not to strike just yet. "There isn't a cent of money for relief," he told them. This tells the story of the internal condition of the United Textiles Workers, and of the AFL, which announced at this very time that it was launching a southern campaign to organize textile workers. Aside from enjoying marginal advantages of being part of the established AFL institution, most of the help that Hoffman received came from Brookwood

37

Labor College devotees. In any case, the decision was taken out of Hoffman's hands: the employees streamed out of the two Marion plants.

On the nineteenth, Clinchfield opened in the face of mass picketing. The governor ordered out state troops who took over both mill villages and effectively broke the strike. In addition, 148 strikers, including Hoffman, were arrested on charges of insurrection as well as other offenses in response to a group of unionists' removing the furniture from a strikebreaker's home. (He had moved in after a striking member had been evicted.) In a further walkout on October 2 following management's wholesale violation of the no-discrimination agreement that had been reached, deputy sheriffs opened fire on pickets: three strikers were killed outright, three were mortally wounded, twenty-five were seriously wounded. All those who died had been shot in the back. The only casualty on the other side was one deputy sheriff who suffered a scratched cheek. In November, Hoffman and five strikers were tried for the furniture incident. The insurrection charge was dropped, but they were convicted of rioting. Hoffman was fined $1,000 and sentenced to thirty days in jail. Three others were given six months on the chain gang. The sheriff and his deputies, tried for murder, were acquitted. That was the end of the Marion strike. The AFL union had fared no better than the red union, although one can make the point that the sentence meted out to Hoffman and others were nowhere as savage as those pronounced against Beal and his friends. B. M. Hart, president of the Clinchfield mill, said, "I cannot see that there is any difference between this so-called conservative union and the Communist union in Gastonia."[27]

6

In the one industry in which Communists had solid support, and which they might have converted into a bastion for their trade union operations, they irresponsibly squandered their opportunities. The needle-trades unions in New York were unique in the twenties in that the bulk of the membership was Jewish, and was part of a Jewish labor community that was heavily swayed by radicalism and sympathy for the Soviet Union. The sectarian battles between Socialists and Communists, unnoticed by (and without interest for) the generality of American workers, were hotly debated by the ranks throughout the needle-trades market. The Yiddish press—the Socialist *Jewish Daily Forward* (supported financially and morally by the Ladies Garment union right-wing administration), and the *Freiheit* (controlled and backed by the Communist party)—were the daily messengers to rally their cohorts when the struggle between the two factions escalated into outright war. The cutthroat character of this anarchic, disorganized industry, affording its volatile force of wage earners only seasonal employment under sweatshop conditions and wages, kept the market in near-constant turmoil, and gave the union contestants plenty to fight about. While the men's clothing and headgear unions were also caught up in the left-right struggle, the decisive battles centered in the International Ladies Garment Workers (ILG) and the Fur Workers International unions, the important contributing factor being the two industries' concentration in New York City.

In 1924, the left-wing faction, led by Communists, took over three major ILG locals in New York, as well as important offices in Boston, Chicago, and Philadelphia locals, and promptly opened fire on the International administration. Morris Sigman, the ILG president, frightened by the strength of the opposition, retaliated with wholesale removal of officers from the three insurgent locals. As Benjamin Stolberg explained in his authorized study of the union, "Naturally the International couldn't tolerate Moscow control at the very center of the union's life. It simply had to get rid of this fifth column in its midst." The ensuing struggle, punctuated by violent exchanges between supporters of the contending sides, threatened to tear the union apart. The left-wing leaders, Louis Hyman, Charles S. Zimmerman, Joseph Boruchowitz, and Rose Wortis, were individuals of stature, enormously popular with the ranks— and there is no dispute that the left wing was backed by a big majority of the New York membership. Its rally at Yankee Stadium was attended by over 40,000 cloak- and dressmakers. To quote Stolberg again, "Obviously the vast majority of the workers were with the left wing and not with the International. But that didn't faze Morris Sigman."

At the stormy Philadelphia convention in November 1925 the Sigman-Dubinsky administration retained control by reneging on its prior agreement to write proportional representation into an amended union constitution (Sigman's control depended on a rotten borough system); and because the Communist high command forced the insurgent delegates to return to the convention after Louis Hyman had led a demonstrative walkout. The left-wingers— the suspended officials had been reinstated under a pre-convention

39

compromise settlement—continued to dominate the New York scene all the same. In a sweeping victory, they gained control of the New York Joint Board. Then came the days of sorrow. On July 1, 1926, the left-wing leaders called a strike of 40,000 cloakmakers to oppose the recommended reorganization and rationalization of the industry as proposed by a commission appointed by Governor Alfred E. Smith. The commission report would have permitted employers to discharge up to 10 percent of their work forces in any one year, while rejecting the 40-hour week and other union demands and failing to seriously restrict the cutthroat jobbing system. The strike was bound to be a difficult one since the economics in the industry were not too favorable. Also, the jobbers flatly rejected both the commission recommendations and union demands. Jobbers supplied materials and samples to the contractors, who in turn supplied the inside manufacturers with parts of the garment and these two sets of subcontractors accounted at this time for 70 to 80 percent of New York's cloak- and dressmakers.

Since most cloakmakers were hotly opposed to "reorganization," the administration leaders soft-pedaled their desire to accept the report as a basis for continued negotiations. Neither the Communist ILG officials nor Communist party experts had the temerity to counsel against a militant action, and the union was permitted to stumble into the strike. In mid-September the left-wing leaders were in a position to make a compromise settlement with the inside manufacturers, reasonable under the circumstances, but they ran headlong again into the faction squabble inside the Communist party. Neither Foster nor Lovestone dared give the word for fear that the opponent would use it against him. Instead, the union leaders were instructed to continue the strike until additional concessions were obtained. To his own cronies, Lovestone admitted that the garment union had been "tossed about like a football" between the factions. It is difficult to say whether the faction rivalry inside the party was the sole cause for the leaders' pseudo-militant light-mindedness. Up until the popular-front days, Communist leaders were never sure when to end strikes. If a compromise settlement was offered, it never seemed good enough, and fighting a little longer would very likely win a better one; if no settlement was offered, then the indicated revolutionary decision was to fight on; if a strike was falling apart, it took many weeks for the party dialectic to catch up with the fact.[28]

Two months later, the Communist-led Joint Board, in desperation, signed a poorer agreement with the inside employers than it could have obtained in September. That was the signal for the Sigman leadership to step in. With both the strike and the union a shambles, and the membership thoroughly demoralized, the International officers took over and liquidated the rest of the strike on whatever terms they could get. (The strike had dragged on for 28 weeks at a cost to the union of $3½ million.) Sigman then ordered cloakmakers to reregister in order to receive new union books. Another battle royal ensued. This time, the International dealt from strength because the membership was exhausted, and the right-wingers were recognized by the employers as the bona fide dress- and cloak-workers' representatives. (In Chicago, the ILG officials were able to expel the Communists who controlled the Chicago Joint Board with the help of Fitzpatrick.) The right wing consolidated its hold in the face of continuing faction turmoil—here and there its campaign supplemented with the help of professional sluggers—but it was in control of a skeleton organization until the NRA surge. The strike had been costly to both sides. The Communists became a stink in the nostrils of many erstwhile supporters of left-wing unionism, and for years thereafter participants continued to equate Communist domination with adventurism, irresponsible phrase-mongering, and financial waste. They never won back a fraction of the influence they had. The one substantial holding in the party's otherwise scrubby mid-1920 portfolio had been stupidly frittered away. On the administration side, the protracted, unrestrained infighting pushed to the fore the hard-shelled organization men for whom the rules of war became the rules of union administration. Morris Hillquit, the ILG's legal counsel and prominent Socialist leader, gently chided them at the 1928 convention for running the union "too much as a business enterprise. There was not enough soul in it."[29]

The Communist party did manage to salvage the smaller fur union out of the debacle. In this union, it had in Ben Gold, Aaron Gross, and Joseph Winogradsky outstanding unionists with an impressive following in the ranks. Here, too, the Communists took over major New York locals only to be ousted by the International officers who were of the same political coloration as the administration leaders of the ILG. By mid-1925 Communists in coalition with progressives were able to put Ben Gold in as manager of the New York Joint Board, and in February of the following year, under Joint Board direction, the New York fur market was shut down by a gen-

41

eral strike. The international officers attempted repeatedly to inject themselves into the strike leadership, and to wean away the membership, but their maneuvers came to nothing; their standing was poor with the ranks, and they were just running a campaign of interference and obstruction. It was a bitterly, violently fought strike, with the 27-year-old Gold and his coadjutors facing the massed opposition of the employers, their own international officers, the AFL hierarchy, and the *Forward* faction organized into a Committee for Preservation of the Trade Unions. The settlement of June 11 was a spectacular left-wing victory. The union won the first 40-hour, 5-day week in the garment industry, a 10 cent hourly increase, 7 paid holidays, and other benefits. The victory led quickly to left wing ascendancy in major out-of-town locals.

To forestall a left takeover of the entire International union, the AFL Executive Council moved in with an investigating committee. Acting on the committee's report, it instructed the International to revoke the charters of the Joint Board and Communist-led locals, and to expel the left-wing officials. The Joint Board replied with a strike on June 3 that again tied up the fur market. The manufacturers came to heel once it was clear that Gold and his friends were in control of the situation, and the AFL beat a hasty and none-too-dignified retreat.[30] The Communists in the fur union displayed a dazzling mastery of tactics to solve complex and varied problems, and ability of a high order to mobilize outside support for their cause. They had better market conditions than did their comrades in ladies clothing, but the one set of union leaders was not inferior in ability or experience to the other, and that underscored the party's culpability for the smashup in the ladies garment union.

THREE · *Red Unionism*

To understand the change in Communist trade-union policy between the New Bedford and Gastonia strikes, we have to turn again
to the Moscow wellspring. The previous year Stalin crushed the
combined Trotsky-Zinoviev left bloc, and Trotsky was banished.
Now Stalin was getting ready to discard his Bukharin right-wing allies, intending to take over, after his own fashion, Trotsky's program
of industrialization. The free-swinging left turn signaled at the
Ninth Plenum in February 1928, and at the Profintern Congress in
March, gathered force at the Sixth World Congress that met from
July 17 to September 1. Although Bukharin was the main congress
reporter, the air was thick with rumors that a break between Stalin
and Bukharin was imminent.[1] Foreign Communists were nervously
scurrying to and fro, trying to guess what was afoot to line up with
the winning side. The congress proclaimed that humanity had entered the "third period," which in Communist parlance signified
that "capitalist stabilization" was at an end, and that "a new revolutionary upsurge" was close at hand. Among other conclusions to be
drawn was that the American party had to stop "dancing a quadrille
around the AFL"—in the phrase of Lozovsky, the Profintern
head—which he now described as "fascist"; the American faithful
were under instructions to proceed forthwith to organize the unorganized into new radical unions.

The package of 1928 decisions preceding and following the Sixth
World Congress disclosed that there was a change in the character
of Moscow's suzerainty over the foreign Communist parties. In the
heroic period, which lasted from the Third International's formation
through 1923, Moscow's instructions—whatever their merits—were
designed to advance the various parties toward revolutionary goals.
Between 1924 and 1928, when the Russian leaders were embroiled
in the struggle over the succession, all the factions unscrupulously
sought to use the foreign parties as pawns in their own game. When
after the Sixth World Congress Stalin emerged as the undisputed
ruler, and the program of "socialism in one country" was doctrinal
writ, the Stalinization of the foreign parties into auxiliary detachments of Soviet national power was worked up into a system. Where

earlier arbitrary decisions originated from the Russians' ignorance of foreign conditions, the proclamation of the "third period" and the instructions to build new unions stemmed from Stalin's internal policies, and his pernicious habit of arbitrarily extending these universally from Paris to Patagonia. To the outsider, the connection might appear remote between Stalin's pell-mell collectivization and forced-march industrialization on the one hand, and "revolutionary upsurge" abroad, "social fascism," and the "united front from below" on the other. But in the Comintern schema, the two were ineluctably linked. So it was that because Stalin decided to drive the Russian peasants into *kolkhozes*, Foster and his associates had to push the unorganized American workers into red unions.

Aside from their unique position in the fur industry, the Communists disposed of no forces to set up a new labor federation. It was something sucked out of their thumbs. Haywood, St. John, and their supporters were able to bring into the newly launched IWW in 1905 the Western Federation of Miners, and could count on the enthusiastic backing of most left wingers in the country. But the Communists' larder was bare, and they had antagonized and disappointed erstwhile and prospective allies. Moreover, 1905 was a year of vast hopes; 1928 and 1929 were years of listlessness and demoralization. Nonetheless, orders were orders, and the TUEL at its fourth convention in Cleveland at the end of August 1929 transmogrified itself into the Trade Union Unity League (TUUL), American section of the Red International of Labor Unions. Independeent unions had already been set up the previous year in textiles, coal, food, then in needle trades; before very long they sprouted in a dozen different fields. Unfortunately, the new federation had few prospects and fewer members. The claim that TUUL unions had a roster of 57,000 at the foundation was not just inflated by several times; it was a meaningless figure. Throughout their lifetime, the red unions (aside from a few special cases) were propaganda organizations. To the extent that they had members at all, these came in during strikes and left when strikes were lost (which they generally were). To compensate for its lack of members, the TUUL did have a ferociously revolutionary program calling for nothing less than "the overthrow of the present system of capitalist ownership and exploitation and the establishment of a Soviet system."[2]

At the time, the new Party policy was considered an unmitigated disaster by many old-time Communist unionists, and castigated by non-Stalinist radicals of every persuasion. They proved to be right since the Communists never succeeded in breathing life into their revolutionary industrial unions. The policy, in terms of its declared purposes, was a failure. The critics forgot, however, that the previous TUEL policy had likewise been cut to shreds in the counterattack of the labor officialdom. It was the collapse of Foster's TUEL perspectives that had earlier pushed the Communists on their own into unacknowledged semi-independent unionism in the Passaic and New Bedford strikes. The fact was that the practice of neither the one nor the other tactic could enable Communist-led formations to prosper in the 1920s. That is one reason why the recurring debate in radical circles over creating independent unions vs. boring from within the AFL unions could never be resolved in that decade. Each side to the debate was more effective in demolishing the position of the opponent than in demonstrating the cogency of its own approach.

By sheer chance, however, the foundation of the TUUL coincided with the beginning of an unparalleled economic crisis, and in the changed environment, impersonal forces worked to provide the Communists a new arena for their agitational and organizational activities. The Great Depression broke down the individualistic philosophy that had been in ascendancy for over a century. The American Dream seemed a brutal jest when unemployment kept climbing year after year until it hit the 15 million mark in March 1933 (a third of the labor force with those on part-time unrecorded). Wages of those fortunate enough to hold jobs plunged 48 percent between 1929 and 1933 (while living costs declined by only half of that).[3] When cruel want became commonplace in the midst of potential plenty, many shared with Edmund Wilson the conviction that the Marxist forecast of capitalist breakdown had come true. An entire era ended for some when a hitherto swaggering industrialist like Charles Schwab of Bethlehem Steel could lament, "I'm afraid, every man is afraid. I don't know, we don't know whether the values we have are going to be real next month or not."[4]

Extensive rents in the social fabric—the breakup of homes, mass migrations, women and juvenile vagrants wandering over the countryside, rise of prostitution, reappearance of antediluvian sweatshops—preceded the devaluing of age-old stereotypes of self-reliance and the "work ethic"; and there was some aimless talk about a revolution. The easygoing, whiskey-drinking, Irish newspaperman Edwin A. Lahey, working out of Chicago, recalled later that the left-wing social philosophy was common in the depression years, and that he also was sympathetic toward left-wing thinking. In the 1932 election, fifty prominent writers declared for the Communist presidential slate because the Communist party "offers the only practicable solution of the crisis—a workers and farmers government."[5] The prominence of a number of the fifty should give no exaggerated notion, however, that a Left landslide was in the making. Many who were aware of the extent of the social cave-ins were amazed, not at the depth, but at the shallowness of the revolt. The same unemployed who in an opinion poll declared for revolution, reacted strongly against Communism and alien radicals. People were asking, "Do you think we are going to have a revolution?"— but asking it "apathetically, as if nothing they might do could either help or hinder it." Theodore Dreiser, a Communist sympathizer at the time, related regretfully in 1932 that "the workers do not regard Communism as their cause," the same year in which the *New Yorker* editorialized that "people are in a sad, but not a rebellious mood."[6]

The Communist party, with a membership of 7,500 in the spring of 1930, had a maximum of 19,000 in 1933. For the entire period from 1930 to 1934, 60,000 filled out application cards and paid initiation fees, but owing to the notorious membership turnover, the actual increase was only about 16,000.[7] More than tripling the membership from 1930 to 1934 may look impressive in percentage terms; as an index of Communist influence in American life in a period of unprecedented crisis, it shows the Communist party was still a marginal sect—although a sect beginning to break down some of the suspicion and revulsion habitually directed against it. One could argue that another revolutionary party with the vigor and devoted corps of activists that the Communists had, but without their internal diseases and the albatross of Comintern overlordship, would have done considerably better. But the temper of America, particularly of its labor ranks, being what it was, an avowedly revolutionary party could not attain a mass following on the order of the German or Czech Communist movements. The depression provided the Communists with larger opportunities; they were limited opportunities, nonetheless. There was a swing leftward, but it was to produce the New Deal, not soviets or farmer-laborism. It was a big swing considering its starting point, but its starting point was Harding-Coolidge-Hoover Republicanism.

2

Few strikes were called in 1930-1932—strike statistics were far lower than the average for the preceding 30 years—and most of those that occurred, were desperate, rear-guard actions to fend off wage cuts. It was a long-standing conviction of labor professionals that strikes and organizing campaigns were to be avoided in depressions because in such periods union treasuries were depleted, relief facilities were eroded, and the bargaining power of those members at work was at its lowest. The Communists now, in a supreme assertion of "voluntarism," sought to overturn past experience, and rebuked those in their own ranks who repeated such views as defeatists who did not fully comprehend "the growing radicalization" of the masses.[8] Since AFL unions had neither resources nor inclination to lead workers driven to unpromising defensive struggles, especially in unorganized industries, the Communists had little competition in taking over responsibility in these nearly hopeless situations. Following the murderous confrontation in Gastonia, they tried to rally support behind their National Textile Workers union in a series of fierce strikes in 1931 on old battlegrounds: at the American Woolen Mills in Lawrence, Massachusetts, and the silk mills in Allentown, Pennsylvania, and Paterson, New Jersey. They led other equally desperate strikes, under the auspices of various TUUL unions, of Mexican field laborers in the California Imperial Valley, of cigar makers in Tampa, of shoe workers in New York. None of these strikes were successful; none resulted in the establishment of stable organizations; the unions remained ciphers.

Before assessing what the Communist party, as a corporate entity, gained from these losing fights, attention must be called to a number of other experiences, the first in what at the time was the Party's most important concentration point, the coal industry. This should have been a rich field for Communist activity since it was a meeting ground between highly motivated labor squadrons with a long, varied tradition of aggressive unionism, and owners in a sick industry bent on slashing already inadequate wages and breaking the mine union in the process. To this explosive mixture was added the catalyst of the John L. Lewis machine in the United Mine Workers. Lewis's cold-blooded resolve to set himself up as the unquestioned autocrat of a union that was disintegrating under employers' blows—whatever the internal opposition or cost—added to the demoralization and chaos and kept the UMW in turmoil for a decade.

The TUEL forces initiated their assault on the Lewis leadership for leaving out the unorganized miners of western Pennsylvania (who had struck on their own) in the settlement of the national 1922 strike. Lewis met the criticism by summarily expelling hundreds of opposition members. He was already well launched on his strategy of lifting charters of the union's autonomous districts that were led by critics, and placing his own henchmen in control: northwestern Canada in 1919, Kansas in 1921, Nova Scotia in 1923. The TUEL countered with an opposition slate headed by George Voyzey, an unknown Communist miner from Illinois. In the election of 1924, he was officially credited with polling 66,000 votes against 136,000 for Lewis. Since Lewis's representatives were notorious ballot-stuffers, it is safe to assume that Voyzey's vote was much larger than the official count; in any case, it was a demonstration of widespread discontent.

Two years later, an enlarged coalition of opposition forces headed by John Brophy and Frank Keeney, in which Communists were active, set up the "Save the Union" committee to oust the hated Lewis administration. Brophy, president of District 2 in central Pennsylvania, was a highly respected figure. A mild sort of Socialist associated with Brookwood Labor College, he was known everywhere as a person of umimpeachable integrity, a trustworthy, unassuming unionist of ascetic appearance and advanced views. Keeney, also an old Debs Socialist, had been president of the West Virginia district, and the hero of the 1920 strike. Edmund Wilson, who visited him several years later, wrote that by reputation, "he can talk to operators as if they were his own miners, and that he can talk to miners like the captain of a ship." The progressives' program—an aggressive organizing campaign, nationalization of the mines, a strategy combining bituminous and anthracite interests, reinstatement of expelled members, district autonomy, a labor party—expressed prevailing sentiments of active unionists. The opposition made a deep impression in the mine districts and among progressive laborites throughout the country.

A like program, particularly centering on nationalization or regularization of the industry, was a necessity, not a luxury. Use of oil, gas, and hydroelectricity was cutting into coal consumption; prices were going down under pressure of lessened demand, aggravated by cutthroat competition. The employers' answer was to take it out of the hides of their workers. In 1920, about 640,000 miners were digging coal in the bituminous fields at a basic daily wage of $7.50. Both the union and its base rate collapsed in the South between 1922 and 1924, wages falling precipitately by 30 to 50 percent.

48

Open-shop mines operating in West Virginia were paying half the union scale or less. At the end of the decade, almost half the coal was mined in the nonunion Southern Appalachian field.

The 1924 Jacksonville agreement with the operators of the Central Competitive Field (western Pennsylvania, Ohio, Indiana, and Illinois) was supposed to maintain the $7.50 rate until March 1927. The agreement became a dead letter within months of its signing. The operators demanded a wage cut, and upon Lewis's refusal, they set out to break the union. When the Mellon-controlled Pittsburgh Coal Company, the nation's largest producer, tore up its agreement, evicted the miners and their families from company houses, and reopened its mines in the summer of 1925 with strikebreakers, war broke out in western Pennsylvania. A reporter for the New York *Daily News* wrote about "thousands of women and children literally starving to death . . . a system of despotic tyranny reminiscent of Czar-ridden Siberia at its worst . . . police brutality and industrial slavery . . . the weirdest flock of injunctions that ever emanated from American temples of justice . . . terrorism and counter-terrorism . . . mob violence and near lynchings." Many lost their lives in the struggle, particularly women and children struck down by hunger, malnutrition, and disease. The combination of armed power and starvation finally wiped out the union.[9]

That the opposition could have successfully hurled back the onslaught is doubtful. Brophy's program for government intervention could not have immediately affected the coal digger's plight. Lewis said to Brophy at this time, " 'There is no chance, John, you know, of getting Congress to agree to regulation of the coal industry, as matters stand now.' "[10] That was correct. A Lewis-sponsored bill introduced by Senator James Watson of Indiana later in 1928 for licensing coal producers as well as underwriting labor's right to organize expired in the congressional hopper. But a program of this nature that would give a perspective to the miners, and a union leadership that would take their wishes and troubles into account, would have slowed the atomization processes. Lewis's regime of bluster and coercion hastened them.

In the referendum at the end of 1926, Brophy was credited with 60,661 votes to Lewis's 173,323. It was widely believed at the time that Lewis had stolen the election. Years afterward Brophy still insisted, "If the phantom districts and locals had been excluded, I'm satisfied that I would have won."[11] By the time the Communists launched their National Miners Union in September 1928, the

49

UMW was a shadow of its former self, and no one knew whether the Lewis machine would survive. The next few years' events showed that the Communists had unnecessarily separated themselves from the main body of insurgents. In 1930, the long battle between the Illinois district and the International flared up when Lewis revoked the district charter and put in his own appointees. The rival union offices in Illinois again became pitched camps. District 12 officials went to court and obtained a decision stating that Lewis had violated the UMW constitution. After many maneuvers and byplays, they joined with Brophy and other opposition leaders to call a convention in Springfield, Illinois, and declared themselves the authentic UMW. Each faction proceeded to expel the leaders of the other union. The Springfield UMW started with two-thirds of the Illinois membership and with Alexander Howat's following in Kansas. After a period of virtual civil war in southernn Illinois (during which the governor called out the National Guard, and police and deputy sheriffs openly cooperated with the Lewis forces), a rank-and-file offspring founded an independent union, the Progressive Miners of America, in the fall of 1932 (several of whose leaders were under Musteite influence in the first few years).* The new union's existence was underwritten when a rival employer's association consisting of some smaller firms decided to recognize the independents. The main body of insurgents had been forced back in the Lewis fold, and the autonomy of the last of the antiadministration strongholds was soon snuffed out. Lewis had again defeated his opponents with money, the strong-arm stuff that money could buy, and establishment support—only to preside over a shadow organization.[12]

The National Miners Union fumbled about for the first two years of its existence, issuing strike calls that scarcely anyone paid any attention to, and sought unsuccessfully to take over local revolts after they had collapsed. Then in 1931 came the Communists' big opportunity. By this time, the miners' living conditions had grown intolerable, their mood grimmer, the social tie to conservatism being torn apart. In May the union held conferences in Ohio and Pennsylvania to ready its forces for a strike in the western Pennsylvania and eastern Ohio area. This might have given birth to yet another grand-

---

* A. J. Muste, founder of Brookwood Labor College, headed a non-Communist left-wing group dedicated to progressive unionism in the twenties and early thirties. Later he tried to organize a new revolutionary party.

iose paper project except that on May 25 the Carnegie Coal Company announced a wage cut, the workers in several of the company mines voted to strike, and then strike delegations, travelling from mine to mine, shut down a big part of the Old Competitive Field. At the high point, 40,000 miners were reported to be out. It turned into one of the major battles of that year.

The TUUL did not have the resources to manage a strike of any magnitude. But as soon as the Communist hierarchs realized how electric the situation was, they rushed in organizers and such other resources as they could. Bill Dunne, one of their union specialists, and Jack Johnstone, TUUL national organizer, were prominent on the scene. Foster himself repeatedly toured the coal fields. The Party's legal and relief auxiliaries moved in full force. Alfred Wagenknecht, the champion money-raiser, set up a Miners Relief Committee. And a special ad hoc executive board, made up of local and outside Communists, took over the running of the strike.

It was an unusually violent one even by mine-strike standards. On June 8, in a bloody encounter near Pittsburgh, two miners were killed and a state trooper was beaten up. At Ellsworth a marching column of strikers and the coal and iron police fought it out at barricades on the highway. In eastern Ohio hundreds of armed miners descended on the New Lafferty mine in St. Clairsville to force a shutdown. When 18 were jailed, 2,000 miners stormed the jail on June 11. In Belmont County a pitched battle between strikers and mine guards resulted in 8 injured. Two days later on June 20 a Communist union official was shot dead while picketing.

The impetuosity of the union attack forced a break in the employers' ranks, but it benefited Lewis, not Foster. In mid-June, the Pittsburgh Terminal Company, the second largest in Pennsylvania, announced that an agreement would be signed with the United Mine Workers, the union that was not involved in the strike, and with which the operators had refused to deal since they tore up the Jacksonville agreement. If they had to choose between Lewis and the Communist outfit, the employers would take Lewis. The negotiations had been conducted in the executive mansion in Harrisburg under the aegis of Governor Gifford Pinchot, one of the noted liberal executives of the time. Frank Borich, the Communist union secretary, led a protest delegation on the Capitol and warned that the agreement would not be permitted to stand. The company obtained a sweeping injunction which forbade the union to picket or gather about company property at Wildwood. There was a demon-

51

stration of 7,000 miners and their families in front of the Washington County courthouse; then an armed clash in Wildwood in which one man was killed and twelve were injured. Forty-two miners were arrested and deportation proceedings were instituted against twenty who were aliens. The strike ebbed rapidly after the agreement with the UMW was signed on June 23, but the violence continued for weeks thereafter. That same day at Arnold City a storekeeper was killed and four men were injured in a battle between miners and armed guards. A week later three truckloads of union pickets were driven out of Ellsworth by deputies armed with clubs and tear gas, and the union answered with a hunger march of 8,000 miners through downtown Pittsburgh. On July 19 in Canonburg, a meeting of the UMW broke up in a riot in the course of which the speakers were dispersed and 100 were injured.

Despite Communist audacity and miner militancy, the National Miners Union was routed and driven out of Pennsylvania. The coal and iron police, the courts, Lewis's machine, and above all, the whip of hunger, were too formidable a combination to defy. In eastern Ohio the strike collapsed even earlier. In these battles of desperation, a strike generally held together as long as relief supplies held out—and no longer. The Communists exhibited the same characteristics that they had in the textile battles. That they could mobilize, or at least set in motion, several tens of thousands of miners in the frightful circumstances of the time, under the auspices of a skeleton union, propelled by an apparatus of a party with limited manpower and circumscribed resources, was a tribute to their organizing capacities, their illimitable drive, their fanatic faith, their passion for achievement. At the same time, this faith and passion obscured under a thick cloud what native sense of proportion and reality they possessed. Shrewdness, energy, creative organization, were at the mercy of doctrinaire bombast and make-believe. Their missionary zeal for revolutionizing workers remained impervious to the rebuffs of indifference and hostility; their reluctance to admit defeat led them to drag out the strike until the first week of August—a month after it had disintegrated. It would be unrealistic, however, to argue that this Communist-led strike could have had another conclusion—given the material and power realities—had these and other pitfalls been avoided.[13]

That same summer a battle raged in the Kanawha Valley of West Virginia, providing the same counterpoint to the Communist-led strikes that the Marion strike imparted to the Gastonia theme in textiles. Frank Keeney, the one-time UMW president of this district and leader in the "Save the Union" committee, who had been a delegate to the Springfield convention, set up a local branch of the rival UMW. When the latter collapsed, he formed an independent West Virginia Mine Workers Union. He was said to have a kitty of $100,000 he had received from northern liberals, and a small corps of dedicated organizers from Brookwood Labor College was on hand. The union was set up along what progressives of that period would have said were sensible, realistic and efficient lines. There was plenty of color and drama, punctuated, as in a Homeric epic, with bursts of violence, but none of the outlandish politicizing that Communists would have introduced. The organization drive was a success story. Keeney—no novice at the game—knew that this would avail nothing unless he got an agreement with the operators. This meant, in view of their unrelenting hostility, that a strike had to be called although the times were hardly propitious for a showdown. On July 6 the miners struck. The operators responded by evicting the strikers from their homes and replacing them with "barefootmen" from the ranks of the jobless. The union set up an elaborate complex of tent colonies to house and feed its members. But by mid-August, money and food ran out, and the miners could hold out no longer. Keeney called off the hopeless fight, and the union fell apart.[14]

It was in the Harlan coal fields that the Communists made their major mark on depression-years labor history. The miners, leading an isolated existence in this eastern Kentucky hill territory, were reduced to industrial peonage by coal operators who ran the enclosed communities like rapacious feudal barons. The United Mine Workers had been crushed in 1921, and since that time the region was ruled with little regard for constitutional or human niceties. When the coal industry went into a steep decline in the depression, the owners imposed one wage cut after another. By 1931 Harlan miners, averaging three days work, took home no more than four or five dollars a week, often paid in scrip, so they had to trade at company stores where prices were higher than at ordinary markets.

In February 1931 when wages were cut another 10 percent, their cup of miseries ran over: "We starve while we work; we might as well strike while we starve." They turned to the unlikely figure of William Turnblazer who headed District 19 of the UMW, which had jurisdiction over Harlan and Bell counties. Turnblazer was a conventional Lewis payrollee, and District 19 was an organization with

53

a charter and no membership. But thousands began streaming into the union when Turnblazer, on instructions from the home office, promised support. In response to the companies' discharge of union members, over 11,000 struck. Violence swept the coal fields, climaxing on May 4 near the town of Evarts when several carloads of deputies, armed with machine guns and rifles, exchanged fire with armed miners. At the conclusion, three deputies and one miner lay dead. The state's criminal syndicalism law was invoked to charge the UMW with conspiracy to overthrow the government, and 28 miners were indicted for first-degree murder

Lewis was not ready for this kind of struggle, and the UMW just walked out, abandoning the miners it had encouraged to resistance. Some weeks later the Communists stepped into the breach—or rather, the lion's mouth. Their ILD (International Labor Defense) took over the legal defense of the indicted miners, Wagenknecht's relief committee set up shop in Kentucky, and assorted organizers tried to function in this industrial no man's land. Since the mine owners, with the power of the state and legal apparatus at their disposal, had blackjacked the miners into submission when they were affiliated with Lewis, they were not about to practice Christian forebearance now that straggling bands of miners had joined with Communists. Everything that moved came under a systematic reign of terror. The Communists were divided in their counsel as to what to do. The local fraction, responding to demands of desperation around them, favored calling another strike. In New York the Communist heads were hesitant in getting tangled in another hopeless campaign after the debacle in Pennsylvania and Ohio. Finally, in November, to give any contemplated action maximum grass-roots support, the party secretariat ruled that a genuinely representative conference would have to make the decision whether to strike or not. Accordingly, it was the district convention of the National Miners Union held on December 13 in Pinesville, Kentucky, that officially took the fateful step by voting to strike eastern Kentucky with the new year.

The strike was a disaster from the first. Unlike the previous strikes in Pennsylvania, Ohio, and West Virginia, there was no shutdown of the mines. The union had signed up masses of blacklisted miners whose immediate interest was to qualify for relief, and when relief became unavailable, they drifted away. Some representatives of working miners who may have intended to call their men out, did not do so when they learned that the union could not provide sufficient relief. Jack Stachel of the Communist trade union high command admitted later in the inevitable self-criticism that "we were wrong in calling the strike when we did," that the union consisted mainly of blacklisted workers who could not close the mines, that the strike should have been called off as soon as it became clear that there was no strike in reality, only a demonstration of unemployed.

If Communist politicizing had a deleterious effect on the strike in Pennsylvania, it was far worse in Kentucky where the miners, of old native stock, belonged to fundamentalist sects. One example: Findley Donaldson, local union chairman and a member of the Holiness Church, was sent up to Chicago for a training course. When he came back, he reported that he never would have joined the union or the Party if he had known that the Communists did not believe in God, were against the United States, and honored Soviet Russia. Inevitably, also, race relations led to ill feeling although no more than 2 percent of Kentucky miners were Blacks. The question came up of whether Blacks should eat in the same soup kitchens or sit at the same tables as Whites. Black miners who joined the Party took the lead in speaking against eating together on the ground that it would hand an issue to the mine owners and police on which to break the strike. But the Communist leaders were adamant.

Outside investigators took the serious view that denunciations by Donaldson and others were the main reason for the defeat, "far more effective in smashing the union," according to H. L. Morris, "than the National Guard could have been." Malcolm Ross thought the strike was cracked "less by guns and whips than the rock-ribbed fundamentalism of the miners." These appreciations do not take into account that the strike did not and could not get off the ground from the day it was announced, but they reflect the horrendous reactions to the crudeness and excesses of Communist "third period" propagandizing. Any and all militant unionism was bound to be provocative and the object of brutal misrepresentation at this time. The Communists compounded their own difficulties by identifying the Party and the red unions—to the disadvantage of both.

If the Communists could not win a strike or build a union in Harlan, they had one considerable accomplishment to record, both for themselves and for the miners. The hunger and degradation in the Harlan mine country had been a condition of life for decades; so had the barefaced police-state regimes in company-ridden towns. No one on the outside cared about it or paid any attention to it until the Communists broke down the walls of ignorance and inattention that had shielded the area. In November, Theodore Dreiser's National Committee for the Defense of Political Prisoners, made up of eight intellectuals (others refused to participate), conducted a tour of the area in the course of which many witnesses, including the Harlan sheriff and prosecuting attorney, were questioned. The committee's hearings, widely broadcast, made Harlan County and its outrages a familiar story to millions across the country. Several months later, when the Communist-led strike was on, another group of writers arrived on the scene with truckloads of food and clothing, to be followed by delegations of clergymen, students, and a committee of prominent lawyers sponsored by the American Civil Liberties Union. The continued arrests, kidnappings, beatings and killings in the area, and the nationwide excitation, led in May to a full-blown senatorial investigation. This typhoon of publicity—a spate of articles in the liberal journals, a series of reports in the *New York Times*, a book of findings by members of the Dreiser Committee, *Harlan Miners Speak*, and many other expositions—made a strong impression. For a while it seemed as if no discussion in advanced circles was complete if it did not include a denunciation of the wicked goings-on in Harlan. One of the best-known labor songs to come out of the depression era, immortalizing the Harlan saga, was written by a union organizer's wife during the strike. The challenging "class-struggle" refrain, "Which side are you on? Which side are you on?" was belted out in a thousand labor gatherings to the tune of an old Baptist hymn, "Lay the Lily Low."

The muckraking and indignation did not benefit the miners, the union, or the Communists on the ground, but the heightened public consciousness probably helped open up the area to unionism some years later; and without a doubt, Harlan was an exotic, cherished, and valuable feather in the Communists' cap. They had dared invade the armed fortress of reaction at its worst when no one else had the courage, and before they had been driven out by superior force, they had made Harlan County a byword for corporation tyranny, and an exemplar of class struggle to break the chains of industrial exploitation. The hastily recruited Communist party membership in the Harlan coal area was just as hastily lost; but the troubadours and minstrels who told and retold the glories of the battle were instrumental in making many more converts to the Party and its auxiliaries in the metropolises of the North and West.[15]

3

In the big strikes, the Communists piled up a perfect negative score; their zeal stood them in better stead in marginal, less conclusive situations, as in the food industry another early entrant into the red trade-union federation. On May Day, 1929, Communists in New York City were able to organize a parade of several thousand cafeteria workers under the banner of the Food Workers Industrial Union. "Such an impressive demonstration spread gloom in the Cincinnati headquarters of the Hotel and Restaurant Employees, especially when it was contrasted with the inactivity or apathy of the regular AFL locals in the field." So recorded Matthew Josephson, who in the course of a checkered career as Paris expatriate and avant-garde editor was also the authorized historian of the AFL hotel and restaurant organization. The red union struck many eateries in the garment center and mid-town areas patronized by thousands of unionists and union friends. Their bold forays in the busy streets, leading to court injunctions and mass arrests, enabled the union to sign agreements with numbers of cafeteria owners. Other owners tried to brazen it out, or to find succor in the arms of the AFL union, which announced its presence and availability; this, in turn, led to further street altercations and lengthy court suits between the two organizations.

While the actual membership was never large in the depression years and fluctuated wildly, the Communist-led union remained a power in the cafeteria field, and the AFL union was being edged out. The left outfit was one of the very few in the TUUL grab bag that was able to take advantage of the NRA upsurge, in part because the AFL union had been reduced to a shell in the Prohibition twenties, its locals in both Chicago and New York infiltrated by mobsters. In contrast to the sleazy officials who had been taken in tow by emissaries of Al Capone and Dutch Schultz, the red union had a number of outstanding talents. The leading spirit was Jay Rubin, the union's secretary (today, the head of the New York AFL Hotel Trades Council). He had been a business agent for the Upholsterers Union in Boston, and later, in the food industry, displayed skills as a union strategist and negotiator. The president, a German waiter by the name of Michael J. Obermeier, was an important left-wing figure in the hotel and restaurant field since the First World War. (He was ordered deported in the cold-war period, and after a long court process and a prison term for perjury, left voluntarily for Germany in 1952. Obermeier, Rubin, his wife Gertrude Lane, also a key organizer in the union, and a number of others had broken with the Communist party by this latter date.)

There was a sensational general strike in January 1934 that crippled major New York hotels, conducted under the aegis of an old, quasi-left independent union, the Amalgamated Food Workers, led at this time by a Trotskyist faction. Despite overflowing enthusiasm on the picket lines, and the support of celebrated New York intelligentsia rallying to the cause of the cooks and waiters, the strike fell apart in the face of the owners' tenacity. Once the Amalgamated disintegrated, the Communist-led union—caught unawares by the revolt in the hotels—emerged as the strongest body in the field. Edward Flore, the AFL food union president, thought that the red union had about 9,000 members in 1934. When the Communists decided (as will be discussed) to reenter the AFL, unity negotiations with the AFL international proved difficult and protracted precisely because the local AFL officials in New York feared that they would be displaced by the abler, more dedicated, more popular left spokesmen. Their fears were justified. The unification was finally consummated two years later, and the red officials took over key locals without any difficulty to become the powerhouse of the New York organization.[16]

4

The pioneering work in the maritime industry was of a different nature. From earliest days, this field had a romantic fascination for the Communist movement. Aside from any Conrad-like allures, there was a certain radical tradition on the waterfronts; seamen were well placed to act as couriers and to establish international links; and it was hoped they would provide shock troops for future revolutionary actions. (Who did not know the role the Kronstadt sailors played in the 1917 revolution!) Here, too, "objective conditions" seemed made to order. After the loss of the 1921 strike and the rout of the AFL unions, the shipowners exercised unquestioned hegemony over their labor forces, and restored the execrable prewar conditions, so that, unlike others, maritime workers enjoyed little prosperity in the prosperous twenties.

It would have been logical for the IWW to become the dominant radical organization. The Wobblies had established a foothold in the maritime industry before the First World War with their own industrial union. Their adherents also headed the growing disaffection inside the AFL International Seamen's Union (ISU). In the AFL's West Coast division, the Sailors Union of the Pacific, the Wobblies were able to elect the editor of the *Seamen's Journal* in 1921 and to take over most of the union offices. On the East Coast, old-line officials were similarly menaced. They put down the rebellion by indiscriminately expelling IWW members and supporters, only to be leaders without followers for the entire decade.

There was another factor which should have made for Wobbly ascendancy. The waterfront of the twenties, a domain of shipowner harshness and casual employment, bred an unusual labor force. Seamen were little affected by conservative shoreside traditions. They had no objection to radicals becoming prominent in their union affairs so long as the radicals' objectives ran parallel with their own economic goals. *Fortune* magazine called American sailors "the true proletariat of the Western world, the homeless, rootless, and eternally unmoneyed [with] no stake in the system beyond this month's voyage." Not only had the Wobblies formulated the basic program (taken over by the Communists when they set up their own union) of job action, rank-and-file control, federation of seamen and longshoremen, and industrial unionism, but the syndicalist tenor was closer to the maritime workers' inclinations and habits than the more intensely political doctrine of the Communists. Yet it was the Communists, not the Wobblies, who led the revival of the thirties. Why?

James P. Cannon, who had been an IWW organizer before joining the Communists, gave this general explanation:

Insofar as the human material was concerned, the advantages were all on the side of the IWW. . . . The IWWs imagined that their actions and their sacrifices so far outweighed the mere doctrinal pretensions of this new revolutionary movement that they had nothing to fear from it in the way of rivalry. They were badly mistaken. . . . The IWW, with its wonderful composition of proletarian militants . . . could not keep pace. They had not adjusted their ideology to the lessons of the war and the Russian revolution. . . . That is why their organization degenerated, while this new organization with its poorer material, its inexperienced youth who had seized hold of the living ideas of Bolshevism, completely surpassed the IWW and left it far behind in the space of a few years.

Transposed into a less ecstatic key, this is a good explanation. When the big upsurge came in maritime, the Communists, with almost no representation among longshoremen and very little inside the industry as a whole, but with the bigger and better trained battalions in the radical movement, could impose themselves on the inchoate labor formations.[17]

The Communists made their initial entry in 1926 when they set up an International Seamen's Club to provide recreational facilities for both ISU and IWW members. This organization went through several metamorphoses until the Marine Workers Industrial Union was organized in 1930. The program was in line with the TUUL ritual: tough trade-union demands climaxed with unterrified calls for the abolition of "wage slavery," defense of the Soviet Union "against all attacks of the imperialist governments by every means in its power," and "the establishment of a revolutionary workers' and farmers' government."

Since the MWIU was not in a position to act on any of these latter planks just then, it concentrated its attentions on more immediate, pedestrian matters. In 1932, the MWIU Waterfront Unemployed Council in New York began a hit-and-run battle with the Seamen's Church Institute, the main charitable organization supplying relief to unemployed seamen. Noisy rallies were staged in the institute's assembly room, protest demonstrations were called, tough-talking delegations were sent in to intimidate the institute directors. At one time, a group of waterfront Communists met with Gerge Mink, one of the red-union leaders (later notorious as a strong-arm man and GPU operative), to confer on strategy when the institute began serving only one meal a day instead of the two it had served previously. Mink gave the committee its assignment: "The first thing you do is fight for two meals, and when you get two meals you fight for three meals, and when you get three meals you fight about the menu; if they give you stew you want roast beef, and if you get roast beef you want steak, and if you get steak you want a choice on the menu. Remember, you cannot demand too much because the workers created it all and until the workers take it all they are not demanding enough."

The MWIU claimed that it called many job actions on East Coast ships after 1932; fifty stoppages on Munson Line ships. The writeups in the *Marine Workers' Voice* are the usual hodgepodge and slipshod verbiage that make up Communist reporting in this period, so it is impossible to determine whether the propagandistic exhortations refer to job actions sponsored by the union, or the customary "beefs" and "quickies," in which Communist seamen participated, that often took place on board the ships. The latter would appear to be the case judging by the comment that "we did not convince the Munson crews to stay on the ships after victories and make it possible to develop company scale action." The union also claimed to have established a "seaman-controlled" hiring hall in Baltimore that for a while accounted for 85 percent of all shipping. This feat was credited by some to Harry Alexander, an engine-room tender, who was with the Party through thick and thin (later pushed out for his reputedly syndicalist proclivities). Jobless seamen who were on government-financed relief—higher in Baltimore than elsewhere—were housed and fed at the waterfront YMCA. Thus, there was a good opportunity for getting them together for concerted action. What the hiring hall amounted to and how much control it actually exercised is difficult to establish—it lasted a very short time only—and the shipowners were supposed to have destroyed it by dispatching crews from other ports.

That same year, the union in San Francisco began to issue a monthly paper, the *Waterfront Worker*, which the comrades ran off on a dilapidated mimeograph machine and sold for a penny (later a nickel) at the shape-up near the Ferry Building. Harry Hynes, its founding editor (the paper was issued on a catch-as-catch-can basis, like most Communist shop publications) was an Australian seaman with the revolutionary sailor's knowledge of foreign countries and international labor annals. (He later died in Spain in 1937, shot through the neck by one of Franco's Moorish marksmen.) He and Harry Bridges, a fellow Australian, hit it off, and an important alliance was struck up by the Communists with a group of longshoremen. The paper had an impact on the waterfront, but few joined the Communist union.

After Bridges became an editor in the fall of 1933, he and his longshoremen circle took over control of the paper. Sam Darcy, the Communist party leader in California, reported, "Unfortunately, our Marine Workers union, after having as many as four and sometimes six full-time functionaries in San Francisco alone, had not a single worker on the docks." What the Communists did have was a trained force that could jump into situations and take advantage of opportunities. Before the great West Coast maritime strike was over at the end of July 1934, the Communist party recruited 25 longshoremen and over 50 seamen in San Francisco, 40 of both categories in San Pedro, and "many more" in the Northwest ports. It thus became an established force in the West Coast Maritime unions.[18]

5

Depression-period Communist activities in the automobile industry are perhaps most representative of the character and limitation of Communist activities in general. Because of its enormous expansion in the prewar years and the twenties, and its high hourly wages, the automobile industry was an irresistible magnet to the young, the vigorous, and the adventuresome from every part of the country— before immigration was cut off, from every part of the globe. The assembly line became the popular symbol of triumphant American technology, and Henry Ford, the major producer of this period, a world-renowned prophet of mass production and high wages. To the workers, of whom only 5 to 10 percent were skilled in the traditional sense (Ford estimated that 85 percent of his workers required from one day to two weeks training), the auto plants were workhouses where they were driven like robots in repetitious and monotonous motions, leaving them in nervous exhaustion at the end of the day. To the unsatisfactory character of the work and a humiliating sub-mission to a supervisory force that rode roughshod over manhood was added the risk of long layoffs. Because the auto industry de-pended on a mass market, the depression struck it harder than most others. Factory sales of cars and trucks fell by 75 percent from 1929 to 1932; the number of workers dropped 45 percent; total payrolls, over 60 percent. In the early depression years, Detroit had the worst relief crisis and the highest jobless rate of all major American cities.[19]

The Communists started their purposeful agitation in the Detroit plants in 1925 during their TUEL period. They had a scattered auto membership in the Michigan area through their language federa-tions. Soon there was a blossoming of shop papers, *The Ford Worker*, *The Dodge Worker*, *The Fisher Body Worker*, *The Chrys-ler Worker*, *The Buick Worker*, *The Oakland-Pontiac Worker*, is-sued under the auspices, not of the TUEL, but of the Workers (Communist) Party itself, reflecting presumably the left zig-zag in the middle twenties. (A member in Detroit wrote all the papers with the exception of the one in Ford.) These little four-page sheets, sold for a penny or given away by Communist distributors at plant gates, were often eagerly accepted; they provided the only news of conditions and grievances inside the plants available to workers. The Communists claimed a circulation of 20,000 (the highest) for *The Ford Worker*, but this is a meaningless figure, like listing circulation data for a throwaway advertising sheet. The primary importance of their pioneering was that in auto, as elsewhere, they were building a select officer corps with some knowledge of the industry and the labor personnel.

In 1928, Communist membership in the auto field was listed as 407, and the party had gained control of the Detroit local of a moribund union, the United Automobile, Aircraft and Vehicle Workers of America. This had been an old union in the field, originating with the wagon workers established in 1891. Suspended from the AFL in 1918 when it refused to accept the decision to stay out of the auto industry, it had some small successes for a while, but disintegrated after the 1921 recession. The Communists inherited very little besides the name, and this they proceeded to scrap. They rechristened the organization the Auto Workers Union, and affiliated it in 1929 with the TUUL. Aside from having a union that flaunted a program of class struggle and the abolition of capitalism, they carried on very much as they had before. The union held conferences, issued pronunciamentos, thickened the air with war yells for a "united front" of all auto workers, and predictably excoriated the companies, government officials, and AFL bureaucrats. Its most significant actions were not in the trade-union field, strictly speaking, but the two hunger marches it organized to the Ford River Rouge plant. In the 1932 hunger march, four young men, one the district organizer of the Young Communist League, were killed, and 23 were seriously injured. Over 50,000 participated in or observed the impressive funeral march down Woodward Avenue sponsored by the Communist party and the Unemployed Councils.

So far as establishing itself in the industry, the union was a nullity; its membership consisted of little more than the Communist apparatus. But it did leave a mark. Frank Marquart, a Socialist who worked in the Detroit shops in the twenties and later was education director of several CIO auto locals, testified that some workers were sympathetic. The CP shop paper "gave them a visceral reaction; it spoke to them about the experiences that impinged on their nerves

63

. . . The paper said what they felt! . . . I do know that those papers played a significant role in preparing auto workers' minds for the union thrust that was to come." It should be kept in mind that there was a certain radical milieu in Detroit in the depression years, and that Communists, Socialists, and members of the Proletarian party (a Marxist dissident group that had some importance in Detroit and Flint), and later, Trotskyists and Lovestoneites, were a leavening influence. "You just cannot underestimate the [role] that these radical political organizations played in helping to develop leaders and consequently influencing the trade union movement."[20]

Organizing the automobile industry was an aspiration common to all radicals; they all exaggerated and glamorized its importance for transforming the social system; and before the advent of the CIO, radicals were the main carriers of the ideas of industrial unionism and militant action. While the industrialists' plants continued to stand as impregnable fortresses, on the plains and in the hamlets were gathering the forces of rebellion. The election of Frank Murphy, a noted humanitarian attorney, as Detroit mayor in 1930 on a welfare platform, and his immense and growing popularity in office, was symptomatic of the trend: liberal currents were gathering strength and would open the passage to unionization of this hitherto open-shop stronghold. Who was to provide the flag? The AFL had no following in the industry; its so-called campaign of 1927—like the one in textiles—relied on convincing the auto magnates of the benefits that they could reap from collective bargaining, and had been similarly ignored.

Roosevelt's victory quickened the atmospherics of expectancy, bringing on a flurry of spontaneous strikes. The first important one in 1933 was on January 23 when 6,000 workers walked out of the four Briggs plants (Briggs was known as the "butcher shop") to protest a wage cut, a speed up, and the dangerous, unsanitary working conditions. Ford, dependent on Briggs for bodies, announced big layoffs, and the strike became a major labor-management contest. Lacking any organization of their own when they went out, the strikers turned to Phil Raymond, secretary of the Auto Workers Union (and the Communist mayoralty candidate in 1930), for help. This was the long-awaited opportunity, and the Communists moved in, furnishing what facilities, experience, and leadership they could. Bill McKie, one of the stalwarts, although a worker at Ford, was elected to the strike committee. Tom Parry, who had been a member of the "Save the Union" opposition in the mine organization, and was now an employee at another auto plant, set up soup kitchens. The front outfits were supplying relief and trying to raise funds. Raymond was at the center of things working up strategy as head of the strike committee, as were the district Party organizers.

With that came a public outcry against Communists and Communism that bowled over the strike committee members. Most of them caved in under the pressure and repudiated the Communists. The Communist triumph was a short-lived one. By the beginning of March, without funds or adequate organization, the strikers drifted back to work; they had won a few marginal concessions, but no recognition and no bargaining rights. The strike, although broken, was not without effect: it dispelled the myth that the manufacturers were ruling over an empire of contented, loyal employees. *Business Week* noted that " 'this first "depression strike" is the beginning of a process which established the limit of pay and hours and treatment which men will stand.' "

Another major strike was led by the IWW at Murray Body. The Wobblies had tried unsuccessfully to gain a foothold in auto in 1913, and now made a new determined effort to build their Metal and Machine Workers Industrial Union. They had been in the leadership of the Briggs strike at the Highland Park plant where two of their members headed the committee; they had gained members and prestige. The IWW now moved into larger quarters, inaugurated a six-day radio program on a local station, and an intensive campaign of meetings at plant gates. Their main organizers, Frank and Tor Cedervall, and Fred Thompson were talented soapboxers, but the union had few resources and was well past its prime. The special circumstances that favored the Wobblies in maritime were absent in the automobile industry. Though workers, in desperation, would accept the leadership of avowed radicals, most of them were fundamentally nonradical and wary of being tagged. Their alliance was opportunistically motivated. Moreover, IWW organizing, centered at the Murray Body plant, developed in an unfortunate way: the big membership influx came on the eve of a layoff for a body changeover.

The new members, convinced that they were being discriminated against, demanded work rotation. Management officials consented to meet with the shop committee, insisted there was no intention to discriminate, but would not agree to work rotation on grounds of practicality. The IWW leaders now permitted themselves to be swept along by the activists' momentary mood of indignation. It was no time to take action since it was the end of the season, and a shut-down would exert little or no pressure on the company. The frustrated negotiating committee was in a frenzy, however, and voted to call a strike at the end of September. The strike was foredoomed; the union members simply wore themselves out in aimless picketing and arm-waving. Six weeks later, their funds exhausted and prospects for a settlement nil, the strike was called off without having won a single concession. The IWW newspaper sounded the cheerful note that the strikers had "learned what the class struggle really means," although it conceded that the union had suffered "a slight setback." Actually, because of its lack of generalship, the IWW removed itself from the arena.[21]

The Briggs, Murray, and several similar strikes were only one manifestation. With the National Recovery Act about to be enacted, William Green, the AFL head, summoned a conference of selected AFL dignitaries to discuss plans for taking advantage of Section 7(a)—the labor clause of the NRA that prohibited employers from interfering with the worker's right to organize. A decision was reached to start an auto campaign, and William Collins, who had been connected with the ill-fated 1927 venture, was dispatched to Detroit. This appeared more menacing than it was. The AFL was totally unsuited and unprepared to challenge the auto magnates. The old-line craft officials were only going through the motions of taking on the industry. They were actually thinking in terms of snatching small groups of workers for their own separate organizations—and of keeping up public appearances. First was the roadblock of their own creation. Collins and his rotarian-type organizers tried to enroll workers in so-called federal locals—an interim bastardized division—regarded as "wards" directly controlled by the AFL Executive Council; their members, at an appropriate time, were supposed to be parceled out to the various craft unions. Even this arrangement was too liberal to suit some hidebound officials. A. O. Wharton, president of the International Association of Machinists, demanded that auto members who fell under his jurisdiction be transferred to his organization forthwith. Green had no choice but to notify Collins that the jurisdiction rights of the various internationals would have to be respected.

Craft narrow-mindedness went hand in hand with penuriousness and bureaucratic inertia. From July 1933 to February 1934, the AFL Detroit headquarters spent about $5,700 on organization work. Between October 1934 and January 1935, another $36,000.

Green reported in 1936 that UAW locals had paid over $181,000 in per capita tax between July 1933 and October 1935, and that during the period the AFL had spent $249,000 in auto—a grand total of $68,000 contributed in 27 months. Antiquated organization concepts and closefisted narrow-mindedness were aspects of the larger reality that the AFL lacked the capacity, the will, the outlook, and the staff for the kind of battle that would have been necessary to compel the automobile manufacturers to come to terms.

Despite its nugatory campaign and policy, almost despite itself, the AFL managed to make some headway, particularly in the outlying areas, where the power of the manufacturers was not so overwhelming. (During the two NRA years, 1,800 federal locals sprang up in the mass-production industries, virtually by the self-organization of the workers concerned.) The fact that the AFL was the established trade-union body, and that its reputation for conservatism and respectability would make it easier, many believed, to gain bargaining rights from employers, gave the AFL an initial advantage in catching the winds of discontent in its own somewhat moth-eaten sails. A number of federal locals called strikes either with no support from the Detroit office, or in conflict with the Detroit office, at Auto-Lite in Toledo, at Seaman Body in Milwaukee, at the Nash plants in Racine and Kenosha, at Hupp Motor in Detroit; they established going organizations and won limited bargaining rights. Communists were major protagonists in both the White Motor local in Cleveland, and the Seaman Body local in Milwaukee. Upon being informed of these infiltrations, Green wrote agitated letters to his representatives informing them that either the Communists must be ousted, or the local charters revoked. In the fluid, chaotic conditions of pioneer auto unionism facing obdurate employer opposition, this was easier said than done.[22]

The early activities of Wyndham Mortimer at White Motor (who later became vice president of the CIO auto union) are evocative of unionism in those days. Mortimer—an old-time Communist from the mines—began to sign up workers in the TUUL Auto Workers Union in early 1933, and invited Phil Raymond to come down to address a local meeting. When word of this got around, organizers of the AFL Metal Trades Council distributed a leaflet at the plant gates with the message, "Join the only bonafide *American* labor union. Join the American Federation of Labor, the only union endorsed by our great President Franklin Delano Roosevelt." Another leaflet read, "Choose between Franklin Delano Roosevelt and Joe

Stalin." After the distribution of these leaflets, "new applicants in our independent union dropped off entirely," said Mortimer. He talked the problem over with several key workers. "These men were anxious to build a union, but felt that a union affiliated with the AFL . . . would be more acceptable." When Mortimer found that his arguments were not changing his hearer's minds, and that some had already signed AFL application cards, he and his supporters cast their lot with the AFL, a federal charter was applied for and granted, and federal Local No. 18463 came into existence.

Our federal charter was presented to us by George McKinnon. He announced that it was the policy and custom of the Metal Trades Council to appoint temporary officers. I arose and asked what had happened to the vaunted AFL democracy? McKinnon was taken aback. "But, Brother Mortimer," he said, "this is a traditional and temporary arrangement for a brief period." "What is a brief period?" I asked. "Not over three months." I did not press the matter further. . . . President George Lehman of our local sent a letter to the White Motor Company requesting a meeting for the purpose of negotiating a contract covering wages, hours, and working conditions. As chairman of the grievance and bargaining committee, I was spokesman for the union. We met at the appointed time and presented to the company's representative (Vice President George Smith) a copy of the proposed contract. To our amazement, we found James McWheeny of the Metal Trades Council already sitting in Mr. Smith's office. We had not asked him to be present, nor had we even told him of the meeting. However, he did not make us wait long before showing us why he was there.

"Mr. Smith," he started off, "the Communists are trying to take over the American labor movement, and my advice to you is, do not sign any contract or agreement of any kind with this local 18463. If you sign a contract it must be with the Metal Trades Council and the American Federation of Labor." Mr. Smith surprised us. "We are capable of handling our own affairs," he replied curtly. Then turning to me and the committee he added, "We will study your proposals and you will hear from us."[23]

Concomitant with AFL activities, another independent union appeared on the scene, the Mechanics Educational Society of America, which was to play a notable part in the unfolding drama. It had been formed in the early months of 1933 by tool-and-die makers, the aristocracy of automobile workers, whose wages had been driven down to decidedly unaristocratic levels. As soon as the NRA was promulgated in June, the MESA broadcast its message and the response was overwhelming. Members were streaming in from Detroit, Flint, and Pontiac. (The MESA was at this time a craft union, and in revolt against the high fees and dues charged by the AFL International Association of Machinists, had no initiation fee, and monthly dues of only 25 cents.) Within a matter of months, the union was strong enough to put wage and hour demands to GM managements in Flint at Buick, Chevrolet, and A. C. Spark Plug. When company responses were deemed unsatisfactory, a strike was ordered on September 21. The strike shut down the tool rooms in Flint, and after a short delay, it spread to Detroit and Pontiac. Though a lot of die work was shipped out of the state, the strike in Detroit hit hard at the big job shops (to which the manufacturers subcontract much of their tool, die, and fixture needs) and at Fisher Body and Ternstedt. In the first flush of optimism, the strike committee announced that it would demand one settlement to cover all struck plants.

MESA officers had boasted that it was unnecessary for their organization to have the support of production workers; a tool-and-die strike would necessarily force the closing of all operations. The strike taught them otherwise. Automobile production was hurt, but not stopped. For weeks the strike dragged on with no negotiations in progress, while the morale of the men was sagging. When the National Labor Board's mediation efforts came to nothing, the strikers resorted to more forceful methods. Guerrilla forays culminated on October 30 with a motorized brigade of 3,000 strikers going on a rampage, smashing windows and furniture, and destroying blueprints in a number of shops. Within the next ten days, the union was able to settle with most of the struck companies. Pay increases were modest, in some cases already covered by the NRA code, but the employers granted union recognition by indirection—at the time, a banner breakthrough. The MESA came out of the strike as a force in the industry, its prestige sky-high. It had taken on the automobile giants in the first national strike, won a partial victory, breached the historic open shop, and doubled its membership in the course of the strike.

A number of Communist tool-and-die makers were swept into the MESA in the elemental upsurge, and they could count on some support inside the union from others who had been associated with the Independent Labor Party or the shop stewards movement in Britain. Because the MESA was a new, small union with no established officialdom, and the national office had practically no finances and hardly any staff, the Communists were able to keep several Detroit locals in perpetual turmoil. During the strike they directed a drumfire of barbed criticism at the national officers, particularly the national secretary, Matthew Smith, who was both the brains and dynamo of the organization, and could trounce them in open debate. The planks of their super-militant program—including a rank-and-file strike committee, united action with the Communist-led Unemployed Councils, spreading the strike to Ford—were either irrelevant, pernicious, or impossible to achieve. One point of their criticism that was very much in order, however, called attention to what, in fact, became the union's Achilles heel—the failure to organize production workers. This, too, of course, required something more than phrasemongering. John Anderson, the Party spokesman in the union, a Scotsman from Glasgow, presided at MESA mass meetings during the strike, at which there was a lot of inflated talk about marching on Dearborn and calling out all production workers. Neither project saw the light of day. The unorganized production workers, who had been ignored by the MESA up until the calling of the strike, could not be commandeered at the eleventh hour in a fight that was neither started by them, nor on their behalf.

When Communist agitation against the leaders became reckless after an unsuccessful second strike in Detroit job shops in April 1934, the union's District Committee expelled the two ringleaders, John Anderson and John Mack, and announced that all Communists would be purged. Anderson managed to have his own local reinstate him by a narrow vote, but was decisively defeated in his run against Smith for national secretary at the end of the year. The Communists continued haranguing for united fronts with their own Auto Workers Union and the UAW federal locals until they dissolved their red union at the beginning of 1935. When it became clear to them that they could neither take over the MESA nor force Smith to unite with the UAW, they withdrew the two Detroit locals they controlled, and were chartered as Local No. 155 by the UAW at the time of that union's South Bend convention. It is likely that they would have succeeded in carrying all or most of the MESA had their prior conduct not been so obstructionist and irresponsible.

Matthew Smith was the most impressive figure to appear on the scene of auto unionism in its initial phase. He came out of the

British shop stewards movement, a freewheeling British-laborite type of socialist. A fluent, effective speaker, a good negotiator and organizer (although with a tendency to run things out of his own vest pocket), he made an excellent impression. Many thought he was the potential spokesman of the big auto union to be. Unfortunately for him, once the MESA was unable to organize the production workers in the wake of its victory, it became an object, not a subject of decision-making. It was caught in the demoralization that preceded the CIO's emergence, rolling over the auto centers after the disintegration of the federal locals when Green and Collins reneged on their promise to call the strike they had been threatening for March 1934.

The process of dissolution was hastened by their agreeing to the creation of the Automobile Labor Board which, in effect, legalized company unions. When the AFL was discredited, not just its own members fell away; there was a catastrophic decline of all union sentiment. The first uprising was over. Then the CIO came into Michigan in force two years later, and Smith had to make the best arrangement he could with its auto affiliate, the UAW. He could play from some strength since the MESA had a sizable contingent of the key skilled workers of the industry, and the MESA reputation was still good. Now Smith's megalomania became his undoing. He devised an impossible program for an all-embracing metal union that effectively cut off any meaningful negotiations or agreements with the CIO representatives—and that was probably his intention. He still lived with the illusion that when the big push would occur, the MESA would again be on top—as in 1933. Once he missed the chance to come in when the UAW was still small, and when he would have been well received, the MESA was stranded as an inconsequential union on the sidelines.[24]

6

It might be thought that the movement of Communists away from their own Auto Workers Union and into AFL federal locals and the MESA represented the triumph of common sense over dogma, that Communist unionists were responding to workers' sentiments in the way Mortimer represented his own conduct in Cleveland. That is not the way important activities were governed in the Communist domain. To understand why the Communists were switching allegiances in Cleveland or Detroit, we have to consult again with the Moscow soothsayers. As early as the Twelfth Plenum of the

ECCI in September 1932 there occurred one of the policy modifications that the seasoned Communist politician was ever alert for. Laboring under the impact of the deadlock in Germany, where Communists led the unemployed and Social Democrats had control of the trade unions, the ECCI mentors, in approved Byzantine style, as if they had never read their own previous decrees, slipped this joker into a new resolution: "The consistent, everyday struggle of the Communists and supporters of the revolutionary trade union movement for the establishment of the united front of the workers urgently raises before all sections of the Comintern and the RILU [Red International of Labor Unions] the question of work *inside* the reformist trade unions. . . . The influence of the trade union bureaucracy . . . is one of the chief hindrances to the development of the class struggle, and cannot be broken down by shouts about wrecking the trade unions for which Communists are not striving, nor by deserting the trade unions, but by persistent work inside the reformist trade unions." Ossip Piatnitsky, the grizzled Comintern paymaster who served, in turn, Zinoviev, Bukharin, and Stalin (and who disappeared a few years later in the purges), clarified the issue in this way: "Some talk can already be heard and questions asked as to what danger is greater, the right or the left. It has already been found that the chief danger is the right danger, and here no changes must be made. . . . But does the fact that the chief danger is the right danger exclude the necessity to struggle against the 'left' danger? Is it for this reason that we don't have to work in the reformist unions? Such an opinion is sectarian."[25]

Before the Americans could get into the intricacies of weaving together red and reformist unions, and right and left dangers, portentous events transpired in Germany. Hitler was appointed chancellor at the end of January 1933, and as he quickly unleashed his terror and consolidated Nazi power, it became clear to the world that the largest Communist party outside of Russia was being annihilated. The train of Third Period follies—social fascism, united front from below, red trade unions, "after Hitler, us"—had immobilized the German labor movement and contributed to a tragedy of historic dimensions. In Europe, both Socialist and Communist ranks were seething; the pressure was intense on all leaders to unite against the common danger.

The Bureau of the Socialist International made the initial gesture on February 19 in a declaration expressing the readiness of its affiliated parties to form united fronts with Communists. In response, the ECCI issued a manifesto on March 18 lambasting the Socialists in typical Stalinist style, and trying to unload full responsibility for the calamity on their shoulders. After dutifully mouthing phrases about workers taking things into their own hands to set up united fronts from below, the authors suddenly shifted the argument to call upon the Communist parties "to make yet another attempt" to come to an agreement with the Socialist parties. They went further in annulling the rhetoric of a thousand proclamations with the recommendation that "during the time of common fight against capital and fascism to refrain from making attacks on Social Democratic organizations."[26] This and other improvisations came to no fruition that year because the Comintern officials received no clear instruction from the Kremlin on how far to go.

Stalin at first adopted a wait-and-see attitude. The German Communists, in their leftist splurge, had made it an article of faith that Hitler was a passing phenomenon, and Stalin wanted to satisfy himself concerning the stability of the Nazi regime. He also wanted time to determine whether Hitler would adopt a Bismarckian policy, now that he held the reins of power, or would follow through on the anti-Soviet fulminations of his barnstorming days. The result was to adopt an official stance of studied calm, as if the Nazi triumph represented nothing more than a routine change of ministries. German Communist leaders, now residing abroad, insisted that they had been right in everything they had done and said, and that the fascist victory only "accelerates the speed of Germany's march towards the proletarian revolution." Fritz Heckert wrote: "The talk about the German Communists being defeated and practically dead is the gossip of philistines, of idiotic and ignorant people." The Thirteenth ECCI Plenum in December put its official stamp of approval to this balderdash. It was a year before Stalin referred in public to what had happened in Germany. Then at the Seventeenth Congress of the Russian party in January 1934 he talked like the Russian nationalist leader that he was. Picking his way cautiously, he pointed out that German policy was proceeding in an anti-Russian rather than a Bismarckian direction. Nevertheless, fascism was not the issue "if only for the reason that fascism, for example, in Italy, did not prevent the USSR establishing very good relations with that country." The issue was simply which countries were for the status quo, and which were disturbing the peace, and the USSR would not hesitate to ally itself with those who were for peace.[27]

The pretense of business-as-usual at Communist headquarters to

73

the contrary notwithstanding, the American commissars decided they had to reorient and gear up the Party, many of whose ranks were either alarmed or bewildered by the German smashup. They summoned the faithful to an extraordinary Party conference in July 1933 for the purpose of approving an open letter to the entire membership. This was well and good, but what to propose? The composition of this letter required considerable ingenuity. They decided on a nondescript potpourri: the reliable Third Period recipe with added ingredients being recommended by the Moscow chefs. They were cautious in moving out in any given direction so that by the time Browder was through explaining the meaning of the Comintern manifesto on the united front, the tactic seemed to resolve itself to conducting better public relations in discussions with members of the Socialist party, Musteites, or AFL unionists. For the rest, the document was loaded with the customary admonitions, scoldings and exhortations to correct mistakes, overcome weaknesses, struggle harder and better.

The Central Committee resolution of October continued to lecture: The line of the open letter was being carried out too slowly, weakly, inadequately. There was still some resistance to "penetrating into the A.F. of L., especially among the newly recruited masses." What line were the comrades supposed to concentrate on? Stachel's elucidation was, "We must stop saying that our main task is to build the red unions and then add, 'and also work in the A.F. of L.' We do not have to reverse the formula. What we need is to build the red unions wherever we can and better than until now, but at the same time work among the A.F. of L. workers wherever they are organized." The comrades also had to "give real serious attention to the Independent unions and adopt a flexible policy toward the building of such unions." Thus, at the end of 1933, the new trade-union line seemed to cover all contingencies: build red TUUL unions, penetrate AFL unions, solidify independent unions. Were the tasks compatible? No one dared ask.

The Eighth Communist Party Convention held in Cleveland in April 1934 continued to edge its way gingerly, under cover of conflicting directions, to the new trade-union line. It gave the order for "a sharp struggle" against "open and hidden opportunist resistance" to systematic work in AFL unions, specifically rapping Joe Zack on the knuckles for the bad tendencies he was displaying in continuing to talk in favor of independent unions. (See note 23.) It added the new amendment to its previous three-layered offering that the

74

TUUL unions should be brought together with the independent unions into a new Independent Federation of Labor. Five months later the resolution adopted by the Central Committee in September continued to regurgitate the formulae.

Only in January 1935 did Browder admit that the line had been changed and that red unions were being liquidated. Actually, the disbandment of red unions had been proceeding apace in the previous year. The National Miners Union was dissolved in late spring of 1934. The Steel and Metal Workers Industrial Union sent its steel people into the AFL Amalgamated Association of Iron, Steel and Tin Workers in the fall, and struck "steel" from its name. The National Textile Workers closed shop during the September 1934 textile general strike. The Auto Workers Union officially gave up the ghost in December. The Marine Workers Industrial Union disbanded in February 1935 and its members entered the AFL International Seaman's Union. The fur workers section of the Needle Trades Industrial Union initiated unity discussions in February 1935, and merged with the AFL union in the summer; its dress members drifted back to the ILG individually. The rump Metal Workers Industrial Union was able to secure a minor agreement with the International Association of Machinists in the spring of 1935. The Food Workers Industrial Union had made unity overtures to the AFL Hotel and Restaurant Union as early as the summer of 1934. The TUUL, the putative overall federation, made an inglorious exit from the labor scene by reconstituting itself in March 1935 as a Committee for the Unification of the Trade Unions. *Labor Unity*, the TUUL organ, announced the change of line in its February issue, and promptly closed down without any further notice or discussion.

Browder explained the change in party line by confessing that "[the 1934] strike movement took place mainly through the channels of the reformist unions, and that the Communists in the main were unable to exercise a decisive influence in the leadership of the workers because we were not entrenched as yet inside the A.F. of L. unions which the masses were entering." This was a good explanation; it was not the real explanation. It posited a self-governing party that was not there. The disorderly movement into the AFL was part of the headlong gallop toward the united front with reformists (a way station to the more inclusive People's Front with liberals). As always, the signal came from abroad. Up to the Thirteenth ECCI Plenum of December 1933, revolutionary ranting continued as the order of the day. The lead article in *Pravda* of January 4 thus summarized the Thirteenth Plenum message, "The Communist International sets the Communist parties the task of preparing rapidly for decisive revolutionary struggles. This means that the Communist parties, in their agitation and propaganda, are to place the question of power in all its greatness before the masses of the workers." The same plenum issued the call for the Seventh World Congress in the second half of 1934, but the congress had to be repeatedly postponed, because the Russian leaders were in the process of shifting course.[28]

As 1934 proceeded, Russia was confronted with a German-Polish rapprochement, rejection by both countries of an Eastern Locarno, and the end of military collaboration between the Reichswehr and the Red Army. Stalin began to shop around for alliances with the Western democracies. In September Russia entered the League of Nations—the same organization that Lenin had called the "robbers' den"; the following May an alliance was concluded with France. That Stalin considered the foreign Communist parties expendable came out in a public incident after Laval's visit with Stalin when the French premier was in Moscow. Journalists surmised at the time that Laval merely wanted the pact to frighten Germany. (In fact, the alliance was stillborn.) But Stalin was not waiting for its implementation. Laval was able to announce on his return to Paris that Stalin had authorized him to say that he (Stalin) favored the strengthening of French military defenses. At one stroke—without worrying about the sensibilities of his coadjutors—the putative world leader of world revolution repudiated the decade-long antiwar propaganda of the French Communists. He was informing the chancelleries that whoever made an alliance with him would also get the support of the native Communist party for the same price.

All through that year, the French Communist party served as the prototype for New Model Communism. On February 12, the reformist union federation, the CGT, called a 24-hour general strike against the fascist gangs, which were becoming increasingly aggressive and violent. In a sharp departure from past responses, the Communist union federation, the CGTU, joined the action. The massive strike aroused the entire country and changed the course of French politics. After repeated overtures, the Socialist leaders signed a unity pact with the Communists on July 27. The treaty to fight fascism and war contained an unprecedented clause: the two parties were not to criticize or attack each other. By October, CGT and CGTU officials held discussions to unify the two trade union federations, with unification achieved a year later. At the same time, the Communist leaders were bombarding the Socialist party, both officals and ranks, with offers to fuse their respective organizations. And already, moving beyond traditional left alliances, Maurice Thorez, French Communist head, was importuning the Radical Socialists (the largest party in France at the time; somewhat similar to Roosevelt Democrats) to become part of the popular front, an offer that they accepted a year later. Thus, it is evident that Browder was carrying through in America the unfolding Comintern policy which had its formal presentation at the Seventh World Congress in July and August 1935, like a lover who has cohabited with his mistress for over a year before taking marriage vows. [29]

7

This excursion into Communist decision-making and line-changing illuminates the otherwise baffling twists and turns of American Communists preceding the liquidation of the red unions. Now let us return for a summary review of several other important activities of the "third period" in which the cadres were hatched, not for anticipated revolutions, but for subsequent popular-front alliances. As one would expect, major missionary efforts in the early depression years were directed toward the unemployed. The red unions not only cooperated with the Unemployed Councils, but they also made united fronts in which the line of demarcation was often effaced; red unions continually hammered away on the need to set up Unemployed Councils; and many union organizers doubled as organizers of unemployed.

The desperate character of the initial struggles in this field was set when the Hoover administration took the position that alleviating elementary needs of the unemployed was the responsibility of private charity and local and state governments. None of these were equipped to meet a crisis of 1930 proportions; funds available for direct relief were very quickly exhausted. Since for weal or woe, neither the AFL officialdom, nor community nor religious leaders wanted to take on the responsibility and the anguish of leading the unemployed, radicals were handed a monopoly of this jurisdiction, and the Communists were the first in the field with their Unemployed Councils. On March 6, designated by Moscow as International Unemployed Day, mass demonstrations were held in major cities throughout the country. The demonstration in New York, consisting of 110,000 according to next day's *Daily Worker*, and 35,000 according to *The New York Times*—numerically impressive in either case—turned into a bloody riot when the leaders defied police orders and marched on city hall to demand a meeting with Mayor James J. Walker. Violence broke out in other cities as well. In Washington police used tear gas to disperse demonstrators before the White House. The Detroit demonstration was broken up by police with drawn clubs, and dozens of demonstrators were jailed. (The leaflet calling on the unemployed to gather in Cadillac Square was signed by the Unemployed Councils, the TUUL, the Communist party, and the Auto Workers union.)[30]

There were criticisms of the Communists in succeeding months and years for their determination to politicize struggles with extraneous demands, their courting violence by their eagerness for confrontations with police, their excessive demands that the unemployed could not take seriously. The Communists' own literature was loaded with self-criticisms concerning deficiencies in organization structure, absence of stability or rank-and-file participation in the councils' inner life, the general disorder, and the like. With due respect to the legitimacy of the criticisms of both friends and foes, it must be kept in mind that other radical groups had no more success in stabilizing organizations of unemployed. The Musteites set up Unemployed Leagues in Ohio and Pennsylvania and led demonstrations and marches; the Socialists did the same in Illinois and New Jersey—with no greater accomplishments to their credit. Their unemployed organizations, too, were utterly dependent on small circles of trained professionals—and when these individuals became interested in other fields of endeavor, the rickety structures would promptly collapse. Moreover, since the human ingenuity of concerted minds has natural limits when working on an identical problem, there was a tendency to homogenize techniques.

Though unemployment was a mass phenomenon in the thirties, the unemployed considered the lack of a job a temporary misfortune, not a vocation. Those whose unemployment continued for several years, instead of becoming more organization-minded, sank under the leaden weights of hopelessness and inertia. To the extent that he had a consciousness of kind, it was a consciousness that the unemployed worker was determined to get rid of, not to perpetuate. Hence, the unemployed proved capable of brief bursts of militancy and violence, but they lacked interest, as well as finances, to set up permanent organizations. When several years later the three unemployed-organizations merged into the Workers Alliance that had been set up by the Socialists, it had nothing to do with the aspirations, needs, or wishes of the unemployed. The unity came about exclusively because of esoteric political goals of the three radical parties that led the unemployed. The Alliance claimed a membership at its peak of 600,000, but it was sheer fantasy, and the organization disappeared once radicals got caught up in the CIO and other campaigns.

Beyond winning relief for some of the needy and making the country conscious of the national problem, the marches and demonstrations, the moving of furniture back into apartments whose tenants had been dispossessed, the countless sitdowns in relief offices and other so-called job actions were important in carving the image of Communists as intrepid fighters for the underdog. This image swelled their prestige in the same way that their leadership of the Harlan strike swelled it. As we have seen, they were not too successful in transmuting prestige into recruitment of workers striking under their leadership.

Did they have greater success with the unemployed? In the first big recruiting drive after the 1930 demonstrations 6,000 members were brought into the party, according to the official account, "largely from demonstrations of unemployed and mass meetings, with absolutely insufficient recruiting from factories and trade unions." In 1932 most new recruits were "won over chiefly through unemployed mass work." In 1933, 90 percent of new members were unemployed. In May 1935 two-thirds of new members were unemployed. It might be deduced from these figures that this was one of the important reasons for the instability of Communist party membership. As noted before, there were 60,000 new applicants from 1930 to 1934, and the membership rolls increased only 16,000 in the same period. But this was an old story. Party fluctuation had been inordinate in the twenties, and remained so in the late thirties when recruitment was predominantly from the employed.[31] It was an outward manifestation of an inner disease. But there was another side to it; this pressure-cooker of activity, recruitment, railway-station turnover, furnished the Party with a force of raw, obedient personnel who were not sufficiently informed and did not stay around long enough to ask embarrassing questions.

Nor should one accept uncritically the claim that unemployed activities accounted for most of the Party's expansion. There has been a reference to the indistinct and shifting line of division between unemployed and trade-union work. It should also be noted that most unemployed recruits were not of the lumpen-proletariat; members of this underclass who did join the party generally drifted away after a very brief sojourn. Very many recruits were students, clerks, office workers, teachers, here and there other professionals, as well as out-of-work blue-collar mechanics. That so many recruits were unemployed in the early depression years was scarcely surprising or revealing, considering the condition of the country. Most joined not in response to any specific Communist activity, but for congeries of reasons that convinced them they should enter the Communist ambiance. They might be initially attracted because of party dedication to the cause of the unemployed, or to one of a dozen other campaigns, but signed on the dotted line for reasons that encompassed ideology, economics, international policy, and not least important, visceral feelings that the party was in league with history, that it was the coming thing.

A word should be said about the Communist fronts of this period whose memberships made up pools that were continually being replenished, and that could be drawn upon for party recruitment. Like attractions neatly arranged in separate booths at a carnival, there was an organization to cater to every taste and preference: International Labor Defense, Workers International Relief, International Workers Order, Friends of the Soviet Union, Friends of the Chinese Soviets, John Reed Clubs, not to mention the temporary defense committees and unity groups. The American League against War and Fascism, which became active in 1933, and the American Student Union, captured from its nondescript founders the following year, became the most important Party-run "mass organizations" as the CP was edging its way to the popular front. The knowledgeable knew that even moderately active Party members belonged to three or four front organizations, that Communist organizers were organizers at the same time for one or another of these auxiliaries, that at the periodic united-front gatherings, the faithful—whether certified members or certified sympathizers—would indiscriminately carry the banners and credentials of one or another group. The Party and its associated groups was like an extended, consanguineous family in primitive society that gave fealty to the same tribal chieftains and idols.

Daniel Bell characterized the "front technique" as "one of the great inventions for manipulation in the mass society" that the Communist party contributed to twentieth-century political experience.[32] Whether it is entitled fully to this billing or not, it was not the machine for entrapment of the uninitiated and innocent that some imagined. It was a myth that tens of thousands were lured into these organizations without any suspicion that Communists were in substantial control. Some joined because they were principled believers in the popular front and thought these organizations were valid realizations of that concept. Some joined to acquire platforms for their private pursuits, and thought they got fair value in exchange for Communists' use of their names and positions. Many affiliated while staying out of the Party more for imagined protective coloration, or to avoid having too many demands made on their time and free movement, than because of naiveté about Communist suzerainty. Even if some proverbial innocents were sucked in without any inkling of what they were getting into, they would have had to be deaf, dumb, and blind not to realize in short order that they had blundered into a Communist auxiliary of some kind. The relationship was blatant in the Third Period when Communists were not hiding their light under a bushel; it was not all that opaque later during the popular front, either.

Heavy Party recruitment from the fronts supports the idea that much of this influx in the early thrities must be credited to the movement's total public image (regardless of what particular activity the new recruit might have checked off on a questionnaire as having led him to sign an application card). Were one to judge by received impressions, one would say that the agitation, campaigns, and demonstrations on major college campuses across the country were the most important endeavors in supplying the Party with new functionaries and colonizers for industry. These were conducted under the aegis of the Young Communist League campus auxiliary, the National Student League, and later, the American Youth Congress—transactions which in the college environment were necessarily more intellectual and less utilitarian than exhortations of strikers or the unemployed. Such colonization only staffed the Party's paper organizations during the Third Period, furnishing red unions with organizers, leaflet writers, and distributors. When the big upsurge came in the later thirties, when jobs were more easily obtainable in industry and there was a demand for dedicated organizers, such individuals, backed by disciplined fractions of old-time workers, could and often did become a force. No one, least of all the top Party leaders, planned it that way. It happened. They were there at the right time and with a bag of tools.

FOUR · *Who Gets the Bird?*

THE NRA (National Industrial Recovery Act) was the catalyst for the 1933-1934 strike eruption. Primarily a mechanism to fix prices under cartel arrangements, the government program required the cooperation of workers while beneficent activities were in progress to get the economic wheels turning and put the jobless back to work. The employers who dominated the writing of NRA codes set minimum wages extremely low; they interpreted Section 7(a), which was supposed to guarantee labor's right to organize and bargain collectively, as sanctioning company unions; or they emasculated the guarantee by discharging employees and breaking unions through familiar methods of coercion. Since in this first New Deal Roosevelt was intent on preventing strikes from interfering with what he hoped was the engine of recovery, the NRA labor complex of government boards and mediation panels became, in effect, an instrumentality for manufacturers to work their will. Confronted by companies undercutting already inadequate wage and hour provisions, and by government inability or unwillingness to enforce the law, labor ranks resorted increasingly to the strike weapon to redress the balance.

It was an exciting two years, like a turbulent spring bursting through the lethargy and despair of a forbidding, too-long winter. Although Section 7(a) gave workers on parchment what they had already secured in the Norris-La Guardia anti-injunction law of 1932, and Hugh Johnson, the NRA administrator, devitalized with his interpretations this already ambiguous pledge, the NRA was a great galvanizer. By ushering in the first upturn since the depression, and emanating from a government that displayed a humanitarian concern after an era presided over by tight-lipped Republican standpatters, the Blue Eagle was, in its first flight, a harbinger of hope renewed, of manhood regained. The bitterness and frustration that accumulated in the bleak depression years now exploded in a riot of union organization and strikes. Workers hitherto deemed untouchable by union organizers, such as taxicab drivers, hotel chefs, shipping clerks, and newspapermen, were caught up by the same current that was propelling blue-collar workers in mass production industries.

82

The Executive Council stated in its report to the 1934 AFL convention, "There was a virtual uprising of workers for union membership. Workers held mass meetings and sent word they wanted to be organized." Hoarse-voiced union missionaries harangued excited crowds with the magic message, "The President wants you to join the union." The coal miners in Alabama sang, "In nineteen hundred an' thirty-three,/ When Mr. Roosevelt took his seat,/ He said to President John L. Lewis/ 'In Union we must be.' " A Kentucky State Federation of Labor leaflet read, "The United States government has said LABOR MUST ORGANIZE." Wrote Edward Wieck about the auto workers, the "faith in Washington during the early months of the NRA was almost of a religious intensity." Wrote novelist Martha Gellhorn, at this time a Federal Emergency Relief Administration investigator in the Carolinas, "Every house I visited—mill worker or unemployed—had a picture of the President. . . . The portrait holds the place of honor over the mantel; I can only compare this to the Italian peasant's Madonna." No matter that this was myth-making on a historic scale—self-serving on the part of labor officials, born of adoration and the craving for a savior on the part of millions of disadvantaged. No matter that Roosevelt was attuned to noblesse oblige, and that in these first years, his concern was economic recovery, not social reform. The need of the hour made the myth a social fact of large consequences.[1]

Two impulses set the NRA strike-wave rolling across the cities. First was the brief economic upturn. The economy revived between March and July when businessmen built up inventories in anticipation of NRA provisions that would raise minimum pay rates. Industrial production shot up by two-thirds, and the President's Reemployment Agreement, or blanket code, promulgated in the latter month, was reputed to have created an additional 2½ million jobs between June and October—mainly through a reduction of the work week; the speculative boomlet had collapsed by July.[2] The recovery, minor in economic terms, performed wonders in ridding workers of their depression jitters and gloom. When they saw more people being rehired, their confidence was restored; they felt they were needed, had a function in society, that by their united efforts they could have a say in establishing the terms of employment in the nation's work places.

This, in turn, made more intense a political atmosphere that encouraged the insurgency. At first, the insurgency was powered by the burning faith that there was a Great White Father in the White House who would help labor regain the ground it had lost in the

83

complacent twenties and the black Hoover years; later, when the NRA was referred to in some oppositionist circles as the National Run-Around, there was faith that new conditions were making it possible for labor not only to hope, but also to achieve. The strike curve, in line with the tendency for economic militancy to rise during upturns and decline in depressions, was extraordinary. There were 1,695 stoppages, most of them in the second half of the year— twice the number of the previous year, the largest number since 1921; 1,117,000 employees were involved, almost four times more than the year before. Man-days lost, which had not exceeded 603,000 in any month in the first half of the year, went up to 1,375,000 in July and 2,378,000 in August. The next year the wave was still rising with 1,470,000 participating in 1,856 strikes.[3]

With the few exceptions to be noted, the AFL hierarchy frittered away a rare opportunity. In the auto industry, Green and his helpers acquiesced in the establishment of an NRA code that included a merit clause and minimum wage rates which provided no pay increases for any but a handful of workers. The code was hailed by *Automotive Industries* as "the first victory of industry over organized labor under the Industrial Recovery Act." As mentioned, when the threatened strike was called off in March 1934 and the Automobile Labor Board was sanctioned, the AFL had shot its bolt; its federal locals in auto began losing members as rapidly as they had gained them the year before.[4]

The crisis in steel proceeded along similar lines with a similar resolution. There was an established AFL union in the field, the Amalgamated Association of Iron, Steel and Tin Workers, which had degenerated over the years into a small-time dues-collection agency. In 1933, it had less than 5,000 members, mostly skilled, covered by contracts with a few small companies. The union president, Michael Tighe, was known as "Grandmother," more for his septuagenarian ways than his age. Much to his surprise, and certainly not because of anything he or the other becalmed bureaucrats did, steel workers began organizing and writing in for charters. The number of steel lodges jumped from 85 to 214 in the latter half of 1933, and in February of the next year the membership was estimated to be 50,000. Young militant leaders, indigenous to the industry, came forward with the influx of new members; soon they formed a closely knit rank-and-file movement. At the union's April 1934 convention, the opposition delegates put across a mandatory resolution calling on all lodges to present their demands by May 21 to the steel companies;

stating that unless the latter entered into immediate negotiations, and agreements were signed by mid-June, the Amalgamated would call a nationwide steel strike.

The opposition movement appeared to be riding high and about to take over the steel union. Not only had it put across its strike strategy, but the convention majority had also set up a supervisory Committee of Ten to make sure that International officers followed through on the program. The appearance was deceptive, however, and the rank-and-file leaders were in the untenable position of trying to bluff when bluffing would not avail. The rank-and-file movement had shot up too rapidly on the false premise of winning fast union recognition by means of a strike. The movement, though substantial, lacked the massive support in the mills that would make a strike practicable. Most steel workers, though friendly to the militants' aims, had many reservations about both the union and a strike; feelings were not as vehement as in the auto plants. The rank-and-file leaders needed time to extend their organization and to build up strike sentiment, time they did not have. They were trapped by their own rhetoric. If they proposed a more cautious strategy, they would lose their activist following. So they plunged ahead in the hope that something favorable would turn up, though their cannier leaders realized that a strike under the given conditions would be a fiasco.

The hoped-for miracle did not occur. The steel masters put in a supply of munitions, strung barbed wire around the mills, held shop elections which purportedly demonstrated that most were opposed to a walkout. They were all set to administer a crushing rebuke to the brash insurgents. Two days before the strike deadline, a special Amalgamated convention opened in Pittsburgh in the full glare of the newspapers' spotlights for the presumed purpose of calling a nationwide strike. In fact, Tighe was determined that there would be no strike, and the rank-and-file leaders were praying that somebody would bail them out. Roosevelt had already secured the approval of Congressional leaders for Public Resolution No. 44 authorizing a steel labor-relations board to investigate and adjudicate complaints. William Green demanded sternly in his address to the convention that the strike order be rescinded in return for the president's pledge to set up this board. When the convention, amidst disorder and confusion, adopted Green's proposal by an overwhelming vote, the rank-and-file movement was finished—and what is more, the AFL was out of the steel industry. Arthur H. Young,

85

vice-president of the U.S. Steel Corporation wrote in a private letter, "I have read carefully the joint resolution, and my personal opinion is that it is not going to bother us very much."[5]

AFL intervention in textiles was, if anything, more disastrous. The NRA cotton-textile code sanctioned a minimum weekly wage of $12 in the South and $13 in the North, did nothing about the stretchout, and handed administration of the code to the employers' trade associations. The final authority, a tri-partite Cotton Textile National Industrial Relations Board was, in fact, run by George Sloan, head of the Cotton Textile Institute. Minor wage improvements introduced by the code had been erased by the reduction in hours and the rise in the cost of living. For months, the aroused textile workers had been flocking into the United Textile Workers union; by the summer of 1934 their patience was at an end. At a special convention held in New York City in August, the delegates, dominated by southern contingents, imposed a mandatory resolution calling for a general strike in cotton textiles on September 1, and authorized strikes in silk, wool, and rayon as well on suitable dates. One feature of the rebellious mood of the delegates was hostility to the NRA and all its works. While steel insurgent leaders had grown disillusioned with what they designated as the National Run-Around, theirs was an elitist reaction compared to the widespread conviction of the "lintheads" that the NRA was a deliberate fraud.

The cotton strike, which extended to the silk, woolen, and worsted industries, was a spectacular demonstration occuring in a largely unorganized industry that had successfully resisted unionization only a few years before. Within a few days, strike ranks swelled to some 400,000, closing down mills along the entire stretch of states from Maine to Georgia, Alabama, and Tennessee. The strikers formed "flying squadrons" on a scale never before seen in labor-management conflicts. Union workers would arrive in trucks and cars to spread the message to the less-organized mills. Often, their mere arrival would be sufficient to set off a strike. If not, they set up mass picket lines and used methods of persuasion meant to accomplish results. The civil-war tremors, already felt in the encounters at Gastonia, Marion, and Elizabethton in the late twenties, now broke into a full-scale industry-wide revolt.

The employers, and state and local officials met the uprising head on. Thousands of armed guards and spies were put on company payrolls, and pressure was brought to bear on public authorities to cut off relief. The National Guard was called out in Rhode Island,

Massachusetts, Alabama, Georgia, and the Carolinas. The guardsmen, supplemented by thousands of special militiamen, forcibly kept many mills open. The reports of the killed and wounded in the many desperate battles and riots read like bulletins from a war zone. By September 22 it was all over. The strike was decisively beaten. The new Textile Labor Relations Board, set up by Roosevelt, went through familiar motions of dressing up a corpse. The textile strike demonstrated, in the first instance, not that National Guard units had machine guns to shoot down strikers, but that the AFL of the period, and its constituent textile union, could no more subdue determined, open-shop industrialists than a ragged band employing bows and arrows could overcome an opposing host equipped with tanks and bombers. The defeats in auto and steel were reversed when the CIO appeared; the setback in textiles was more lasting.[6]

2

The AFL record of ineptitude and mismanagement stood out in bold relief because three union heads who became leaders of the CIO showed what could be done in the turbulent NRA climate. With the passage of the act, Lewis threw the entire mine-union treasury into an all-or-nothing organizing effort.[7] The response stunned the operators (and union officials as well). The elaborate anti-union defenses crumbled everywhere except in Harlan County. The union even gained a foothold in the hitherto impregnable captive mines operated by U.S. Steel. A year later, Lewis spoke for an organization that again boasted a membership of 400,000. Dubinsky of the dress union put himself at the head of a concerted campaign in all garment centers. Hundreds of volunteer organizers responded to the union call; blitz strikes broke down the resistance of the die-hards. When the jubilant delegates gathered at the next ILG convention in May 1934, Dubinsky was able to report that membership had risen from 40,000 in May 1932 to about 200,000. Sidney Hillman, president of the men's clothing union, the Amalgamated Clothing Workers, enrolled 25,000 shirt workers and additional thousands in the tailor's division so that the ACW dominated all sections of the industry. If this union's growth was less phenomenal than that of the other two, it was because Hillman had held the men's clothing union together more successfully in the lean years than had Lewis and Dubinsky their unions.[8] These were all organization prodigies, but prodigies in industries with a long tradition of unionism. They recovered ground that had been held before.

What caught the imagination of the nation were three upheavals in 1934 that blew up into regional civil wars, in which newly organized ranks broke through tightly held breastworks, palisades, and concentric fortifications to force traditional open-shop chieftains to terms.

Although unrelated, all three took place at approximately the same time: a strike at the Electric Auto-Lite and associated companies in Toledo from April 12 to June 4; the general truck drivers strikes in Minneapolis from May 15 to May 26, and from July 16 to August 21; and the West Coast maritime strike that shut down operations along 2,000 miles of coastline from May 9 to July 27. All three exhibited similar characteristics. (1) They were led or propelled by radicals who maintained their position in the face of sustained barrages from employers, press, public officials, and conservative AFL leaders. (2) All three were settled only after the opposing sides took each other's measure in physical tests of strength. Strikers, reinforced by masses of outside sympathizers and unemployed engaged in pitched battles with special deputies, strike-breakers, police, and National Guardsmen; bricks, rocks, street-paving and lead pipes against clubs, guns and tear gas. It was industrial war at its most raw. (3) Despite the hysteria against Communists and communism, and the featured charges in the press about conspiracies and plots to overthrow the government, the strikers enjoyed widespread support from the public, including sections of the middle class. The humiliations of the depression years had their effects. The political spectrum had shifted leftwards, and industrial barons and bankers had been knocked off their pedestals. They retained power but had lost some legitimacy. (4) The shooting down of strikers produced outcries for a general strike. The demand was actually pushed through in San Francisco over the opposition of old-line officials, and would have been realized in Toledo and Minneapolis as well had the strikes not been settled before new incidents thickened the atmosphere. (5) Unlike so many poorly prepared and conducted NRA strikes, these were victorious. All three initiated the formation of strong labor movements in their locales and industries.[9]

In the light of this concatenation of circumstances in which labor upsurge, AFL helplessness, and discreditment of NRA officials and government mediators were linked as in a chain, bypassing the TUUL closed the book on red unionism. The Minneapolis strikes under the aegis of the AFL Teamsters union were led by members of the dissident Trotskyite faction. The Auto-Lite strike under the aegis of an AFL federal local was turned into a mass altercation by Musteite supporters who headed the Lucas County Unemployed League. And the Communists struck gold on the West Coast only because Bridges, who allied with them following his own trajectory, had emerged as leader of the AFL longshore union. In order to participate in the leadership, the Communists had to abandon their Marine Workers Industrial Union and embrace Bridges and his circle.*

TUUL isolation had little to do with their having committed the cardinal sin of engaging in dual unionism. Dual unionism was a bugaboo devised by the AFL officialdom to justify its claimed monopoly of the trade-union business. It was the repeated smashup of militant independent unions—for reasons little related to dual unionism—that gave the AFL's propaganda catchword its seeming validity. There was nothing to it. A union with an authentic base in an industry—like Hillman's Amalgamated Clothing Workers, or the subsequent CIO breakaways—could flourish without AFL benediction; all the more so, since in so many industries the AFL lacked organizations to which another union could be dual. The problem of the Communist unions was not that they were dual, but that they were Communist. Even under favorable circumstances, the Communist identification was like a bar sinister warning off the citizenry. This was brought out in chemically pure form in the unsuccessful Communist attempt to join forces with the steel rank-and-file committee. Here was an opposition movement led by heretics who were taking advice from a brain trust of four left-wing journalists and economists. The heretics had no bias against radicals and desperately needed help. A meeting of the Committee of Ten and the four brain trusters was set, to which were invited representatives of the Steel and Metal Workers Industrial Union to determine what the Communist outfit could offer. The meeting, described by one participant, went this way:

---

* There were attempts in the next decade to have Bridges deported as a Communist alien. The question explored at many hearings and proceedings of whether he was legally a Communist party member is academic for purposes of this study. We can assume that his legal status was precisely what he claimed. Sociologically, however, he was an ally of the Communists, conferred with Communist leaders, adhered to Communist policy, and helped build up the Communist faction inside his union. He was also an egotistic, opinionated, and willful individual who must have given many hours of agony to the commissars assigned to handle him. But the latter is of importance only to those considering Communist internal administration, not for a study of the Communist faction in relation to the labor movement.

"The first thing that happened was that the date of the strike was set for June 16. Then the executive board of the SMWIU was asked in. John Egan, their secretary, presented their case. They wanted the rank-and-file group and the SMWIU to issue a joint statement from this meeting, a joint call for a joint convention to focus public attention on the issues, and local organizations to issue joint statements and call joint mass meetings. It was perfectly clear that they wanted to formalize the whole affair and be sure that the SMWIU was in the limelight as an organization. As soon as they had withdrawn, the rank-and-file group voted thumbs down on the proposition. We'd have been smeared immediately as Communists if we had accepted. The sense of the meeting was that the two organizations should cooperate informally on a local basis wherever there was such a possibility. Number Three [of the braintrusters] had a hell of a job persuading John Egan not to print anything about the meeting in the Communist press."

Harry Bridges reported the same reaction. He was urging sailors to join the Marine Workers Industrial Union in 1933, but admitted that despite individual desperation and the AFL union's abidcation, seamen refused to affiliate with a Communist outfit.[10]

It stands to reason that in the American environment where radicalism is generally suspect, beleaguered workers would try to build their protective organizations under the most respectable auspices available, and even those who saw some good in one or another variety of radicalism were apt to value the protective coloration afforded by accepted or tolerated institutions. It was pathetic that the Communists who learned all this at the start of the twenties should have had to unlearn it at the end of the decade—in response to foolish directives from abroad, and at such high cost to their own fortunes.

3

The Party moved into the popular-front era under the direction of Browder, since the expulsions of Cannon and Lovestone in 1928 and 1929 had cleared the way for a Stalinized regime. At the time, the expulsions appeared to the Party as an insignificant bloodletting in the course of its consolidation. The numbers that left were, in truth, tiny. But the forced suppression of factions, and the forced elimination of their leaders, had the effect of snuffing out the remaining sparks of independence, making total the Party's subservience. Just as a captive's will is finally broken when he believes resistance futile, the almost effortless destruction of Lovestone, supported by a majority of the Party before his defiance, drove the lesson home that to question Moscow was quixotic and suicidal. True, the new generation of leaders that came up had only a hazy knowledge of the faction struggles of the twenties. Nonetheless, they had been weaned and attained their majority on a slave diet, and knew no other regimen.

Browder, who had been a lieutenant of Foster's, became acting secretary in 1930, superseding Max Bedacht, an interim appointee, after it became clear that Moscow did not want Foster to take over Lovestone's old spot. Whether Browder scrambled up the Party's greasy pole of leadership thereafter on his own or with Moscow's assistance is unclear. At any rate, he was firmly ensconced after a heart attack in 1932 eliminated Foster for three years from active duty.[11] A few words should be devoted to both their biographies; Browder exercised undisputed control in the decade of the Party's greatest influence; Foster, though relegated to the sidelines (at one time, even threatened with expulsion), continued as a grey eminence until he assumed the Party chairmanship after the war. Between them, they oversaw the party over its entire Stalinist phase.

Browder, born in 1891 in Wichita, Kansas, was 41 when he assumed the purple. Of Welsh and Scotch stock going back to colonial times, his father was one of the unlucky ones, and Browder had to leave school before he was ten. Eventually he worked to become an accountant, and also completed a law-school correspondence course when he was 23. Before becoming a Communist, he had been in the Socialist party, and Foster's prewar IWW offshoot, the Syndicalist League of North America, and held membership in an AFL Bookkeepers and Accountants local in Kansas. He served prison terms for his opposition to the war on charges of working against the draft and nonregistration. In the Communist party he was a faithful adherent of Foster's until in 1926 he began his international wandering. For a year he acted as the American Communist party's Profintern representative in Moscow, and the next two years in China as a member of a Comintern delegation. At the Sixth World Congress he held himself aloof from the Foster-Cannon bloc, though joining in its attacks on the Bukharin-Lovestone "right danger." He sought to conduct himself as an independent free of and above the warring factions, a position that stood him in good stead after Lovestone's elimination.

Among top officials in the twenties, Browder had the reputation of a hard-working, conscientious, reliable functionary, but a distinctly second-line figure, lacking both the personality and flair for independent leadership. Possibly he was downgraded because of his drabness—although these faction sharpsters were fair judges of their opponent's qualities and lacks. Despite his world travels, he never lost a pedestrian, slightly seedy appearance. In the popular-front days when he addressed big audiences and was accorded the respect befitting the leader of the foremost left party, it was always a distinct shock to the nonbeliever that the touted great man was a colorless figure emitting a stream of pseudo-statesmanlike platitudes punctuated by wooden gestures. Who can say now whether real political acumen went into bringing the Communist movement to its high point of wartime influence, or whether Browder was demonstrating that a second-rate bureaucrat could make a splash when carried forward by the momentum of the wartime alliance? Certainly, his books and articles on the "spirit of Teheran" and postwar perspectives read today like parodies, and in the end he was a pitiable figure when he was unceremoniously dismissed like a used-up retainer; a forlorn subaltern broken trying to ride the two horses moving in opposite directions: subservience to Moscow, and advocacy of a quasi-populist American nationalism.

If he could have abstracted himself from the man-eating Communist apparatus, Foster was the kind of individual who should have provided a leadership of creativity and level-headedness. He was the archetypal proletarian of a Diego Rivera mural. Born in Taunton, Massachusetts, of Irish and English-Scotch parents, he also had to quit school when he was ten, and for two decades he worked all over the country in a variety of trades, a restless, footloose, rebel worker. He joined the Socialist party in 1901 when he was twenty, was out eight years later with the expulsion of a syndicalist faction of which he was a member, joined the IWW, then left to form his own radical group when he became convinced that the only right policy was to "bore from within" existing AFL unions. He got his first big chance to put his ideas into practice in 1917 when working as a car inspector in Chicago. On his urging, the AFL central labor body set up a committee to organize the Chicago packinghouse workers, with John Fitzpatrick as chairman and Foster as secretary of the committee. The organization campaign was an outstanding success; over 200,000 workers were enrolled, and Foster emerged as a big figure. The next year he was able to enlist Gompers' cooperation through the good offices of Fitzpatrick for a similar nationwide committee to organize the steel industry, again acting as secretary of the committee. Although the strike was broken, 365,000 had fought under his leadership against the steel masters—a masterly achievement at the time that earned Foster a national reputation.

In the protracted, complicated negotiations required to maneuver a dozen squabbling, narrow-minded and egocentric AFL union heads into cooperating in this major organization effort, and then to keep them from undercutting each other during the bitterly fought strike, Foster displayed tact and dexterity of a high order. In addition to being a capable strike organizer and tactician, he was a crafty politician; he had the streak of adaptability in him. This enabled him to work with conservative AFL officials, and after his pact with Moscow, to rise to the top in the unfamiliar milieu of the Communist movement. But this adaptability also became his undoing as step by step he had to give way before the inexorable Comintern machine. When Browder beat him out for the leadership, he was no longer the free-wheeling rebel of yore; he had become a hardened Stalinized politician for whom "principles" had been superseded by "power."

As a personality, he was not in the same class as Debs or William D. Haywood, but he was persuasive on or off the platform. People felt they were in the presence of a bluff, straight-shooting, clear-thinking working man. Before his style got hopelessly corrupted in the double-talking Stalinist factory, he had shown native literary gifts. *The Great Steel Strike and Its Lessons* (New York: Huebsch, 1920) is a classic of its genre. He continued giving advice between illnesses, particularly on trade-union matters, in the Browder decade. He was not his true self, however, being humiliated, disregarded, and shunted off to "literary" activities by people whom he considered his inferiors. Roy Hudson, a Party spokesman in maritime, later stated that "from Browder you could get answers," whereas Foster offered little guidance. If that was true, it was probably owing to Foster's caginess with Hudson, not to his having become tongue-tied. By the time Browder was deposed and Foster had at long last come into his bequest, he was a 64-year-old punch-drunk veteran disoriented by a quarter century of zigzags and unscrupulous in-fighting, more concerned with establishing his place in "history" than in saving the Communist party from disaster.

One other official who was important in perfecting the Party's apparatus is worth mentioning. As Bonaparte had his Fouché, and Franklin Roosevelt his Farley, so Browder had Jack Stachel. In the high politics of the faction wars, in the arts of infiltration and maneuver, it was he, the organization secretary (and at various times, head of the trade union department), who was the keeper of the organization keys, the coordinator, the "apparatchik in chief," holding and manipulating the diverse threads. Stachel was born in 1900 of Polish Jewish parents who emigrated to America when he was nine. He joined the Socialist party when a youngster and switched to the Communists in 1924. His energy and effectiveness in factional activities quickly brought him to the attention of party leaders. When Lovestone took over the national office in 1927, he moved Stachel in to head the organization department. Stachel betrayed Lovestone, with whom he had conspired, without a tremor when the latter fell from grace. Following Foster's heart attack in 1932, he became acting head of the TUUL. When that job terminated, he reassumed his old post as organization secretary, and for the next ten years served as Browder's man Friday as he had previously served Lovestone. Short, dark, humorless, intense, he gave the appearance of an industrious needle-trades shop foreman. He had none of the attributes of a public spokesman or political leader, and consequently posed no threat to Browder (or Lovestone before him). With his eye on the main chance and the timely intrigue, his administrative aptitudes, enhanced by a deceptively conciliatory manner, made him the perfect achiever to maximize the Party's gains whatever the venture or the line. If honors were to go to individuals for the Party's expanding influence during the Browder regime, no one had a better claim than "this dour, cynical, opportunistic arch-functionary."[12]

Three unique men, three disparate personal histories—yet all of them processed by mechanical rollers and presses to fit their party personalities for Stalinist programming. Their power was that of the corporation, whose human cogs achieve efficient coordination by obeying an authoritarian superior. Their weakness was the weakness of the corporation in which self-interest and bureaucratic complacence blurs vision and sense of purpose.

4

The swing of the Communists into the AFL while gleefully tossing overboard from their ark some Marxist-Leninist ballast, could not have come at a more providential time. Dimitrov's discovery of the beauty of democracy and the virtue in alliances with reformists, liberals, and progressive bourgeois elements came when sections of the American middle classes, cut adrift from their conservative moorings, were scanning the shores for new alliances; and inside the AFL there was the maturing of an insurgency that had lost patience with its case-hardened officialdom. The atmosphere could not have been better for the reception of the message that the Communists were starting to trumpet. Voicing a widespread opinion of the time, the *Nation* averred that although Communists had made mistakes in the past in the unions, they were indispensable for providing the labor movement with "much-needed vigor,"[13] something they were given the opportunity to display with the formation of the CIO. John L. Lewis made his fight for industrial unionism at the Atlantic City AFL convention in October, and dramatized his determination to see the issue through by a solid punch to the jaw of "Big Bill" Hutcheson, the near-300-pound president of the carpenters union, and a major leader of the craft unionists' ring. The next month Lewis launched the Committee for Industrial Organization with the support of Hillman, Dubinsky, Charles Howard, president of the typographical union (who joined in an individual capacity), and several lesser union heads. Within a matter of months, the surging waters for a modern unionism, thwarted by frightened AFL business agents, overran the barriers and banks in a historic labor advance.

Communists were present at the creation. (See Appendix I.) A few weeks after the CIO opened offices in the Rust Building in Washington, Brophy, the organization director, called in Len De Caux and offered him the job of publicity head. De Caux was an old-time Communist adherent whom Brophy knew when De Caux had been assistant editor working with Oscar Ameringer on the *Illinois Miner*, the paper of the UMW Illinois district that fought Lewis tooth and nail in the inter-union wars of the twenties. At the same time, Lee Pressman, a lawyer in the Agricultural Adjustment Administration, got his close friend Gardner Jackson to introduce him to Lewis, then secured an appointment as general counsel to the CIO Steel Workers Organizing Committee, and became general counsel for the CIO—in effect, Lewis's personal attorney. Jackson was the libertarian newspaperman from Boston who had become a battler for unpopular causes with his initiation in the Sacco-Vanzetti case. He knew everybody in Washington; was, so to speak, liked by

95

everybody; and was on very friendly terms with Lewis at this time. Pressman, according to his own later testimony, had joined the Communist party in 1934 and left it in 1936.

Although one must assume that the dates are correct, his was only a legalistic, a tactical withdrawal. Pressman remained a fellow traveler in close association with others of the same breed for the next 15 years. In his own person, he refracted some of the fierce passions of the period which led romantic intellectuals to speculate that Roosevelt was merely the Kerensky of an ongoing revolution. A high-powered operator, an adroit tactician, Pressman won the complete favor of Lewis, and was accepted in the national organization as one who had the ear of the big boss. Yet this career-minded sharpster, with his eye on the main chance, so cool, calculating, operational, who never failed to submit big invoices for his valued legal services, remained with the party's periphery, and when faced with a choice of either-or, opted to go with the Communists. (Two years later he bitterly regretted his decision, but it was too late to retrace his course.)[14]

Pressman and De Caux in the national office was a secondary conquest compared to the hide-and-hair participation of the Communist party in the steel campaign. Steel was supposed to be the CIO's major objective, so that by enrolling in this event, the Communists were right in the cockpit of the struggle to come. According to Foster, of the approximately 200 full-time organizers on the Steel Workers Organizing Committee (SWOC) payroll, sixty were Communists. "In Ohio," said John Williamson, the Party district organizer at the time, "our entire party and Young Communist League staffs were incorporated into the staffs of the committee. This included Gus Hall, in charge of Warren and Niles [presently national secretary of the party], John Steuben, in charge of Youngstown, and many others." William (Boleslaw) Gebert, who had been president of the Polonia Society, the Polish division of the IWO (after the war, he became an official in the Polish Communist regime), was appointed by Murray to mobilize the foreign-language fraternal societies. An important conference was held in Pittsburgh in October 1936 with delegates representing Lithuanian, Polish, Croatian, Serbian, Slovenian, Ukrainian, and Russian societies, chaired by Gebert, and addressed by Murray and Clinton Golden. Another national conference of Black groups was held in Pittsburgh in February 1937 organized by Benjamin Carreathers, a Black Communist functionary, also on the SWOC staff. According to other testimony,

31 or 32 out of 33 SWOC staff members in the Chicago area were attending the Communist caucus. Similar although less-extensive hiring of CP'ers occurred later in connection with the packinghouse campaign headed by another administration stalwart from the mine union, Van Bittner.[15]

That a hard-bitten, crafty, Churchillian warrior like Lewis who had dealt ruthlessly with Communists inside the UMW in the twenties, and whose union boasted a constitutional clause barring Communists from membership, should have reversed his course so drastically signified a calculated decision. This had to be even more pronounced in the case of his lieutenant, Philip Murray, who was a practicing Catholic, a political conformist of decided conservative bent, not the buccaneer adventurer and plunger that his chief was. Lewis would breezily wave aside charges that he was harboring Communists with the comment, "I do not turn my organizers or CIO members upside down and shake them to see what kind of literature falls out of their pockets." Why did Lewis do it? His rule of the mine union (and of the CIO national office, for that matter) was no less autocratic and absolute than in the past. His inner nature was not altered. Saul Alinsky, his semi-official Boswell, gave Lewis's thinking on the matter:

> He had no choice but to accept the support of the Communists. Even after the debacle of 1933 and 1934, when the American Federation of Labor smashed the spirit of unionism, it was the left-wingers who zealously worked day and night picking up the pieces of that spirit and putting them together. . . . The Communist Party was then operating in a climate of mass disillusion and bitterness. A generation was growing up that did not know the reality of a job in private industry. The frustration and common misery of the people created a sympathetic interest for all those bearing a gospel of and guidebook to the promised land of security. . . . The CIO was waging economic war, and as do all organizations and nations in time of war, it welcomed allies wherever they could be found. The fact is that the Communist Party made a major contribution in the organization of the unorganized for the CIO.[16]

When Dubinsky remonstrated with Lewis about hiring Communists, and insisted that it was going to create big problems for the CIO, Lewis asked magisterially, "Who gets the bird, the hunter or the dog?" Some years later during the war, after the mine union had

97

withdrawn from the CIO, Dubinsky talked with Lewis for the first time since the two parted company in 1937. According to Dubinsky, he reminded Lewis of his remark, and said, "Tell me now, John, who turned out to be the 'hunter,' and who the 'dog'?" And a subdued Lewis is supposed to have admitted "that he had been 'overconfident,' and had underestimated Communist capacity for mischief." James B. Carey, for many years secretary-treasurer of the CIO, wrote in the same vein in 1948, "Initially, John L. Lewis welcomed the party liners. . . . Lewis desperately needed trained organizers in the early days of the CIO—and your seasoned Stalinist, to give the devil his due, is often a hot-shot labor salesman. . . . We made one mistake in that first flush of organizing ardor: We let the party liners in."[17]

If Dubinsky and Carey's impressions are correct, then Lewis had the choice of letting the Communists in or keeping them out but committed a monumental mistake in thinking he could control them once he opened the door to them; had the contrary policy been followed, perhaps the Communist problem that embroiled the CIO for six years or longer could have been avoided. Not only are these the implications of Dubinsky and Carey's remarks, but an entire school of publicists have worked up these ideas into an article of faith. Consequently, it is of some importance to disentangle and appraise the various strands that make up the proposition; all the more so since such a critical consideration also discloses the dynamic interplay that occurred between business unionists, Communists, and labor ranks at the time that masses were restless and sought forceful leadership.

As Alinsky indicated, when the CIO undertook to organize steel and lead the assault on other open-shop strongholds, Lewis and his associates embarked on the fight of their lives—as they well understood. Not only could civil war be anticipated in major industrial centers, but the CIO was also moving toward the kind of massed confrontation in which labor had always come out the loser. Labor history was dotted with the tombstones of lost strikes and crushed organizations. It was precisely the superior power of big capital in physical encounter and collision that had bred the AFL's habits of caution and temerity, producing eventually its spiritual ossification. Consequently, Lewis was not merely disposed to accept whatever allies were available in the desperate war that was in the offing. He could not do without the support of the radicals—and in the 1930s, radicals meant primarily the Communists. It was not that man-for-man Communists were necessarily superior organizers or agitators than non-Communist radicals. The contrary was demonstrated in the Minneapolis and Toledo strikes. But whatever their qualities, non-Communist radicals were few in number. The American Socialist party was only a shell, and the radical splinter groups, so-called, were less than that. [18]

5

Without knowing or caring very much about the intricacies of Marxist exegetics, Lewis was entirely conscious of how the various radicals fitted into his schemes. The original team of CIO representatives who were sent into the great battles that were erupting—the Akron rubber strikes, the RCA strike in Camden, New Jersey, the General Motors strike in Flint, etc.—were all non-Communists. The roving team consisted of Powers Hapgood, Adolph Germer, Leo Krzycki, Rose Pesotta, on occasion, John Brophy—to name only the high-powered stars. Brophy, Hapgood, and Germer had been Socialists, opposition leaders in the mine union to Lewis; they had been thrown out of the union and the industry, and now were called back by Lewis to active service in his do-or-die crusade. Krzycki, for years a field man in Hillman's Amalgamated Clothing Workers, had been an under-sheriff in the Socialist administration in Milwaukee, and was an old-style soapbox orator. Pesotta had been a left-winger in the twenties' faction struggles in the ladies garment union, of anarchist persuasion. She continued working on and off in her dressmaking trade when a union official, and had an appealing shop-worker's presence that went over with labor ranks. It will be noted that these unionists were all radicals, or more accurately ex-radicals, of one or another non-Communist variety, all falling into the category that labor officials denominate sometimes, with a hint of contempt, as "missionary" types.

It might be wondered why Lewis did not employ many of his mine officials in the organizing drives. He did, but primarily in bureaucratic capacities. He knew his associates. In the ferocious internecine battles inside the mine union in which he consolidated his absolute rule, the one and often the only quality he demanded of his subordinates was absolute and undeviating loyalty to himself. If they had ability, all the better, but that was not the desideratum. "As a consequence the union staff was overloaded with mediocrities, yes-men, alcoholics, sycophants and relations." Shortly after its foundation, when the CIO's name was magic and Lewis was the hero to millions, the hacks of the mine union machine saw a little of the glamor rub off on them—but not for long. These self-styled veterans of the coal fields very quickly revealed themselves in their true guise of talentless machine politicians, unable to compete with the energetic and articulate activists being thrown up from the serried ranks.[19] Lewis understood completely that he needed different spokesmen to arouse and enlist the millions of underprivileged. The reason he did not take on more individuals of the Brophy-Hapgood-Germer stripe was that they were not at hand. For the same reason, the two garment unions did not lend more organizers of the Krzycki-Pesotta kind. They were not available.

Furthermore, the question is not exhausted when one remarks that Lewis was mistaken in his belief that he could control the Communists, and could discard them if they became unruly or were no longer needed. That happens to be precisely the way it worked out in the case of the national office appointees and the steel organizing staff. So far as Pressman and De Caux were concerned, they held prestigious positions, but it would be ludicrous to suppose that working for a boss like Lewis, and later like Murray, they could carry out any policy except the one dictated to them. The importance of their positions to the Communist party was peripheral: they lent distinction to the Communist operation; they could be used to impress those whom the Party needed to impress; they could transmit proposals to Lewis and Murray; they could get the word out as to what was transpiring in the CIO's inner councils; occasionally, they were able to recommend Communists for editorial or organizing jobs in other unions. All this was important, but quite limited. When in 1947 the drive against Communists was on in earnest, De Caux and Pressman were summarily dismissed—with no tremors in the ranks anywhere—like the hired hands that they were.

In the case of the steel organizers, Communists were simply removed from the payroll, district by district, once the union established itself in the industry. This could be done in routine, administrative fashion because for six years the Steel Workers Organizing Committee functioned as a topheavy, centralized Lewis-Murray, then Murray, dictatorship. There were no conventions, no elections, no autonomous locals or districts. All decisions were made in theory by the original Steel Workers Organizing Committee appointed by Lewis. In practice the organization was run by Murray in consultation with the inner council of appointed top directors. Only in 1942 was the formal structure of a union adopted, and even then the national office maintained its overcentralized grip on funds, staff, and policy.

In the circumstances, though Communist field workers could utilize their positions for Party recruitment and individual proselytizing, they had no say in forming union policy, and lacked any instrumentality within the union to conduct meaningful propaganda. As early as 1939, David McDonald, the SWOC secretary-treasurer, publicly attacked them in the union paper, *Steel Labor*, not for anything they were doing, but as ideological preparation for squeezing them out of the union. Murray's justification for the delay in setting up a union structure and authorizing elections was the weakness of the union after the failure of the Little Steel strike, and because intricate, time-consuming preparatory work had to be completed. The real reason was that Murray did not want to go ahead until Communists had been pushed out.[20] When they were, there were no repercussions. The Communists were victims of the dictatorial arrangement they had tacitly accepted. Thus, the Lewis program for kicking aside the dog and seizing the bird worked out successfully in the steel union.*

The Lewis program did not work out precisely where he had nothing to do with inviting the Communists in, and could not have kept them out if he had wanted. It was in the auto, electrical, maritime, transport, metallurgical mining, and lesser office and public workers fields that the Communists became important, and where they created the "Communist problem." Had Lewis known in 1936 what would transpire after the war, he still would not have barred the door to Communists had he wanted to create the new mass industrial-union federation in the conditions then prevailing. The problems of one period cannot be arbitrarily imposed on another. Lewis became America's major labor leader—probably the greatest union leader in this country's history—because he had the

---

* In later years, in another dreary round of "self-criticism," Foster blamed the Communist defeat "on errors and shortcomings, typical of the Browder period." According to him, "the Communists . . . were in a strong enough position locally at the time to have insisted that representative steel workers be brought into the top leadership, but they failed to do so" (*History of the Communist Party*, p. 351). They could have insisted only if they wanted to break the entente cordiale with Lewis and Murray, and be prepared to lose their vested position in the CIO. Good relations with the progressive union leaders were essential for maintaining the popular front, however. Foster had little to lose by declaiming in 1952. What he was proposing retrospectively was to have his cake and eat it too.

fortitude to utilize the forces available, the cool nerve to unleash a social conflict, and the self-confidence that he could control the forces unleashed for his limited purposes of building stable unions and winning signed contracts with the major business corporations. Once he gambled on Wendell Willkie, his megalomania and autocratic excesses came to the fore, and he was never again a national spokesman. But in the five decisive years from the CIO's formation to the 1940 presidential campaign, no other union leader came near him in his ability to grasp the union tasks of the day, to articulate and dramatize the aspirations of millions, and to convert the new industrial-union movement into a social power.[21]

1. Girl textile workers, Gastonia, N. C., attempt to disarm National Guardsman during 1929 strike.

2. In 1934 textile general strike, pickets at Macon, Ga. overturn car in which three company officials sought to enter plant.

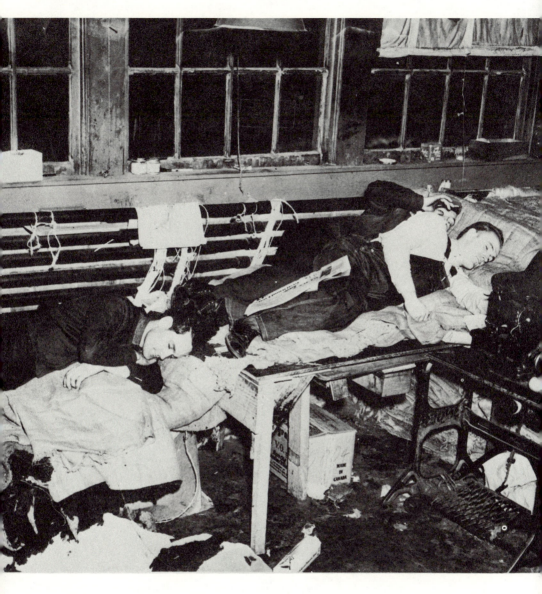

3. Strikers, enveloped by tear gas, use paving stones to combat state troopers at Auto-Lite in Toledo.

4. A section of the mile-long demonstration during the breakthrough Goodyear strike in Akron.

5. In support of General Motors strikers, sit-downers settle in for the night at company supplying cotton stuffing for Chevrolet and Buick cars.

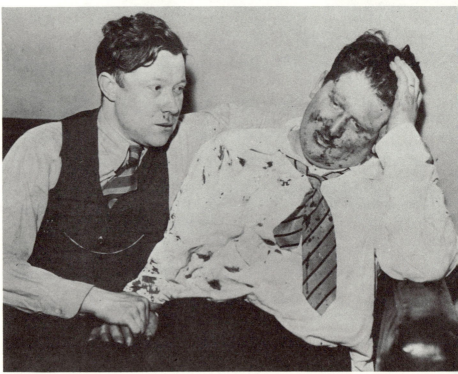

6. Ford Company service men beat up Richard Frankensteen at River Rouge, May 1937, after union representatives tried to distribute literature.

7. Reuther and Frankensteen console each other after beating.

FIVE · *From Akron to Flint*

FOR Lewis and his mine union associates, unionization of the steel industry was at the top of the list of CIO objectives. That inevitably came to Lewis's mind when he made his speech for industrial unionism at the AFL convention in Atlantic City: the mine union had a "selfish" interest in the matter, he told the delegates; it wanted to eliminate the threat to itself represented by the open shop in the steel industry's captive mines. And since Lewis dominated the thinking of the CIO, the organization of the steel industry became the major preoccupation of the national office in the first year of the committee's existence.

In January 1936 Brophy warned the executive council of "serious consequences" if the AFL did not take immediate action to organize steel. A month later Lewis wrote Green offering $500,000 toward a fund of $1½ million for the organization of steel on industrial lines. After Wharton of the machinists union refused in an open letter to Green to contribute anything until the CIO was kicked out of the federation and until all affiliates of the AFL declared themselves in favor of an organization campaign; and after other members of the executive council were equally unencouraging and lackadaisical in their responses, Lewis leveled his guns at the Amalgamated Steel union's convention due to meet at the end of April. Faced on the one side with Lewis's ultimatum that he intended to proceed with a half-million-dollar-funded steel campaign, with or without Amalgamated cooperation, and on the other side with inertia and indifference, Tighe and his fellow officers had no alternative but to capitulate to Lewis and the CIO. The agreement in June provided for the creation of the Steel Workers Organizing Committee, and, although Tighe and Joseph Gaither were named to the original SWOC of nine, for the demise of the Amalgamated.

There was an immediate response from the steel masters to the union announcement. The American Iron and Steel Institute publicly declared war on the CIO in full-page advertisements carried in 375 metropolitan newspapers. "The Steel industry will oppose any attempt to compel its employees to join a union or to pay tribute for the right to work . . . The Steel industry will use its resources to the best of its ability to protect its employees and their families from intimidation, coercion and violence."[1] A week later on July 6, an embattled Lewis flung down the gauntlet in characteristically over-laden rhetoric on an NBC radio national broadcast. It was a speech that had been eagerly awaited by millions, and made a deep impression. It is worth quoting from to convey the flavor of the events even after time has deprived the declarations of their immediacy:

> Let him who will, be he economic tyrant or sordid mercenary, pit his strength against this mighty upsurge of human sentiment now being crystallized in the hearts of thirty millions of workers. . . . He is a madman or a fool who believes that this river of human sentiment . . . can be dammed or impounded by the erection of arbitrary barriers of restraint. . . . The statement of the Institute is an open warning to representatives of recognized and firmly established labor unions that if by any legal and peaceful methods . . . they are so bold as to attempt to persuade steel workers to become members of recognized, standard labor unions, the brutal and ruthless forces of the steel oligarchy will be unloosed against them. . . . Moreover, it is to be emphasized that when the pronouncement of the Steel Institute states it "fears" industrial strife and dislocations may develop, it really means that as the organizing campaign of our Committee is meeting with success, the steel corporations themselves, through their private legions of armed guards, despicable undercover spies, and agents provocateurs will deliberately provoke strife and bloodshed, and attempt to place the blame for its occurrence upon the representatives of legitimate labor. . . . I wish solemnly to warn those who represent the steel industry that their unlawful, ruthless tactics of former years will not be tolerated by our Committee. . . . No greater truth of present-day significance was ever stated by a President of the United States than the declaration made by President Roosevelt in his speech at Franklin Field to the effect that America was really ruled by an economic dictatorship which must be eliminated before the democratic and economic welfare of all classes of our people can be fully realized.[2]

Two things are obvious from the speech. Lewis concluded that the right way to approach labor masses in mid-1936 was to appeal to the tradition of populist-progressive struggle against the "money trust" and the "invisible government" of "finance capitalism"; and the country was put on notice that a titanic labor war would be waged shortly in all the communities that housed important plants of the steel industry. He was not bluffing. Murray was put in charge of the SWOC with a drawing account of $500,000 at his disposal, quickly supplemented with additional funds. (It has been estimated that the steel campaign cost $2½ million in the first year alone, most of the money coming from the mine union treasury.) Murray wasted no time in setting up lavish headquarters on the 36th floor of the Grant Building in Pittsburgh, and soon 240 organizers, some part-time, were in the field.

But that is not how the battle developed.[3] Already in the first months of the year, Akron became the cockpit of the industrial war and the architect of the CIO's potent weapon, the sit-down strike. "Quickie" stoppages swept through the immense plant of Goodyear, the major rubber producer, from the end of 1935, in protest against the company program to introduce the 8-hour day (the rubber industry in Akron had gone on a 6-hour day in 1931 to spread the work) and to reduce piece rates proportionately. On January 19 thousands braved a blizzard to hear Lewis at a rally in the Akron Armory. At the end of the month, a sit-down strike closed the main plant at Firestone over the firing of a union committeeman. The company gave in within 24 hours, reinstated the employee, agreed to pay strikers for 3 hours for each day lost, and to negotiate the pay rate. The Goodrich management similarly capitulated in the face of a sit-down on February 8 in its tire division. A week later, 137 tire builders in Goodyear Plant No. 2 shut off the power and sat down to protest the layoff of 70 fellow workers (preparatory, they assumed, to introducing the 8-hour day). When news of the Goodyear sit-down spread, Akron ignited. Rubber workers stormed the local union halls to sign membership cards. The inexperienced rubber-union officials, unsure of themselves, overwhelmed by events, and fearful of the sit-down, marched the tire builders out of the plant for a conventional strike—a formidable undertaking, as the Goodyear properties extended 11 miles and there were 45 gates.

What was to become the CIO roving team descended on Akron, accompanied by McAlister Coleman, a newspaperman associated with the opposition in the coal fields in the twenties, brought along to direct publicity. Immediately these legates demonstrated that they had what the AFL representatives lacked, that they knew how to ride the winds of discontent. The strike, which went on for five weeks, kept the town in a high fever and converted it into a bastion of unionism. In that interval, the company secured an injunction banning mass picketing, the central labor body issued a warning that if force was used to reopen the plant, a general strike would be called, the former mayor launched an Akron Law and Order League to break the strike, while a Youngstown detective agency shipped in carloads of professional thugs. By March 18 the Goodyear president, realizing the tide was against him, made concessions, and several days later the union ranks accepted the breakthrough, but circumscribed proposals (not a signed contract) on the strong urging of Germer and the other CIO envoys. Between the date of acceptance and June there were at least 19 more sit-downs in the Goodyear plants, and another 2-month-long strike at Firestone, concluded at the end of April when the company signed the first basic contract in the industry granting the union exclusive representation.

What set off the Akron hurricane? It is insufficient to point to the immediate grievances and resentments of rubber workers, for there had been grievances and resentments of equal moment over the years without leading to this kind of revolt. The rubber experience closely paralleled the one in auto in this formative period. Federal locals mushroomed during the NRA, went through similar punishing collisions with AFL officials, and by early 1934 saw their memberships dropping away. There was the same decline and demoralization for the next year and a half. Then came the revival, and it came first in Akron, and it came there with a rush. The Wagner Act, which was to shape the character and contours of labor-management relations for an entire epoch, was not the catalyst. It had no part in the initial CIO upheaval. Although it had been signed by Roosevelt in July 1935, the law was immediately challenged by employers in and out of the courts, and their attorneys tied the labor-relations board into legal knots until the Supreme Court, faced with the president's "court-packing" proposal, affirmed the law—but that was in April 1937.

The general circumstances favoring the Akron and forthcoming upsurges were similar to those that had set off the NRA upsurge. A pronounced economic upturn that lasted from 1935 to the recession in the fall of 1937 brought with it a restoration of self-confidence among wage earners. The other background factor was the buoyant political climate that reassured workers they were in understanding hands, that there was somebody in authority from whom they could get a fair hearing. This was not a bookkeeper's calculation, for federal mediators were rarely helpful before the unions became a power. McGrady spent two days bustling around the principals at the end of February and all he could propose was his stock solution of that period: strikers should return to work and submit the issues in dispute to arbitration. No, it was the continued faith overcoming rebuffs and disillusionments, that the man in the White House was a peerless humanitarian, that in him labor had the greatest friend that American politics had ever produced.

This reverence was given institutional expression that summer as Lewis and his coworkers set up Labor's Non-Partisan League to round up the labor vote for Roosevelt and the Democrats. They contributed $770,000 to the campaign chest (60 percent of which came from the mine union), hammered out a de facto bloc within the Democratic party, and were credited with swinging Pennsylvania, Ohio, Illinois, and Indiana to the Roosevelt column. This energetic, purposeful mobilization of labor behind the Democratic candidates was an innovation; it transformed the old Gompers policy of casual and largely symbolic endorsements of labor's friends, to open a new chapter in unions' political involvement and rise to national influence.[4]

The dramatic event that exploded the volatile elements of the mix was Lewis's formation of the CIO and the announcement of the steel campaign. This was the signal from the watchtower that at long last a labor leadership had come to the fore with the ability, foresight, and resources to take on the industrialists, that workers seeking to win bargaining rights would be aided, not thwarted. The AFL's presiding helplessly over major defeats had brought on an 18-month discontinuity; the CIO's appearance on the scene was the touch of the wand for a rejuvenation.*

---

* Communists were active in the 1936 Akron strikes. According to Williamson (*Dangerous Scot*, pp. 114-122), the Party had members on the Firestone committee, the chief picket captain of the Goodyear strike was a Party leader, and James Keller, the CP Akron organizer, was invited to address a meeting of all the picket captains. Later, the Party won a small voice on the International executive board through several sympathizing local presidents who were board members, and B. J. Widick, a Socialist left-winger was replaced as union editor by Robert Cruden, a Communist supporter. However, the provincial atmosphere of Akron, the center of the union and the industry, was a damper on Party progress. During the war, when the major Akron locals were swept by wildcat strikes, the Communists—in line with their wartime policy—were supporters of the Dalrymple administration against the insurgents. So, their influence was decidedly minor when the power struggle broke out in the top leadership in 1948. The opposition headed by George Bass, president of Goodrich Local 5 of Akron, was exclusively a trade-union challenge to the more conservative administration of Buckmaster, who had succeeded Dalrymple; it was little affected by the presence of an occasional Communist or Trotskyist activist in several

107

2

Akron was a major CIO victory, although the United Rubber Workers union was not yet formally an adherent. It was the crest of the gathering swell that was to break with a thunderous roar to make the following year labor's *annus mirabilis*. There was the month-long RCA strike at Camden, New Jersey, in June and July that put the fledgling United Electrical union on the map. The Maritime Federation of the Pacific called out its unions on October 30 for a battle that was to last 99 days. The West Coast strike, in turn, led to the Curran rebellion inside the AFL International Seamen's Union, and the walkout on November 6, led by insurgents, of all Atlantic and Gulf seamen.

Thus, when the torch passed from the rubber to the auto workers toward the end of the year, the CIO design was already bent out of its original shape. Considerable attention will now be devoted to developments in the auto union. This would be justified in any case because of the big role that the Communists played in this key union. Beyond that, all major conflicts that beset the CIO were played out in this union in classical form; the formation and clash of opposing factions found here their freest and fullest expression; the union practiced a democracy and was able to elicit a rank-and-file participation in its affairs that was only partially or episodically achieved by others; the history of the union was like a typology for sociological representation of underlying trends in blue-collar industrial unionism; and finally, the postwar campaign against the Communists was fought earliest and most extensively in the auto union, and it was there the resounding victory of the conservative camp was important for actuating the anti-Communist campaign throughout the CIO.

The Communists were able to extend their influence in the auto union in an organic way because they had integrated themselves during the formative stage when devoted workers were at a premium. The floundering and bureaucratic stupidity of Collins, Dillon, and the other AFL walking-delegates, which reduced auto unionism in 1934 and 1935 to a core of die-hards and zealots and a handful of outlying locals, played into the hands of Mortimer and his

---

of the locals. Bass lost to Buckmaster by a vote of 808 to 810, although Bass's coworkers were able to win a majority of the incoming executive board. The opposition then overreached itself when it removed Buckmaster from office. Buckmaster won his appeal to the 1949 convention, and went on to win reelection and to reestablish his regime.

friends. They stood forth as battlers for the formation of an autonomous industrial union at the National Council convened by Green and Collins in June 1934 as a substitute for giving the auto workers an international charter. They were floor leaders at the first UAW convention in August 1935 in the fight against the restricted AFL charter and Green's appointing all officers. Mortimer (and Tom Johnson, another Communist delegate from the paper Ford local of Detroit) was a member of the elected delegation of five to protest these decisions to the AFL Executive Council and to the convention.[5]

It is not incorrect to refer to the next year's UAW gathering in South Bend, at which Dillon threw in the towel and the convention assumed control over its affairs, as under left-wing control (as some labor historians have done), but it can be misleading unless it is understood that most delegates making up the left-wing caucus were left-wingers in relation to Green, Dillon, and the AFL hierarchy, not in relation to Lewis, Hillman, or American liberalism. The general mood of workers in 1936 was militant, at times radical, and the auto delegates reflected that, sometimes, in their exuberance, in exaggerated form. But it was a leftism of mood and style, not of political persuasion. It was an inchoate leftism that could move further along the political spectrum or recede to its origins, depending on the possibility or impossibility of achieving limited objectives. Mortimer and his comrades were able over the previous several years to solidify alliances with unionists in pursuit of specific union goals. The paths of the two converged for a period. These alliances, while they lasted, gave the Communists influence and authority. But because they were alliances of convenience, not of love, they were shallow, and as events quickly revealed, transitory. The idea then being propagated that many left-wingers were elected to the new executive board must be modified in the same way: they were in one union caucus with the Communists, or the Communists were in one union caucus with them; but these nonpolitical activists were neither fellow travelers nor sympathizers. Mortimer, elected first vice-president, was the only Communist in the top leadership.[6]

The two substantial allies of the Communists were George F. Addes, the new international secretary-treasurer, and Walter P. Reuther, then a newcomer, elected to the executive board at this convention. Addes had been secretary of the amalgamated federal local in Toledo, and at the time was thought of primarily as an industrious, competent administrator. A dark, compact, attractive figure

109

of Syrian antecedents, he soon demonstrated organization talents of a high order. But he lacked political sensitivity, the ability to see necessary connections between tactical positions and larger political trends outside the union, so that, when in difficulty, he was apt to rely on makeshift combinations, and put his trust in deft patronage deals. Through all the vicissitudes and changes of allegiances and loyalties that rocked the union in the next decade, he remained the central, magnetic figure of the left-wing caucus; it was he, not the Communists, who determined the basis and limits of the bloc.

Reuther was a special case. He was 29 at this time, technically an auto worker since he had been employed at Ford; later he and his brother Victor spent two years at the Gorky auto works in Russia. In truth, Walter and his two brothers who became active in the UAW, Victor and Roy, belonged to the class of semi-professional activists thrown up by the depression. Coming from a Socialist home—the father, a Debs enthusiast, had been a union official in Wheeling, West Virginia—both Walter and Victor were busy giving lectures after their world junket in 1935 on the situation in Russia, speaking at rallies for the Spanish loyalists, attending radical conferences. Roy, the youngest, had a fellowship teaching at Brookwood Labor College, and later got an FERA job in adult education in Flint. Victor spent several months in Brookwood as well, lectured for the American Friends, and taught at the antiwar encampment at Commonwealth College in Mena, Arkansas, in the summer of 1936. The Socialist party, of which they were members, was in its period of greatest left ferment, and the Reuthers were enveloped in the popular-front effluvium that suffused radical milieus of the time.

At the South Bend convention, Reuther was not only part of the left-wing caucus, but he was also on intimate terms with the Communists. They considered him a close friend, and that was the way he thought of himself. It was only this close association that made it possible for him to be a delegate at the convention at all. The charter for the Ternstedt local that he represented had been secured from the International only a few months earlier by a handful of radicals who had not signed up the 15 paid-up members required by the union constitution, and Reuther had never worked at Ternstedt. His credential was challenged at the convention on that ground, but he managed to get seated because of the false testimony of a woman delegate, Helen Tombor, who maintained that he had worked for two months at Ternstedt under an assumed name. (Helen Tombor's credential was also challenged because the plant she represented, Universal Cooler Company of Detroit, did not manufacture auto parts, but here too another delegate came to the rescue with testimony that the company did at times put out some auto parts.) The looseness of union procedures at the time, the questionable character of a number of the credentials, and the left wing's connivance, permitted him to slip in. It had been arranged ahead of time in cooperation with the Communists to fatten the left wing's representation. Reuther almost admitted as much in subsequent years.[7]

The delegates left South Bend with high hopes that the way was cleared for unionizing the industry now that the dead hand of the AFL craft leaders was removed, and they had the backing of the CIO, but they represented no more than 20,000 members at a generous estimate. Organization progress was slow in the next months. It was early August before the executive board appointed fifteen paid organizers and Richard Frankensteen was named director for Detroit. He had been head of the Automotive Industrial Workers Association, the so-called Coughlin union (it had been backed by Father Coughlin, the famed Catholic "radio" priest who presided over the Shrine of the Little Flower) that had a following in some of the Chrysler plants. He now received the seat on the executive board left vacant for a representative of the independent unions. Mortimer, already at work in Flint, was confirmed as organization director for that city. Ed Hall, the second vice-president, who had been leader of the Seaman local, was put in charge of Indiana. The CIO promised to support the campaign and assumed responsibility for the wages of three organizers, apart from the help being given by Germer and Krzycki, both of whom had been assigned to Michigan.

Communist ranks had been enlarged, as we know, by John Anderson and his cohorts from the MESA who received the charter for Local 155, the east-side tool-and-die organization. Nat Ganley, the new business agent for the local, a shrewd and capable tactician, had been a TUUL organizer sent into Detroit in the early thirties. His ability carried him forward to become the Communist spokesman in the UAW, but he was handicapped by his Semitic appearance, decided Brooklyn accent, and abrasive personality. Communist leverage was also augmented with the appointment of Maurice Sugar as legal counsel for the union. Sugar was a resourceful labor attorney, well known in the city, and was associated for years with Communist causes and front organizations. When Mortimer agreed at

111

the end of September to leave Flint (there were complaints against him for his Communist proclivities), he was replaced, at his request, by Robert Travis from the Toledo Chevrolet local, who was more discreet but of the same persuasion. Travis called in Henry Kraus, a graduate of Western Reserve University in Cleveland, a Communist long friendly with Mortimer, to direct the union's publicity and publication program. Kraus had been the unpaid editor of the *United Auto Worker* published by the Cleveland auto council, the first editor of the International union paper, the *United Automobile Worker*; now he began to issue the *Flint Auto Worker*, the first number of which appeared at the end of October.

On the west side of Detroit Reuther was hard at work. Aided and abetted by the Communists (Dave Miller, an active Communist supporter at the time, gave Reuther the initial money to pay for the local union hall), Reuther persuaded the members of six paper locals, including Ford, Ternstedt, Universal Cooler, and Fleetwood, to consolidate their forces (they had a combined book membership of 78), and were chartered as Amalgamated Local No. 174 of which he became first president. In the course of organization efforts directed at the Kelsey-Hayes Wheel plant, several of his Socialist confederates managed to get jobs with the company: his brother Victor; George Edwards, a Harvard graduate and American Student Union leader (later a UAW organizer, now a federal judge); and Merlin Bishop, his former roommate, a Brookwood College alumnus and the union's first national education director. Robert Kanter and several other Socialists also became active in Local 174 at that time or shortly thereafter.[8] In those popular-front days when many Socialists thought Russia was the workers' fatherland, there was no differentiation between what the Communists were doing in Local 155 and what the Socialists were doing in Local 174. As a matter of fact, anti-Stalinist radicals in the union thought that Reuther was part and parcel of the Communist operation, and Reuther was criticized inside his own party for being too close to the Communists. According to Marquart, "some of the comrades almost came to blows when members . . . accused Walter Reuther of becoming 'too footsy' with the CP faction in the UAW."*

Frank Winn, a graduate of the University of Texas, the UAW's

* Nat Ganley claimed in a private memorandum that Walter Reuther was a secret member of the Communist party at the time, that he collected his dues, and that Reuther remained in the Socialist Party in agreement with, and as an agent of, the Communists. (Ganley Papers, Wayne State.)

112

first publicity director, and a Socialist supporter of Reuther's, cogently described these relationships and attitudes:

Walter Reuther at that time was not himself an active functioning member of the Socialist Party, although he had been before he went to Europe and Asia in 1933. The Socialists who were active in the union, including myself and a number of others, looked upon him as a leader generally of our point of view. . . . Walter himself was too thoroughly tied up and immersed in union activities to pay any attention to the activities of the Socialist Party. The union members who were Socialists and active in the Socialist Party actually operated in the union, not as representatives of the Socialist Party, but as trade unionists. In fact they were often criticized by the leadership of the Socialist Party outside of the union, because part of the leadership felt that they were working too closely with the Communists. . . . One has to realize the spirit of the times then as it existed among the union and the radical parties. While there were many sharp ideological differences between the Socialist and Communist Parties, the Communists were looked upon by a part of the Socialist Party with a great deal more tolerance than they are looked upon now. . . . And it must be recognized that in those years the Communists were, for the most part, functioning as good trade unionists.[9]

Roosevelt's victory in November accompanied by the election of the popular Detroit mayor, Frank Murphy, to the governorship of Michigan were accepted as the sign in the sky that the time had come to move. The initiative came first at the Bendix plant in South Bend, one of the UAW's more conservative outposts. For eight days starting on November 16, a thousand workers occupied the plant in what was at the time the longest sit-down strike. Although the final settlement set forth a complicated face-saving formula for the company, the UAW had eliminated the company union and won exclusive bargaining rights. Two days after this settlement, the sit-down came to Detroit: 1,200 day-shift workers occupied Midland Steel, which supplied body frames to Ford and Chrysler. Eight days later on December 4, the strikers marched out, having won the greatest victory up to that time in auto union history. In this debut of the sit-down strike in Detroit, the Communists did themselves proud. John Anderson was in charge of the strike. (Management tried to bar him from negotiations because he was a known Communist—he

113

had been the Party candidate for governor in 1934—and an anonymous handbill was distributed to the strikers exposing the Communists in the strike. This was as chaff in the storm that was now starting to rage across Michigan.) Ganley was editor of the strike paper and general factotum. Mortimer had a hand in the negotiations. Dorothy Kraus, the wife of the *Flint Auto Worker* editor, materialized as head of the food committee. If any Midland Steel strikers or well-wishers failed to receive copies of the *Daily Worker*, which was reporting the strike in ecstatic and copious detail, it was certainly not for lack of industriousness on the part of Communist distributors.

With the Midland victory, Detroit went into a fever of union agitation and organization. Workers would repeatedly call up union offices demanding that an organizer be sent to their shop to sign them up, or take care of their grievance, or call a strike. Delegations would descend on union headquarters for union books and equipment. There were sit-downs at Gordon Baking, Alcoa, National Automotive Fibres, Bohn Aluminum, and Kelsey-Hayes. The last was the most important. Kelsey-Hayes was a producer of wheels and brakes and the 10-day sit-down threatened to stop production at the Ford River Rouge plant. This strike, also concluded with a notable union victory, brought Walter and Victor Reuther to public attention for the first time. Before the strike, Local 174 had signed up at most 200 of the company's 4,500 employees. After the strike victory there was a wholesale enrollment. December saw the first appreciable membership growth of the entire UAW as well.[10]

3

The relatively easy victories at Bendix, Midland Steel, and Kelsey-Hayes, and the failure of the companies or of public officials to eject the sit-downers created the illusion at first that the ultimate weapon had been forged to ensure strike success. The tactic unraveled the conundrum that had baffled workers and union organizers in the open-shop industries. They had been unable to enroll the mass of workers in the face of the employer's spy systems and ruthless firing of union members. They had been held back from retaliatory strike action because the employer had the force to cut them down before the union could bring its potential resources into play. With the sit-down, a determined, disciplined minority could close down an entire plant and, because of the integrated nature of the industry, cripple thereby an entire line of manufacture, at the same time blocking attempts to start a back-to-work movement with scabs and strikebreakers.

As the tactic was more widely employed, it was learned that in solving one set of crucial problems, another set of equally crucial problems had been brought to the fore. It was one thing where the sit-down was a "quickie" involving one department or line over a simple grievance, and where the action lasted from a few minutes to several hours. When the sit-down turned into a prolonged test of strength, there were a number of prerequisites for its success: an elaborate organization on the outside to feed the strikers; an educational service to maintain morale; a program of activity to keep the link at white heat between strikers on the outside and those inside the plant; above all, a favorable political climate so that the general public would at the least tolerate striking workers occupying company properties, and public officials would hesitate to enforce injunctions and court orders. In other words, a tactic that challenged property rights so markedly—even though the strikers had no revolutionary intents or thoughts, and brushed away all but utilitarian considerations—could be practiced only in the special circumstances that prevailed in the United States at the height of the New Deal or in France with the victory of the popular-front government.

Despite the euphoria that the initial sit-down victories engendered, all were aware that the scattered agreements with parts companies would remain provisional and the entire position precarious until the union came to grips with the automobile manufacturers, particularly the Big Three that dominated the industry. This meant concentrating efforts on either GM or Chrysler (which Germer had advocated), since Ford workers were for the time being cowed by the company's internal terror organization, and the main citadel of the Ford empire, the River Rouge complex, seemed unapproachable. After the event, history was rewritten, mainly by Kraus and Mortimer, to make it appear that the union had a well-planned strategy to close down the General Motors empire. It was not enough for the Communists that they played a considerable role in the General Motors strike. They had to enhance that role by portraying themselves as the omniscient planners and architects of the entire project.

In truth, the UAW was in too chaotic a state in 1936 to be able to plan any kind of firm national strategy. It had too few members in the GM plants to force a confrontation. The Bendix and Midland

Steel strikes thrust it into the vortex of a mass upheaval so that it was responding tropistically to events, not controlling them or determining them. Addes in later years put the matter in a realistic context:

> Questioner: Was General Motors selected or did it just happen to fall before any of the others?
>
> Addes: It happened to fall before any of the others. . . . It may have looked like we concentrated on GM. Frankly, we worked just as hard in Cleveland, Detroit and in Wisconsin, but things worked faster in Flint.
>
> Q: Had they really planned on having a sitdown strike or did that just pop up?
>
> A: There was no plan, that is, an early plan.
>
> Q: Had there been some feelings that things were getting ripe now?
>
> A: A lot of discussion about it, but nothing definite. Plans were made only a few hours before it actually took place.[11]

In the light of Addes's explanation, the flittings to and fro across the stage of a number of the union's leading actors can be given their proper evaluation. There was great restlessness in many GM plants across the country when the sit-down fever struck Detroit. Fred Pieper, the executive board member from Atlanta, a close ally of Homer Martin, the UAW president, had been a hotspur for a GM shutdown since the Toledo Chevrolet strike of April 1935. And there is little question that grandiose visions of a labor empire were already beginning to shimmer in front of the eyes of the ex-preacher from Kansas City whom fate had tossed to the head of the auto union, and that Martin agreed to or acquiesced in most of Pieper's actions during the fateful next month. The Fisher Body workers in Atlanta staged a sit-down on October 30—which was quickly settled. The local presented demands on wage rates to the company a week later, and Pieper wrote the members of the union's GM Advisory Council, with Martin's knowledge, asking what support he could count on should Atlanta Fisher Body be struck. Pieper received promises of support from the Fisher Body and Chevrolet locals of Norwood, Kansas City, and St. Louis, and Chevrolet locals of Toledo and Janesville. Travis wrote back that he would try to get the executive board of the Flint local to give backing. These promises were of dubious worth, coming as they did from representatives all but one of whose plants were largely unorganized. On November 18 there was a sit-down at the Atlanta Fisher Body plant over the discharge of several workers who had flaunted union buttons. The sit-downers evacuated the plant next morning upon management's agreement not to operate until the dispute had been settled. The following week the strike spread to the Chevrolet plant, which in any case shut down for lack of bodies.[12] This was all generalship of the lowest order since work at the Atlanta plant could be readily transferred to another unit of the company, and the local was poorly organized and not ready for a prolonged contest.

Three days after the Atlanta strike began, the irrepressible Martin sent out telegrams to GM locals instructing them to "stand by" for action. The telegrams left the other international officers, Germer, and local officials, stunned. None of them had any notion that a national strike against GM was contemplated, nor had they been consulted about such a decision. (According to Frank Winn, Martin assured him that the telegram was just a bluff to "scare" General Motors.)[13] The executive board, by a vote of 7 to 6 (Martin was characteristically absent), decided on December 4 against an immediate strike, in effect repudiating Martin's action. It was bound, however, by an earlier decision, to support the Atlanta strike. On December 15 Glenn McCabe, president of the Flat-Glass Workers, called a strike at Libbey-Owens-Ford, thus jeopardizing GM's supply of plate glass. The next day the GM strike spread to the Kansas City plant over the firing of a union employee. Martin made a statement that the Kansas City strike, which concerned his home local, would have to be settled on a national basis. On December 18 Martin, Mortimer, Hall, Brophy and McCabe conferred with Lewis in Washington. There was a general awareness that the situation was heating up rapidly at the GM plants, and that the union might have to go over to strike action some time in the coming year.[14] Brophy was sent to Detroit to help Martin draft the communication to GM requesting a national conference to discuss outstanding questions. On December 22, William S. Knudsen, then executive vice-president, met with Martin and Addes to inform them that all grievances had to be taken up with plant managers. A few days later Martin renewed his request for a general conference. Knudsen's reply was already overtaken by the spread of the strike to Flint.

117

Let us now turn our attention to that city. Flint was the seat of the GM empire, to auto's number one producer what Pittsburgh was to steel, or Akron to rubber. Out of a population of 160,000 in 1936, over 47,000 were GM employees. If it could not be called a company town, it certainly was a company-dominated one whose police department viewed itself as an outpost of the corporation. If there was to be a GM strike, Flint would be the major battleground. Travis had been left there in charge of organization at the beginning of October. Mortimer had not made much progress in signing up members during his stay, and not too much was accomplished in October either. In early November a few "quickies" took place in the big Fisher No. 1 plant. On November 13 there was a sit-down when three welders who had participated in a quickie found on arriving for work that their time cards had been pulled. Bud Simons, the union steward, ordered a shutdown of the body-in-white department. The plant manager, anxious to keep production moving, agreed to reinstate the men and to pay the sit-downers for time lost. The news of this department victory spread throughout Fisher Body and led to the first sizable enrollment of members. That month GM was also beginning to take the union threat seriously. It announced a general wage increase, time and a half over forty hours, and a Christmas bonus. The concession, which might have undercut UAW efforts earlier, only added to the electricity, coming as it did when the tension was reaching a climacteric. Recruitment continued in December; by the end of the year the Flint UAW had a paid membership of 4,500 compared to 150 at the end of October, and possibly 1,500 at the end of November.[15]

According to the Kraus-Mortimer thesis, there was a definite union decision for a showdown with GM; there was a blueprint for an organizing schedule; there was a January 1 strike deadline; there was a union strategy to cripple the empire by shutting down Fisher No. 1 in Flint and Fisher in Cleveland, since all Chevrolet stampings originated in Cleveland, and Flint Fisher No. 1 was the sole supplier of body components for Buick, Oldsmobile, and Pontiac. From internal evidence in both the Kraus and Mortimer books, as well as the Mortimer and Travis interviews, it is possible to reconstruct that Travis, Mortimer, Kraus, and undoubtedly other Communists discussed the Flint-and-Cleveland strategy in their private bull sessions.[16] Travis had been one of the militants of the Toledo Chevrolet strike of 1935; he had seen how the shutting down of a single strategic plant could progressively disable an entire line of

118

production. The Toledo Chevrolet strikers had been unsuccessful in spreading the strike to other centers, but now with the CIO on the scene, and given the explosive mood, such a shutdown in Flint and Cleveland would have a different issue. So far, so good. The distortion of the Kraus-Mortimer thesis consisted of converting their private expatiations and hopes—they were no more than that—into a union strategy, a union decision, a union timetable.

Furthermore, they were not in control of their putative private scheme. They had only gained some ability for decision-making in Flint Fisher No. 1 in December. The union still had only minor groups of supporters in Chevrolet, and almost none in Buick and AC Spark Plug. (The Travis-Mortimer connection with Fisher No. 1 was augmented by the presence inside the plant of an effective Communist trio of union devotees consisting of Bud Simons, the leader of the November 13 sit-down, Walter Moore, selected as mayor of the Flint sit-downers when the big strike began, and Joe Devitt, another committeeman. All three had worked together in auto plants and were accustomed to cooperating with each other. Curiously, there was another larger radical contingent in the Fisher plant of members of the Michigan group mentioned earlier, the Proletarian party. It included several able individuals who later became known in Flint labor affairs. Whatever the doctrinal differences between Communists and Proletarians, the relation of the two in Flint was similar to that of Reuther and the Communists in Local 174.)

The Mortimer-Travis axis had no control over the Cleveland end of the project at all. Despite Mortimer's blithe assurance that "the Fisher Body plant in Cleveland was already fairly well organized, since that was my home town," the Cleveland Fisher Body local had virtually no membership at the time of the South Bend convention, and according to Williamson, who was on the scene, had only 300 members at the end of the year in a plant of over 7,000. Although there were a few important Communists in the local, both the president and some of the other officers were unpredictable and on the conservative side. The sit-down in Cleveland on December 28 set in motion the most momentous single strike in American labor history, the testing field that determined the fate of the CIO and the entire labor insurgency of the second New Deal. It was a spontaneous, undirected protest over a local grievance, and an indirect expression of the tension building up against the company. Only after the bewildered local union president called Mortimer in Flint, and Mortimer rushed to Cleveland, rejected the mayor's peace plan to resume

119

work pending negotiations, and announced publicly that the strike would have to be settled on a national scale, did the Mortimer-Travis bubble become a strategy.[17] (See also Appendix II.)

The Communists now had the opportunity of playing the same kind of role in the strike of the century that they had played in the Midland Steel strike. It was a Marxist's wildest dream come true. The tableaux could not have been improved upon. Here was a classic labor-capital confrontation encompassing scenes of corporation executives intent on beating back the union challenge, property-minded judges issuing sweeping injunctions, sheriffs and police with drawn guns, vigilante leaders trying to organize a back-to-work movement, grimly determined workers, heroic wives, excited labor agitators—the works. And the Communists were in the center of it all. Mortimer was one of the negotiators, the only UAW officer present in the decisive stage of negotiations. Travis was the Flint director. Kraus was running the union newspaper and publicity. His young wife was in charge of food supplies and distribution. Sugar was legal counsel working in cooperation with Pressman, also on the scene. Veteran Communists were in the leadership of the Fisher sit-downers. (Bud Simons wrote his wife that if there was an attempt to seize the plant, "I will be here to do my duty as a warrior of the working class. If anything happens it will be for the best cause on earth.")

The three Reuthers, Merlin Bishop, and other Socialists, all important in the strike, worked in kinship with Travis and the Communists, since on union matters they saw eye to eye. The same was true for Powers Hapgood, the CIO representative. Roy Reuther, who had been hired as a UAW organizer in November, and was Travis's lieutenant throughout the strike, said that Travis "was a good dedicated trade union guy," and did not think he was "political" at the time. Roy Reuther was mistaken on the latter score; what is telling is that his attitude tallied exactly with that described earlier by Winn.[18] The Communists also had a representative on the staff of the La Follette Senate Civil Liberties Committee, whose auto findings were important for the strike. Charles Kramer, the Committee's chief investigator in Detroit (he was replaced in January by La Follette on Germer's request), was later identified as a Communist. Not that his close association with Travis distinguished him from other non-Communist La Follette Committee staff people in Michigan. At the time, these young lawyers saw themselves as allies of a great union battling for social justice against the soulless minions of a billion-dollar corporation, not as sternly neutral researchers developing value-free data.

As one would expect, the Communists did not neglect this golden opportunity to "politically develop" the workers. The *Daily Worker* covered strike doings extensively and knowledgeably, given its inside connections; and literally tons of the papers were distributed around the town. On one occasion, when there was an objection made in Fisher No. 1 to the *Daily Worker* coming into the plant along with the other newspapers, Simons delivered a pep talk that it would be unconstitutional and undemocratic to censor reading matter, that it was up to the strikers themselves to determine what they did or did not want to read. Communists or fellow travelers were at all sorts of places carrying out various union tasks and assignments; for "politicals" it was clear that the Communists were well supplied with finances. To what extent the Party made special funds available is unknown. Possibly, it had no need to. There was a UAW Mortimer-Travis account, handled solely by the two of them, through which some $200,000 passed. Once the strike started, big contributions came in from other unions, and there were numerous individual contributions, as well. Mortimer originally opened the account in his own name with the approval of the other international officers in order to circumvent the possibility of union funds being seized through a court order. Whatever the wisdom of the arrangement, all through the strike both Travis and Mortimer wrote checks on the account to cover strike and relief expenses.[19] Numbers of Communists were able to receive expense moneys for undertaking sundry union and ancillary, as well as party-related assignments. Not that money was not paid out to others for taking on responsibilities, but control of such sizable funds gave the Communists a striking advantage in selecting secondary personnel.

4

In subsequent hearings of the House Committee on Un-American Activities, witnesses asserted, and the Committee chairman Martin Dies concluded, that it was all a Communist plot, an example of a strike instigated, directed, and controlled by Communists.[20] This is reasoning based on demonology. Its working method consists of stripping away from a social phenomenon the causes, the contradictions, the dynamics that make corporeal a society's behavior in order to account for unruly events by the arbitrary machinations of villains and devils. That Communists were

121

prominent in the conduct of the strike is established. That Communists were the creators of the social conditions that made the GM clash possible, or that a strike of that magnitude and ferocity could have taken place because of the conniving of Communist agitators, can only be believed by those bereft of social understanding. What is of concern to labor historians in determining the question of control is not how many Communists worked in the strike commissary or cranked mimeograph machines at strike headquarters, but to what extent Communists devised and dominated strike strategy. No sooner is this question posed than one is struck with the realization that the point is academic. Just as Roy Reuther saw eye to eye with Travis on strike matters, so there was a similar consensus between Lewis, auto-union officials, and Communists. Some, like Dies, wanted to draw from this datum the conclusion that the entire strike, or the CIO as a whole, was a Communist enterprise. Others, by the same reasoning process, argued later that Roosevelt was a Communist dupe since he and Stalin agreed on many immediate war aims. That does not cut across the reality that different individuals with both varying and conflicting social philosophies get momentarily united behind a strategic objective in a major social conflict. Only that made it possible for Communists to move around so prominently.

In the most important tactical difference that arose in the negotiations, concerning a decision that could have affected the fate of the strike, it was Brophy and Lewis—not Mortimer, not Travis, not Maurice Sugar—who were the unrelenting radicals. Brophy was against the agreement to remove the sit-downers from the plants in return for the company's promise to start negotiations.

> We insisted [Brophy stated in his account] that an organization called the Flint Alliance, which had been created as a combination of company union and vigilante outfit, must not enter into the negotiations in any way. The company gave a vague promise but refused to put anything in writing. I was not satisfied . . . The company made too much of the "concession" involved in even talking to us. I advised against accepting the proposal. If we pulled out the sitdowners without any comparable concession from the company, and we would be giving General Motors a chance to reverse itself and leave us stranded. But the UAW people were wobbly, especially Martin, who had shown up late in the day. I telephoned Lewis, taking Martin with me, and asked him to see if he could get Martin to understand what had to be

done. He demurred at first, but finally agreed. Martin yessed Lewis on everything, but five minutes later he was up in the air again. So we finally had to accept the promise to negotiate later as the best we could get.

When Brophy learned the next day that a United Press reporter had found out that GM was planning to negotiate with the Flint Alliance as well as the UAW, he decided that the agreement for the evacuation of the plants had to be blown up. He talked heatedly to Martin over the phone about it.

"Homer," I said, "this is a doublecross, one of the worst I've ever heard of. We've got to countermand the orders to the sit-downers, tell them to stay put tomorrow morning. We've got to see the governor, and we've got to tell the newspapers that it's all off until GM comes to its senses." I told him to come to my hotel—we were back in Detroit by this time—and we went to the governor's apartment. Murphy was very much upset by this development. . . . Martin sent word to the sitdowners to stay put. I stuck to him like a brother, talking constantly about "doublecross, doublecross." I figured that he could at least remember the word if I repeated it often enough. . . . Knudsen's move was really a break for us. It gave us a chance . . . to spread the strike to more plants, and to get rid of the absurd "preliminary agreement."[21]

If we would personalize the major social forces that went to produce the strike victory, we would say that in the final decisive weeks it was John L. Lewis who provided the steadfastness and imperturbable resolve that forced a bourbon corporation to give in. And high-minded New Deal personnel, Governor Frank Murphy, Secretary of Labor Frances Perkins, as well as President Roosevelt, in refusing to base their decisions on what Perkins called "legal technicalities," made it possible to restrict the struggle to an Indian wrestling match in which the specific strengths of the labor camp could prove more telling than the financial power of the corporation. The two made it possible for the sit-downers and union warriors to fight their way to a victory. (Later that year Roosevelt felt he had to redress the balance. After the Memorial Day shooting in the course of the Little Steel strike, he declared publicly, "a plague on both your houses.")

What did the Communist party gain from its admittedly influential position in the GM strike, and in the prior Midland Steel strike? There was the general prestige that accrued to the Party in left and liberal circles. In the normal course of things, this should have been translated into increased membership and press circulation, and those figures should therefore provide the most reliable indicators. In the case of the Communist party, this is not easy to measure. Its unusual structure made irrelevant ordinary comparisons with other organizations. For one, there was the incredible membership turnover that diluted the meaning of recruiting figures and gave the Party something of the character of a religious encampment. For another, the apparatus was staggeringly top-heavy. Gitlow stated that in 1925, of some 13,500 members, 2,000 were Party functionaries—one out of seven. That was clearly exaggerated, but only if he meant direct Party functionaries. According to Epstein's estimate of early 1939, there were 10,000 job holders of all sorts, including those in government employment, who owed their jobs to the Party's good will. If we use the rather high Party membership figure of over 70,000 cited by Browder for that time, we again get a ratio of one to seven. If we summarily exclude numbers in clerical and government positions that added little or nothing to the Party's combat potential, the ratio might drop to one to nine, or one to ten. In early 1937, in other words, approximately 4,000 to possibly 5,000 full-time and part-time organizers were at the disposal of, or associated with, the Party. It was this unique apparatus that gave the Party the ability to maneuver forces with what passed, on a comparative basis, for military precision.*

The membership figures proper were relatively small: 37,000 registered in January 1937, and 55,000 in January 1938, almost a 50 percent increase (then only 44,000 in early 1942, undoubtedly reflecting losses during the Stalin-Hitler-Pact period.) The auto membership rose more rapidly from 550 to 1,100 in 1939 (then fell twice as heavily to 629 in 1942.) Party membership, however, constituted only a part of the Communist sphere of influence. Communist officials were known to boast that there were ten periphery supporters for every member. There is no way of accurately measuring this more amorphous mass, but every student of the Communist apparatus knew that it existed, and that membership figures had to be multiplied possibly by three or more to estimate the Party following. Press-circulation figures are an even less trustworthy gauge because of an opposite consideration. The national office was con-

* Of the 766 delegates registered at the Party's 1938 New York State convention, three-quarters were functionaries: 106 full-time Party officials, 253 functionaries in "mass organizations," and 208 functionaries in trade unions.

124

stantly pressuring section and local bodies to accept larger bundles of newspapers and to engage in all manner of sales campaigns and "Red Sundays." Tens of thousands of these newspapers, after gathering dust at branch headquarters, would simply be given away on the streets to make way for new incoming bundles. Tens of thousands more would be finally consigned surreptitiously to the furnace or garbage heap. *Daily Worker* readership was always lower than Party membership, and the *Sunday Worker* readership—the so-called mass paper—no more than 15 to 18 percent higher than Party membership. Of the big circulations of a number of pre-World War I Socialist newspapers, the Communists never had a trace. On the other hand, they were the only left-wing organization that for many years could pack in 20,000 in the old Madison Square Garden in New York, and during the popular-front years, hold big meetings in other major cities.[22]

The figures do bear out other observations that the Party was making progress up to the end of 1939. If we take the auto union membership of this latter year and (in accordance with an arbitrarily set formula) multiply it by three, we get a figure of 3,300 Communist supporters. Whether that figure is considered big, small, or medium depends on the standards of measurement and the tasks that the host is called on to perform. Set against the auto union membership, the figure was insignificant. Set against the Socialist party's and all other radical groups' auto membership, it was huge. In the light of the policy-making power that the Communists sought to wield, their organizational influence was far in excess of their ideological influence. Certainly, they could never have carried against the administration at a UAW or a CIO convention 30 to 35 percent of the vote that the Socialist delegation chalked up against Gompers at the 1912 AFL convention. It is true that labor officials often control their organizations by bureaucratic manipulation, not because of membership attachment. Other rules came into play for Communists, however, who, at the head of labor unions, could expect to be subjected to pressures both within and without their organizations that would necessitate their having the unstinted loyalty of the ranks if they were to survive.

In line with ahistorical sociologies of totalitarianism prevalent in the fifties, Philip Selznick generalized Communist conduct into a totalitarian organizational principle. "It is convenient," he wrote, "for a subversive group to seek sources of power that may be won without bidding for direct popular support."[23] There was no totalitarian principle of this sort. The Communists were simply forced into organizational alliances and maneuvers by necessity, not by preference or propensity. They did bid for popular support time and again, but the response was inadequate. While a Party with a wildly fluctuating membership and a top-heavy professional staff simplified the leadership's task of running an authoritarian organization, and could intervene forcibly for tactical gains, it also aggravated the Party's vulnerability in an unfavorable environment. A generation of anti-Communists exaggerated the capabilities of and were overimpressed by the resources of the so-called combat party; at the same time they underestimated or ignored the precariousness of its position.

SIX · *Factionalism and Anti-Communism*

THE UAW's sensational victory over GM cracked the industrialists' front against the new unionism, and the surge to the CIO became a tidal wave. In the fall of that year, the CIO claimed a membership of 3.7 million—larger than the AFL. The figure was somewhat inflated, but official membership statistics have traditionally been on the high side; in any case, it was incontrovertible that no trade-union movement had made such progress in so short a period. "CIO" became an incantation, a watchword, a call to battle. In auto the way was cleared to unionize the entire industry. In March-April the UAW won an equally substantial victory at Chrysler, followed by agreements, with or without strikes, with most of the independents and the parts producers. By the time of the convention in August, the union had 350,000 dues-paying members. It was on the way toward becoming one of the largest labor organizations in the country.[1] Just as a sudden change in the fortunes of an impecunious relation has been known to unsettle that person's self-possession, so the prospects of high status and power shattered the inner poise of the UAW. The union was thrust into a savage faction fight that threatened its survival. It would simplify matters to be able to follow some of the anti-Communist journalists who wrote about it at the time, to be able to say with Benjamin Stolberg that the raging battle was all due to "Stalinist rule-or-ruin tactics."[2] Unfortunately, in the social sciences, as in the other learned pursuits, there are times when neatness has to be sacrificed to authenticity. It was not that monochromatic then—or later. Let us take up the major factors that led to the fight, without at first attempting to integrate them or to ascertain their relative importance.

The position of all the leaders, and even of spear-carriers who aspired to become leaders, was transformed as soon as the UAW metamorphosed from a pariah group to a power structure. Here is a plant employee bursting with anger at the exploitation and abuse that he and his fellow workers are subjected to. In a great act of heroism, he risks his job by joining the union, or leading a sit-down strike. On the morrow of the successful campaign or strike he finds himself lifted out of the shop where he is a mere cog, and installed

127

in an office as president or secretary of an important local union. Foremen who used to shout orders to him as to a bondsman, and a superintendent who did not deign to notice his existence, now treat with him as a person of importance. Newspapermen interview him and write down his opinions as something the public will want to know about. Our shop worker has a changed status. This does not necessarily mean that he is no longer concerned about improving the conditions of those he represents, but he now sees his tasks from a different vantage point, and he now has his own special status to protect.

What applies to local union officials or organizers applies even more to international officers and board members. The union militant has been transformed into the union careerist and bureaucrat, or he is in the process of being transformed. Homer Martin, the hill-billy Baptist preacher who had to get a job at the Chevrolet plant in Kansas City, is catapulted into place as one of the country's major labor leaders. Richard Frankensteen, the 200-pound ex-football player working his way through Dayton University, pushed by the depression into Detroit's Dodge plant as a 49-cents-an-hour trim operator, now confers with mayors and governors, and negotiates on equal terms with industrial barons. Nor should it be thought that political radicals were immune to the lure of status and power. It merely took different forms with them. With an ex-Socialist like Walter Reuther, ambition is colored by social awareness. Not that social vision is permitted to inhibit the scramble for posts or the means used; one simply justifies or internalizes the scramble for the purpose of realizing higher social objectives, as an ecclesiastic might explain that his maneuvers are a means to realize the Deity's purposes. In the case of Communists, ambitions are not less ardent, but more corporative. In fixing their deals, they are battling for "history," for which enterprise they have assignments from "history's vicars" to grab up posts for themselves and their associates. The contestants cannot come to a compromise agreement on how to order their raging ambitions within a fixed hierarchy because of the rapidity with which the UAW passed from a struggling aspirant to a far-flung payroll-bearing concern. The membership is still too turbulent to permit the imposition of a settled bureaucracy, and the would-be leaders have to appeal to the ranks against each other.

This brings us to the second proposition, the mood of the membership. The GM settlement provided for de facto (not contractual) exclusive representation in 17 struck plants for a period of 6 months;

128

in all others, recognition for union members only. In order to sweep the unorganized workers who constituted the vast majority in all plants into the union fold in this period of time, the UAW had to demonstrate fighting spirit and effectiveness. It had to challenge a supervisory personnel which had been trained to exercise unquestioned authority, and which had strong doubts that the arrangement with the union would last beyond 6 months. Many under the direction of superiors were trying to hold the disciplinary line as close as possible to the pre-strike position. On the other side, workers were in an exalted and defiant state of mind. They felt their hour had come for redress. They had devised this matchless weapon, the sit-down strike, and with it, had forced arrogant corporation moguls to the bargaining table; now that same weapon was available to teach foremen and supervisors the lesson that the old workhouse regime was finished.

The post-strike contract agreed to on March 12, which contained a clause outlawing stoppages until a lumbering, multi-stage grievance procedure had been exhausted, underlined in effect the unresolved, provisional nature of the original settlement.[3] With the corporation determined to hold on to most of its power, and the shop ranks determined to materially change work relations, it was obvious that it would take additional tests of strength before a new power balance was struck. The stage was thus set inside the union for a debate on centralization and discipline vs. militancy and local autonomy. Although the March contract was negotiated by Mortimer and Hall (aided by Brophy), no sooner did the question become entangled in the inter-union rivalries than those associated with Mortimer and Hall used the agreement unscrupulously against Martin. From that point on, the question of unauthorized stoppages and the authority of the international office continued to run like red threads through the developing struggle.[4]

Next, the existence of a tightly knit, clandestine Communist faction was bound to produce counterorganization and the clash of factions as a matter of political tropism. There was the same response in less volatile unions. Here the law of self-defense was the more pressing since the Communists constituted a major power bloc by virtue of their alliances with influential leaders and payrollees. It was not necessarily this or that nefarious plot being hatched that would embroil the union in a disruptive struggle; the very existence of a secret power caucus had a menacing character. It carried an implicit threat against those outside its circle and called for protective

129

counter-measures. Whether in this case it was the Communists or Martin who struck the initial blow is as difficult to determine as the question of ultimate responsibility for the first Balkan war. What is certain is that when flaming matches are tossed into a powder magazine, at one point or another there will be an explosion.

The character of the contest was initially obscured by the personality of the union president, Homer Martin, who became one of the independent causes of the struggle. There is little question that he was not cut out to be the head of a union, much less the head of the auto union. He was an orator of the evangelical, stem-winding school, and had some of the talents associated with the public orator—facile intelligence, flashiness, an ability to draw fire from an audience, and an actor's adaptability to altering circumstances. In the formative period, his forensic gifts, his popularity with the ranks, and his image of an ex-minister devoted to the cause of social justice, were invaluable assets to the young struggling union. When the UAW began to emerge from the shadows, Martin was out of place. He lacked the interest and capacity for sustained work, he could not apply himself to any of the grueling tasks required of a union leader, whether it was administration, negotiation, planning a union campaign or a faction intrigue. Of the traits possessed by most important union presidents he only had the vanity and ambition. Brophy, associated with him during the GM crisis, thought him flighty. "I would make an agreement with him on some point of policy, and he would reverse himself within a day. . . . He flitted in and out of wage conferences, leaving most of the job to subordinates, while he rushed off to make a speech somewhere. People like Germer and Krzycki were soon as exasperated with Martin as I was." Mortimer, who was incapable of crediting an opponent with any but the basest motives, did fix on one of Martin's traits with devastating accuracy: "Martin had the habit of just getting up and putting on his hat and walking out." There were important conferences in hotel rooms where those present, seeing Martin leave in the midst of the discussion, thought he had gone off to the bathroom. When he had not reappeared after an interval, someone was sent to investigate, only to report back that Martin had taken off. Next day, an item would appear in the press that Martin had addressed a meeting in Rockford, or had made some remark to a newspaperman in Tarrytown. Unreliable, impulsive, irresponsible, unstable, were a few of the assessments by some of those who had dealings with him. This solving of unpleasant or tedious problems by geographical mobility, this attempt to metamorphose a labor official's existence into a glamorous round of speech-making and curtain calls was expressive of a Peter Pan personality that had been inappropriately and mistakenly deposited in the unfriendly environment of a labor union.[5]

Whatever his failings, he was no fool. He quickly realized that he was losing the respect of fellow officers and CIO representatives. However he had been hoaxed into leaving the GM negotiations, it was a fact that he was out on the road, like an itinerant salesman, when the epoch-making agreement was signed—without his signature. He remembered how Francis Dillon had been cashiered at the South Bend convention, and he decided that he had to shore up his defenses if he was to avoid a similar fate. There was no question in the spring of 1937, after the GM strike, that he was the object of a whispering campaign. Martin was portrayed in a variety of unflattering roles ranging from buffoon to hysteric, with the Communist caucus specialists supplying the words and lyrics. Already before the GM strike, Martin distrusted Mortimer and invited the complaints of the old AFL group in the Flint local. It was their accusations that Mortimer was trying to build "a Red empire" in Flint that led to his being replaced. Now in April Martin began to cut down the opposition. Roy Reuther and William Cody were transferred out of Flint. Victor Reuther, who had directed the desperate battles at Anderson, Indiana, was sent out to the "sticks." Kraus was removed as editor, Winn as publicity director, Travis was demoted, Mortimer was dispatched to St. Louis. The opposition, aroused and frightened, struck back by mobilizing its forces into the "Unity" group; the Martin supporters were gathered into the "Progressive" group; and the fratricidal war was on.[6]

2

What guaranteed that it was going to be unlimited war was the bizarre alliance with Jay Lovestone that Martin blundered into. Bewildered by the strange relationships into which the union was being drawn, panicked by the stridency of Communists and Socialists whose dramaturgy he understood imperfectly or hardly at all, Martin felt the need of friendly counsel from those who had experience in both unionism and Marxian radicalism. The advice to make Lovestone his confidant came from Dubinsky, and Martin entangled himself in the fraternization with his customary thoughtlessness and abandon. While Lovestone had the discretion

131

to remain for the most part in New York, Martin was soon surrounded by a clutch of Lovestoneite lieutenants who took administrative charge of the national office, the newspaper, publicity, and
other departments.

How Dubinsky came to recommend Lovestone is a separate story
only the barest outline of which can be recited here. After Lovestone's expulsion from the Communist party, he set up his own sect
called the Communist party (Majority Group). This nomenclature
was derived from Lovestone's being in the majority at the 1927
Party convention before Stalin pronounced the anathema. The
Lovestoneites went through a series of name-changes corresponding to the group's changing positions: Communist party (Opposition), Independent Communist League, finally, Independent Labor
League. Since the Lovestone faction had opposed the TUUL line,
its supporters in the needle trades remained or returned to ILG,
and several became prominent again, particularly Charles Zim-
mermann, manager of Local 22. He was in a loose alliance with the
Stalinist group in the local in the early thirties, then went over to
Dubinsky toward the latter end of the decade. It was through his
good offices that Lovestone began to receive commissions from
Dubinsky, who soon was convinced that Lovestone was ready to
stand and be counted as a fellow fighter against Communists no matter how unpleasant or slippery the assignment. Strangely, the
Lovestone group did not abandon its pro-Russian orientation until
after the trial of Bukharin and his associates in 1938, and the group
was not formally dissolved until two years later, but the anti-
Communism, which became almost a monomania with Lovestone
and his remaining adherents, was already asserting itself when he
tried out his expertise in the auto union. The same unscrupulousness and brutality that had been his hallmark in the faction fights
inside the Communist party he now sought to employ against the
opposing faction inside the UAW.[7]

Both Dubinsky's advice and Martin's acceptance of it were insen-
sate and led to Martin's undoing. While Martin would probably
have consummated his self-destruction as a labor leader without
Lovestone's help or presence, the arrangement hastened his
Gadarene plunge down the abyss. The bringing in of the Lovestoneites was unwise for at least two reasons. First, it compromised
Martin's anti-Communist crusade and made it easy for opponents to
accuse him of hypocrisy, or to portray the struggle as a cat-and-dog
fight between two rival groups of Communists. Before very long,

organizers who were only recently punch-press operators or cushion builders, who neither knew nor cared about Marxism, could discourse on how Lovestone had been expelled from the Communist party for being aligned with the right wing, and demanded to be told why Lovestoneite communism was more acceptable than Stalinite communism. At one point in the battle, when a UAW delegation of local presidents went to Washington to confer with Lewis, that was precisely the question he put to them, "What is the difference? Why is one better than the other?"

There was some attempt to portray Martin as a battler against Stalinist disruption "from the left," and as Stolberg had it, "with a new attitude and a new vocabulary, completely different from the old Red-baiting stuff of the reactionary A. F. of L. oligarchy." At one point, the Lovestoneite mentors tried also to build him up as an apostle of peace against what was described as the collective security warmongering line of the Communists. When the executive board, under the aegis of its Martin majority, endorsed the amendment sponsored by Congressman Ludlow calling for a referendum before there could be a declaration of war, the *Daily Worker* accused Martin of aiding Japan and fascism. To this the *United Automobile Worker* replied that collective security was "company unionism applied to foreign policy."[8] The claim that the Communists were being fought "from the left" was used effectively as a leitmotiv, or a piece of incidental ornamentation, by Reuther a decade later. Martin could not do much with it because the union, in its heroic phase, was seething with conflict over problems closer to home. Engaged unionists, scarred in industrial warfare, were suspicious of "porkchoppers" and would-be "labor statesmen" who wanted to centralize authority, no matter how leftist their rhetorical pretensions, and regardless of their position on peace (which was not a paramount issue in the union at that time).

The second reason why the Lovestoneite invasion was counterproductive was because of the nature of the advice that they proffered. While Lovestone saw himself as an expert par excellence on fighting Communists, and was subsequently accepted at his own evaluation by Dubinsky and George Meany, he represented a one-sided strategic school. For years Lovestone had been on the receiving end as AFL officials made use of administrative machinery to control conventions, exclude and count out insurgents, and successfully crush oppositions by mass expulsions. His experiences strengthened his natural inclinations to rely on ruthless power plays. In the given UAW situation, where a light-minded adventurer like Martin needed to be restrained from his bent for solving his leadership difficulties by autocratic assertion, he was incited instead to dispose of his opponents by proscriptions and purges.[9] Of all places that might have been chosen, the auto union in the 1930s was the most unlikely place in the entire labor movement for such an experiment. It was out of the question to get away with Lewis's tactics of the 1920s.

Unauthorized strikes, union discipline, constitutional powers of the international leadership—the three were interwoven, into what one might assume was the one issue of substance dividing the Unity and Progressive caucuses. Any straightforward debate was precluded, however, because both factions succumbed to demagoguery, with the result that programmatic declarations became tactical expedients designed to solve the major question in their favor—the major question being who was going to run the show. Leaders who ran their own locals like baronial estates insisted on looseness in international arrangements because the opposing faction was in control. Leaders who issued local newspapers that violently criticized international officers identified with political counterparts in other unions who tolerated no dissidence.

The riotous August convention in Milwaukee could not lay down the law. Although it gave Martin some additional constitutional authority, it did not end the factionalism since the Unity group remained in effective control of almost half the union including the largest units in Detroit. The dilemma became excruciating the next month when the 1937 slump came on and the GM contract was up for renewal. The corporation said it would not negotiate until it received effective assurances that unauthorized strikes would be eliminated. The executive board thereupon approved a provision to allow the company to fire workers engaging in wildcat strikes. Negotiations were then started and by November a new agreement was ready for ratification. It registered no gains at all; all union demands had been ignored; and with the new disciplinary provision, it was a worse contract than the union had before. The ranks were in no mood for that kind of a retreat, and both sets of leaders were tossed about in the ensuing gale. The Unity spokesmen made militant noises, but they were as much hostages as instigators of workers' disgruntlement. Martin, deeply involved in negotiating the agreement, made a turnabout when confronted with the hostility of the delegates to the GM conference, roundly repudiating his own hand-

134

iwork. The conference proceeded to reject the agreement by a unanimous vote.

In this crisis atmosphere a strike broke out at the 14,000-man Fisher Body plant in Pontiac over management's refusal to shorten hours. The plant was occupied when the company fired four committeemen and stewards whom it held responsible for the wildcat. Five days later, the sit-downers, in response to Martin's appeal to them to let the issues be submitted to arbitration, evacuated the plant. The Pontiac strike then became a cause célèbre inside and outside the union. Martin used it to lash his opponents as Communists or tools of Communists, and to spread the word that it was the Communists who were behind the calling of innumerable unauthorized strikes to keep the union in turmoil in the fulfillment of their nefarious scheme. The *United Automobile Worker* reprinted verbatim an article from the *New York Times* depicting the Pontiac strike as the work of the Communist party, and this became a widely accepted version of what was at issue in the faction fight inside the UAW. That it was propagated by Stolberg is understandable since he believed in painting with a broad stroke; but even a conscientious scholar like C. Wright Mills repeated it simply because, through repetition, it was accepted by anti-Communists as an uncontroversial statement of fact. [10]

Disentangling the knot has relevance for understanding Communist party attitudes and the difficulty that Martin's attack put them in. The Party supported Roosevelt in 1936; it was becoming a force of sorts in left-liberal politics; the leather-jacket-and-low-heels days of red proletarian bohemianism were being left far behind; the quest was for acceptance and respectability. The Party had not yet attained the peaks that it was to reach during the war, but it was on its way. It had a de facto alliance of limited scope with CIO national leaders which it was not disposed to upset even when provoked. It did not challenge Murray when Party organizers were unceremoniously dumped from the steel setup. It did not challenge Murray and Hillman later at the 1939 UAW convention when they insisted that R. J. Thomas, Martin's recent lieutenant, had to become the new president (although the Addes-CP combination had a majority at the convention and theoretically could have elected Addes in the face of Murray-Hillman disapprobation). [11]

Consequently, there was the urge to emphasize responsibility and statesmanship, to demonstrate to all and sundry that Communists were not wild-eyed obstructionists, to convince allies that

135

Communists were practical people who understood the complexities of questions, ready to cooperate with all reasonable progressives. That is why Browder lowered the boom on Michigan Communists in the summer of 1937 for opposing the decision of CIO leaders to have the sit-downers at Chrysler evacuate the plants during the strike. "Even if their fears had more solid foundation," he lectured, "it was necessary to proceed with much more tact, foresight and consideration. . . . We are a fully responsible party, and our subdivisions and fractions do not independently take actions which threaten to change our whole national relationship with a great and growing mass movement." He told the rank-and-file members not to forget their proper place. "We do not attempt to estimate such difficult and complicated trade union problems by ourselves, in isolation."

The search for respectability had important internal consequences. It was in this period that the initial shift took place in the relationship between the Party and important union officials. Coalition politics have a logic of their own. The Communist union leader, if he is to operate successfully, has to adapt himself largely to the union milieu, which in the United States is saturated with the mores of a status-conscious society. Like other union officials, he becomes a bureaucrat who must set himself up as a power broker mediating between his constituents and powers representing employers, public spokesmen, government; he becomes a person of some stature disposing of influence and finances.

The Communist "outsider" has acquired a "base" of his own. An early manifestation of his new position is his intolerance toward the traditional Party fraction. In Communist constitutional theory, the fraction is an embodiment of the Party's internal democracy—the mechanism whereby members of a subdivision make decisions by majority vote binding on all. In practice, fractions, like other subordinate bodies, become sounding boards to give resonance to the leaders' directives. But the very mechanism—with its egalitarian implications—has become an irritant, for the high Communist union official, like other union officials, is convinced that much of what he and his associates do is confidential and cannot be aired at a town hall gathering. Moreover, he is not prepared to have his decisions questioned, much less overridden, by nondescript members he considers untutored or unseasoned. It is true that Communist leaders inform him from time to time of decisions that may disturb his internal alliances, and that until the cold war the Party was gen-

136

erally successful in having these honored. That does not negate the fact that a social-democratic strain was affecting its system, and that had the trend continued, in time Communist union officials would have balked at Party supervision of any sort.

The new model unionism did not disturb the discipline with which the ranks carried out instructions and assignments, but Party functionaries acted like parliamentary whips to line up union ranks behind their officials, and relied on personal liaison with the latter to gain adoption of party policies. Clayton Fountain, a Communist auto unionist during this period, related that he never saw either Mortimer or Travis at a Party meeting, but Weinstone and Gebert "praised them up to us often." When the decision was made to switch signals at the 1938 Michigan state CIO convention, "I remember vividly how we comrades were hastily rounded up and called into a caucus to have the party strategy spelled out to us. . . . Thirty or forty comrades of lesser rank, like myself, sat around listening while the powers of the party gave us the line." In the new system, Communist union officials, particularly the important ones, became an elite that had to be treated with kid gloves by Party functionaries. Relations were never as autonomous as in the old Socialist movement: Socialist leaders expected Socialist trade-union figures to support Socialists in elections; for the rest, they did not believe it was the Party's business to mix into trade union doings. As the popular-front era progressed, a similar undercurrent of thought could be sensed. Williamson, the Party organization secretary during the war, one of those moving with the times, stated in a report, "We must put an end to anything that might be interpreted as interference with the normal functioning of the trade unions, including those with Left and progressive forces in the leadership."

In later years, Max Bedacht, a Communist founding father, argued that the abolition of fractions made the Party leaders utterly dependent on the Party union leaders. After Browder's downfall, Williamson reported along similar lines when he proposed the reconstitution of fractions. In the semi-hysterical Dostoyevskian three-day plenary session in June 1945 at which Browder had the blocks put to him by his erstwhile adulators, Peter Cacchione, one of the two Communists on the New York City Council, lashed out at the Communist trade-union officials—referred to in the Party as "submarines"—who lacked the courage to admit their membership. "If the trade union leaders have not come out openly as Communists in three and a half years of easy sailing," it was "idealistic" to believe they would do so in the next period. He said the Party ranks were critical of the Communist union leaders, and referred caustically to those who draw big salaries and "contribute nothing to the CP, who do not even attend meetings." David Davis, an official of the UE, joined in these remarks. He said that bureaucracy was widespread, above all, in the Communist unions. He knew of cases "where there is complete disregard for the feelings and needs of the members where comrades are leaders in these unions."[12]

3

This fast excursion to the other side of the hill will help to set the Pontiac strike in perspective. The strike was spontaneous, though George Method, chairman of the bargaining committee and one of the four fired workers, was reputed to be a Communist. Like most unauthorized sit-downs, it blew up over an unsettled local grievance on which the company had been stalling, and it was undoubtedly spurred by the GM National Council's rejection of the new agreement. That was one section of the tableau. In another part of the scene, the Communist party was facing accusations that it had engineered the strike, and was reputed to be provoking countless other sit-downs. In truth, the Party was not guilty, although some members, as in the case of Pontiac Fisher, may have participated in, or been ringleaders of, such actions. These members were acting in their individual capacities, and in the spirit of the Party's older tradition, however, not on Party instructions. Anxious to clear itself of this type of accusation, the Party adopted a high-level decision to speak out forcefully on the issue. As a result, the December 2 *Daily Worker* ran a statement of William Weinstone, Michigan state secretary, declaring "unequivocally and emphatically that the Communists and the Communist Party had never in the past and do not now in any shape, manner or form advocate or support unauthorized and wildcat action and regard such strikes as gravely injurious to the union's welfare." Lawrence Emery, the local Party correspondent, at first reported the Pontiac action in an approving spirit of exuberant militancy. He was quickly straightened out. The December 5 *Daily Worker* carried a feature article of his in which he quoted fulsomely Homer Martin's condemnation of the strike.

Then, in the center panel of the tableau were the UAW Communist leaders and their Unity allies—and their gestures are puzzling. It is known that Communist and other Unity caucus spokesmen did their bit to tear up the GM agreement. While the executive board was recorded as voting unanimously not to authorize the Pontiac strike, Mortimer and Reuther had spoken earlier in favor of authorization to put additional pressure on GM for new contract negotiations. All this while the *West Side Conveyor* was hurling one broadside after another at Martin. (Reuther's West Side local was an interested and influential party in the matter since it included three major GM plants: Ternstedt, Cadillac, and Fleetwood.) In March 1938 the GM contract was renewed unchanged, with an even poorer grievance procedure spelled out in a supplementary agreement. This time, neither Martin nor the Unity officers dared refer the contract to a delegate conference. The executive board ratified it. And again, many Unity locals protested vehemently, with West Side Local 174 in the van. The *West Side Conveyor* scored "the secrecy in which the negotiations were handled," censured "the undemocratic manner in which the agreement was signed," rejected out of hand "Martin's claim that the agreement was the best that could be had at the time."[13]

Despite the deafening shouts issuing from both faction centers, and the heated exchanges between the editors of the international newspaper and the sundry local opposition sheets, the sit-downers had no authoritative spokesmen to represent their point of view. Had there been in the union an influential IWW faction, there could have been a genuine debate between centralizers and decentralizers, a counterposition of theories of "responsible unionism" vs. anarcho-syndicalist unionism or shop-steward-oriented unionism. But the sit-downers, who must have numbered many tens of thousands, were voiceless. They had not elevated their anarchic actions into a concept. And their putative champions of the Unity group had no different theory of unionism than did Martin and his adherents. The oppositionists merely acted as voice boxes for native frustration; they were content to utilize dissatisfaction to advance their own faction fortunes. Hence, the debate degenerated into guerilla sniping and belligerent posturing on the one side, and unscrupulous denunciations of Communism and of Communist disruption on the other side.

A factional struggle carries a heavy freight of overhead costs because it diverts energies to besting rivals rather than employers, and consumes finances for building caucuses, not locals. But the organization proved strong enough to weather the ordeal, and the sharpshooting and wirepulling produced, as a byproduct, a generation of labor sophisticates. It was a tribute to how deeply the union put down its roots that throughout the soul-searing struggle the loyalty of the ranks remained intact. The UAW, systematically exploited and tortured by self-seekers, martinets, and quacks, exhibited extraordinary stamina and powers of recuperation.[14] What brought it to the edge of disaster was not factionalism per se, but the recourse to violence, to the use by both sides of flying squadrons—the Galahads of a dozen picket lines now degraded to praetorian house troops. When with the violence came Martin's turn to administrative sanctions, the fight went into a death grapple that threatened to undo the heroism of 1937. It was not the union's finest hour, and no one on either side earned laurels. As for the Communists, instead of raising the debate to a more principled level—their alleged strong suit—they competed with their erstwhile national secretary in matching intrigue with intrigue, and got so engrossed in maneuvering and scheming as to lose sight in the process of who they were supposed to be.

By the time of the special Cleveland convention at the end of March, Martin's secession movement to the AFL had been reduced to a splinter group. With the disgrace of the Martin faction, and the penitent return of his erstwhile associates to the CIO fold, one might imagine that the path was cleared for Unity-Communist hegemony. That is not how it worked out. The Unity group had been disunited since the Communists executed their fancy maneuver at the Michigan CIO convention in April 1938. They had induced Frankensteen to pull out of the Martin camp while he was virtuously calling for the dissolution of all caucuses, and the Communists, in turn, promised to support him for UAW president, and successfully backed Richard Leonard, a Martin supporter, for secretary-treasurer of the state body against Victor Reuther. The Communist-inspired spectacular, carried through in an atmosphere of Borgian conspiracy, did not disintegrate both factions, but panicked Martin into suspending his fellow officers. It was only the need to unite in the face of a mortal threat that kept the anti-Martin ranks together.[15] As soon as Martin was out of the way, the Communists had the second payoff on their intrigue. Reuther and his friends—the original group rested primarily on three large Detroit locals, West Side 174, Briggs 212, and Chrysler 7—hastened to announce their independence, as well as their abhorrence, of the Communists. At the convention there was also a sizable number of delegates who had supported Martin; too cowed to form a faction of their own, they looked to R. J. Thomas, the acting president, to be their spokesman.

For the rest, the convention was in the hands of the Addes-Frankensteen-Communist combination, a kind of reconstituted Unity faction which on paper had the votes to install Addes as the union's president and to take over the international office. In later years, after the Communists in the CIO were struck down, they castigated themselves for letting the presidency slip out of their hands.[16] This was not wisdom after the event; it was day-dreaming. Addes and Frankensteen would not have consented to defy Murray and Hillman, even had the Communists been disposed to do so—nor would many delegates. The UAW was still in a critical position; it needed CIO support to consolidate its mastery over the defecting Martin troop. On another level, the "self-criticism" revealed how thoroughly these would-be Marxists, whose specialty was supposed to be the analysis of social trends and forces, had succumbed to caucus calculations. Had there been no CIO influence, and had Addes become president, he would no longer have been dependent on his alliance with the Communists. In that case, given the pressures of the times, the nature of the man and his outlook, and the thinking of most in the so-called left-wing caucus, the probability was that instead of being crushed by Reuther during the cold war, the Communists would have been crushed by Addes.

Employing the same yardstick that was employed at the South Bend convention, journalists concluded that left-wingers emerged from the Cleveland convention with a controlling vote. This had even less reality than the analysis of three years before. The pundits arrived at their startling conclusion by crediting the Communist forces with every board member who was not friendly to Reuther. Actually, the Communists—although they did not realize it either—were already in decline, for the entire contretemps with Martin had tarnished their reputation more than they understood. Rather than controlling the new executive board, they had been effectively removed from the top councils when their solid man Mortimer was pushed out, never to be returned to the inner sanctum. To break the deadlock between Addes-Frankensteen and Reuther, who could not agree on the number of vice-presidents, the CIO representatives proposed the elimination of the office altogether. Mortimer was not purely the victim of Murray-Hillman guile;[17] he had not been elected a delegate from his own local; neither was any effort made to select him as the board member from the East Ohio

141

region after his vice-presidential post had been pulled from under him. His basic burden, of course, was that he had become known throughout the union as the enduring party-liner and mouthpiece. What passed muster at South Bend was no longer acceptable at Cleveland. If his Party affiliation was the major cause of his elimination, it can be said with equal validity that he never would have attained his prominence had he not been the Party's chosen instrument. In his favor it can be said that he was industrious, persistent, and dependable, that he had the appearance of an honest mechanic; but he lacked verve or presence and had no superior tactical or organizational gifts. On the level of personal assets, he could not compete with Addes, Reuther, Frankensteen, or other lesser luminaries. Instead of being an impassioned people's tribune, the UAW No. 1 Communist was a colorless organization man.

Also defeated for the board was John Anderson of previous MESA fame, and Tracy Doll from the Hudson local who was known to work with the Communists—both attractive and capable unionists. Of a board of 18, the Communists' only true friends were Leo LaMotte of the Plymouth local (a somewhat erratic fellow traveler), Lew Michener of California (a distinct lightweight, at this time a Party member), and George Burt of Canada who at times cooperated with them. Reuther, their redoubtable ally of yesterday, was now an opponent. Aside from the three and from Reuther's supporters, the board was composed of regulation trade-union politicians who, like Frankensteen and Addes, made or unmade alliances as called for by their organizational and careerist objectives. Communist theoreticians could have concluded that their position in the union had improved only by their assumption that calling the Addes-Frankensteen combination a left-wing group really made it so. After their preeminence in the ouster of Martin, and with their allies in control of the union, the fact that the Communists in auto could be raked over mercilessly by CIO dignitaries with impunity and relegated so unceremoniously to the second-tier benches, demonstrated anew that they had made little headway in ideological penetration.[18]

In addition to laying the groundwork to isolate the Martin split-off, the Cleveland convention's other major achievement was to decentralize the union. The dolorous Martin episode had created a consensus among activists that diffusing power was the only way to ensure membership control. They had come, by their own groping, to a fundamental rule of political craftsmanship: breaking the power bloc into discrete units and forcing leaders and factions to compete are the true guarantors of democracy. Never in the history of modern unionism had a constitution been examined so meticulously and revised so drastically by convention delegates. "Politicals," both Reutherites and Communists, were concerned that the sentiment for decentralization was getting out of hand. Emil Mazey cautioned the delegates against trying to write a constitution in order "to take care of Homer Martin." George Edwards said, "According to all this discussion at tonight's meeting, what the delegate body would be voting for would be a loose federation of local unions, without any international." S. Levine of the Plymouth local, from the other faction, seconded Edwards' remarks, "We know that there must be some authority of some kind"; and Morris Gottlieb from Cleveland Fisher Body emphatically concurred.[19] When, clause by clause, the new constitution emerged from the convention mill, the authority of the president had been pruned, the powers of the executive board augmented, the yearly convention brought back, the rights of locals increased, and control over collective bargaining protected through a structure of intracorporation councils of delegates from the plants. The UAW came out of the Cleveland convention the most democratic union in the country. It was under this basic constitution—and the competition of factions—that it became the prodigy of the American labor movement.

4

Before the year was out, the Communists were to undergo another trial by fire. Overnight, five years of painstaking, popular-front workmanship were discarded. Alliances with liberals, support for Roosevelt, collective security against fascism—the Mosaic tablets—all went by the board. The war, the preparations for which they had enthusiastically and noisily supported, was now disqualified as a war between "rival imperialisms for world domination." Roosevelt the emancipator became Roosevelt the warmonger. And instead of admiration for the grand alliance of the democracies proudly arrayed against fascism, the slogans now were "Keep America out of War" and "The Yanks Are Not Coming." The Communists bore the double onus of resisting American mobilization and of doing so at the behest of a foreign power. It was in the public domain that their recently refurbished revolutionism had been prompted by Stalin's pact with Hitler, and Molotov's discovery that fascism was "a matter of taste."

143

Some commentators thought that while Communists lost heavily among intellectuals because of this somersault, they held their own in the CIO.[20] They did not. They had become too prominent to be able to get away with brazen flip-flops the way they were able to in the twenties. Several fortuitous occurrences—and the return to popular-frontism within less than two years—masked both the blow absorbed and the internal hemorrhaging. But their moral position had been irreparably compromised (as they found out a decade later). In the national CIO, the Communists were saved from the worst consequences of their preposterous left turn by Lewis's providential break with Roosevelt. In his egotistical misreading of the power balances, Lewis imagined that his kitchen coalition with the Roosevelt camp was a full-scale, European-style coalition; that he, the head of the powerful industrial union sector, was entitled to honors and perquisites customarily accorded a political partner. The flaw in his reasoning was that the labor movement was split into two warring federations, that most of Lewis's fellow officials in the CIO had no such exalted view of their own political weight, and that most CIO members considered Roosevelt, not Lewis, their political leader. However, Lewis's split with Murray and Hillman on the political course to follow in 1940 made the CIO national office a house of confusion and uncertainty.

There was a similar muddle over foreign policy. Here, in contrast to his challenge to Roosevelt, Lewis was reflecting prevalent thinking of labor ranks. When war broke out in Europe, both the AFL and CIO declared themselves against American participation. At large, the antiwar feeling was strong enough to induce both major political parties to include noninvolvement planks in their platforms, and both Roosevelt and Willkie felt constrained to give pledges that American boys would not be sent to fight in foreign wars. As the struggle for public opinion was heating up, Hillman, supported by Reuther and a scattering of officials, favored all-out aid to Britain; Lewis was associated with the so-called isolationist wing that ran the gamut from Senator Robert Taft, the Republican conservative, to Norman Thomas, the Socialist pacifist. Since a stand for American neutrality was very much in the labor mainstream in 1940, the agitation to keep America out of war did not, per se, isolate or even distinguish the Communists.

What did distinguish them was that everybody, so to speak, was aware of the source of their antiwar and anti-Roosevelt professions; and no one was unaffected by the campaign of exposure. There was a rehearsal for the more orchestrated postwar performance upon the Red Army's invasion of Finland (the one country, Herbert Hoover reminded us, that had paid its wartime debt). The League of Nations, never before known for its resoluteness, summarily expelled the Soviet Union from its councils, and the United States government gave the signal that Communist leaders were no longer respectable folk when in 1940 Browder was sent to jail for passport fraud committed years before; and in succeeding months, other Communists were convicted on old charges, some of these going back over ten years. On the liberal front, the first hint of the postwar anti-Communist crusade came when Reinhold Niebuhr and James Loeb, Jr. formed the Union for Democratic Action (the precursor, initiated by the same two, of Americans for Democratic Action).

While he was president, Lewis, for his own reasons, muffled the blows directed against the Communists; he was not interested in stopping them. Already in 1939 he gave the Communists notice that their alliance with CIO leaders was shaky. At the conclusion of the CIO convention in San Francisco in October (where he blocked an anti-Communist resolution), he spoke at the executive board meeting against outside interference, warned the Communists not to press their luck, and curtailed Harry Bridges' jurisdiction from West Coast director to California director. The board then adopted a resolution which stated "that we are, and always shall be, unalterably opposed to any movement or activity of subversive character, Trojan horses, or fifth columns, which are aimed against our nation and government, or the basic free and democratic institutions upon which our Republic has been founded." The following year at Atlantic City, though the convention was dominated by the Lewis-Hillman clash, and the Communists shielded themselves by clinging to Lewis's coattails, they were again savaged with a resolution holding that "we firmly reject consideration of any policies emanating from totalitarianism, dictatorships and foreign ideologies such as Nazism, Communism and Fascism. They have no place in this great modern labor movement." Both resolutions were adopted unanimously—and better than that, the 1940 one was introduced by Lee Pressman, secretary of the resolutions committee. He was not an apostate; he was carrying out a Party decision. "It was a 'smart' move to save the necks of the Left," De Caux later explained, "The Left avoided an ugly showdown at a dangerous moment." It was an accumulation of such "smart" moves that helped in time to bury the Communists. By voting hypocritically for resolutions that de-

145

nounced them, they appeared as unprincipled tricksters whose dubious associations and ideas could not stand the light of day. De Caux confessed that "in submitting like this, the Lefts seemed to lack strength, principle, or guts. Uncharitably, the right assumed they lacked all three."

The dangerous current moving against the Communists had been partially deflected by Lewis's split with Roosevelt, and his consequent estrangement from Hillman and then Murray. Now that he stepped down from the CIO presidency at Atlantic City, would they not be more exposed? Hostilities were already under way in many city and state CIO bodies. The one in New York was especially important: as the seat of a strong labor movement, with a long tradition and an extensive network of associations inside and outside unions, it was an ideological pacesetter. Here, Hillman's clothing union would not affiliate with the city CIO council that was controlled by Michael Quill, Joseph Curran, and the Communist caucus, but clothing-union representatives with textile union and other allies controlled the state body. At the 1940 state CIO convention in Rochester, preceding the national gathering, the right-wing majority barred many delegates from Communist-led unions and whipped up demonstrations against Communists and Lewis supporters, whereupon other delegates walked out of the convention. Were it not for the drastic changes that occurred in 1941, the incipient split in the New York city and state CIO would have presaged the finish fight that started after the war.[21]

Naturally, the Communist party was shaken like a ship that had lost members of its crew in a storm. Browder later insisted that the Party actually enhanced its position in this period—*Daily Worker* circulation reached its peak, and he won 14 percent of the vote when he ran for Congress in January 1940—because it was the beneficiary of considerable antiwar sentiment. This is an attempt at having the best of two worlds. It is irrelevant to discuss whether a consistent left-wing party would have tapped deep pools of antiwar discontent. Possibly. For the Communists it was a different story. Even if they snatched odds and ends of this constituency, it meant breaking up old alliances that had been put together on different premises, and reenacting a revolutionary melodrama before an audience that questioned the sincerity of the performance. Besides the mass flight of intellectuals, fellow travelers in the leadership of important front groups like David Lasser, head of the Workers Alliance, and Joseph Lash of the American Student Union, hastily decamped. Transient allies like A. Philip Randolph resigned from the National Negro Congress. The exodus from the American League for Peace and Democracy and the American Student Union was so general that these organizations collapsed. Party membership declined for the next two years. The budding and proliferation of local Community Peace Councils and Peace and Civil Liberties Committees, capped in September 1940 with the formation of the American Peace Mobilization, was a tribute to the Party's energy. It served to narcotize the members from the realization that they had been seriously wounded. It did not mean that the abrupt switch to pseudo-Leninism was to go unpunished.[22]

5

The preservation of organizational positions inside the national CIO concealed from view that they were in trouble in component CIO unions. In places where there had been conflict before, the conflict was renewed on terms more favorable to Communist opponents. The International Woodworkers of America was a case in point. The Communist issue, deployed from the outside by its jurisdictional rival, the AFL Carpenters Union, was taken up by sections of the IWA, exasperated by the high-handedness of their top officials. By 1939 the faction fight inside the IWA was headed for a denouement. The Communist-led international administration, in an editorial in *The Timberworker*, called the opposition a "fifth column," and counseled that "the enemy within the walls is far more dangerous than the one outside." In reply, Harry Tucker, president of the large Aberdeen local, stated that he agreed there was a fifth column at work. "We differ only in opinion as to who are the members of this 'fifth column.' " The issue was joined when the three executive officers, Pritchett, Orton, and McCarty brought concocted charges against the Aberdeen local leaders for conspiring with employers to destroy the IWA.

The Klamath Falls convention in October was uproarious, bedevilled, as in the case of the auto union, by the attempt of the leaders to solve a political schism by means of charges, trials, and expulsions, except that it was the Communist administration that was taking the initiative for this extermination game. The convention results were indecisive, and the struggle continued after the convention in pitched battles at major local meetings. (Despite preoccupation with internal adversaries, the Aberdeen local won its first

147

formal collective-bargaining agreement with the operators; the AFL Carpenters union at Grays Harbor was unable to take advantage of the IWA's disunity.) When the union seemed to be on the verge of a split, the national CIO intervened. The opposition proposed that the CIO bypass the factionalism by launching an organization drive under its own supervision. After considerable balking, the IWA officers were obliged to sign a formal agreement giving the CIO authority to name the campaign director who was to have sole charge of campaign personnel, including the right to hire and fire. Germer, of mine-union and Michigan wars, was shipped in to take over. When in September 1940 the left-right tussle broke up the convention of the Washington State Industrial Union Council, Lewis peremptorily removed the left-wing council secretary and replaced him with Harry Tucker.

Germer did two things in the Northwest. He ran a successful campaign at Everett and Longview concluded with the signing of agreements with Weyerhaeuser and Long-Bell, the lumber industry leaders; and he sided with and aided the opposition. The tension inside the union rose perilously again at the Aberdeen convention in the fall of 1940. Pritchett, a Canadian, denied entrance into the United States, handed over his presidency to O. M. Orton, the vice-president, also a Communist adherent, while the CIO regional directors of Oregon and Washington lined up with the opposition. The anti-Communist caucus already represented a clear majority of the membership, but the administration controlled the convention because it was backed by numerous small locals outside the major lumber areas. After the adjournment of another inconclusive convention, the opposition leaders held a rump session; claiming to speak for 70 percent of the dues-payers, they petitioned Lewis to take over the IWA until the internal difficulties were resolved. The administration forces countered with the demand that Germer be recalled. Moves and countermoves—which included court injunctions and the setting up of a CIO investigating committee—continued to be made until the Communist line changed again with the Nazi attack on Russia. Now Orton and his friends became intensely unity-minded. It was too late. In a referendum election following the 1941 convention, the administration candidates were voted out of office, and the opposition slate headed by Worth Lowery, a respected ex-Wobbly logger, took over direction of the union. Also adopted by a 2-to-1 vote was a constitutional amendment barring Communists from membership.[23]

An opposition solidified against the Communists in another union they ran, the Mine, Mill and Smelter Workers. As in the lumber field, there had been a powerful IWW influence in metallurgical mining in pre-World War I days. In fact, Mine Mill was the rechristened Western Federation of Miners that had been the centerpiece of the old IWW, and had furnished the great leaders of industrial unionism insurgency, William Haywood and Vincent St. John. Too much should not be read into this history, however. In both industries, the unions consisted of new labor forces inside a country vastly changed from the United States of the past. While the nature of the occupations in logging (not in sawmill production), and hardrock mining (not smelting and refining), gave a unique stamp to their workers, just as coal mining produced a distinct breed, by the thirties the political and social attitudes of these workers differed little from those elsewhere. The great American engine of acculturation had been at work in Montana and Oregon no less than in Michigan and Pennsylvania, and their workers fell under the sway of technological and social standardization.[24] Unionization went through the same succession of patterns since the NRA as in other industries. It was unique only to the extent that every industry is *sui generis*.

Because the Communists had in Reid Robinson a free-swinging, brash official facing a disorganized and inept opposition, they were uninhibited in politicizing and infiltration labors. Robinson had been elected president in 1936 as a conservative. A year later, when he unaccountably moved into the Communist orbit, he brought in a full-blown braintrust from the outside. The first rift in the leadership occurred once this kitchen cabinet became the counselor, adviser, and policy maker, and the members of the executive board were shunted aside. The rift widened as Robinson sought to entrench his machine by isolating opponents or skeptics, and in the developing undercover tug-of-war, accusations of Communist control began to reverberate around the union. Communist propagandizing went beyond the official paper's noisy pronunciamentos and denunciations, for Robinson was one of the Communist celebrities of the peace crusade. Accompanied by delegates from a number of locals, he attended the mass rally in Chicago at which the American Peace Mobilization was set up, and accepted a vice-presidency. He was scheduled as the main speaker at the American Youth Congress convention in February 1941, but had to have his speech read since he was a member of the CIO committee of three to investigate dissension in the lumber union, and the committee was to meet at the same time as the youth convention. In both Waterbury, Connecticut, and Butte, Montana, where the membership was heavily Irish, he made impassioned pleas to keep America out of war, coupled with warnings of the danger of one-man rule represented by Roosevelt. In Connecticut, he succeeded in having a delegation sent to an American Peace Mobilization conference in New York City. At his urging, the Butte organization sponsored a mass meeting at which he inveighed against Roosevelt and war alongside Senator Burton Wheeler. At the end of June, for less than arcane reasons, Robinson and his coworkers reversed themselves to urge "full material aid to all peoples fighting Hitlerism, including the Soviet Union and England." And in the Mine-Mill edition of *CIO News*, Robinson went to great lengths to explain to a partly antagonistic membership that he was following a logical and consistent course.

He might have brazened his way out of his political contortions had he not at this time tried to follow Homer Martin's example, as well. He came to the Joplin convention in August 1941 fully prepared to purge his opponents on the executive board. When this became clear to his intended victims as well as to the delegates, the convention was thrown into bedlam. He had badly misjudged the delegates' temper. He had to retreat, and face the humiliation of having the convention, over his fierce opposition, order the discharge of Harold Rossman, the imported editor, for having sent out a factional letter to local unions. The opposition retained a majority of the executive board posts and believed it had come out ahead at the convention. It was a badly disunited, jealousy-ridden, opportunist group, however. It had not used its majority at the convention to good advantage, and was to see its plans checkmated because of its own lacks as the contest was renewed in succeeding years.[25]

It need only be referred to briefly here—since chapter 11 takes up the electrical union—that the Stalin-Hitler-pact flip-flop also precipitated a war inside their jeweled preserve in the CIO. James Carey, the UE president, who had stood shoulder to shoulder with Communist officials since the union's formation, now broke ranks. In July 1940 he came out demonstratively for Roosevelt when the other officials were sheltering themselves behind Lewis in order to oppose a third term. At the September convention, the same battle over endorsement of Roosevelt occurred as in other unions where

Communists had influence, and the Party machine managed to push through a vacuous compromise motion. Several months later, Carey carried the fight further by stating in his *UE News* president's column that a local provision to bar Communists, Nazis, or Fascists from office was not in conflict with the union constitution. When the *UE News*, in the summer of 1941, bounced back to status quo ante, Carey drove the shaft home. "Political acrobats in pink tights," he wrote, "posing as labor leaders are a disgrace to the union and insult the intelligence of the membership." The lid blew off at the convention of that year over the Communist issue. Carey was forced out of the presidency by a vote of 635 to 539, and was defeated on barring Communists from office by over 2 to 1. The fight, suitably modulated, became a perennial until it roared into a consuming blaze after the war.[26]

As one would expect, the auto union responded to the new currents blowing through the nation; and the debates at its 1940 convention were more brutally candid than elsewhere. What had started as a conjunctural division was building up a dynamic of its own to harden the factions into durable parties alerted for issues. There was a lot of impassioned, finger-pointing oratory and de facto unanimity on the major task facing the convention, the organization of Ford, the only holdout of the Big Three. It was generally recognized that the Frankensteen-Reuther debate on Ford organization at the previous convention had been pure farce—an unedifying spectacle of two politicians squabbling clumsily to make factional capital out of the cadaver of an unsuccessful union engagement. An understanding was reached now, so that at the conclusion of the convention, the executive board requested the CIO to assign a capable organizer, and the CIO responded by sending in Michael Widman, the CIO organization director. Both sets of leaders had come to the realization that neither faction could take over the Ford campaign, and that if the Ford workers were eventually to be enrolled in one of the factions, they would first have to be organized into the union.[27] As for Widman, unlike the CIO representative previously dispatched to head the lumber drive, he kept strictly to his role as a nonpartisan, concerned solely with getting everybody's cooperation for Ford organization. He could not have carried on otherwise in the auto union.

If the differences over the main trade-union dispute could be readily compromised, national and foreign policies provided a cornucopia to differentiate the factions and solidify loyalties. In its first incarnation, the Reuther faction's hostility to the Communists had a leftish flavor. Now, because of the implications of anti-Communism in the defense period, the original faction was getting fleshed out with the adherence of conservative and regulation unionists, many of whom had previously supported Martin, and of Catholic unionists who joined for ideological reasons. At this time, too, the Association of Catholic Trade Unionists came on the auto-union scene; the first issue of the *Michigan Labor Leader* (later called the *Wage Earner*) was issued in September 1939 and the publication very quickly became a prime organizer of anti-Communist formations. The attempted division along the line of Communism was magnified because of the division inside the national CIO; Reuther identified with Hillman and the right wing, while Addes put his wager on Lewis (who was being ballyhooed by the Communists).

Because of R. J. Thomas's leaning toward Reuther at this time, the latter's followers dominated key convention committees, so that the assault on the Communists dominated proceedings and came in the form of majority recommendations. The line of attack was the same as in other union conventions: endorsement of a Roosevelt third term, and condemnation of Soviet Russia alongside the other "brutal dictatorships" of Germany, Italy, and Japan. A further resolution disqualifying for office members of subversive organizations was a refinement of other such resolutions, probably drawn up with the aid of an attorney. It barred from any union office or position members of organizations "declared illegal by the government of the United States through constitutional procedure." The Communists had all their big guns roaring away, but a strange thing happened: they lost their faction allies. Frankensteen and Addes, after offering them soft-soap rhetoric of their unalterable opposition to red-baiting, joined in the condemnation of Russia and in support of a Roosevelt third term.

Ganley remarked bitterly in later reminiscences, "Under the theory that the Communists that were in this coalition bloc had no place to go anyhow . . . [Addes and Frankensteen] made an agreement with Reuther in attacking the Soviet Union . . . thus isolating the Communists to a small defensive group." There was no agreement with Reuther, nor was Reuther in need of an agreement on these issues. Addes and Frankensteen were simply resolved not to get tarred with the Communist brush (the two resolutions coincided with their own thinking, as well), and as Ganley correctly observed, they did not think their Communist allies were in a position to form a third faction. Thus, the Communists stood exposed as a very small group with a diminishing influence; not the locomotive of the Addes-Frankensteen train, but the caboose. Observers estimated that only thirty to forty delegates out of 550 supported their positions even partially.

The actual strength of the expanded Reuther faction could not be gauged accurately until a year later, but Reuther and his allies stepped forward as leaders in formulating an altered political ideology for the union; Addes and Frankensteen, still probably the majority faction, were bringing up the rear.[28] Reuther's abrupt switch from an ally to an arch-opponent of Communists, rather than compromising his cause or career, worked to his advantage. Unlike old-line AFL'ers or later recruits to anti-Communism, he, his two brothers, and his close political friends, could convincingly fight Communists with the rhetoric of militant unionism because they had a heroic record in strike struggles. They naturally and effortlessly became stellar performers of a CIO troop that included John Green of the Shipbuilders, George Baldanzi of the Textile Workers, Lowery of the Woodworkers, and Carey and Harry Block of the Electrical union. It should not be thought that the resolution barring Communists from office was taken literally by anybody at this time; its significance was understood to be purely symbolic. The entire struggle between the two factions was of that character: a preliminary engagement for the ferocious battle staged a year later when Reuther made his bid for dominance.

How can one explain these anti-Communist eruptions in one union after another? What moved the actors? The big majority of American unionists—high, medium, minor officials, rank-and-filers—want to have their union considered a respectable enterprise. They want to be accepted as responsible citizens who adhere to the nation's ongoing traditions and precepts, and are uncomplicatedly loyal to the government. Worker and official alike have this in common with the general run of the middle class: their belligerently asserted Americanism is a compound of the same shibboleths and platitudes derived from an adherence to predominant values of our society. Dispensations of individualism and nationalism that find favor with the diners at the country club are accepted without demur at the bar of the neighborhood saloon. But unionists cannot take their ideology, like whiskey, neat. Because of their special position in society, they have to blend strident nationalism with a diluted populism. Until recently they were locked in desperate battle with employers and were themselves bespattered with accusations, thrown at them by local dignitaries and government officials, of illegal trespass, disloyalty, even Communism. So on the one hand they build up resistance to the thunders of official public opinion which they defied before and may have to defy again; and on the other hand, they seek to compensate for their equivocal status by eager displays of political conformity and community-mindedness. Despite labor's growing self-confidence, there remains a strong element of an earlier feeling that workers constitute a minority group that requires alliances if it is not to be trampled upon; that labor has to have friends at court, so to speak, if its needs are to receive attention; that unions can prosper only with the approbation of the larger society. Hence, when anti-Communism became part of the American creed, it was a matter of course that it would be embraced by the unions. Other things being equal, most unionists would no more refuse to vote down, condemn, or expel Communists, when that is required, than they would refuse to pledge allegiance to the flag. This was the governing impulse on which all else was dependent.

Ideology ranked lower. Whereas it was the lure for gathering in recruits for anti-Communism in the liberal camp, in unions ideology tended to slide into unadorned conformity or patriotic assertion. Once it lost its pristine unction when confronted with the need of justifying tactics in the roughhouse of union politics, it became a mélange reflecting the disparate beliefs, backgrounds and ambitions of diverse labor constituencies. For those indifferent to ideology and cynical about the popular clamor, anti-Communism was a common-sense matter of public relations. Whatever the rhetoric fastened upon, Communists had to be eliminated because they compromised labor's reputation for political orthodoxy. This was supplemented for some with the conviction that the Communists made up an indigestible and dangerous power group with allegiances outside the union community, who therefore could not be trusted and had to be eliminated. On the other end of the spectrum were the social-democratic-minded, most closely akin to embattled liberals, for whom anti-Communism was a fighting cause. These had joined their traditional or new-found hatred of Communists to the Wilsonian universalism that was then the source of liberal perspectives. At their tail stood a handful of anti-Stalinist leftists whose zealotry was in inverse proportion to their sparse numbers, for

154

whom fighting Stalinite Communists was part of their life's work of returning American leftism to its Augustine purity. For another distinct sector made up of Catholics, the animus against Communism came from its being an abhorrent doctrine of atheism, an anathema to their church.

Of course, individuals and groups combined these appreciations, borrowed freely of each other's arguments and prejudices, changed their emphasis or personal attachments with the changing drifts. All major spokesmen were sharply aware not only of public-relations imperatives, but of the career opportunities in riding with the tide; here and there, some disappointed office-seekers saw the crusade primarily as an opportunity to win posts. Many Catholics, caught up in the spirit of their milieus, were moved less by religious fervor than the urge to establish their bona fides of orthodoxy, etc. But as experience was to show, while the crusading was on, in most situations all of them could work in unison because they had a common enemy and purpose, and they were moving with, not against, the political current.[29]

SEVEN · *Political Strikes in Defense Period*

WHEN the turn was made to the creation of a war machine in mid-1940, Roosevelt decided he had to change his course if he was to forge the national unity that he needed to carry through the defense-mobilization program. He had said in 1936 during his reelection campaign, it will be recalled, that big business forces were unanimous in their hate for him, "and I welcome their hatred"; that "we have only just begun to fight" for more reforms; that he would like to have it said that in his second administration these forces had "met their master." His attempts after his landslide victory to enlarge the Supreme Court with additional liberal judges and to purge reactionary Congressmen—both unsuccessful—intensified the animus against him; therefore, at this time newspaper opposition was more venomous than in 1936, though the New Deal, for practical purposes, had ground to a halt two years before.

He signalled the new political course by placing Henry Stimson at the head of the War Department and Frank Knox at the head of the Navy Department, both prominent, arch-conservative "interventionist" Republicans. Concomitantly, the great corporations were invited to send representatives to Washington to direct the newly created production and procurement divisions; the Vinson-Tramnell Act, which limited profits on shipbuilding and aircraft, was suspended; and business was permitted to write off capital expenditures over a five-year period instead of the customary twenty years. As corporation executives and lawyers descended on Washington, like the Bourbons returning to Paris after Waterloo, took charge of defense agencies and procurement boards, and began elbowing New Dealers aside, the political scales tipped rightward. Rexford Tugwell, the veteran New Dealer, wrote:

> Washington had become a kind of madhouse . . . There had descended on the capital flocks of businessmen and their various satellites in pursuit of profitable war contracts, or of escape from regulations, or in search of favors of other sorts. They buttonholed congressmen, made themselves at home in executive offices, entertained lavishly in hotels, and generally created confusion and

sometimes near scandal. It became more and more difficult to keep the economic expansion orderly, to avoid flagrant profiteering . . . Cynicism spread out from this vortex . . . It was in these circumstances that [Roosevelt] succumbed to the pressures exerted by the conservatives for a more sympathetic White House attitude toward business.

Those who objected that mobilization was being used by corporations to enrich themselves were accused by newspapers and congressmen of interfering with the defense effort. Strikes were branded as unpatriotic and often ascribed to the machinations of Communists or their dupes. Many in Congress and the business world were convinced that the opportunity had come to regain ground lost in the preceeding decade. At a later press conference Roosevelt took note of the changing times with his announcement that Dr. New Deal had been replaced by Dr. Win-the-War.

Immense government orders, meanwhile, led to an industrial boom. Soon huge masses of workers were streaming into factories and shops, so by the time of Pearl Harbor, unemployment was wiped out—something the New Deal had been unable to accomplish in seven years of pump-priming and press-agentry. With the headlong economic expansion came price rises and, what is usual in such periods, increased activities on the labor fronts.[1] Because labor unions were far stronger and more audacious than in the period of the First World War, it was inevitable that they would demand greater concessions and recognition than they had been satisfied with under the previous wartime leadership of Gompers and the Old Guard. Their officials, grown self-confident and combative in recent industrial wars, saw not only dangers, but opportunities, in the new configuration. Some administration officials were sympathetic to labor; Roosevelt, in any case, had to take cognizance of labor's increased strength in maintaining social equilibrium in order to meet defense-production schedules. It so happened that this also coincided with his technique of running government: to play off one bloc against another, to act as the broker adjudicating competing interests in order to reinforce his position as final arbiter of administration decision and policy.

The strike movement built up gradually. In the aggregate, 1940 was not a big strike year. The number of stoppages was the smallest of any since 1937, the number involved was the smallest since 1932, the number of man-days lost, the smallest since 1931. The CIO accounted for a little over 25 percent of the strikes compared with the AFL's over 60 percent. Nevertheless, in the changing political climate it was becoming clear that strikers would face some of the opposition and opprobrium that had been customarily accorded them in pre-New Deal days. With each strike, conservative public figures, congressmen, and editorial writers developed the habit of agitatedly demanding that the President do something about it, lest disaster overwhelm us. The decibel count rose when the French army collapsed in May.

At the end of the month Roosevelt responded by setting up a seven-man National Defense Advisory Commission—a characteristic Roosevelt creation, with loosely defined powers and securely tied to executive prerogative. It was the first of the defense agencies that was soon to beget numerous offspring and successors to adorn and overcrowd the Washington landscape. Hillman, who became Roosevelt's labor amanuensis for the next eighteen months, was made a member serving as a kind of commissar for labor affairs. Lewis felt affronted by the appointment because he, the head of the CIO, had not been consulted, and because, as he understood too well, Hillman would be representing Roosevelt in labor councils, not labor in White House councils. He began to press Hillman hard, and under this continual pressure Hillman forced through a policy that defense contractors had to comply with federal laws.

This blew up a denunciatory storm in Congress and the press, whereupon Roosevelt hastily retreated. He ordered Hillman to ignore labor-law compliance until after the elections. Hillman also persuaded Murray to delay a projected strike against Bethlehem Steel in order not to embarrass the administration. The first important strike affecting defense production, called at the Kearny works of the Federal Shipbuilding Company by Hillman-inclined leaders of the CIO Shipbuilding Workers union, was called off after two days, without achieving its purpose, in order to avoid charges of obstructing defense. In this brief time, the strike had been branded "treason" by Congressman E. E. Cox of Georgia and had led Congressman Clare Hoffman of Michigan to call for a law to outlaw defense strikes.

Then, patriotic fury was unloosed on the strikers at Vultee Aircraft in Los Angeles in mid-November. The strike, involving 3,700 workers called out when negotiations for an agreement to raise wages from 50 to 75 cents an hour proved fruitless, was important to the UAW to plant its flag in aircraft. Now that Roosevelt called for the production of 50,000 planes, aircraft was due to become a major industry, and although the UAW had jurisdiction in aircraft, it was being successfully challenged by the AFL Machinists union. (The AFL enjoyed the favor of the manufacturers, and had agreements by this time with Consolidated, Lockheed and the big Boeing company in Seattle.) The Vultee strike was vulnerable to attack because Mortimer, who had been assigned to the aircraft organization campaign in California to get him out of the Michigan area, was the man in charge, and several other Communists were on the campaign staff. The propaganda campaign against the strikers, the union, and Communist "saboteurs," was shrill. The FBI issued a public statement that the strike was "fomented by subversive elements." Robert H. Jackson, then attorney general, denounced the strike as Communist in origin. There were further congressional demands for outlawing defense strikes. There were even calls in the press for the removal of Hillman (who had intervened to get the strike quickly settled). R. J. Thomas flew to Los Angeles to direct negotiations. When he walked into the lobby of the Biltmore Hotel accompanied by Mortimer, newspapermen questioned him about Communist influence in the strike. "You boys notice that nobody is calling me a Communist, don't you?" was his response. The strike was settled after twelve days on the basis of a 62½-cent hourly wage and paid vacations.[2]

There was a bizarre, minor scandal that came out at the conclusion concerning a Major Sidney Simpson. The major had jumped to the labor relations branch of the War Department from a teaching post at Harvard Law School, injected himself into the negotiations, and was accused of holding up a settlement because of his drunkenness; there were also suggestions that he was improperly involved with the wife of a local citizen. Simpson was quickly recalled to Washington; the incident, however, brought to public attention a new fact of mobilization politics, that the military was intervening in labor-management disputes. The War Department, under Stimson, expanded its labor subdivision with corporation lawyers who would henceforth intrude in the settling of defense strikes. It was common at one period to have representatives of the Labor Department, of Hillman's office, of the Army and of the Navy all jostling each other in strike-settlement efforts. More telling than these brash incursions was the War Department's needling of Roosevelt to support more stringent legislation to control labor, and to incite Congress and the

159

press against labor stoppages. Its labor section began in 1941 to collect and forward strike data to the White House and Congress on a daily basis, and to release strike statistics to the press to build up public hostility. Stimson also brought in John McCloy, another prominent lawyer, to direct the department's antisubversive program, and pressed for an amendment to the 1918 Sabotage Act that would make it a criminal offense to slow down or obstruct defense production for subversive purposes.

Disturbed by the increase of strikes, beset by the continual agitation of the War Department, harassed by outcries from Congress, Roosevelt set up in the following March a tripartite National Defense Mediation Board to bring some order in the regularization and conciliation of labor conflicts. It was composed of three members for the public, four for employers, and four for labor, the AFL and CIO sending in two each. Technically, the board was only a mediation agency; it could hold hearings, issue findings of fact, and recommend terms of settlement. In practice, as time went by, the board (so long as labor cooperated) could virtually dictate settlements because it could call on other agencies of government to take punitive actions against recalcitrants.

2

The board's career was not to be a pacific one; 1941 was a banner strike year. In all categories the figures were very high. The number of strikes and man-days lost was exceeded only in 1937, but more workers were out, and they constituted a bigger percentage of the work force. One out of every twelve workers took part in a strike at some time during the year; interestingly enough, this was the identical proportion as in 1916, the Preparedness Year preceding United States entry into the First World War. Economic boom and labor shortages had explosive properties when coupled with rising prices and blatant profiteering. To the uninformed, labor complaints and stoppages appeared inexplicable, proof of the workingman's greed or the overweening ambitions of labor bosses, or both. Were not jobs plentiful, wages better than before? It is undeniable that for most workers, neither the conversion nor the subsequent war meant economic hardships but often improved living standards.

That is only the starting point for a serious inquiry. Man is a social animal, and sociology as much as biology usually determines his wants and aspirations. The defense-and-war period started another mass migration in American history, disrupted settled routines and family relationships, later brought the tensions of battle casualties and draft call-ups into the lives of loved ones, injected into the stream of a nation's consciousness uncertainty, instability, acute feelings of comparative deprivation. Masses were crowded into communities that lacked the facilities to properly house and furnish the minimum amenities of urban living to the new arrivals. Workers exhorted on all sides to work harder for patriotism's sake found themselves gouged by real-estate operators, overcharged by old-time residents, hooked by speculators; they encountered on all sides people, many in exalted positions, intent on using the emergency to enrich themselves at the expense of others. Workers, after a decade of deprivation, wanted to make a new economic start, and union officials seized the opportunity to push old claims.

The greatest single contributor to the 1941 strike record, measured in terms of workers participating and resulting idleness, was Lewis's mine union. There was the general bituminous strike in April of some 350,000, the captive mine strike in September of 53,000, the supporting strike in November of 115,000. There were the two state-wide strikes, of Illinois coal miners in April and of Alabama coal miners in September-October, as well as the strike of 90,000 anthracite miners in May. Time lost was 4½ percent of available working time, a figure almost five times larger than the largest figure in any other industry. By 1941, Lewis was estranged from other labor heads. While going through the formalities of cooperating with the defense agencies, he set on the path of using the nation's desperate need for coal to squeeze maximum advantages for the mine workers and union. In his colossal self-confidence, he felt he could force through improvements that had been impossible to garner in preceding years, and he succeeded: wage differentials were eliminated between North and South; wage standards went up in the anthracite fields; the union shop was nailed down in the captive mines. He had another purpose in addition to the union official's endemic quest for power, status, and revenue. He wanted to impress labor ranks throughout the country that only he had the audacity and vision to be the labor movement's top spokesman.

The strike at the Ford River Rouge plant in April, the final stroke of a five-month campaign that recreated the charged atmosphere of 1937, swelled the figures for that month. In the final stages, department sit-downs and physical encounters were being set off like activated mines throughout the huge fortresslike complex of plants,

161

until union officials formally called the strike and ordered workers to vacate the premises. They did not rely on the sit-down this time, but set up a vast barricade of automobiles that blocked off all the main arteries leading into the enclave, while UAW picket squads made up the sole policing force of a ten-square-mile area. The UAW won by a landslide vote the NLRB (National Labor Relations Board) election held on May 21. With that, Ford, the bare-knuckled feudalist among the auto manufacturers, made an about-face and signed a contract granting the union more far-reaching concessions than it had won from either GM or Chrysler, including the union shop and checkoff of union dues.

There would have been, as well, a shutdown of all plants of the Little Steel corporations that had broken the 1937 strike of the SWOC, except for their timely surrender under union and government pressure. The heat flashes indicated that a showdown was at hand. A pitched battle took place at the Lackawanna, New York, plant of Bethlehem Steel in the course of a 38-hour strike at the end of February over the firing of a group of unionists. A month later, on March 25, there was widespread violence when the main plant at Bethlehem, Pennsylvania, was struck. In both cases, as in the cases of brief strikes at the company's plants at Johnstown, Pennsylvania, and Los Angeles, management, sensing the mood, gave way quickly in order to resume production. After the SWOC won NLRB elections in all Bethlehem Steel plants, the other steel companies agreed to abide by the results of an NLRB cross-check of union membership cards against payrolls. Negotiations with the Little Steel companies proved long and arduous; it was only in August 1942 that contracts were signed embodying the terms of a War Labor Board award.[3] Thus the CIO reversed its two humiliating setbacks of the thirties and completed the organization of the automobile and steel industries.

By and large, public reaction to defense strikes was adverse. The theme propagated by much of the press had been struck in the fall of 1940 by the *Saturday Evening Post* (Aug. 10, p. 26), namely, that Hitler conquered France because France was a rich, soft nation in which hours had been shortened and wages unduly raised; that the United States had to discard the luxuries of union conditions if it was to produce in time the necessary equipment for national defense. This laid the foundation for loud denunciations of strikes and of unconscionable labor bosses accompanied by stern lectures that there were no strikers in the foxholes. This labor-baiting, which continued through both the defense and war years, helped to mold a body of public opinion convinced that union labor and union bosses were unpatriotically taking advantage of the crisis for their own selfish ends. Whenever a sizable group of workers would walk out, press excoriations would swell, to be matched with threatening talk in Congress and the introduction of punitive bills. Since both houses were in the hands of conservative blocs increasingly hostile to Roosevelt and New Dealers, such threats carried weight, prompting defense officials to implore and prod union officials to get their members back to work and trust to government mediation, lest they provoke Congress to harsher restrictions.

Communist officials, for obvious reasons, were the easiest butts. From the Vultee strike to the end of June 1941, they were singled out for rubber-truncheon treatment. Hatton Sumners, chairman of the House Judiciary Committee, stated in relation to the Allis-Chalmers strike leaders, that if the interests of the country required it, neither he nor the other committee members "would hesitate one split second to enact legislation to send them to the electric chair." This hit an extreme note, but one not out of keeping with other parts of the conservative score. Nor was the attack restricted to the Communists. Lewis was an even more frequent target for the fusillades of indignant newspapermen and congressmen. The storm of abuse and denunciation would rise menacingly from one strike to the next. "Traitor" and "betrayer" were epithets repeatedly hurled at his head. When he closed the captive mines, the AFL joined the chorus. In the summer, Daniel Tobin, the Teamsters president, had identified Communist-led strikes as being "strikes against the government," and declared that Communists were "doing more to help place on the statute books adverse legislation against labor than all the enemies of labor combined." Now in the fall, Philip Pearl, the AFL publicity head, called the mine strike "a dastardly and indefensible betrayal of the best interests of all labor" and described Lewis as "the most cordially hated man in America." He blamed Lewis's "headstrong and insane" leadership for the new antilabor bills being introduced.

Toward the end of the year, both the AFL and CIO had to take cognizance of the fact that plans were under review in some quarters to housebreak unions, for which egotists or fanatics inside the labor movement were not responsible. The Executive Council reported to the AFL convention "that certain labor-hating members of Congress have seized upon the present emergency to endeavor to black-out many of the gains made by labor over a long period of years." Murray reported to the CIO convention that "strong forces inside and outside of Congress and supported by the powerful anti-union press, planned . . . to use the national defense emergency as a smokescreen for driving through the most drastic anti-labor legislation ever proposed in any democratic country."[4]

What was the responsibility of the Communists for this strike eruption during the period when they were out to fan the flames of industrial strife? The mediation board, created in March, collapsed in November when the CIO representatives withdrew over the captive-mine finding. In this 9-month period, 118 disputes were referred to the board; in the case of 64, workers were on strike; in the case of 45, strikes were threatened. If we assume (to overstate the case) that a strike was Communist-led or Communist-inspired because Communists were prominent in the local leadership or had control of the governing national union, the following listing shows 9 Communist-led strikes of a total of 64, and 8 threatened strikes (with 5 eventuating as strikes) of a total of 45. (See Tables 1 and 2.)

It is also worth noting that the average number of monthly strikes in the six months of January through June was 345; the average number in the succeeding 5 months, July through November, after the Communists turned patriotic, was 415, or 20 percent higher. (With the outbreak of war on December 7 several strikes in progress were immediately called off, and several planned strikes, even when strike votes had been taken, were cancelled.)

Because Communist-led strikes accounted for only 13 percent of the total referred to the mediation board, it does not follow that public concern over "political strikes" was without foundation. But it is immaterial to ask—as some did at the time—what the Communists would have done if they had greater influence in the labor movement than they did have. The historian is now called upon to discuss what took place, not what might have taken place; and government officials were called upon to deal with existent problems, not those that their imaginations and fears could conjure up. The data makes clear that in the hysteria of the time and later in the cold war the dimensions of the problem were vastly overstated, that politically motivated strikes were carelessly equated with sabotage, that publicists were more interested in playing up the issue for its sensational, not its scholarly possibilities. When we place Communist-led strikes in the context of general labor unrest, it is unmistakable that Communist officials were taking advantage of—not originating—a widespread labor insurgency in the course of which one and a half million new members were added to union rolls; that in many cases they were responding to substantial pressures of their union constituencies as well as the guidance of Communist party mentors.

With this as background, the Allis-Chalmers and North American strikes can be taken as case histories in the issue of political strikes during the defense period. The two have not been selected fortuitously. They were the most important Communist-led strikes in defense industries, received the most extended treatment by the

TABLE 1 · COMMUNIST-LED-STRIKE DISPUTES CERTIFIED TO NATIONAL DEFENSE MEDIATION BOARD, MARCH-NOVEMBER 1941
(Total number of strike disputes certified to Board: 64)

Case No.	Employer and Location	Labor Union	Date Certified	Strike Period
4	International Harvester, Chicago, East Moline, and Canton, Illinois; and Richmond, Indiana	Farm Equipment, CIO	March 27	In progress for a number of weeks before certification. Strike called off at board's request.
6	Allis-Chalmers, Milwaukee	UAW, Loc. 248	April 2	Strike: January 22-April 7
10	Phelps-Dodge, Elizabeth, New Jersey	UE, Loc. 441	April 8	Strike: April 7-May 2
11	Sklar Mfg., Long Island City, New York	UE, Loc. 1225	April 9	Strike: April 4-May 12
12 and 37	California Metal Trades Assoc., and Bethlehem Shipbuilding, San Francisco	IAM, Lodge 68, AFL	April 15	Strike: April 7-28, May 12 - June 24
19	American Potash and Chemical, Trona, California	Mine Mill, Loc. 414	April 23	Strike: March 15-July 2 (strike broken)
32	Allis-Chalmers, LaPorte, Indiana	FE, Loc. 119	May 9	Strike: May 7-May 15
58	Ohio Brass, Barberton, Ohio	UE, Loc. 747	August 1	(Strike began on June 16; continued to Sept 16)

SOURCE: National Defense Mediation Board, BLS bulletin No. 714, pp. 45-48, 91-262; also, author's personal knowledge and interviews with participants.

TABLE 2 · Communist-Threatened-Strike Disputes Certified to National Defense Mediation Board, March-November 1941
(Total number of threatened-strike disputes certified to Board: 45)

Case No.	Employer and Location	Labor Union	Date Certified	Strike Period
13	Minneapolis Moline Plow and Hopkins Moline Plow, Minneapolis and Hopkins, Minn.	UE, Locs. 1138 and 1146	April 15	No Strike
22	Minneapolis-Honeywell, Minneapolis, Minn.	UE, Loc. 1145	April 28	Strike: May 22-24
26	Allis-Chalmers, Pittsburgh, Pa.	UE, Loc. 613	May 3	No Strike
31	Twin Districts Logging, Puget Sound area	Int. Woodworkers of America	May 9	Strike: May 9-June 16
35	E. W. Bliss, Brooklyn, New York	UE, Loc. 475	May 22	No Strike
36	North American Aviation Inglewood, Calif.	UAW, Loc. 683	May 22	Strike: June 5-June 9 (Army seizure)
38	Aluminum Company, Cleveland, Ohio	Nat. Assoc. of Die Casting Workers, CIO	June 4	Strike: June 9-June 11
40	Bohn Aluminum, Detroit	UAW, Loc. 208	June 9	Strike: June 10-June 11

Source: Same as for Table 1.

media, made the greatest impact on the public mind, and figured as prime exhibits then and thereafter in both government and private surveys.

3

Local 248 of the UAW, which conducted the Allis-Chalmers strike, was Communist-oriented from its early inception to 1947, and a dominant force in both the Milwaukee and Wisconsin CIO. It was, therefore, a major Communist operation whose influence radiated out well beyond its immediate confines. The plant over which the local had jurisdiction is located in West Allis, a working-class suburb of Milwaukee. It is the largest and most important of the 15 Allis-Chalmers plants scattered around the world, a key producer of many lines of motors and electrical equipment, as well as tractors, and construction and farm machinery. Employment at the Milwaukee plant, 8,000 in 1937, rose to 12,000 during the war period.

Harold Christoffel, the local head, was the leading spokesman for unionism from NRA days when Milwaukee went into the unionization paroxysm experienced by other industrial centers. He was a tall, lanky militant with the serious mien of a theological student; very capable, very devoted, very aggressive. He first appeared on the scene as a member of the company union Works Council bargaining committee. When the AFL tried to gain recognition, he was on the bargaining committee of the electrical union and chairman of the joint bargaining committee of AFL crafts. In the fall of 1936 union members abandoned the craft unions and flocked to AFL federal Local 20136, which by January 1937 was reputed to have over 2,000 members, with Christoffel again at the center of the action. In March, the Allis-Chalmers workers led the exodus from the AFL into the CIO, making official the split in the Milwaukee and Wisconsin labor movements. The AFL federal local was chartered as Local 248 of the UAW, with Christoffel as president. When the Milwaukee County Industrial Union Council was formally set up in August, Christoffel was elected its first president. He was 25 at the time. In March, Local 248 won a signed contract with the company, gaining recognition on a nonexclusive basis. In January of the following year, the local became the exclusive bargaining agent after it won an NLRB election. Thus on a local and regional Christoffel recreated Mortimer's early career. He was a founding father of the local and of the CIO in the city. An abler organizer and speaker than Mortimer, he was also more open in supporting Communist causes.

Christoffel denied he was a Communist party member, and was convicted and jailed in 1950 for perjury. As with Bridges, it is irrelevant for purposes of this study to delve into the legal technicalities. For practical, extra-legal purposes, he was an integral part of the Communist movement. According to Arthur McDowell, who was labor secretary of the Socialist party in the thirties, Christoffel as a young student at the Milwaukee Industrial Trades School in 1933, was a member of the Socialist party. McDowell considered him a Communist infiltrator or supporter, but his proposal to expel him was overruled by the local organization. He remained a Socialist party member until he was finally expelled several years later. What happened in Milwaukee was that the once powerful Socialist organization was in a state of disintegration. When the Communists turned to popular-front politics, a number of influential Socialists, convinced that the Communists were the new virile force of the Left, went into the Communist orbit. This included Meta Berger, Victor Berger's widow, Josephine Nordstrand of the

167

later Wisconsin Conference for Social Legislation, Frank Ingram of the Workers Alliance. Whatever the precise year of his conversion, Christoffel was part of this trend.[5]

Another factor important in the evolution of both Christoffel and the Local 248 activists was the obdurate character of the management they were bargaining with. Despite the admitted ability of Christoffel and his associates, and the intensive nature of organization, far beyond what was usual in other locals, the contracts that Local 248 extracted from the company were inferior to many others won by unions with lesser leaders and weaker organizations. From early days, the company exhibited a stiff-necked determination to retain most of the prerogatives of its open-shop past.

Before the 1939 contract was signed, the local engaged in a hard-fought 27-day strike. None of the major union objectives—union security, joint agreement covering the Boston and Pittsburgh plants, wage increases—were obtained. The only important concession the company offered was a verbal agreement that it would discipline any person who acted against the union in the shop. In line with this understanding, the company discharged five workers aligned with George Kiebler, Homer Martin's appointed administrator over Local 248 during the UAW civil war. The 1940 agreement registered no gains over the previous one. Again, however, the union won a victory over its plant opponents. Two were discharged; four others given warning to cease anti-Local 248 activities were subsequently discharged; and five members who had been fired, were reinstated with back pay. The company also issued a letter over the signature of William Watson, company vice-president, that no employee would be permitted to engage in labor activities on company premises except as provided in the contract with Local 248. Christoffel acknowledged that the Watson letter and "the general cooperative attitude" of company officials were "big factors in inducing the union to accept the company's proposals to avert a strike."[6]

The bargaining history of the local through 1940 shows that the union leadership was conciliatory, even modest, in the kind of contracts it would (and had to) settle for, but that it was extremely sensitive and stubborn on the question of union security. This arose from the internal difficulties faced by the Christoffel administration. First, the Martin-Unity conflict tore at the Milwaukee CIO more fiercely than elsewhere. The Martin-Kiebler faction refused as far back as 1937 to recognize or affiliate with either the Milwaukee city central or Wisconsin state organizations. It made use of the UAW

168

District Council to wage guerrilla warfare. After Martin suspended his opponent officers, Christoffel was deposed and Kiebler appointed a local administrator. Pitched battles followed between the two factions; charges of Communism and Lovestoneism were freely exchanged; each side sought a court injunction against the other.

In October the national CIO leaders worked out a compromise: the Christoffel leadership was reinstated, but the administratorship was continued with a new representative. Christoffel would not give an inch. Meetings of Local 248 became so violent that the new administrator suspended further meetings for 90 days. Throughout 1938 and 1939, Christoffel kept the upper hand and his group was recognized by the company. He used his control to ruthlessly drive Martin supporters out of the plant. A series of stoppages in 1940 were intended to force management to get rid of remaining Christoffel foes.

Was the company the innocent victim of a Communist drive for plant hegemony? The company maintained that it sincerely accepted collective bargaining, and was pledged to a hands-off policy in the union's internal affairs. Outside observers concluded that it was not the disinterested bystander that it pretended to be. Dr. John Steelman, head of the U.S. Labor Department Conciliation Service, was of the opinion that Max Babb, the company president, was hostile to unions, and in order to keep the CIO off balance, encouraged AFL craft organizations to come into his plants. The native combativeness and taste for ruthlessness of Christoffel and his friends was thus fed by the need to solidify a leadership that was repeatedly being harassed and under challenge. (This was not just an emanation of the Stalin-Hitler-pact period. When the line was switched again, Christoffel turned war patriot with the best of them so far as his political pronouncements went. But all through the war years, the processing of grievances was pushed belligerently, and a grim tug-of-war with the company continued inside the plant.)[7]

To what extent was this firebrand provoking the very opposition he had to contend with? It is a question that cannot be conclusively answered. The fight with the Martin forces would have occurred in any case, although it was aggravated by his flamboyant Communist operation. Would the company have been less willful in dealing with a non-Communist leadership? Its record was not reassuring. True, in the fifties, after anti-Communists took over, relationships stabilized, but by then dominant corporation opinion on a national scale had shifted to acceptance of unionism. The matter is thus

169

moot. What is incontrovertible is that the Christoffel crew raised the threshhold of conflict and violence. The belligerence in the GM plants in 1937 became the norm in the Milwaukee Allis-Chalmers plant.

Two additional points are important for understanding the Christoffel internal administration. It had none of the sangfroid, the easy-going routine, of the average union leadership. It fought like a Savonarola in fifteenth-century Florence for members' allegiance. The education program was both elaborate and distinct. The local ran its own newspaper; after Martin cracked down on local papers, the same purpose was achieved by utilizing the *Wisconsin CIO News*, which the Communist faction controlled. A qualified full-time education director was brought in who set up an extensive program of classes, drama programs, movies, and town halls; prominent lecturers were invited, special meetings held for wives, sweethearts, unemployed workers. Local 248 was not unique in this kind of an undertaking. What was unique was the program's great intensiveness and extensiveness.

The classes and related education activities aimed at indoctrinating members along general CIO lines of thought, the ideology was more heavily tinctured in this case with populist "class-struggle" approaches. Publications like George Seldes' *In Fact* (a quasi-fellow-traveling sheet until Tito's break with Stalin) were utilized to make the Communist slant acceptable. The big Communist party positions were faithfully and noisily put forth in the newspaper and at meetings. Up to August 1939 articles came out strongly in favor of collective security, Roosevelt's foreign policies, the boycott of Japanese goods. After the Stalin-Hitler pact, Christoffel lectured the membership that Roosevelt, not Lewis, had deserted the New Deal, and the newspaper ran a letter from Senator Burton Wheeler congratulating the local for its opposition to Lend-Lease. By July, the CIO Council called for all-out aid to Britain and the Soviet Union, and a subsequent local membership meeting adopted the same position "unanimously."[8]

Local 248 also had its elite corps, the flying squadron. As we know, formations of this kind were employed by many CIO unions, particularly the larger UAW locals in Michigan, to furnish strikes with what the military could term specialized armed mobile units. These squadrons, misused by faction leaders on both sides during the internal civil war, lost their popularity. After the UAW reorgan-

170

ized, they were disbanded or disappeared as regular union subdivisions. Instead, ad hoc special squads were formed when needed. Local 248's flying squadron had the same origin, and was similarly subverted and "blooded" in the course of the struggle with the Martin-Kiebler forces. But since the Christoffel bunch lived in a charged atmosphere of permanent crisis, it tried to make the flying squadron a permanent institution, a semi-military, politicized arm of the administration with multiple functions. It was not just to use in Local 248 strikes, but to aid strikes of other unions; not just for union purposes, but for use in "peace" struggles, "political-action" struggles, "solidarity" displays; not just a local patriciate to preach loyalty to the union, but a strong-arm squad to protect the administration.

New members joining the formation were required "to take an oath of loyalty to Local 248 and its duly elected officers." Captain Heideman explained, "We want no men who are not 100 per cent for 248. And when you are 100 per cent for 248, that means 100 per cent for Chris and the other officers who have worked so hard to build this local." The October 8, 1938 *Wisconsin CIO News* carried the information that fifty squadron members participated in demonstrations for Czechoslovakia, as well as these additional items: "A meeting of an independent union for Allis-Chalmers workers was visited by the Squadron, outnumbered the independents, and broke up the meeting. The Squadron assisted the Harnischfeger local union in picketing." The next issue provided a touch of military glamour. Under the headline, "248 Ladies Thrill at Own Movie Stars," the reporter asked, "Doesn't it make you feel proud to see one of your men marching with the Squadron?" Nor was the work of politicizing neglected. The squadron's Ten Commandments included admonitions "to be on the alert for anti-union tendencies"; "to judge all union members by their union activity"; "to fight against racial, religious and political intolerance or discrimination"; "to attend the meetings faithfully and to be floor leaders."

At local union meetings, when it was necessary to build up hysteria, or to intimidate critics, squadron members would march up to the rostrum, lift Christoffel on their shoulders, and march around the hall to the cheers of a supporting claque. Squadron members also used threats against oppositionists. Again, in this case what was a specialized union sub-formation employed only in a crisis period elsewhere was converted into a permanent feature of the Christoffel

171

administration. It was this that gave Christoffel the reputation of running Local 248 with a "goon squad."*⁹

Why did he need it? The evidence is strong that Christoffel was a popular leader. His ability and dedication were widely recognized and appreciated. He and his co-workers fought indefatiguably to improve conditions. A National War Labor Board panel criticized him for overzealousness—an overzealousness that enhanced rather than diminished his popularity with the ranks. The Communist faction was able to maintain control through the war years and until 1947 without the help of the special squadron. However, in the thirties the squadron was at hand, and bringing it into the fray accorded with Christoffel's siege mentality: he was constantly beset by enemies who could be subdued only by the use of every available weapon. Not that the enemies existed only in his mind, but he was part of a faction that ensured the continual appearance of opponents that his enterprise was designed to overcome. He was like a manufacturer who created the demand for his product.

The deployment of a semi-military body inside the union would be sufficient, by itself, to stamp the Christoffel administration as undemocratic. By its nature, it is an instrument to overawe and intimidate potential critics. It would be an error, however, to consider it as more than a convenient adjunct of the machinery of control. What was decisive was the de facto one-party regime in which opposition to the officers was equated with disloyalty to the union. A Communist-led administration, disposing of the union's electoral, administrative, and bargaining controls, cannot be effectively challenged, unless it is hampered by a countervailing force. The congenital tendency to impose its viewpoint and to ride roughshod over dissenters, the habit of confronting a dispersed scattering of members with an elaborated program, a sophisticated rationale, and a battle-ready apparatus, acts to snuff out opposition or to prevent its appearance. The only Communist-led administrations that permitted an appreciable amount of democracy were in those unions where oppositions were strong, and could not be rough-housed without splitting the organizations. Even then, Communist officials were disposed to try—as in the Woodworkers and in Mine Mill— until and unless stopped by a superior force. Did Communist-

---

* Contrary to extreme opinions that had credence during the cold war, Communist organization is not exempt from customary influences of time and tide. When full employment and lots of overtime occupied the Allis-Chalmers workers after 1941, the flying squadron atrophied and disappeared.

controlled undemocratic administrations differ from non-Communist undemocratic administrations—by no means a rarity in American unions? This is discussed in detail in chapter thirteen. Suffice it here to say this: the major difference was political. The mechanics of control were similar, often identical, except for the Communists' more intensive (generally unsuccessful) indoctrination efforts, and the evangelistic atmosphere of consecration with which they sought to uplift the organization.

4

The negotiations for the 1941 contract led to one of the most publicized "political strikes." The local was in the midst of a mop-up drive at the time. At the close of the midnight shift on December 18, 1940, an auto occupied by two former members was surrounded by unionists who tried to persuade the two to pay up their back dues and fines. The driver suddenly stepped on the gas and a union member standing in front of the car narrowly missed injury. The incident raised tempers inside the plant, and Christoffel demanded that the two be fired. The company suspended the two workers, and also six Local 248 members who participated in the action. On the overriding and perennial matter under discussion, union security—the issue that had dominated the negotiations for the previous three years—the company offered no concession. The union called the men out on January 22—the 1940 agreement was not due to expire for another three months—in a strike that was to go on for 76 days. The response to the strike call was overwhelming; immense picket lines ringed the plant; and other CIO unions of Milwaukee responded sympathetically. But for our knowledge that the local was Communist-led and that the Communist party was at this time a "peace" advocate, the strike had all the earmarks of a standard union battle. The strike leadership was in an exposed position, however, on this count, as well as that of military necessity: the plant was an important defense producer in fulfilling the company's $40-million Navy contract for turbines and generators. And the country's mood was grimmer after Congress had adopted in mid-September the first peacetime draft in American history.

After several weeks of deadlock, Hillman took the dispute out of the hands of the Labor Department and worked out with both principals a "maintenance of membership" compromise formula. Both Babb and Christoffel agreed in private sessions with Hillman in Washington to accept Hillman's memorandum, and this was announced publicly on February 15. When Christoffel got back to Milwaukee, he was supposed to have boasted at a meeting that the agreement was a step toward the closed shop. Upon receiving word of this, Babb refused to accept any such interpretation. The difficulty was supposedly smoothed over after R. J. Thomas persuaded the union to accept the Hillman memorandum without any additional interpretation. [10] But Babb's complaint was apparently only a pretext to continue the struggle. On March 1 the company, as well as the two workers involved in the automobile incident, now members in an AFL Machinists local, filed complaints with the State Labor Relations Board challenging the validity of the strike vote. At the same time about a hundred women, allegedly wives and mothers of strikers or of company employees, gathered at the Schroeder Hotel to plan a mass meeting in favor of a new strike vote. An organization was formed, Allis-Chalmers All-American Women, headed by the president of the former company union. Babb took another trip to Washington to convince Knox and Office of Production Management co-director William S. Knudsen that the strike vote included 2,000 fraudulent ballots.*

Buttressed by this testimony, Knox and Knudsen, bypassing Hillman's office, wired peremptory orders to both company and union officials on March 27 that the plant had to be opened at once. The *Washington Post* was enthusiastic: "This is the most favorable piece of news that has come out of the strike situation in recent months. In effect, Messrs. Knox and Knudsen have undertaken to break a strike." Murray, in contrast, sent a telegram to Knudsen in which he demanded to know "by what power are you and Secretary Knox authorized to issue ultimatum?" The Knox-Knudsen-sponsored back-to-work movement resulted in the return of 1,200 workers to the plant. There followed three days of rioting and bloodshed. Feeling in the city against the company and state troops was running so high that Governor Heil withdrew the militia and ordered the plant closed again. In Washington, Stimson was demanding that the local leaders be prosecuted for ballot fraud, and that the army be permitted to take over the plant. Roosevelt turned

---

* Later investigation by handwriting experts showed that the actual ballot count was 3,758 for strike and 758 against. Since a restrictive Wisconsin law required an absolute majority of employees of a bargaining unit for a strike call, the local leaders had stuffed some 2,000 additional affirmative ballots into the ballot box in order to claim compliance with the state law. The company was hoping that a new supervised strike vote would fail to bring out a majority of the plant work force.

aside his pleas and ordered the strike certified to the newly created mediation board. Within a week, a settlement was reached along the lines of the original Hillman proposal.[11]

The question remains: To what extent was this a regulation union strike? To what extent was it a Communist-provoked "political strike"? The subsequent congressional report that the strike delayed important defense production for periods up to six months does not help answer these questions, for man-days and production would have been lost in a 2½-month strike whatever the political complexion of the union leaders. The anti-Communist literature of the period and later is equally unhelpful on this score. Eugene Lyons wrote, "The seventy-six-day strike involved nothing more momentous than the charge that a tiny number of A.F. of L. workers were engaged in their own union propaganda." Max Kampelman stated, "No issue of wages, hours, or conditions was at stake." These and dozens of similar statements are tendentious. They have no analytical value to establishing their claim that the strike was a Communist plot. Government officials who were close to the strike were inclined to blame both sides for the protracted struggle. That was the position taken by William H. Davis, chairman of the National Defense Mediation Board, in his testimony before a House committee. That was Hillman's view also: that there were fanatics on both sides. The Davis-Hillman proposition, while dividing the blame, does not necessarily invalidate the hypothesis that the strike was Communist-provoked.

The only direct proof adduced was the testimony of Louis Budenz, the ex-Communist testifier. He claimed that Christoffel met with Eugene Dennis and several other Party leaders at the home of Meta Berger prior to the calling of the strike. According to Budenz (who was not present at the meeting), Dennis said that a strike had to be called to interfere with defense mobilization, and Christoffel opined that there were enough plant grievances to justify a strike. "But I know that if Christoffel had not agreed, he would have been ordered to call a strike, and as a Communist he would have had to obey." Testimony of Budenz, unsupported from other sources, has to be viewed with caution since he was the author of known fabrications. Assuming that such a meeting took place— entirely likely—the probability is that Christoffel was not getting orders but consulting with Party leaders on whether calling a strike in the given situation was the thing to do. In any case, this testimony does not advance our knowledge materially, since Christoffel was already known as a Communist supporter, and the Communist party was known to favor strike struggles at this time.[12]

When one applies general reasoning to this problem, it is clear that one cannot divide the psyche of an individual like the Christoffel of 1941, and say this part impelled him to act for political reasons, this part impelled him to act for trade-union reasons. To try to separate one from the other would be like the Theosophist's separation of the astral from the physical being. There were clear and justifiable trade-union reasons for a strike flowing out of the history of labor-management relations. In later interviews, anti-Christoffel unionists who worked at the plant in 1941 insisted that the strike was popular with the ranks.[13] Indeed, how else could one get several thousands of workers to picket for 76 days, and to battle with police and state troops in the final outburst before the settlement? On the other hand, the contract still had three months to run; the union had not yet exhausted all mediation possibilities; there is no evidence that Christoffel feared rapid demoralization of his ranks unless he took precipitate action. Hence, one is led to the conclusion that the Communists' hopped-up state of mind, their fevered resolve to "emancipate" the masses (in the words of Gil Green, one of their national leaders) from the "Roosevelt myth," entered into the decision-making process. In that sense, the strike was political.

5

The next case history concerns the strike at North American Aviation in Los Angeles, then a subsidiary of GM. Here, the acute competition between the CIO and AFL to gain hegemony in the aircraft industry took a virulent turn. During the civil war in the UAW, the North American local had voted to affiliate with Martin's UAW-AFL. An NLRB election was held in February 1940 in which neither union obtained a majority. The UAW-CIO finally was certified as bargaining agent in a new election it won over the AFL's International Association of Machinists by 70 votes out of 6,016 cast. The local that entered contract negotiations in April 1941 was consequently a very insecure one. The leaders felt they had to rapidly build a record if they were to hold their ranks together. Before and during negotiations, they were hard-pressed by the IAM's anti-Communist broadsides. The AFL union was using testimony given by the Dies Committee and Jackson's attack on the Vultee strike to good advantage, and these negotiations dragged on with no results; the company refused to grant a general wage increase to bring its wages up to the level then prevailing in plants represented by the IAM. Most North American workers were earning the minimum 50-cent hourly rate while other plants were up to a 75-cent minimum. The union leaders were all the more nervous about their position since the company was hiring thousands of new workers who had never belonged to a labor organization before. Once it became clear that a strike was brewing, the case was certified to the mediation board on May 22. Thus far, the conflict followed the normal pattern of defense disputes.

From this point forward, the conduct of the local officials became increasingly suspect. As is established, Communists dominated the leadership even more pronouncedly than they had at Vultee. The local president, Elmer Freitag, was a known Communist. There were several other registered Communists on the bargaining committee. Lew Michener, UAW regional director, was a Party member from 1938 to 1944, according to his own later testimony. Mortimer was the leader, although he had been assigned to Seattle, and was in Los Angeles ostensibly on a personal visit. The Kraus husband-and-wife team were working in the aircraft organization office. Several international organizers were in the Communist camp. Moreover, the CIO in the area was under heavy Communist influence. Communists controlled the Industrial Union Council, and Philip (Slim) Connelly, a prominent Party-liner, headed the California CIO organization. Despite the excitation and confusion inherent in a strike-threatened plant in which most were newly recruited members in their early twenties, policy decisions were being made calculatingly by Mortimer and his associates.

After the certification, Frankensteen, the UAW and CIO aircraft director (the aircraft campaign was under joint aegis after the Vultee strike), went to Washington accompanied by his assistant Walter Smethurst, Michener, and three members of the bargaining committee. There was a delay in getting a panel assigned for a hearing; an understanding was reached, however, that any agreement would be retroactive to May 1, and that no strike would be called until three days after the board had published its recommendations. (According to Mortimer, the agreement had a further point that if a strike was called, the retroactive pay would be lost. This did not invalidate the agreement not to stike during the mediation, as he tried to argue.) This was on May 27, the same day that Roosevelt proclaimed an unlimited emergency. The atmosphere in which the negotiations occurred can be sensed from some of the articles in the

177

Los Angeles Times. The May 30 issue, under the headline, "Harbor Guarded in Sabotage Plot," ran a story that municipal and special police blanketed Los Angeles harbor after a mysterious report of possible sabotage over the Memorial Day weekend. The same issue reported that at the hearing of the Dies Committee in Washington, Freitag was sharply questioned concerning the charge that the Communist party was cooperating with the German-American Bund to bring about "bigger and better" strikes.

A week later the six committee members on the West Coast decided in a telephone agreement with the three committee members in Washington that they were being stalled and that an immediate strike was necessary. What was the real reason for this extraordinary decision? Mortimer's explanation was that "further delay would be perilous to the continued strength of the union, since many men were quitting the organization and others were beginning to heed the call for wildcat action coming from provocateurs and other dubious elements in the plant. It became a question of either striking unitedly with the full force of the union behind such a strike, or allowing wildcat actions to dissipate the strength of the union." This sounds like a reasonable explanation—but it has a flaw. If this was the real reason—and it is a reason that unionists can readily understand—it is strange that Mortimer never offered it in the course of his lengthy philippic at the 1941 UAW convention. Did he remind himself of it only thirty years later when putting together his memoirs? Neither did Freitag nor Michener give this explanation in their oral history interviews nineteen years after the event. Furthermore, it quickly became evident—and the Communist leaders must have realized it beforehand—that this strike could not be called "with the full force of the union." Thus, the explanation appears to have been devised after the event. Aside from their own exalted state induced by political fever, there is a strong hint that they suspected that there would be slim pickings from the mediation board and decided to take the offensive while they could.

As soon as Frankensteen received word of the projected strike, he telephoned the local leaders, told them a strike was unauthorized and the men should be kept at work. They refused to comply. On Thursday, June 5, picket lines were set up as the night shift left. By next morning, what was described as the largest picket line in the state's history shut down the plant. Frankensteen rushed to Los Angeles the next day. He called a meeting of the bargaining committee and all the union's international representatives. He informed the group that the strike had to be called off while the union fought the issue through the mediation board. He got a very cold response. He then turned to Mortimer and asked, "What is your position?" Mortimer answered, "My position is with the rank and file." Frankensteen informed him then and there that Mortimer had just joined the rank and file. He proceeded to fire as well a number of other organizers and the publicity head who associated themselves with Mortimer. That evening he spoke over a nationwide hookup on CBS radio calling on the strikers to return to work. He blamed the strike on the "infamous agitation, the vicious maneuvering" of the Communist party, and threatened the workers with suspension if they did not follow UAW policy. When he appeared at the strike mass-meeting at the beanfield the following afternoon, he was jeered by organized squads parading around with banners depicting Frankensteen as a rat, a skunk, and a snake. He was furiously attacked by a number of speakers preceding him as one who sold out for thirty pieces of silver, and was heckled mercilessly and shouted down when he tried to speak.

In Washington, the army was readying itself for action. Stimson had advocated seizure of the plant as soon as a strike was in the offing. Murray told mediation-board members that the strike was engineered by Communists and that he had authorized Frankensteen "within the hour . . . to take charge there, clean these fellows out, get the men back to work." William H. Davis, the board chairman, related that this led to the calling of a conference through Francis Biddle's office between Biddle, the army, and the mediation board. "Our objective was to postpone any action by the Army until Phil [Murray] had a chance to do his work. . . . We came in, and there were eleven lawyers representing the Army, and John McCloy . . . was at the head of them." After Frankensteen's failure at the beanfield meeting, Hillman came over to the army position. As recorded by Stimson in his diary, "Sidney Hillman acted very well and was more vigorous almost than any one else against the strikers and in favor of taking over the plant." When news of the beanfield demonstration, and reports of rioting as police tried to breach the picket lines, reached Washington the day after, Hillman, Undersecretary of War Robert Patterson, McCloy, the assistant secretary of war, and Attorney General Jackson, went to the White House to propose a government seizure. Roosevelt signed the Executive Order, and over 2,500 troops moved in with fixed bayonets to disperse the picket lines and open the plant. Within two days it was all over.

179

Political Strikes in Defense Period

A number of local officers and strike leaders were banned from
plant facilities on army orders. Draft boards announced that they
were cancelling deferments of any strikers refusing to return to
work. Frankensteen, with R. J. Thomas's approval, withdrew the
local charter, suspended the members of the bargaining committee,
and reorganized the local. He was also excited enough to issue a
statement that if skilled workers failed to return to their jobs, the
UAW would send in replacements from other UAW shops. The
Communists, for their part, apparently overestimating their hold on
the ranks, were anticipating a prolonged struggle. On June 8
Freitag sent a defiant message to the White House that "the armed
forces will not break our strike. Bombers can't be built with
bayonets." That same day, Orton, the lumber union president,
broadcast his commendation: "We are united with you in maintaining the American democratic way of life." Two days later, when the
army was moving in, and the strike leaders had been suspended,
Connelly addressed the strikers from a sound truck: "Army occupation does not mean you are to return to work until your demands are
met." It was only after 8,673 out of 11,236 had returned to work by
the second day of the occupation—the figures are Frankensteen's—that Mortimer announced, "It is time for a stategic retreat."

Though the strike was conclusively broken, the fearful scene of
June 10 was not easily forgotten in either the Los Angeles or national labor movements. Labor relations inside the plant were chaotic, the ranks were sullen, it was weeks before production schedules
were restored. But the Communists' notion that the army seizure
was intended to break the union showed that they were still thinking in the past, that they did not yet comprehend the subtleties of
the new coercive controls. Breaking the union was not what either
Roosevelt or his coadjutors had in mind. Colonel Charles Bradshaw,
the officer in charge, was under instructions to uphold the authority
of Frankensteen and his crew. A labor adviser from Hillman's office
was assigned to advise and work with Bradshaw. The shop-steward
system at the plant was continued and recognized. But it was slow
going for the cooked-up Frankensteen substitutes. When Walter
Smethurst, Frankensteen's assistant director, appeared before the
steward body, he narrowly missed being ejected. Bradshaw, recognizing the realities of the situation, recommended that the mediation board come up with a plenty good ruling if Frankensteen's
friends were to retain control. Patterson then wrote to Hillman, "It

180

is my view that if an agreement can be brought about promptly by the mediation board, the better elements in the Union . . . would then have proof of their power and ability to get results."

Now, the Defense Mediation Board did not drag its feet. A new panel was promptly set up which recommended that the company grant the union's wage demands, and threw in, for good measure, a strong maintenance-of-membership provision. "There was an urgent need," according to the official report, "for reviving the union in order to assure stable labor relations." When company officials wanted to argue about the union security clause, the board peremptorily told them that the army would remain until management acquiesced. The North American officials gave in and on June 28 Roosevelt returned the plant to company control.[14]

6

Why did the Communists provoke the crisis? It was unique among all the strikes conducted under Communist influence during the defense period. Most of them were regulation contests and were settled in the same manner as other CIO strikes. Even in the sensational Allis-Chalmers struggle, the local had the formal backing of its own international and of the CIO, and the prolongation of the strike in the final month was the doing of the company rather than of the union.

The closest analogue was the Puget Sound lumber strike called in early May. The mediation board made a reasonable compromise proposal on May 23 which was accepted by the employers. The union angrily rejected the proposal several days later, embellishing its rejection with the gratuitous militant proclamation, "Our problems will be solved only through the action of the membership and not through the intervention of federal agencies." Orton released another bombardment in Washington: the board, he said, was "an all-out labor busting and strike-breaking device," and the strike would continue, "Mr. Dykstra's [first board chairman] phony propaganda and bulldozing to the contrary notwithstanding."

The next day, under a two-line banner headline, the *Seattle Post-Intelligencer* carried a story of Murray's stinging rebuke to Orton. He had personally recommended acceptance of the board's terms, Murray explained. Orton's statement was "a most reprehensible, lying defamation" of himself and the other CIO representative on the board. At this juncture, Bridges intervened. Orton was again summoned to Washington, and within a week the men re-

181

turned to work amidst a welter of confusing amendments to, and reinterpretations of, the May 23 recommendation. Although the confrontation with the board, with malice aforethought, as lawyers say, was common to both disputes, Orton did not carry the struggle through to the doctrinaire length that Mortimer did—probably owing more to inability than to a belated visitation of prudence.[15]

There is evidence that the Communists in Los Angeles, in first perfecting their strategy for an anti-Roosevelt stroke, made a miscalculation. Michener stated in his interview, "We did not feel that the troops were actually going to enter until they actually did show up." This was not just Michener's lightheadedness. An echo of a related thought is to be found in Mortimer's remarks at the UAW convention: "I said that if the strike was authorized the Army would not come in. I still believe that was true." (He had induced the international to authorize the Vultee strike after it had been in progress and may have had a notion that he could successfully repeat the tactic at North American.) Whatever the preliminary analysis, it was obvious when Frankensteen arrived in Los Angeles brandishing the authority of the UAW and CIO presidents, firing Mortimer and others, that the strike would be fought tooth and nail by the national organization, and that the army would come in if the strike was continued. By then romanticizing took over. Some had illusions that they could defy the government in the way Lewis had defied it in the coal fields; so Mortimer and his associates were set for a historic confrontation in which they would show up all of labor's enemies in all their hideous colors from Roosevelt to Murray to Hillman, and in which a political victory would take precedence over the immediate fate of the local strike.[16]

As it turned out, they had neither a political nor a trade-union victory to comfort them, but a reversal of policy two weeks after the strike was broken. While the Christoffel leadership came through in good order from its 76-day ordeal, and the Orton group was defeated in the lumber union for reasons antedating the Puget Sound strike, the Communist leadership was wiped out at North American. The officers suspended by the army were never reinstated, the organizers fired by Frankensteen were never returned to the payroll, Communist influence in aircraft was never revived. The adventure cost the Party dearly.

Analysis of these strikes helps to place in perspective Sidney Hook's dictum that "in labor organizations, the existence of Communist leaders is extremely dangerous because of their unfailing use of the strike as a political instrument at the behest of the Kremlin." First, the Comintern gave no instructions to the American Communist party to call this or that strike. With the war in Europe cutting off communications, the American heads had to deduce their tasks primarily from cribbing Soviet and Comintern publications. The "line" was cast so as to justify and buttress Stalin's diplomacy— which was uncertain and shifting in the period of his pact with Hitler. Stalin wanted to gain time from the pact; a protracted, stalemated war in the West would have suited his purposes; the rapid collapse of France and the withdrawal of the British from the continent, rather than reinforcing his position, upset his strategic calculations. It dismayed Stalin and his entourage.

Second, the Party's assignment—as its leaders understood the message—revolved around mobilizing masses for its "peace" crusade and countering what was seen as the drift to reaction, repression, and war. Like Lewis, but for different reasons, the Communists were indifferent to defense mobilization; his objective was to get more for the miners; their objective was to involve masses in "struggle." Finally, their use of the "political strike" was not unfailing, but exceptional. They could permit their pseudo-Leninist exuberance to determine strike policy only in circumstances when this could be synthesized with an authentic, explosive union mixture. That is why the record of "political strikes" was so spotty.[17]

How they intertwined with, and shared aspects of, ordinary labor activities was illustrated in the sequel to Hillman's recommendation to call out the troops. It came as no surprise to anyone that Foster wrote, "When President Roosevelt sent Federal troops against the aviation workers and broke their strike, it was a taste of the Hitleristic terrorism that Wall Street capitalists have in mind for the working class. . . . The strike was symptomatic of the widespread resentment among millions of workers at being forced to pay for a criminal war to which they are opposed." It was another matter when Lewis lashed out at Hillman at a CIO conference, and put through a resolution denouncing the dispatch of troops to break strikes. Murray felt obliged to join in the denunciation, and to condemn, for good measure, the mediation board for attempting to impose a system of compulsory arbitration. *Labor*, the highly regarded publication of the railroad unions, gave voice to widespread uneasiness when it asserted that "in the space of a few hours, labor was deprived of rights which had been won in more than a half century of struggle." It would have been one thing if a spy nest had been uncovered in a plant and ferreted out by the FBI; it was something different when the army broke a strike and fired strike leaders.[18]

7

Inside the auto union the issue of "political strikes" was grist to the Reuther-faction mill. By the 1941 convention, Reuther had built up his forces to the point where he was the co-power. Aside from his personal acumen and drive that went into the caucus-building, his argument to attract a following was anti-Communism, a platform afforded superlative appeal in the twenty-two months of the Stalin-Hitler pact. The Reuther forces now swept into Buffalo in an ultra-confident mood, buoyed by the national anti-Communist wave that threw the Communists on the defensive. They hoped to crack the Addes faction by whipping up the convention with the Allis-Chalmers and North American *causes célèbres*. There was the possibility that the Communists could not even make a stand as they had done at St. Louis the year before since the convention was taking place in August, and as luck would have it, the Communist-party line had changed again; its stalwarts were holding the bag of a discarded cause. Reuther had another ace in the hole: he succeeded in detaching Frankensteen—who had been damned by the Communists at North American—from the opposing faction. The two had driven to Buffalo together with their wives, and had agreed on a bloc which could readily dominate the convention, isolate and discredit the Communists, elect each other to vice-presidencies, and force out Addes as secretary-treasurer. Both convention arithmetic and the fervor of the times gave the Reuther whips the conviction that this was the right moment to make their lunge for leadership.

Through the preceding months when both factions were electioneering at high velocity, Reuther had his own campaign sheet in the *Michigan Labor Leader*, the Association of Catholic Trade Unionists' paper. Well edited, forcefully written, widely distributed and read, the paper had become the virtual mouthpiece of the right-wing faction. In its first issue the editor had timorously rejected working with Socialists. "Theoretically we can collaborate with Socialists on sound trade union principles," he explained, "but practically it is almost impossible because the Socialists have set themselves up as a political bloc aiming at control of the unions." These virginal scruples were rapidly swept away by the practicalities of the anti-Communist crusade. The May 23, 1941 issue reprinted an article by Blair Moody, *Detroit News* columnist, to make clear to its readers that Reuther's leadership should be unqualifiedly accepted. A previous issue carried a report that the Milwaukee ACTU had begun publication of the *Wisconsin Labor Leader*, and reprinted the detailed story on the vote fraud perpetrated by the Communist leadership at Allis-Chalmers. From that point on, the paper directed a steady drumfire against Communists at Allis-Chalmers, North American, and elsewhere. The preconvention issue ran a denunciation of Addes for failing to repudiate Communist-party endorsement of his candidacy. The same issue carried a detailed report of "a remarkable radio address" delivered by Walter Reuther over NBC in which, while opposing the use of troops against a legitimate strike, he placed the blame for the use of troops at North American "squarely on the shoulders of the Communist Party." The *Michigan Labor Leader* and Walter Reuther had an identical idea: combine anti-Communism with patriotism, social meliorism and labor aggressiveness. It was a heady brew. Certainly on the part of the ACTU, it was an alliance based on strategic agreement, not just momentary convenience.[19]

At first, everything seemed to be going according to plan. Before the convention's opening gong had sounded, delegates knew that the Allis-Chalmers blockbuster was to be unloosed. The hotel lobbies were buzzing with rumors of showdowns and juicy revelations to come. On opening day, the minority on the credentials committee jumped the gun with its own report to seat the Local 248 delegation. A nasty wrangle ensued, halted only with the agreement to instruct the credentials committee to report on Allis-Chalmers as the first order of business the following day. When the convention was called to order the second day, Frankensteen rose to call attention to the California delegates' table on which were displayed toy tanks, airplanes, and lead soldiers with a sign reading, "Frankensteen's Local 000." "Although I disapprove of troops," he said, "I would rather symbolize the American army than the Red Flag of Moscow"; whereupon the California delegates mockingly waved little American flags, and the opposing delegates cheered Frankensteen. R. J. Thomas requested the California delegates to remove the display, which they did.

Tom Doherty then gave an inflammatory report on behalf of the Reutherite-committee majority arguing not to seat the Local 248 delegates. This was no minor technical matter, he made clear. "Hitler and Stalin believe that treaties are scraps of paper. They believe constitutions are only made to be broken, and the majority of this committee believe that the ruling officers of Local 248 believe the same thing." The election of the delegates was "undemocratic, illegal and strictly unconstitutional"; "they were elected in the same manner as Hitler and Stalin hold their elections." The ground for the accusation: delegates were nominated and elected at the same meeting, whereas the UAW constitution specified nominations at one meeting and election at another, with at least one week to elapse between the two. The committee minority pointed out that the international executive board had held up election of local offiers and convention delegates. The local hurried along the procedure to be able to send in their delegates' credentials in the required time. All previous conventions had excused technical violations of constitutional provisions where "good and sufficient reasons are shown."

With that came the free-for-all. Addes (himself a practicing Catholic) denounced the ACTU as an "outside organization creating factionalism within the auto union." Leonard appeared to be attacking the Local 248 leaders for continuing their strike in the face of the Knox-Knudsen demand to reopen the plant, and bore down on the use of fraudulent ballots. Walter Reuther said that the issue was whether "the highest tribunal of our organization is going to put the stamp of approval on the worst kind of strong-arm political racketeering . . . or whether we are going to support . . . democratic procedure and the international constitution." Miley read a telegram from Lewis to Christoffel praising him for "a magnificent achievement" in an "epic struggle." Clearly this was a test case of delegates' loyalties—the arguments for not seating duly elected Local 248 delegates were flimsy—and the Reuther faction won the first test vote resoundingly. The minority report was lost 1,744 to 1,257. Thomas then appointed a committee of three, pursuant to convention instruction, to proceed to Milwaukee for a new election of convention delegates. There was another prolonged wrangle about who was and who was not eligible to participate in the vote (the 1,200 or 1,500 workers who heeded the Knox-Knudsen call to return to work were fined by the local and not permitted to vote until they paid their fines and delinquent dues). This was resolved by giving the committee the extraordinary authority to set the rules on eligibility.

On the sixth day (the convention went on for two weeks) Charles Bioletti gave another inflammatory report on behalf of the committee of three. He prefaced his remarks by informing the convention that Christoffel had called a number of officers "phonies, rats and Hillmanites" and the convention delegates "a bunch of bastards." He then related that agreement had been reached with Christoffel on arrangements so that members could vote if they paid up dues delinquency fines without paying the other fines. The negotiations broke down however on Christoffel's insistence that he would chair the meeting that would pass on eligibility. Two of the committee members informed R. J. Thomas over the phone that owing to a lack of cooperation they thought a fair election could not be held. Thomas then ordered them to return to Buffalo.

Bioletti's report was meant to set the stage for a lynching bee— and as of that moment, it achieved its purpose. One of the members of the committee of three, James Jennings, had broken with Bioletti and was ready to give a minority report. He was temporarily forgotten in the fury against Christoffel and his cohorts that was sweeping over the convention. Ed Hall, now an international representative, one of the deputies of the Addes caucus who had previously talked in favor of seating the Local 248 delegation, was apologetic. He could not condone the actions reported by the committee; if they were correct, he did not propose to plead with the convention any further on behalf of the Local 248 delegates. But he thought one thing should be done; Christoffel should be given an opportunity to explain why he took the positions that he did. Emil Mazey followed with the proposal that the executive board be empowered to revoke the charter of the local, Christoffel to be suspended forthwith, and the convention to prefer charges against him. Harvey Kitzman, who invited Reds at various conventions to take the next boat to Russia, made this contribution: "I don't see how any man has guts enough to plead that a leader of that type should take up the time of this convention to come before this convention and give you a pack of lies like he has been doing in Wisconsin for five years." Thomas related a story of how the Local 248 financial secretary had threatened to get him. When he invited "Brother Christoffel to come out of the gallery and come down here and let us see if he can defend himself," it was like a hanging judge asking the prisoner at the bar if he had any remarks to make before sentence was passed.

Mazey's remarks indicated that the Reuther people thought Christoffel would try to apologize his way out of his dilemma, and both Mazey and Victor Reuther hastened to cut the ground from under that kind of plea. They were to get their comeuppance.

Christoffel's was a remarkable performance. He began matter-of-factly, reviewing the three lengthy discussions he had with the convention committee, and how detailed agreements were arrived at on procedures to be followed for the holding of an election. He even agreed that members who were fined would be permitted to participate without payment of the fines if they paid up their back dues and delinquency fines—though this violated the rules that had been previously approved by the international executive board. Only two questions remained: whether Christoffel would chair the meeting that would determine eligibility, and whether the polls would be open an additional day on Monday. Christoffel explained that his only reservation on the extra day related to how long the convention would be in session; there was little sense in electing delegates to a convention that had already adjourned. It was agreed that another meeting would be held the following morning at 8:30 to conclude the arrangements. He waited in the union office for the committee, but the committee did not show up; instead he received a telegram that the committee was returning to Buffalo because of lack of cooperation on his part. "Somebody changed his mind."

Christoffel proceeded to lift the cover from the struggle going on in Milwaukee that was at the bottom of the Reuther faction's alleged concern for strict observance of constitutional punctilio. A leaflet signed by "Rank and File Committee of Local 248" was distributed at the plant gates conveying the information that the convention "had justly refused to seat delegates picked by Christoffel bureaucracy at the FAKE election July 13 . . . DO NOT VOTE for the Christoffel delegates whom the International Convention refused to seat." The leaflet was distributed by paid agents and Christoffel had a statement from one of them that he was paid by Nordstrom, the UAW regional director. He then displayed to the delegates different mimeographed sheets, the first discarded stencil, as well as typed press releases that had appeared in the Milwaukee papers, to demonstrate that both the leaflet and the anti-Christoffel newspaper stories had been ground out at the regional office and paid for by union funds. "All these people are so clever . . . but they forgot to empty their wastebaskets." At the conclusion of this part of his presentation, he flung out his challenge: "And let no man infer that Harold Christoffel has anything to apologize for. I am just as proud of my record in the labor movement as any man can be, because I have given everything that is within me to fight for American workers." As Christoffel went on, the attitude of many delegates changed; hostility turned to sympathy; his sallies were punctuated by increasingly demonstrative bursts of applause. When he came to his peroration, it was obvious that he had reversed the convention's mood. The neutrals had switched. The convention proceedings read "prolonged applause" at the conclusion of his remarks. In truth, it was an ovation.

Christoffel's speech set off another acrimonious debate. The committee report was rejected; and a new enlarged committee of seven was sent to Milwaukee to conduct the election for delegates. On the ninth day, the committee reported back that an election was held, 1,475 ballots were cast, 20 candidates ran, and the same 10 delegates were reelected (receiving roughly three times as many votes as their opponents). The proceedings read, "The Allis-Chalmers delegates came into the hall carrying a large United States flag and a banner of their local union, and received an enthusiastic reception." The Reuther faction overreached itself and was rebuked. Reuther and his friends could not attack the Allis-Chalmers strike itself because the strike had been authorized by the international union. They could not associate themselves with the Knox-Knudsen back-to-work order because that had been condemned by CIO and UAW leaders. They could not openly espouse the cause of those who had gone through the picket line because that would have left them open to the charge of scabbery. So they hung their case on a technicality while hurling an anti-Communist broadside. When this backfired, several hundred votes shifted to the other side on this question.[20]

8

Intertwined with Allis-Chalmers was the lengthy, intermittent debate over North American. On the fifth day, the grievance committee underwrote in its report Frankensteen's charge "that the wildcat strike was engineered by Communists, inside and outside the union"; it condemned the use of troops against labor, but deplored "those conditions under which the use of troops was widely accepted by the public"; commended Murray, Thomas, and Frankensteen for their conduct in the strike; and in view of Michener's malfeasances, and the need to free the region "from all outside interference and domination," the committee recommended that the region be placed under an administratorship. This was the strongest case the Reuther people had against the Communists, but they could not exploit their advantage because their alliance with Frankensteen had unravelled. Allan Haywood, Murray's representative at the convention, had been meeting with Frankensteen and advising him that the CIO was opposed to any attempt to remove Addes from the secretary-treasurership. According to Haywood's arithmetic, with the support that the CIO representatives could muster, Frankensteen could have a vice-presidency without Reuther's support. As a result of this intrigue, Frankensteen moved away from the Reuther camp and made advances to Addes.

There was an unformulated personal reason that reinforced Frankensteen's decision to put distance between himself and Reuther. By 1941 the Reuther phenomenon had burst over the UAW. It was not that he was the ablest of the national leaders, although, on balance, he undoubtedly was. In specific talents he did not outshine his main rivals. He was a fluent speaker, but no spellbinder, no orator, and not superior to a dozen others in presentation or intellectual prowess. He was a capable organizer and negotiator, but again, not in a different class than his rivals. In certain respects, his rivals had the advantage. Frankensteen had a more appealing, a less stilted personality; he was the more effective mass organizer; he had more of the qualities and bearing of the successful American politician. Addes, less flamboyant and more intellectually cramped, was an accomplished floor man and a gifted executive; at the time, he was the most respected figure of the three. What set Walter Reuther apart was the combination of traits; high tactical skills powered by unrelenting perseverance. It was this that made him a phenomenon to those who admired him, and a menace to those who did not.

Eli Ginzberg's exploratory study of the labor leader provides an insight into the Reuther makeup. While one or another characteristic of the ideal type that Ginzberg describes does not necessarily apply in this case, the description fits sufficiently to disclose the inner mechanism that impels an individual to battle without letup for the mastery of his environment. To transpose Scott Fitzgerald's remark about the very rich into another key, Reuther was not like other auto union officials who avidly sought power; it was as if he were biologically structured for the quest. Ginzberg wrote:

> Some people have an inordinate need for power, and it is no accidental matter that they achieve it, for they devote their every waking hour to getting ahead. They are driven as if by the furies, and they can no more retire from the race than retire from life itself. . . . These men [great captains of industry] were ruthless.

190

To achieve their ends they used every weapon at their command, not hesitating to transgress law or custom to avoid defeat. . . . It is noteworthy that their ruthlessness was directed not only towards opponents, but also towards close associates and friends. The primacy of their aggressive needs was reflected in the doggedness with which they sought to enhance their power. Their need for power was so overwhelming that they made short shrift with all other emotional and social values. . . . The leader is lonely. He has many followers, some associates, but no intimates with whom he can share his work and worries. In the last analysis he can trust no one, for his goals are always personal. The power that he wields and the power that he seeks are eyed greedily by others. He knows that his competitors, like himself, would not hesitate to use every advantage.

Already at Buffalo, some expressed uneasiness about what would happen to the auto union if Reuther was the man in charge. It was quickly apparent to Frankensteen that in the Reuther-Frankensteen bloc he himself would be the captive. So would anyone else with independent strength who sought an alliance with Reuther. That was what eventually forced Leonard to break with Reuther and go over to the other side. It was the key as well to Murray's intervention. Just as England in its heyday did not want any one power to dominate the continent, Murray did not want the leading union in the CIO under the control of an empire-builder. That Reuther should convey the strong impression of a single-minded seeker of power was the more remarkable since the ambition was not alien to other officials around.[21]

The Communists were now in desperate need of revamping their alliances; consequently, they were more than willing to play Frankensteen's game. A horse trade was concluded. Mortimer and the other fired organizers were abandoned, the Communists were going to admit that they made some mistakes. In return, they secured the protection of the Addes-Frankensteen forces, and Michener (who was popular with the West Coast ranks) was to be let off with a slap on the wrist. The formal question on which the debate occurred was thus narrowed down to administratorship or no administratorship, and what penalty for Michener. After the caucus politicians reduced the policy question to administrative pettifoggery, the committee returned with three reports. The majority report, supported by

191

Reuther, proposed to bar Michener from holding any office for one year. The minority report of the no-compromisers proposed to expel Michener from the union, and to appoint an administrator over the region. The super-minority report proposed that Michener be disqualified for election to the board for one year (making possible his appointment as an international representative). Under fiery challenge, all parties to the patched-together Addes bloc had to do more talking than they had anticipated would be necessary. Mortimer made a long speech in which he tried to duplicate Christoffel's feat, but he lacked the ability, the material to work with, and the encouragement of either the Addes or Party forces. Frankensteen had to take the floor for an extended statement on his role in the strike in which he displayed sufficient agility to defend his activities, flay the Communists, and urge leniency for Michener. In the end, the lines of the bloc held, and the super-minority report was adopted by the narrow vote of 1,570 to 1,465.[22]

It was on the proposal to bar Communists from any union office that the Reuther faction reaped its harvest. This was the final debate before the voting on officers and board members, and the opposing spokesmen hurled their most powerful ammunition at each other in a supreme effort to draw a convention majority for their side. The arguments to bar Reds from office ran along well-trod lines: It was the only way to preserve democracy in the union and the nation; and the union could not organize the unorganized in aircraft and elsewhere so long as there were those within the organization receiving instructions from agents of Stalin, Hitler, and Mussolini. The counterattack disclosed again that the Communists were a small minority. Anderson of the East Side tool-and-die local was the only delegate to defend Communists and their rights within the union; and Montgomery of the West Coast was the only one to make a civil liberties argument and to deplore witch hunts against radicals.

The Addes caucus spokesmen gave little comfort or consideration to their Communist allies. James Lindahl, who reported for the committee minority, took his position "four-square behind democracy and American principles." He was against all foreign "isms," and to drive home his point, insisted that members of the Socialist party also had to be included in the interdiction. Addes was for eliminating from the union all Communists, Socialists, and adherents of other radical groups. He held members of these groups responsible for "all the bickering that has been going on in this

192

union." This counterposition was supplemented by a fierce personal attack on the Reuthers: they had sent out a letter from Russia with the message "to carry on the fight for a Soviet America"; and Walter Reuther was a draft-dodger (he had asked for a deferment on grounds of being the sole source of support for his wife). A special handbill distributed to convention delegates summed up the personal and political case against Reuther.

The counteroffensive was a failure. Victor Reuther insisted that the letter from Russia was a "phony." Actually, the basic letter was authentic, but the many delegates who knew it was authentic understood that the Reuthers had some years ago changed their minds about both Russia and a Soviet America—and the letter was therefore not germane. The draft-dodging accusation was blunted by the fact that both Murray and Thomas had endorsed Reuther's request for a deferment. On the substantive issue, delegates were not being asked to decide whether Communists should have or should not have a constitutional right to run for office, but whether Socialists should be barred, as well. Despite Lindahl's major oratorical effort buttressed by numerous quotations culled from the Socialist press, to depict the Socialist party as another disciplined, power-seeking group similar to the Communists, the delegates were unimpressed. While most knew little and cared little about the operations and aims of the Socialist party, in a common-sense way they understood that Socialist adherents did not constitute a disciplined formation within the union. (Walter Reuther left the Socialist party in 1938; others resigned in 1941 because they took issue with Norman Thomas's pacifism. In the debate, the Reuther speakers simply rested their case on opposition to groups that were agencies of a foreign power.) After all, the anti-Communist impulse was in response to the felt need to proclaim to the world the union's respectability; that the union could be counted on as a patriotic organization. Socialists, it was felt, could get in under the wire of this requirement; Communists could not. As Kitzman explained, "We have some sixteen states in the United States which barred the Communist Party . . . I don't know of one single state that has barred the Socialist party. That is the difference."

Because this (as well as factional advantage) was the fundamental motivation, Addes's earlier attack on the ACTU drew no blood. On formal grounds, if the principle was valid, the ACTU should have been barred along with Communists. The ACTU caucuses were directed by outside chaplains and worked up their strategies outside the union. Since the ACTU was a peripheral organization attached to the church, and justified its activities by Papal encyclicals, it could be defined as subservient to a foreign power. Beyond that, the ACTU's organizational structure closely resembled the Communist one; labor priests had studied Communist operations and copied some of their techniques. Kermit Eby, the CIO education director in the forties, made a comparison between the two: "There are two extreme poles of power attraction in the CIO, the Communist pole and the ACTU pole. Both receive their impetus and inspiration from without the CIO. Both believe the control of the CIO is part of the larger struggle for control of the world." The formal case against the ACTU notwithstanding, the Addes forces could not do anything with it. They did not dare to press their attack by including the ACTU in their proposed list of proscribed organizations. The days when masses could be mobilized against the Pope and his American legatees were past. The Catholic Church was now accepted in official society as a loyal American body as well as a leading participant in the anti-Communist cause. Any attempt to proscribe the ACTU would have redounded against its authors—which the politicians in the Addes camp were quick to grasp.

The anti-Red clause was adopted by an almost two-to-one vote, 1,968 to 1,027, the sizable majority augmented by Frankensteen's honoring his earlier public commitment on this question. On the decisive organizational challenge, Leonard v. Addes for secretary-treasurer, Reuther was set back, but the Reuther camp showed great strength. Despite the loss of Frankensteen and his supporters, despite the active electioneering for Addes on the part of CIO dignitaries, Leonard received 1,313 votes to 1,754 for Addes. The vote was piled up to remove the top man in the opposing caucus, not for inefficiency or inadequacy, or dereliction of duty, but for his refusal to repudiate his Communist allies.[23]

It would be logical to assume that Reuther came out of the convention with enhanced prestige, but such was not the case. He was just barely reelected to the executive board. At one point, a tabulating error made it appear that he was defeated, and one of his friends (Leonard Woodcock, the recent president) went out to break the bad news to him. He had excited too many suspicions and fears about himself. Frankensteen in 1941 was the floating kidney of the UAW body politic. His swaying to and fro left him in a precarious position. The Reuther people considered him an apostate; the Addes people were wary of this overflexible operator. As for Addes himself, a fixture since the South Bend convention, he managed to retain his office only with the help of CIO well-wishers. Even more pronouncedly than the year before, major delegations refused to swear allegiance to either camp; instead, they deliberately supported now one side, now the other, and apportioned their votes for executive-board candidates so as not to give undisputed control to either faction. The neutrals who held the balance of power wanted their leaders to compete and watch over each other. In this, they reflected the wishes of the ranks more faithfully than the faction enthusiasts. The three major leaders therefore left Buffalo with less personal authority than they had when they arrived. Although the convention moved emphatically to clear the union's skirts of Communist taint, it would not increase the authority of the anti-Communist politicos.[24]

EIGHT · *War Years—I*

ACCORDING to Joel Seidman, the war "brought in its wake a degree of national unity such as America had seldom, if ever, experienced." Unlike 1917 or 1898, there was no meaningful antiwar movement. On the Left, with the Communists turning super-patriotic, opposition was confined to hole-and-corner revolutionary and pacifist sects. There had been extensive opposition to getting into the war, with the America First committee drawing sustenance from many in business circles and certain ethnic minorities. That ended once America became a combatant. Still, war patriotism had a stereotyped quality to it. It lacked resonance and the commitment was shallow. Frederick Lewis Allen, the chronicler of the decade, remarked that whereas "there had been a lively crusading spirit" in the First World War, there was a minimum of it in the Second, for "the popular disillusionments" that followed Wilson's crusading "had left their marks." Everyone wanted to beat Hitler and the Mikado, but on the cheap. Wage earners read about war contractors reaping huge profits, became indignant about rising prices and black markets, and saw no reason why they should not combine war patriotism with better living standards. The imperatives of war leading to an upheaval in the economy, society, and people's lives, referred to in describing the defense period; the reigning individualism finding new outlets; the insatiable demand for labor; and the headlong expansion of unionism—all this bred a turbulence and an assertiveness that continued to mount with every year of the war.

The problems that labor leaders, particularly CIO leaders, faced during mobilization, were now aggravated. Their abilities for manipulation and maneuver were tested repeatedly and to the utmost in holding their members to confining government regulations, while at the same time trying to satisfy grievances and to bring additional millions into the labor fold. They had all subscribed to the no-strike pledge and entered the newly created War Labor Board (WLB). Even Lewis declared, "When the nation is attacked, every American must rally to its defense. All other considerations become insignificant"; and Thomas Kennedy, the mine union secretary-treasurer, accepted a place on the board. In return, the labor leaders were granted union security by means of the previously worked-out "maintenance of membership" formula. The rationale, explained by Frank P. Graham, one of the public members and past president of the University of North Carolina, was this: "Management in the war industries has the guarantee for the duration of the war of continuous business, without the usual risks to investments. The unions, with the unusual risks of the war pressure against strikes and general wage increases, except in the nature of equitable adjustments, need some security against disintegration under the impact of war."

This may have appeared reassuring, but with the passing months labor representatives found it harder to keep their equipoise. Initially, the War Labor Board voted for wage increases on various grounds of equity as well as employers' financial abilities. In July this came to an end. The board came up with the "Little Steel formula" in response to the steel union's demand for a dollar-a-day increase. Basing itself on the Price Control Act passed in January, and the president's 7-point anti-inflation program of April, the board ruled that workers had no right to expect higher wages during the war. Since, according to BLS figures, the cost of living had risen 15 percent between January 1, 1941 and May 1942, and the steel workers had already received an 11.8 percent increase, all they were entitled to was an additional 3.2 cents per hour. They were granted another 2.3 cents for an alleged time inequity, making for a total of 5.5 cents per hour. Henceforth, the "Little Steel formula" became the standard yardstick against which to measure all wage demands. "These are hard days for Labor men who are trying to keep the wheels rolling," Daniel Tobin, the Teamsters' boss, lamented to Roosevelt. Then in October there was a further freeze. Under this presidential executive order, the board could authorize wage increases that would in its opinion require price increases only if approved by the newly created director of economic stabilization, to which post Roosevelt appointed James F. Byrnes, a rock-ribbed conservative ex-senator from South Carolina.

Thus a board set up by agreement between labor and industry had been converted into an agency to prevent wage increases; with the exception of the wage freeze, the other six provisions of the President's anti-inflation program were in limbo. The formula became labor's bête noire based as it was on the legal fiction that prices were being stabilized when in fact they continued going up. In early 1943 came the dénouement: the miners union wanted wage concessions going beyond the formula, and Roosevelt, acting on Byrnes's recommendation, issued a "hold the line" order that stripped the board of authority to grant increases even on grounds of inequality.

AFL and CIO leaders limited themselves to protesting and issuing vague warnings, but Lewis mounted a massive economic challenge. He began to broadcast across the country blood-curdling denunciations and belligerently couched appeals. At a conference with the coal operators in March, he thundered, "The coal miners . . . are ill-fed and undernourished below the standard of their neighbors." Men with hungry children will not accept a "miserably stupid" formula drawn up by a board of "labor zombies." "If I had a yellow dog I would hate to have his standard of living fixed by this man Davis and the men who are doing his dirty work on the WLB." The union's full weight was put behind the demand for a $2-a-day increase and additional portal-to-portal pay. When the members of Truman's Senate War Investigating Committee tried to pillory Lewis in open session, they were flung back on their heels. Lewis accused the government of abetting inflation with cost-plus contracts to industry that underwrote enormous profits. Senator Ralph Brewster broke in with the remark that under existing and proposed tax legislation "we will hope that the rich will not get richer out of this war." Lewis answered, "We all hope with you, but hope deferred maketh the heart sick." Senator Harold Burton wanted to know "if we restrain industry and finance, are you willing to work on holding down the wages?" Lewis's reply was a sneer: "My dear Senator, whenever you have restrained industry and finance, just call me on the telephone and let me know."

A general coal strike was set for April 1, and from that date to the final breakthrough in November Lewis kept industry and government in a state of turmoil and crisis. He refused to appear before the WLB, which assumed jurisdiction of the dispute, and announced that a walkout would take place at the end of a new truce deadline on April 30 if a new contract was not signed by then. Miners in Pennsylvania and Alabama left the pits a week in advance of the deadline. On April 29 Roosevelt threatened to use troops if the walkout was not ended by May 1. Instead, on that date the entire soft-coal industry was shut down. With that, the vials of public wrath overflowed. The media linked Lewis with Hitler; union officials enlisted as strike critics. Roosevelt decided to ignore Stimson's importunities to let the army take over and instructed Harold Ickes, the Solid Fuels Administrator, to seize the mines. Ickes proclaimed that the miners were now working for the government and had to return to their jobs. Lewis continued his harassing game and demonstrated his strength. He set another 15-day truce as of May 4, and only on that day did the miners troop back to the pits. This tenacious struggle went on for the next six months through a succession of three general strikes, interrupted by new truces and new deadlines, scorching arraignments and threats led off by the President himself, and returning salvos of defiance from Lewis. In the midst of the uproar Congress in June passed the Smith-Connally antistrike law over Roosevelt's veto, in which veto message he suggested several even harsher measures than those contained in the law.

At issue at this point was not only the Little Steel formula, but the authority of the War Labor Board, and the cooperation of the labor officialdom. If the no-strike pledge could be successfully flouted, the board might be wrecked, while AFL and CIO officials would find their entire position eroded. The dangers inherent in the Lewis revolt were made manifest at the Michigan state CIO convention convened in Detroit after the passage of the Smith-Connally Act. By a 2-to-1 vote, the delegates recommended to the affiliated auto, steel, glass and other unions that "unless assurances that were made to labor are immediately and effectively put into operation," the no-strike pledge be withdrawn. This recommendation was adopted in defiance of the entire top leadership. Haywood, Brophy, Thomas, August Scholle, the Michigan CIO president, not to mention the leading Communist spokesmen, all vehemently fought the proposal, and to no avail. By another overwhelming vote the delegates overrode all suggestions to criticize Lewis and pledged instead unconditional support to the mine union. It was a vote of no confidence in the top leadership. Neither the delegates, nor their constituents, were really ready to defy the government and to break with the WLB. The restlessness and discontent was not that well defined, and not that resolutely led. But it was palpable, had been fortified by the mine strikes, and the delegates were giving voice to it, and it might have further consequences.

The board officials and labor officials, at the receiving end of the revolt, could not adopt a philosophical attitude. In defense of their bureaucratic positions, both of them worked themselves into advocating actual destruction of the mine union in the higher interests of the war effort. Said Wayne Morse, noted liberal and WLB compliance officer, in response to Frances Perkins' objections, "In time of war, when a union seeks to defy the government of the U.S., I am

199

all in favor of breaking that union. I am all in favor of the Government's using whatever power is necessary to destroy that union." Van Bittner, a former district director of the mine union, felt the same way about it. The issue, he said in his exhortation to the board was "whether or not we are going to act as Americans and meet an enemy head on." The Communists were not in on the conferences, but they made up in zeal what they lacked in inside influence. The *Daily Worker*, whose public denunciations of Lewis had from the beginning of the strike threat pierced through the ozone, sent its then managing editor, Louis Budenz, and others, into the coal fields to try to organize back-to-work movements. Julius Emspak, the UE secretary-treasurer and member of the president's Labor Victory Board, urged Roosevelt to crack down with everything he had. Responding to all these entreaties and somber warnings, Roosevelt issued an executive order empowering the WLB to impound the union's funds, seize its property, halt the checkoff, and that also authorized Selective Service to cancel strikers' draft deferments.

But the offensive did not work in this case. The miners held firm. With a new strike starting at the end of October, and chaos in the offing in the coal fields, Roosevelt again seized the mines and directed Ickes to negotiate a contract that Lewis could accept without further ado. When the nerve-shattering experience was over, Lewis had come out with a substantial part of his program achieved. The miners were granted $1.50 per day increase, although in order to pretend that the Little Steel formula remained intact, the award was justified as an allowance for portal-to-portal time and a reduction in the lunch period. The mine strikes had punctured a hole in the formula, and other labor leaders now hastened to take advantage of the Lewis initiative that they had denounced by negotiating so-called fringe benefits relating to travel-time allowances, paid vacations, holiday pay, and the like. At the CIO executive-board session hurriedly assembled after Roosevelt's announcement, Murray bared his soul as to what the leadership would be up against. "[The campaign for higher wages] involves a tremendous amount of responsibility; our organization may suffer from certain sources castigating the leadership and even the unions themselves. Nevertheless the situation has reached such proportions—I mean insofar as the clamor of the membership is concerned, the membership of my union particularly—that it seems to me the time has come for the Executive Board to provide guidance in the thinking of our various International unions. . . . Unless we provide the proper guidance for our people, I am afraid that our people will provide guidance for us."[1]

The fanfare was more impressive than the play. At the CIO convention proper in November 1943, Murray went through a familiar routine. On the one hand, the no-strike pledge was reaffirmed "without any qualifications or conditions," and a great show made of the CIO's patriotic exertions on the many fronts of the war. On the other hand, in a lengthy argumentative resolution, the CIO called attention to the failure of the government's anti-inflation program and demanded a new more realistic wage policy. This "guidance" afforded only minor relief because the unionists were tied to the WLB and the WLB adjudicating machinery had been devised to be cumbersome, dilatory, and wage-freeze prone. The steel union's demands, supposed to break ground for the CIO's wage campaign, were permitted to slowly wend their way past the bureaucratic obstacle courses so that it was a year before the board rejected the union's basic demands to award it several secondary fringe benefits. This epitomized the dilemma of the labor leaders. The repressive war machinery was paralyzing their bargaining abilities on the outside; the dissatisfaction in the ranks was undercutting their authority on the inside. But they had become adept at the games of shuttlecock and back and fill.

The next year their ingenuity was sorely tried. By mid-1944 over 2 million workers had gone out in 5,000 wildcat strikes, and Murray lamented that union officials had been turned into labor policemen: "A very substantial portion of the monies collected by each of the international organizations is now being used to enforce the directives of the National War Labor Board which, in the first instance, we do not believe in." It should not be thought that this was limited to moral suasion. Sanctions were repeatedly imposed—members suspended or expelled, locals put in receivership or charters lifted, company firing and draft board induction of strikers and local officers ratified—so that there existed in a number of CIO unions a state of warfare between large sections of the membership and high union officials.

In the steel union Murray managed to isolate and squelch insurgencies before they progressed very far, bringing into play the presidential cult fostered and fastened on the union by the staff. Disciplinary action had to be resorted to only rarely, and then the well-oiled, centralized machine could smoothly work its will. But in the auto union, the entire leadership, time and again, was in danger of losing control. The WLB had to intervene as a strike-breaking agency by using maintenance-of-membership as a punitive weapon. In 1943, the board withdrew the provision in Chrysler plants for six months. Later, Ford and Briggs made the same demand on the board. Under the pressure of growing numbers of wildcat strikes, and increasingly insistent company demands for safeguards, the international executive board assumed sweeping powers to intervene in local unions, to discipline offending members and officials, with stewards, committeemen, and local officers made responsible for the repression of unauthorized strikes. Since local union officers suspended by the international were generally voted back into office after administrators were removed, it was a question whether international officers could long endure. In the rubber union all Akron rose in revolt against the international administration headed by Sherman Dalrymple; the "big four" locals were united in a bloc demanding the rescinding of the no-strike pledge. The guerrilla battles, involving wildcat strikes and the expulsion of hundreds of members, were climaxed in June and July of 1945 with long strikes at both Goodyear and Firestone, halted only when both plant complexes were taken over by the army. The unbending Dalrymple, having lost control of his union, had to resign.

With the gathering tensions, Murray warned the board at the end of 1944 that unless it moved expeditiously, CIO representatives would be forced to withdraw. This was just "tough talk." He did not mean it, as he speedily demonstrated. In the spring of 1945 the board was ready to raise minimum rates in southern textile mills from 50 to 55 cents and to grant some fringe benefits. It was overruled by Fred Vinson, the complacent border-state politician who was Byrnes's successor. An outraged Emil Rieve, the textile union head, resigned from the board, revoked the union's no-strike pledge, and called on the CIO to pull out its representatives. Murray squelched the revolt. He explained that for the CIO to withdraw from the WLB meant that it would have to revoke its no-strike pledge, as well. That, in his judgment, with the nation at war, would be tantamount to signing the organization's death warrant. Though the WLB was faulty, it had protected union security. Should the organization decide on a course of irresponsibility, he told the CIO executive board, he could not continue as president. Except for the textile representative, the members voted to back Murray. No one (including Rieve, who led a very weak union) was really of a mind to follow in Lewis's footsteps. (Vinson's myopic ruling cut across the WLB's desire to ease some of the pressure by granting small fringe benefits. He walked away from the small crisis he had foolishly created by resigning, only to be replaced—in

Washington's game of musical chairs—by William Davis, the WLB chairman.)

AFL officials, with a more diffused membership, one less concentrated in mass-production industries, were not as emphatic in protesting and criticizing. They were more in the Gompers business-agent mold. That did not mean that their less politically articulate membership was unmoved by currents of unrest. In 1943 AFL unions engaged in 37 percent of all strikes, the same proportion as CIO unions. The CIO accounted for more than twice as many workers and some 50 percent more of man-days idleness only because their unions were in larger enterprises; with the percentages fluctuating slightly, similar proportions obtained in 1944 and 1945.

In summary, the defense-and-war labor turbulence marked the second upsurge and period of exceptional union growth of the Roosevelt era. From 1940 to 1945 labor unions jumped from 8,717,000 to 14,322,000, or from 27 percent of nonagricultural employment to almost 36 percent. This was not the breathtaking expansion of 1936 to 1939 when the rise was from 3,989,000 to 8,763,000, or from 14 percent of nonagricultural employment to 29 percent; 5,615,000 new members in 5 years entailing an enlargement by a third of a much more sizable labor force was a spectacular expansion, nonetheless. The growth was accompanied by labor unrest, which built up into a revolt in several CIO unions against the no-strike pledge. This revolt kept gathering force until it exploded at war's end as another epochal strike movement, qualitatively of a different and more successful order than the one at the conclusion of the First World War.

Wartime strikes had a different character than the insurgency that established the CIO. They lacked the thirties' sense of desperation. There was little of the resolve to battle for the holy cause come what may, and to push aside leaders who would not heed the call. Except for the special circumstances of the mine strikes, workers were giving vent to frustrations, not resolution, as in Akron and Flint, to tear down the iron gates of industrial servitude. These were struggles based on a sense of relative deprivation tempered by the realization that their absolute standard of living was improving. Average weekly earnings in manufacturing rose 70 percent between January 1941 and July 1945, while the cost of living rose a third. Real weekly earnings, $24 in 1939, were over $36 in 1944. Continuous demand for labor had other exhilirating effects. Many who had been employed at low-paid nonmanufacturing jobs were now working at better-paid manufacturing jobs. Many who had been working part time or intermittently were now working full time with overtime. The statistical number of breadwinners per family had risen. Some families now had two.

These larger pay packets were distributed very unevenly. There were many in less-favored industries and localities who bore the burden of inflation without compensating benefits in take-home pay. It was in the most vigorous sections of the labor movement, however, that the wage improvements were greatest. In war-production centers workers were buying household goods and cuts of steak that they could not afford in the thirties despite shortages, rationing and black markets. Needless to say, no wage earners, even the most skilled putting in long hours of overtime, became millionaires. Industry profits and farm income shot up more dramatically. Workers read how Congress knocked down the proposal for a ceiling of $25,000 net on salaries and passed a tax law "providing relief not for the needy but for the greedy." So they kept pushing their tin plates forward to obtain larger helpings of the ill-distributed opulence, and government officials kept pushing their plates aside, while the press ran leaders on the need to sacrifice, and Congress thundered imprecations. All this made for exasperation, not desperation. The intensity of dedication to a struggle is determined by the source of the indignation. Envy is less pressing than insecurity. The feeling in labor ranks that those who were giving them lectures were cashing in on war opportunities while they were frozen to their jobs and their wages were being held down made for heady outbursts, but outbursts that lacked sustaining power.[2]

Union leaders tried to compensate for members' sacrifices and their own patriotic exertions by winning new positions of influence for the labor movement in the changed environment of a nation at war. Green called for effective labor representation "of its own choosing in all defense planning and execution," the AFL reiterating plaintive pleas along this line from time to time. The CIO was more insistent and demanding even if not more successful in gaining its objective, starting with the 1942 CIO convention at which Murray made this a special theme in his report. "This is a people's war," he intoned. "In order to gear our country for total war, the CIO has repeatedly urged full and equal representation of labor in all government agencies dealing with war problems."

204

Nothing too much came of all this huffing and puffing. Despite the presentation of numbers of "win-the-war" programs, the earlier Reuther Plan for "500 Planes a Day" that caught Roosevelt's attention, and the later, heavily touted Murray Plan for labor-management industry councils, labor representatives were successfully relegated to advisory roles in the war agencies. The Tolan Committee reported that "recommendations of the [Labor Production] Division [of the War Production Board] are ignored. . . . Employees of the Division not infrequently are treated as outsiders and their presence resented by industry branch representatives." That was the universal fate of the different labor advisory boards and divisions. Although 5,000 labor-management committees were theoretically set up in the course of the war, most of those that functioned at all did little more than distribute inspirational literature, tack up posters in the plants, and conduct occasional rallies for community funds or blood donations. Those committees that attempted to occupy themselves with production quickly aroused management suspicion and hostility, and disintegrated or became dormant. Business would not tolerate labor getting a foot in the door of management prerogatives.

Contrary to radical expectations, the commonalty of workers did not resent the cavalier treatment accorded their leaders and their patriotic offerings. Working men and women were little moved by these aspiring labor programs. To the extent that they were aware of them at all, they accepted them as part of the public-relations rhetoric of the labor movement. The issue that provoked wartime militancy and wildcat strikes was more money (except for the battles of Blacks for jobs and nondiscriminatory treatment, and a corresponding backlash.) Where militancy attained a programmatic level and found articulate spokesmen, the demands stemmed from the ranks' same excitation over wages and working conditions, not from demands for increased labor representation in the agencies. It was this excitation that was at the origin of resolutions to revoke the no-strike pledge and to break with the War Labor Board.

One labor writer speculated that had the AFL and CIO been united, the labor movement would have won a position in government comparable to that acquired by labor in Britain. He was mistaken. Not that mutual wrangling and mutual undercutting were not damaging to labor's progress, but neither the country, nor liberal friends of labor, nor union ranks thought in terms of labor in government. When Lewis offered himself as a candidate for the vice-presidency in 1940, Roosevelt was utterly taken aback, and Frances Perkins related the incident with incredulity. Such arrogance! It was not simply Lewis the person whom Roosevelt rejected—although he did that, too. The idea of a labor running-mate struck him as preposterous. The day had not yet arrived when for the broad electorate labor representation would be an asset, not a liability. Because the American labor movement was economically strong, but politically weak, it made a different impression on the public than did labor in Britain. In Britain, no sooner was the war ended than the electorate returned Churchill—the war hero, but Tory expositor—to private life. In the United States, business executives recovered a good part of their pristine image since they were credited with the "production miracle," while labor leaders were blamed for wartime stoppages.[3]

2

The war proved an intoxicating experience for American Communists. It carried them into a *union sacrée* and the flood tide of their importance. No sooner did the press wires carry news of the Nazi assault on the Soviet Union than the Party reversed itself with breakneck speed. For the comrades, this was the capitalist intervention that had been feared for so long, the final fruit of the Munich pact to open the eastern road to the Nazi legions. Their response was a conditioned reflex, having none of the indecision and confusion that preceded the switch of 22 months before. All their training had prepared them to don battle dress at such a moment and hasten to defend the socialist fatherland. The imperialist war was now transformed into a people's war against Hitlerism. "The Yanks Are Not Coming" was whisked out of sight; the new slogan of the hour was "Defend America by giving full aid to the Soviet Union, Great Britain, and all nations who fight against Hitler." Within a month Foster was beating the drums for full-scale entry into the war. (Browder was in jail until May 1942.) Those who were merely proposing all aid "short of war" were guilty of "spreading pro-Hitler propaganda." Labor leaders who were demanding "special concessions for labor" as a condition for their support of the defense program were nothing less than "enemies of our class as well as of our nation." By the time of Pearl Harbor, the Communists had already been at war psychologically for five and a half months. They had plunged in their violent 180-degree turn to the conservative end of the spectrum.[4]

Because of the providential meshing of events in December 1941, the Communists could be both Russian patriots and American patriots. For once, they could have the best of both worlds. Relying on the shortness of human memory, and the need of harassed union officials to cooperate with whatever allies were at hand, they could work to reforge the broken links and to forge new ones for a bigger and better all-national popular front. They could be part of the general labor coalition opposing strikes and calling for more production. At the same time, to retain their status as a distinct left grouping, they could criticize big business for the inadequacy of its sacrifices in the common cause, beat the drums for a labor voice in decision-making, and call for a populist deepening of war aims.

But in these unprecedented circumstances when its policy dovetailed so neatly with that of labor officials and liberals, the Party displayed the extremism, the lack of judiciousness and scruple that was endemic to its inner character. The moment Browder and his acolytes felt the first stray breezes of acceptance, they had delusions of grandeur as if the task of producing war matériel and placing American armies on the European continent had fallen primarily on their shoulders. Discarding one obsession meant taking up another. The conceit that they were now plenipotentiaries in the world of *hochpolitik* pushed the Communists time and again into needless, stupid fights with a variety of labor officials and Black spokesmen, and in general brought into question their sense of balance. Suddenly they were the 150 percent Americans while regulation unionists and Black reformers were practically fifth columnists—a case of charlatanry vying with chutzpah. The statesmanlike pose of the refurbished Browder did not alter the reality that he remained a Stalinist hack politician beset by the furies of a Comintern heritage. When at the height of his wartime eminence he was able to correspond indirectly with Roosevelt, a good part of his letters were filled with fulminations against a variety of individuals and publications whom the president was urged to be on guard against. The list of enemies included Dubinsky, Reuther, Carey, Roger Baldwin of the American Civil Liberties Union, James Wechsler of the *New York Post*, whom he called a Trotskyite, as well as the *Nation*, the *New Republic*, the *New Leader*, and *PM*. Placed in the enviable position of being able to gain access to Roosevelt's ear, he had little better to offer than the stale reports of a third-rate intelligence operative.

Starting in the thirties with a proposed united front with Socialists, the Communists quickly graduated to a popular front with liberals; now they were calling for a national front ranging from

J. P. Morgan to Earl Browder. (When a reporter from a liberal daily twitted Browder that he would get along fine with representatives from the National Association of Manufacturers, Browder solemnly avowed, "I'm awfully glad to hear that.") By moving far to the right of the labor-liberal stance, they undercut traditional divisions between conservatives and liberals; they made their popular-front allies and potential allies suspicious, without winning over or interesting any of J. P. Morgan's associates.[5]

How much of a force in the unions were the Communists at the start of the war? The then current analysis generally exaggerated. Hostile publicists and Red-hunting congressmen were prone to impart demonic abilities to Communists. Since they wanted to convince the country that the menace was great and growing, they would interpret every random boast in the *Daily Worker* as a hard fact of Red triumph. Their inflated estimates were supplemented by non-Communist left-wing writers who would unconsciously compare Communist successes with the miniscule influence of other radical sects—and on that screen of comparison the Communist party was blown up into a gargantuan monster.

The statistics never lived up to the billing. Of the 50,000 members claimed in a report to the National Committee in early 1942, less than half were in industry. Let us say, for the sake of argument, that 25,000 were in unions; this at a time when, according to Troy's knocked-down figures, there were 8.4 million union members and 2.6 million CIO members. After including all sympathizers, fellow travelers, and friends of varying degrees of dependability, we still arrive at a minute ideological penetration.

In organizational control, they suffered noticeable losses from the high point of the late thirties, but losses difficult to measure statistically. They had been ousted from national leadership in the wood workers. They retained their grip on Mine Mill, but were facing a substantial opposition. They had been cut down in the auto union so that their hold or influence was limited to a number of scattered, though important, local unions. They had been cut out administratively from the steel union, and had been cut down in the packinghouse union. Their strength had ebbed in several central labor bodies. But they did retain control of 18 international unions of which UE, Mine Mill, the two maritime unions, the New York-based transport workers, and the fur and leather union were consequential. According to Troy's compilation, these 18 unions had a membership in 1941 of 457,000 or 17½ percent of the total. In the AFL, Communist influence was limited to local enclaves: stagehand and talent unions in Hollywood studios, New York hotels and restaurants, New York painters, a machinists lodge, carpenters and several other locals in the San Francisco area, and marginal infiltration through individual office holders in a scattering of locals around the country. The sum and substance of this was that they had emerged from the Stalin-Hitler-pact slough not intact, somewhat battered, but—in tribute to their resiliency—still a faction to be reckoned with.[6]

At first the Party resumed its long-abandoned and profitable popular-front journey. In the first months of 1942, it busied itself with war-bond sales, built up the movement for Russian War Relief, campaigned to free Earl Browder. It howled against strikes "FOR ANY REASONS!" and hurled maledictions at Lewis, whose "opposition to the Roosevelt administration constitutes, in plain English, sabotage of the nation's war effort." It solemnly advised Roosevelt that he had to take stern measures against the Fifth Column. The Party's good works were quickly acknowledged. In May, Roosevelt gave the signal that the Communists were back on board by commuting Browder's sentence "in the interests of national unity." Julius Emspak, of UE, was appointed one of the CIO representatives along with Murray and R. J. Thomas on the Victory Labor Board that met with Roosevelt occasionally. At the CIO convention of that year, Murray came out for the Second Front. At the UAW convention, Victor Reuther introduced the resolution for the Second Front, enthusiastically seconded by Nat Ganley, and passed almost unanimously by the delegates. Harry Bridges was one of the speakers at the convention, and a resolution was adopted asking Roosevelt not to permit Bridges' deportation "in the interests of our nation's war effort." It seemed that Communist rehabilitation was complete. But the Communists did not know when to desist.

It was an evil hour when Browder, like a new convert who wants to impress higher authority with the profundity of his piety and zeal, rushed to champion the cause of incentive pay. The plunge to disaster started with his taking on unsolicited the task of war manager on the home front. As befitted a statesman surveying the entire panorama of war mobilization, one whose thought transcended the narrow preoccupations of this or that economic interest or group, Browder called for a central administration to control and direct the

209

entire economy as a superstate capitalist enterprise. This, at one stroke, would eliminate the cross-purposes, bottlenecks, and confusions bedevilling the production program.

Others outside Communist ranks might have been interested in some such program for national planning, and believed that since the government was becoming the biggest customer, this was a propitious time for introducing the proposal. Even on this assumption, such a presentation could have had a useful impact only if the advocates took into consideration national circumstances, political lineups, and were at pains to move within the orbit of their potential allies. But Browder seemed to have an instinct for self-caricature. His proposition coincided with a press campaign for a czar to be put in full charge of war production, and industrialists and New-Deal-killers found this a handy stick to belabor and undercut "that man" in the White House. Roosevelt had already ridiculed the idea that the country's fate depended on making someone a combination Czar, Pooh-Bah, and Akhoond of Swat. His coolness to the idea stemmed from the knowledge that an all-powerful economic chieftain could usurp his domestic power. As it was, the building of a defense establishment under business aegis had shifted the balance in his disfavor. As explained in the official Bureau of the Budget history, "the issue in large measure was who was going to run the defense program. Given the strength of special interests in American society and the shortage of leaders generally regarded as attached to the national interest, the issue of who was to control was posed sharply by the demand for the appointment of a single defense czar. This suggestion clothed a variety of motives. Some people believed that such an arrangement was absolutely essential but others advocated it in the hope that the President would abdicate a large part of his responsibility to some person more to their liking."

By brushing aside all such mundane preoccupations in favor of undisciplined skywriting, Browder was guaranteeing that his project would get a hearing only within the confines of his own organization. His opus on national planning would have remained another extravagent think-piece to be relegated to the shelves of forgotten works had he not hit on the idea of incentive pay as the key to doubling production. By the end of the year, as he summoned his cohorts to fight for this signal contribution to the war effort, incentive pay became the operative section of his grandiose plan. He knew there were problems in putting it across. He reported to a Communist conference that in instances where workers increased pro-

duction "they find all they have accomplished is to add to the profits
. . . while throwing themselves out of a job for an indefinite period
of time or at least making their employment irregular." He related
that the UE negotiated a piecework program with a major corporation only to have management lower rates in violation of the contract after production was increased. But, like a seeker of the Holy
Grail, the setbacks increased his ardor for the quest, in the course of
which he was revealing a touch of megalomania. "To the extent that
we can bring forward the sharpest posing of the issue of victory, we
will split the bourgeoisie away from the defeatist leadership . . . and
help the bourgeoisie to crystallize the will to victory." He summed
up the problem to another assemblage of New York unionists, "we
have to find out how to make the capitalist system work. And since
the capitalists themselves, who are in charge of that, are not doing a
job that satisfies us, we have to help the capitalists to learn how to
run their own system under war conditions."

It is immaterial where Browder got the idea that Communists
should become crusaders for piecework and speedup. The idea was
in the air at the time. It was talked about by various management
people. An authoritative piece appeared in *Advanced Management*
by Albert Ramond, president of the Bedaux Company, who argued:

> The question of wage incentive plans as a means of stimulating
> increased labor productivity takes on special significance at the
> present time because of the wage stabilization program. We have
> now reached the stage where wage rates for all workers are being
> confined within very narrow limits. . . . Under these circum-
> stances, labor as a whole, including those sections still recalcitrant
> with regard to incentive plans, is likely to take a more sympathe-
> tic view of wage plans making extra pay dependent on extra effort
> or skill.

Ramond hit on the crux of why a campaign at that time might
overcome labor's traditional hostility once workers were confronted
with the alternatives of no more wage increases, or more pay for
more work on an incentive pay system. In October, when wages
were, in effect, frozen, the labor board ruled that individual wage
increases would be allowed when based on increased productivity
arising from piecework or bonus schemes, and the War Production
Board had set up a panel to devise guidelines and procedures. What
had to be beaten down was unionists' opposition arising out of
decades-long dolorous shop experiences. Piecework, incentive, and

bonus systems were generally based on 50-50 sharing; an employee receiving $1-an-hour base rate to produce 10 pieces per hour, would receive $1.25 to produce 15 pieces, not $1.50. More important in the unionist case than operators' not receiving the full benefits of increased production, was that the system led to inequitable wage spreads and differentiations; that managements habitually retimed operations and lowered rates when production was increased; that by pitting workers against each other, the system tended to break down solidarity. Instead of blaming the employer for an inadequate wage, high producers would blame low producers. Hence, the call for the elimination of piecework had been one of the prime objectives of leading CIO unions, and its abolition in auto and other industries was viewed as one of labor's cherished accomplishments. That the Communists became leaders to move the union clock back, that they permitted themselves to become embroiled with labor officials over an issue of this kind can be explained by two theories which are not necessarily mutually exclusive: (1) that Browder was a Mad Hatter directing a membership unaccustomed to talking back; (2) that Communist hearts were in Moscow and Stalingrad. Workers' concerns about production speeds and an extra dime an hour seemed picayune if not frivolous to Communist global strategists when the fate of mankind rested on the Russian battlefronts. In the light of the realities of how decisions were made on lend-lease allocations and troop dispositions, the incentive-pay crusade represented a mating of fatuity with effrontery.[7]

3

Browder's first major success in putting across the piecework line was in the electrical union. This was in the order of things, because Communists dominated the leadership and because this union had never eliminated the system in most shops under its jurisdiction; but what had been considered an unavoidable and temporary evil now became a positive good. Beginning with a pronouncement of the top officers in January, union functionaries kept up a steady bombardment to indoctrinate the ranks. In a special 128-page pamphlet distributed wholesale, the union declared, "We of the UE will produce more than we have ever produced. We will cooperate with industry wherever industry is working to arm the nation." The pamphlet authors noted that there is only "a small percentage of UE plants remaining entirely on straight day work. In some of these the local unions, while desiring to remain on day work, seek means of

212

obtaining increased pay for that extra effort from which their members have not benefitted. In such instances the need is acute for the guidance afforded by the experience gained by a majority of our members in other plants." When the president of General Motors asked the UE to cooperate with the company in establishing an incentive-pay system, Matles answered pointedly, "The majority of GM employees under contract with the UE work under one or another [piecework plan]."

At the end of the year, as we have seen, the CIO convention, under Murray's guidance, demanded the scuttling of the Little Steel formula. The *UE News* dutifully printed the statement of CIO wage policy along with another statement signed by Fitzgerald and Emspak reiterating UE's stand for incentive pay. Using a familiar public-relations technique of argumentation by insinuation, they pretended that the two wage policies were in beautiful harmony. In later years, the anti-Communist rival IUE, set up by the CIO, charged that "the UE held numerous conferences and meetings designed to advance speedup systems . . . UE sanctioned [these] to an extent that they were still in contracts three and four years after the war ended."

The incentive-pay proposition was never brought up directly at the national CIO convention. The UE delegates remained silent in the discussion on wage policy, while the two Communist-liners who spoke, Lewis Merrill of the office union and Reid Robinson of Mine Mill, associated themselves with the official resolution. Only those in the know could sense the undercurrent of animosity within the formal unanimity: Merrill plumped for "political action," Robinson for not becoming confused "by the theme song of Lewis" and for stabilizing and rolling back prices, while Reuther demanded "equal pay for equal work" and R. J. Thomas ridiculed the slogan for a price rollback. Pretending obliviousness to the rude interpolations, Murray presided over the unity. In an earlier CIO executive board meeting, Bridges did have a tiff with Murray. Bridges said the emphasis should be on stricter price control, and Murray answered that there had to be some wage increases to compensate for price increases in order to keep the loyalty of the ranks. But on the whole, Communist union officials finessed the issue inside the national CIO so as not to provoke open clashes with Murray or other accredited national CIO leaders. What the Communists designated in their inflated jargon as the left-center bloc was not to be endangered.

In their own bailiwicks they were less circumspect. Bridges discarded diplomatic niceties when he spoke to the San Francisco CIO Council. (His speech was later used by the IUE to discredit the Communists.) "If we place stress on hours and wages so that we interfere with the fighting," he declared, "we're slackers and selling out our unions and our country. . . . The majority of the time of officers, of grievance committeemen, of the unions as a whole, must go to winning the war. How? Production. I'd rather say speedup, and I mean speedup. The term production covers the boss, government and so on. But speedup covers the workers—the people who suffer from speedup are the workers. To put it bluntly, I mean your unions today must become instruments of speedup of the working class of America." (No wonder the commissars found Bridges hard to handle. He had the unfortunate habit of reducing windy rhetoric to barebone essentials.)[8]

UE involvement and Bridges' tough speeches were all very well, but Browder—his eyes set on national goals—understood that the incentive-pay blitz would fall apart unless it broke out of the confines of the Party-led labor enclave. This led him and his fellow warriors to their ill-fated march on the UAW—by 1943 the largest union in the country and the country's main war producer. A bizarre turn misled Browder into believing that he could stampede the auto union into adopting his scheme, and in the process, dismember the Reuther faction. Communists had scored a coup in winning over Addes and Frankensteen to their way of thinking on this question. Though neither fellow travelers nor clients, the two got hooked because of a miscalculation. Labor leaders, it has to be recalled, particularly in such a volcanic union as the UAW, were in a bind. There was a government wage freeze and job freeze while prices were rising and meaningful collective bargaining was at a minimum. The ranks were restless. More-militant leaders were replacing more-complacent ones in local unions. With Lewis's challenge, wildcat strikes were becoming more prevalent. Buffeted by strong winds, officials were searching for some formula that would relieve the pressure on themselves. Frankensteen was especially sensitive to these currents for he was the aircraft director, and his organization campaign had been dealt a heavy blow when the WLB turned down a requested wage increase for West Coast aircraft workers at the beginning of March. He had to be in a position to offer prospective members something, or aircraft organizing would become bankrupt. As he candidly explained his reasoning to the subsequent auto convention:

214

My job during the past year was to deal with the unorganized workers, trying to bring them into this organization. We have not been able to promise wage increases, but we have promised them . . . a militant, fighting union, and better than 250,000 of them have joined our ranks in the last year. If we were to meet manufacturing companies such as the Grumman company, where they were able to raise wages through incentives . . . I say organization among unorganized workers in this country would come to a standstill, because wages will be granted in unorganized shops and their wages will go so much above the wages of the plants we have organized that we would have to reconsider our policy.

Frankensteen then read a letter of Murray's demonstrating that Murray too was flirting with an incentive-pay program. (The steel industry's pre-union-days system had not been eliminated. Most production workers were still under tonnage or piece rates. Incentive-pay systems also obtained in the clothing, textile, and rubber industries.) Murray's letter, dated July 16, 1943, to Davis, WLB chairman, stated, "I urge the National War Labor Board to establish a Steel Panel for the industry which can proceed to explore the entire situation in the endeavor to have the industry adopt a wage policy which will assure increased production of steel and at the same time afford the steel workers increased earnings for such increased production."*

One incentive for the incentive pay formula therefore was that it would facilitate continued organization of new workers. The other argument, this one taken over from Browder, and stripped by Addes of its spread-eagle fustian, had an equally persuasive ring: since our union favors more production to help the war effort, and since under the government wage freeze workers are not being compensated for their increased production, an incentive-pay plan makes sense. It will permit workers to get more money while bypassing the War Labor Board. Here was a formula to make everybody happy: the government would get more goods; the workers would get more money; the union officials would breathe more easily. Unfortunately for Addes, Frankensteen, and the Communists, the ranks rejected this logic.

At first it appeared that the UAW would dispose of the issue in

---

* Questioned in April about his attitude, Murray had answered that he was personally opposed, but "it is up to the various international unions to decide whether or not they want incentive pay. The CIO is neutral."

routine fashion. At its March 10 meeting the board adopted without contest a motion made by Reuther that the union reaffirm its traditional opposition to incentive plans; where members in a local plant wanted an incentive plan, it would have to conform to certain set standards and be approved by the international union. A committee was then set up to study the matter further. The *Detroit Times* correspondent wrote, "The unanimous vote on Reuther's motion was surprising inasmuch as several board members stated last week that they were in favor of some kind of incentive pay. Their retreat on the issue was probably attributable to an avalanche of protests from rank and file members throughout the country." Six weeks later Frankensteen came to the board's April 19-21 meeting resolved to make a fight. In the interval several things had occurred: Roosevelt issued his "hold the line" order which definitively closed all avenues out of the wage freeze; and the CIO, under Murray's tutelage, to emphasize Lewis's isolation, accepted the policy and officially placed its reliance on the President's promise to roll back prices. (As we have seen, Murray had to change course, or at least, his rhetoric, six months later after the mine demolition of the Little Steel formula.) Frankensteen now proposed that the UAW drop its opposition to incentive pay for the duration of the war. In addition to the other arguments, he warned that if the union did not bite the bullet, the War Production Board would move ahead regardless, fastening unsatisfactory incentive systems on the workers.

This time the board split, the Reuther members succeeding in tabling Frankensteen's motion by a close vote. The UAW was already seething with debate, and literature was freely circulating. In March the Michigan Communist party had sent a letter to the FBI demanding that it "discover and expose" the sponsors of leaflets being distributed in plants throughout the city that accused the Communists of trying "to bring back the Bedaux piecework system." The next day the *Detroit News* carried a forceful statement from Paul Ste. Marie, president of the Ford River Rouge local, that he took public responsibility for the leaflet. When the General Motors Council resolved that the union should oppose "any and all forms of the so-called incentive pay plans," Reuther discarded the conditional position he had sponsored in March, and now advocated opposition with no reservations or exceptions. In regional conferences called by the International at the beginning of May in response to the high excitation, the Addes-Frankensteen proposition was overwhelmingly rejected, and in the most important of the conferences, the one in Detroit, Frankensteen was called upon to with-draw from the War Production panel studying piecework plans.

The Communists decided rashly to press their attack. Browder delivered a violent speech in Detroit, printed as an advertisement in the *Detroit News* in mid-May, in which in Moscow-trial fashion, he lumped together Reuther and Lewis, accused Reuther of "con-ducting the same type of wrecking in the airplane and automotive industry," and of blocking the incentive-pay solution by "unprinci-pled demagogy and lying propaganda." Then he pronounced the anathema, as though he were the power he imagined himself to be: "Labor will be unable to give leadership until it settles accounts de-cisively with Lewis, Reuther and Co." With the determination of lemmings, the Communists now pushed into the surf and dragged a bemused Addes and Frankensteen along with them.

When it came to questions of production and wage rates, the lowly worker had a better grasp of realities than officials manipulat-ing large abstractions. He knew that neither he nor his union was the decision-maker in setting production schedules and devising basic company policy, that the elevated talk about "guarantees" and "no cutting of standards" would evaporate in the heat of the shop assembly lines. Workers did not want to be speeded up for the benefit of increased company profits during the war; they feared working themselves out of jobs after the war; and they had a Darwinian concern for their own health and life span. Patriotic rhetoric did not alter the fact that the previous employee-employer economic relationship remained intact. In the world of manufactur-ing plants and shops, production rates were being set and argued about in the manner that they had been set and argued about in prewar days. Workers had no more intention than employers of making patriotism and production rates interchangeable.

It may be doubted that the introduction of new incentive plans or patriotic exhortations to produce more led to higher labor produc-tivity. Labor productivity is the grand result of numerous factors, many of which are outside the individual worker's ability to deter-mine or regulate. Most economists believe that labor productivity growth actually declined in the war years from the previous decade. Dewhurst estimated that output per man-hour rose possibly 1.5 per cent each year between 1940 and 1944, the peak year of the war ef-fort, so that "average productivity of the entire working force may have increased less rapidly than usual, if indeed it increased at all." Where output per man-hour increased dramatically on tanks,

217

airplanes, and ships, it was due to the application of automobile assembly techniques, not new technology or patriotic exertion. The
overall growth falloff, in turn, was due to causes other than the refusal of workers to bestir themselves: manufacture, under wartime
necessity, of high-cost innovative or synthetic products, dilution of
the work force, lengthening of the work week, etc. It would appear
that the campaign was wrongheaded from a trade-union point of
view, and largely irrelevant as it related to increasing production.

In his verbal assault, Browder included the charge that "[Reuther]
has also created an ominous wave of strike sentiment." There was an
element of truth here in that agitation against piecework, WLB rulings, employer stonewalling, added to the general unrest. Why did
Reuther, who was up to the brim in war-mobilization activities and,
because of his effectiveness, had been offered the post of deputy to
Ferdinand Eberstadt (a major power on the War Production Board),
seize the incentive-pay issue to stage another Donnybrook Fair?
Why was he able to carry his faction, with its many conservative
adherents, with him?

Reuther was trying to carve out a middle-of-the-road position for
himself. On the one hand, assessing the mood of the ranks more accurately than his rivals, he was placing himself at the head of the
militant oppositionists. In opposing incentive pay—which became a
symbol of militancy, a resolve to do something to alleviate the many
frustrations of the previous year and a half—he was also announcing
his determination to resist and upset Washington's wage- and manpower freeze. On the other hand, he refused to move out of the
orbit of the CIO leadership, and rebuffed his more leftward followers by standing shoulder to shoulder with Murray, Addes, and
Frankensteen in repudiating Lewis and condemning the mine
strikes. As for the conservatives in his own faction, opposition to
piecework was one of the auto union verities; it did not impinge on
larger political loyalties.

It was Richard Gosser—the board member from Toledo who
epitomized business unionism, and was shown up a few years hence
for financial corruption—who made the most provocatively radical
talk at the 1943 convention. "Are we," he demanded to know, "the
almighty militant UAW that we speak of? If we are . . . let us unite
ourselves on this basis, that we throw the Little Steel formula to the
hell out, that we either correct the War Labor Board or throw it to
the hell out, that we stabilize the wages in this industry and that we

don't say to our membership, 'Work like hell so you can make a couple of more pennies.' "

The Reuther forces had been handed a winning issue by the Addes-Frankensteen-Communist combination, and they were resolved not to be deprived of it. When Addes realized that popular sentiment was going against him, the minority of the resolutions committee came in with a very watered-down report in which it tried to shift the issue to the question of local autonomy. When that did not get far in the ensuing debate, the minority amended its report to prohibit international officers from promoting incentive plans. With that, the two reports were almost indistinguishable. (The *Daily Worker* called the minority amendment "opportunistic.") Victor Reuther, the resolutions committee chairman, tried to stop the maneuver. Then he drew back for fear of having the issue lost in procedural disputations, concluding that the lines of demarcation had been drawn anyhow. He was not mistaken. The majority report was carried by a clear voice vote.

What was taking place off the convention floor was more compelling than the speeches being made at the convention. For several days, Reutherites kept the delegates in high hilarity and swept the boards with a jingle sung to the tune of "Reuben and Rachel." The first two stanzas of an endless number (some of them unprintable) went:

> Who are the boys who take their orders
>   Straight from the office of Joe Stalin?
> No one else but the gruesome twosome,
>   George F. Addes and Frankensteen.
> Who are the boys that fight for piecework,
>   To make the worker a machine?
> No one else but the gruesome twosome,
>   George F. Addes and Frankensteen.

Indignant Communist delegates tried to get R. J. Thomas to confiscate the song sheets on no less portentous grounds than that "they cast slurs upon the integrity of our great Russian ally" and were "harmful to the unity of the United Nations." That did not help their cause any. The Addes braintrusters then commissioned a lyricist in their camp to work up a competing jingle:

> You have given the workers nothing
>   Except hot air and lots of steam,

219

And when the votes have all been counted
  We'll still have Addes and Frankensteen!
You have fought a dirty battle,
  You've yelled RED, you've lied and schemed.
We know you by this time Reuther
  So we'll take Addes and Frankensteen!

But by common consent of the literary critics among the neutrals and attending newspapermen, the Addes-Frankensteen product was not on a par with the Reuther offering. The "gruesome twosome" represented the triumphant fusion of policy and poetry.

The incentive-pay controversy almost gave Reuther the coveted prize. Leonard again ran against Addes and was edged out by the vote of 3,746 to 3,676, a bare 70 votes out of 7,422 cast. This time Reuther won the first vice-presidency over Frankensteen by 347 votes, 3,881 to 3,534. But when Leonard tried to win the other vice-presidency by running against Frankensteen, he was voted down by 255 votes, 3,842 to 3,587. Many neutrals were still there, and still did not intend to hand over national leadership to one faction.

By their bumbling and miscalculation, Addes and Frankensteen had almost dispossessed themselves from their offices (although the lineup on the new executive board was little changed). Communist intervention had cost the Addes-Frankensteen faction dearly, and for the Communists themselves, it was a disaster. They bore most of the blame for the ill-starred proposal, and their reputation in the UAW, which had plumbed new depths in 1941, suffered a blow from which they never recovered. Roy Hudson, a Party trade-union expert, by comparing the convention vote with the vote for incentive pay at an earlier union conference, determined to his own satisfaction that "the convention showed that the struggle for a union incentive wage policy is gaining ground and those who oppose such a policy are losing ground." It is possible that he took his pronouncement seriously since the Communists often dwelt in a make-believe world of their own creation. Years later, Ganley wryly admitted that Reuther's "most effective slogan was 'Down with Earl Browder's piecework.' "[9]

4

Because of the thin margin by which Addes was reelected, there was speculation in the Reuther camp, in the course of convention post-mortems, that he had been saved by the Black vote. There were 150 Black delegates at the convention representing approximately 400 to 500 votes, and a majority of these were cast for Addes. Of course, in an election won by a narrow margin, it is easy to point to this or that bloc or sub-group without whose support the results would have been reversed. Since Addes was re-elected by 51 percent of the total convention vote, the focus has to be on the nature of his entire majority, without which all accretions would have had no consequence. Communist advocacy of special Black representation, taken up by the Addes faction, shook the convention nonetheless; similar proposals were to disturb different unions in subsequent years; and because of the nerves it touched on, the issue had social significance inside and outside the labor movement going beyond the maneuvers for advantage of two sets of caucus politicians.

The riot that had taken place in Detroit determined the nature of the convention debate. As soon as Michigan became a major war production center, there was an ingathering of masses of new workers, many from the South. By mid-1941 in Detroit alone there were over 350,000 new workers, 50,000 of them Blacks. No provisions worth talking about had been made to accomodate the newcomers. All facilities were monstrously overcrowded; there was an acute housing shortage; the Blacks, who were forced into decaying, infested ghetto slums and were hemmed in by walls of hatred, turned sullen. Here and there, flurries of wildcat strikes staged by White workers opposing the transference and employment of Blacks on defense work agitated the industrial scene. The growing antagonisms, flourishing wherever war industries attracted many workers of both races, found release in early 1942 over the Sojourner Truth government housing project, intended for Black occupancy.

An armed mob surrounded the buildings when the first tenants tried to move in. The project was thereupon closed down and remained closed while the city fathers procrastinated, and dispatches flew between Detroit and Washington as bureaucrats sought a compromise solution. Only in April, on new Washington instructions, was adequate protection provided by several hundred state troopers to allow the Black families to occupy the premises. That did not quiet the city. Tensions between Blacks and Whites continued to mount and skirmishes became commonplace. A year later, in April 1943, 25,000 Whites struck at the Packard plant in retaliation for a brief sit-down of Blacks protesting their not being promoted, and R. J. Thomas was jeered when he tried to get the strikers to return to work. In June the accumulating social dynamite set off the blast of a major race riot that went on for three days, resulted in 34 dead, hundreds injured, millions of dollars lost in property damage, and was only quelled when federal troops were moved in. The conduct of all UAW officials was exemplary in trying to defuse the hostilities.* Later, they boasted that while the streets were gory with blood, there was no violence in the plants, presumably because of the beneficent effects of trade-union education. The fact that a majority of White and Black workers were absent from the plants because they were doing mighty battle in the streets probably accounted for the plants remaining "an oasis of sanity in a city gone mad."

That same month, White servicemen stationed in and around Los Angeles stormed through the Mexican districts for four days, assaulting the so-called zoot-suiters, beating them up, stripping off their clothing, and chopping off their hair. (Many lower-class Mexican youths, caught between rival traditions, sought status in their own ethnic "Pachuco" gangs, adapting as their own a distinctive costume that had originated in Harlem. The costume generally consisted of a long jacket, trousers tightly pegged at the cuff and deeply pleated at the waist, long hair sometimes gathered in a ducktail covered by a broad felt hat.) The city police, following the mobs, looked the other way while the mayhem was in progress, jailed the victims, not the attackers, and the Hearst *Herald and Express*, suffering from the same misdirected vision, blamed the riots on zoot-suiter hoodlums. Shortly after, on August 1, at the other end of the country, Harlem exploded when a false rumor spread that a White

---

* The CIO changed the face of race relations in American unionism. The affiliated unions opened their doors to all Black workers on an equal basis. Gone were the constitutional bars, segregated locals, secret Jim Crow rituals that disfigured the AFL and Railroad Brotherhoods. It was an achievement of the first order. The limitations were twofold: (1) Preoccupied with winning bargaining rights, the CIO did not concern itself with employers' hiring practices. Hence, what was won benefitted only those with jobs. Since Blacks were discriminated against at the hiring gate, comparatively few were able to profit from initial CIO accomplishments; (2) Inside the unions, the nondiscrimination policy often looked better on parchment than in practice. Age-old ingrained prejudices and disabilities could not be wiped out overnight. Gunnar Myrdal thought in 1942 that CIO officials would face the alternative of either "following rank-and-filers' anti-Negro attitude or being exchanged for new leaders." The problem proved more tractable on a shop and union basis. A modus vivendi was fashioned that lasted for the next two and a half decades. The color-caste system in hiring and job allocation was moderated, and other less manageable complications were pushed out of sight.

policeman had killed a Black soldier. The root cause, here as in Detroit, was the Blacks' frustration and restiveness: the war rhetoric for
the Four Freedoms and the brave new world to be was making them
increasingly impatient with their second-class status. Under New
York Mayor LaGuardia's open-minded leadership, 1,500 Black volunteers were deputized for police duty, and the police acted with
circumspection. Nonetheless, before the rioting was over, six Blacks
were dead and 300 injured.

The scene was therefore set at the convention in October for a
tumultuous encounter as the two factions brought in opposing reports on Black representation. The Constitution Committee minority (Addes group) report, presented by Ganley, proposed a special
minorities department headed by a Black, to be elected by the entire convention, who would be a full member of the executive
board. To placate the opposition, Ganley made a verbal concession
by removing the mandatory provision that the director had to be a
Black. Instead, he declared that he was confident that the convention "would want to demonstrate to the entire nation our policy of
racial solidarity by electing a Negro member to this post." The
majority (Reuther group) report proposed a minorities department
with the director to be appointed by the president with the approval
of the executive board. It appeared as if the difference between the
two reports was secondary. In actuality, the undercurrents of racial
antagonism—the auto union, no less than other institutions of
American society, understood these inadequately, and was trying to
control them by flimsy devices—surfaced in the convention with
these two presentations.

Because both reports were tangential to what was confronting the
union, the remarks from speakers on both sides dealt glancing
blows, if any, to the problem at hand. Later, when a resolution was
unanimously recommended by the resolutions committee opposing
racial discrimination and calling for disciplining instigators of "hate
strikes," the tide of white bigotry broke through the conven-
tionalities. An unidentified delegate from Detroit stated, "I have no
objection to the Negro participation in our economic life, but I do
not believe that this convention should go on record as endorsing
their participation in social life . . . I would never go to any union
function and take my wife and daughter when they were supposed
to mingle with the Negro race." The convention at this point was
close to pandemonium. Another delegate from Milwaukee said: "I
have nothing against the Negro race, but I think it is just incidents

223

like this, resolutions of this kind, that bring these things to a head.
. . . It is unnecessary to have these things brought up in a convention
to get everybody heated." A delegate from the Detroit Dodge local
also held that the resolution should never have been introduced. "It
has no business on this floor. . . . Have you got guts enough to go
back and tell your rank and file that you voted for the colored
people, that they have social rights equal with you? . . . In regard to
the locals disciplining people in local unions for taking a stand . . .
[that] is a joke . . . Some locals will follow it, yes, but will the majority follow it? You know and I know that they won't. It gets my goat
to see these things passed annually. To what purpose? What is
gained by it?" This *cri de coeur* provoked Victor Reuther to declare:
"I think it has reached a very bad state of affairs when things that we
write into our constitution are publicly mentioned as a joke that no
one takes seriously. Your committee does not think that passing a
resolution by this convention is going to solve the racial problems
that we have in our unions, in our industry, and in our public life,
but at least we ought to have the guts to spell out a program that will
act as a guide."

The delegates exhibited a frustration in which bigotry vied with
bafflement, in which sullenness was reinforced by the conviction
that both sides were using the Negro issue as political grist. The
convention was in disorder through most of the debate, and at the
conclusion the delegates voted down by voice vote both the Reuther
majority and Addes minority propositions.

Since the leaders of both caucuses called for a special minorities
department, it might seem logical that the two would have tried to
reconcile their viewpoints. But Walter Reuther insisted that the
dispute covered a matter of high principle. "The other morning," he
stated, "before the election of officers, 80 Negro delegates met up-
stairs and Brother Frankensteen and Brother Leonard and myself
were asked to come up there and state our positions, and I said to
those Negro brothers in all sincerity that my opposition to this
Negro Board Member at large was a principled matter . . . I said
that even though I didn't get a single vote of a Negro delegate I
stood opposed to this because of the principle involved." What was
this principle that transcended votes? According to Reuther, the
minority device represented "reverse Jim Crowism." Victor
Reuther earlier explained: "If there is a special post for Negroes,
then in all justice there should be a post for the Catholics, the

224

women, the Jews, the Poles, and all the rest. That is not in keeping with democracy or true trade unionism."

The argument of "reverse Jim Crowism" was widely used in the forties and had general credence among liberals and progressive unionists. It was considered to be a ringing affirmation of the liberal creed of equal rights for all, special privileges for none. It was on a par with bourgeois equality before the law. It was no part of the liberal imagination of the time that formal equality was undermined by social and economic inequalities, or that Blacks' traditional disabilities would remain untouched unless special provisions were made on their behalf. Only in the sixties, after cities were burning and squads of desperadoes gutted sections of ghettos, did the country become aware that the rhetoric of equality would not suffice, that special measures were in order if civil strife was to be avoided or abated.

Part of the Reutherite animosity came from the Communist sponsorship of the Negro board member proposition. This was, for Clayton Fountain, "an unscrupulous maneuver." "We Reutherites took our stand for the promotion or upgrading of the Negro . . . because we really believed in equality. The Communists fought the same kind of battle because they wanted to win the support of Negroes for the CP line." Horace Sheffield, a Black Reutherite from the Ford River Rouge local, made a similar accusation on the convention floor. "There are those who sent this resolution to the Constitution Committee who have no interest and no desire to see the minority problem worked out. . . . I consider the Negro in this convention has been made the victim of political demagoguery." Were Fountain and Sheffield right? Assessing human motives is always a hazardous enterprise, all the more so when factions are fishing for votes. The general argument that Communists were insincere, not really interested in the welfare of the Black or worker, only trying to exploit legitimate grievances for their own ends, was tainted. Communists tried to "use" people the way all politicians try to manipulate people for their own purposes. But in their case, the purpose was not personal aggrandizement or self-seeking; they had courageously championed the Black cause when to do so was as popular or rewarding as the championship of Christianity in the time of Nero. If they fought fanatically and often unscrupulously to win people to the Party line, it was because they thought that on that line humanity was destined to advance to its salvation. There are

225

moral ambiguities and ambivalences in all behavior, and we do not know that finding a common language with some white supremacists in their midst was entirely alien to a number of Reuther caucus organizers.[10]

With that said, it must be admitted that there was demagogy in Communists' wearing the Gracchian mantle during the war. Anti-Communist Black reformers charged them with wanting to suspend the struggle for Negro rights in the interests of uninterrupted war production. Wilson Record, who tried to tie together the available evidence, stated, "For most of the war [the Communist party's] main activity was to stifle Negro protest and to urge black workers and soldiers to get into line on the white man's terms, just as it urged unions to get on with the production job, on the bosses' terms if necessary." And again, "by late 1943 the party's Uncle Tomism had become so transparent that its leaders felt that at least a few gestures should be made toward advancing Negro rights. To that end the Communists used such organizations as the NNC [National Negro Congress] and the SNYC [Southern Negro Youth Congress] to launch occasional protests against racial discrimination in the military and in industry. Such objections, however, were feeble, and when some party project threatened to develop into strenuous opposition which might even remotely endanger production or military effectiveness, the Stalinists were willing to protest for the record and then hastily call the whole thing off."

The initial setback for the Communists was their isolation from the March-on-Washington movement, the most effective gathering of Black dissent in the early years. It meant that Blacks were finding new spokesmen to sponsor mass actions, and that Communists had lost the monopoly in their chosen field. At first the Communists criticized A. Philip Randolph because the movement was not radical enough to suit them. This was still in the first months of 1941. Randolph was preparing for a mass march on Washington in the midst of defense mobilization to demand jobs in industry for Blacks because despite the calls for more production, Blacks at this time were being systematically excluded. Myrdal pointed out that by April 1941 Employment Service placements for nonwhites had fallen to 2.5 percent, and that some industries, like aircraft, were totally closed to Negroes. Thus, Randolph centered his attention on jobs; the defense program he took for granted as an objective reality. That did not satisfy the Communists; because he was not opposing defense preparations for an imperialist war, they worked him over.

Next, Roosevelt succumbed to the Randolph threat and promulgated Executive Order No. 8802 setting up the Fair Employment Practices Committee (FEPC). This was on June 25, three days after the imperialist war had become the people's war. Now the Communists had a different objection. The mass meeting held in Madison Square Garden in mid-1942 showed dangerous tendencies: "The general tenor of the speeches were anti-Administration and anti-white. This caused grave concern . . . regarding its dangers to the war effort. . . . The progressive forces . . . were more than ever convinced of the need of taking steps to unite the Negro people for support of the war and for winning greater rights" (*Communist*, July 1943). What were the Communists, in the guise of the "progressive forces," so disturbed about? Randolph and the NAACP leaders were integrationists, liberals, and in friendly association with CIO and Roosevelt administration officials. Not one of them was a Debsian or pacifist opponent of the war, not one a separatist. The Communists were disturbed because they were being excluded from the festivities. Randolph, the man who originated the March-on-Washington idea and ran the organization, was on their hate list. He had dealt their National Negro Congress a body blow when he demonstratively resigned as president in 1940 and slammed the door behind him with a ringing anti-Communist declaration. He was on the other side of their barricades once he set up the March-on-Washington movement that kept them out.

But his movement declined after it accomplished its main purpose, and neither Randolph nor the NAACP leaders had the continual relationship with Black masses that CIO leaders had with their ranks. The Communist party proceeded to stake out positions in different localities and organizations battling for Negro rights by varied and energetically pursued efforts. Record's conclusions are valid, but they are not the whole story. It is well to grasp that in the labor movement, though the Communists lost heavily in the auto and other unions after advocating piecework, elsewhere they either retained strength or advanced their fortunes by other activities. So was it among Blacks whose organizations lacked labor's cohesiveness, and whose aspirations found expression in many groups and forms. It was a distinction for the Party when Benjamin Davis was elected in 1943 the first Black councilman in New York City on the Communist ticket. It was a matter of symbolic importance to Blacks across the country in those years that Paul Robeson was appearing on Broadway in *Othello* and delivering a stage kiss to a white Des-

227

demona. Communists found favor among Black activists in unions by repeatedly and forcefully advancing their demands, many less controversial than the proposition put forward in the auto union. Ray Marshall's researches led him to conclude "that almost every organization that adopted special equalitarian racial machinery [during the war] either was Communist-dominated or had a strong Communist faction." On the political front, Vito Marcantonio, unofficial communist-front representative in Congress, stepped forward as the redoubtable champion of FEPC. From the time that he introduced the first FEPC bill in June 1941 to the end of the war, he was in the forefront and in the limelight, lending his considerable parliamentary skills to jousting in Congress with white supremacists and industry surrogates.

So, while one cannot take issue with Record's assertion that "the party in the Negro community never recovered from its wartime desertion of the racial struggle"—and this is indirectly confirmed by Philip S. Foner, the Party's own apologist—it should not be taken to mean that the Communists did not retain some status and influence among certain groups. Many were not aware of the fluctuations and nuances of Party policy, and most Blacks were not affected by growing public rejection of Communists to the same extent as were Whites. Most Blacks mistrusted the Communist party because they were suspicious of all White organizations. But they were too alienated from American society to embrace readily the anti-Communist convictions of middle-class NAACP officials or Harlem intellectuals. Hence, the emergent postwar picture was muddier than committed protagonists understood. Communist recruitment figures are of limited usefulness as an index of Black feeling; for whatever they are worth, they show no falling off of appeal in the war years. In 1935-1936 Black recruitment was 15-17 percent of the total; in 1943, 31 percent; in 1944, 37 percent. However, Black membership turnover was even more extreme than white. Black membership, reported as 5,000 in 1938 after a big recruitment drive, was 3,200 in 1942, some 7 percent of the total, and the percentage probably never rose much despite continued recruitment. But membership turnover was another story not necessarily related to the Party's standing in Black communities.[11]

8. Lewis, flanked by Murray and Hillman, founding CIO convention, Pittsburgh, November 14-18, 1938.

9. Automobile tie-up employed to block access to Ford River Rouge plant, April 1941.

10. Sixteen thousand UE members walk out at Westinghouse plant in East Pittsburgh, April 1951, to protest suspension of a shop steward.

11. Communist-led group demonstrates against Curran administration of National Maritime Union, 1948.

12. Police intervene in battle between AFL Seamen and CIO Marine Cooks and Stewards at a San Francisco pier, 1953.

13. Harry Bridges (right), International Longshoremen's president, before a House Labor subcommittee in connection with a West Coast dock strike.

14. John Bugas, for Ford Motor Company, and Walter Reuther, for UAW, at a contract-signing, June 1951, that first established the Supplemental Unemployment Benefit Plan.

NINE · *War Years—II*

ALL through the war yeoman efforts were under way to transform the Communist party into an accepted fixture of American political life. The strategies of the popular-front thirties were pushed to extremes in all major fields. As soon as Browder took over the reins again on his release from prison, he proceeded to buttress the Party's agitation for a *union sacrée* with a theoretical justification. In *Victory and After*, which became the Party's ideological guide, the rationale for the new orientation was spelled out:

> The prevailing "American way of life," which is dominated by its capitalist foundation in many and most decisive ways, determines that our national unity cannot find expression in the forms and modes followed by the Soviet peoples . . . In the United States, national unity can be achieved only through compromise between the conflicting interests, demands, and aspirations of various class groupings (primarily between those usually spoken of as "capital and labor"), a compromise which agrees to reach at least a provisional settlement of all disputes through arbitration. The motive power behind such a compromise can only be something which all parties hold in common—that is, patriotism, the common determination to win the war. . . .

> The Communist Party of the United States has completely subordinated its own ideas as to the best possible social and economic system for our country . . . to the necessity of uniting the entire nation, including the biggest capitalists. . . . The Communist Party of the United States foresees that out of victory for the United Nations will come a peace which will be guaranteed by the cooperation of the United States, the Soviet Union, Britain and China. . . . This will make possible the solution of reconstruction problems with a minimum of social disorder and civil violence. . . . We offer our cooperation to all like-minded persons and groups.

When Roosevelt, Churchill and Stalin issued their joint declaration at Teheran at the end of 1943, Browder saw this "as the greatest turning point in all history," verifying his original perspective. It meant to him that the United States and Britain had "closed the books finally and forever" on opposition to the Soviet Union. Foreseeing and banking everything on a long-term postwar collaboration, Browder proposed to make the "Teheran Agreement," as he interpreted it, the touchstone of American Communist policy. It was in this spirit that he uttered his winged phrase, "If J. P. Morgan supports this coalition, I as a Communist am prepared to clasp his hand and join with him in realizing it. Class divisions or political groupings have no significance now."

Naturally, the Party internal mechanism had to be restructured to suit the new ideology. Williamson, the wartime organization secretary, reported how this was to be done:

> Too often the branch is bogged down in old practices and routines, and while intensely active, separates its branch activities from the win-the-war neighborhood activities of the community. The branches which are exceptions to this general weakness, with their public participation in service flag dedications, salvaging metal and rubber scrap, setting up booths to sell war bonds . . . and mobilizing the neighborhood for blood donation, show the greatest possibilities for establishing the closest ties with their neighborhoods through serving their country's war effort.

Since one after another Marxistic obstacle to the realization of national unity had been discarded as unnecessary ballast, the question inevitably arose: was not the existence of a separate Communist party itself a bar to the perfect realization of post-Teheran cooperation? As brought out earlier, Browder did not shrink from the consequences of his analysis, nor did the lieutenants drag their feet. At his behest, the convention converted itself into an unobjectionable association "of Americans which, basing itself upon the working class, carries forward the traditions of Washington, Jefferson, Paine, Jackson and Lincoln, under the changed conditions of modern industrial society."*

* To anticipate the later story, toward war's end Browder was denounced for all manner of deviations and removed from leadership. (See Philip J. Jaffe, "The Rise and Fall of Earl Browder," *Survey*, Spring 1972, pp. 42, 52-54, 59-62.) This was due to a Kremlin intrigue to make sure that the American party got no exalted notions of its own independence, not because his wartime activities cut across the Stalinist course. Not only were they in consonance with the policies enunciated by the international Communist press and with those followed by the French party policy-setter, but Browder also received a number of approving signals from abroad. When in

Many on the outside watching these incongruous proceedings thought the transformation of Stalinist revolutionaries into Fourth-of-July populists was no more than a cynical masquerade. They failed to take into account the hypnotic state of the participants. Repeated ideological shock treatments had housebroken the Communists into overdeveloped operators and underdeveloped thinkers. They had become politicians for whom tactics were everything while the purpose of the tactics was entrusted to the keeping of higher authority. The complacency with which they turned away from their older tradition was due to their being seduced as well as induced. They were seduced by visions of power. After years of rough voyaging, they caught the glimpse of the heroic Party, now accepted on all sides at its true worth, leading serried millions to the morning; 1944 was the year when the wartime popular front attained its zenith; and the Communists thought they were on their way. Just as the formation of the CIO had provided them with unprecedented opportunities in industrial unions, so the CIO's major electoral campaign could give them the opening for a political breakthrough.[1]

The CIO executive board set up in July 1943 a Political Action Committee (PAC), and Murray appointed Hillman to head it. Both of them were frightened by the passage of the Smith-Connally anti-strike law and the hostility manifested toward labor by preponderant sections of Congress. They were concerned that if labor's response in 1944 would be as apathetic as it had been in 1942, more punitive legislation might be in the offing. They agreed between themselves that a supreme effort was called for to ensure a fourth term for Roosevelt and the election of liberals to Congress, a resolve fortified by a subsidiary need to discourage dissidents from launching labor- or third parties. The Michigan state CIO convention, meeting the

---

January 1944 he moved to reorganize the Party into a political association, Foster took the occasion to criticize Browder's so-called Teheran thesis, only to be roundly upbraided by other members of the national committee. He then asked Browder to send his private letter of disagreement to Dimitrov, which Browder transmitted to Moscow in code. Dimitrov sent back a reply to Foster through Browder to withdraw his opposition. At about this time Browder also received a letter from André Marty, the French Communist leader who had gone from his refuge in Moscow to Algiers to become part of De Gaulle's provisional government. Marty praised Browder's presentation which he had just read in *Inprecorr* as a "beautiful speech," and informed him that "we are now publishing it in our theoretical magazine." In the Communist communication system by smoke signals, this meant that Browder had Moscow's blessings.

231

week before, which had defied them on the no-strike pledge, had also declared that the Roosevelt cause could best be advanced through an independent labor party, and there were similar flareups elsewhere. Murray gave the campaign a big sendoff at that year's convention. His introduction of Hillman was like a fanfare of trumpets, "a great labor leader and a distinguished American." Hillman gave a long rousing speech in which he announced that affiliated unions had sent in $700,000 to get the good work under way. When he finished his remarks, Murray was again profusely complimentary: "All hail to president Hillman and the members of his committee! . . . Thank you, president Hillman, for your magnificent report, and I believe that I can definitely assure you the wholehearted cooperation of every unit affiliated with the CIO." It was clear that the convention was not adopting another pious resolution. The CIO meant business.

With the formation of the PAC Hillman returned to the scene as a national leader for the first time since he had been discarded by Roosevelt when the OPM was replaced by the War Production Board. He had suffered a heart attack, possibly brought on by his humiliation, and had thought at the time that his active life was over. Now, seeing the PAC as his big opportunity for a comeback, he was determined to make a success of it. He was convinced that if the PAC was to be as big as he envisaged it for 1944 and beyond, it would need the energy and zeal of trained, dedicated people. With that thought, the alliance with the Communists was inevitable. He had the identical need that Lewis did several years before, and there was no other group to turn to for this kind of support. True, the CIO was a large organization now; it could mount a respectable political campaign by utilizing its organizers and committeemen. For a spectacular effort, however, that was not enough, and Hillman knew it. For a spectacular effort, he had to have the self-sacrifice and fervor of a sizable ginger group, one that could bring into the enterprise the fresh capital of prominent figures, middle-class left-liberals, philanthropists, and the like. Not only did he make the same kind of decision that Lewis had made, and for the same reason, but, like Lewis, he was also completely confident that he was the hunter and would get the bird.[2]

There were no formal meetings between Hillman and Communist officials; none were required. It was done by signals, and almost at once the Communists knew where they stood. A national PAC headquarters was set up in New York; John Abt, a Communist lawyer, formerly with the NLRB and counsel for the Amalgamated Clothing union, became PAC's attorney and Hillman's assistant. Pressman was enlisted as co-counsel. J. Raymond Walsh, a popular-frontist and former Harvard faculty member, took over as research director. C. B. (Beanie) Baldwin, a resourceful executive and reliable Party-liner, who had served under Wallace in the Department of Agriculture, became assistant chairman. He was the day-to-day administrator who directed the activities of the 135 full-time workers in the national and regional offices. Communist union officials and members functioned through regular PAC committees set up by their respective unions. In those that they dominated, they sponsored and directed the entire undertaking. The 162-page *UE Guide to Political Action* showed that they had made a close study of legal technicalities and vote-getting techniques; it was not a generalized inspirational tract, but a tightly knit "how to do it" manual full of practical suggestions and specific information. Similar materials poured out of other CP-led unions. Particularly useful for their labors were the many CIO industrial union councils that they controlled in part or in whole, since central labor bodies customarily busied themselves with political activities.

The CIO-PAC was only part of the operation. In June 1944, Hillman set up an additional organization, the National Citizens Political Action Committee. This organization was a convenient device to get around one of the provisions of the Smith-Connally Act prohibiting labor organizations from making contributions in federal elections. The other more important reason for its being was to surmount the CIO limitation, to make the PAC evangelical effort an all-national one with an appeal to professional, civic, and consumer groups. The Citizens was formally a non-CIO, independent organization, in practice an adjunct of the PAC; Hillman chaired both, and Baldwin was no less dominant in the one than in the other. Because the new outfit was nominally independent, however, both Hillman and the Communists could let themselves go. Hillman, the favorite labor leader of liberals and social workers in the twenties, had accumulated connections and enormous expertise on how to work with representatives of other milieus. The Communists we know about. The community leaders they enrolled under the Citizens banner made the old American League Against War and Fascism look like a scrub team. George W. Norris, the redoubtable, aged senator, became honorary chairman; other officers and board members included James Patton, head of the National Farmers Union,

Freda Kirchwey, publisher of the *Nation*, Elmer Benson, ex-governor of Minnesota, Gifford Pinchot, ex-governor of Pennsylvania, A. F. Whitney, president of the Brotherhood of Railroad Trainmen, Max Lerner, editorial director of *PM*, an assortment of philanthropic big-business men and bankers, various CIO dignitaries, and many others.

The Communists ran the Citizens administratively, but it was not a fellow-traveling organization. Hillman stood at its head, and had to be heeded. He was no less sensitive to the nuances than were Communist or fellow-traveler organizers, and they were no more prone to try to outwit him than Pressman would try to outwit Lewis or Murray in the CIO office. Just as Lewis used mine union officials in early CIO campaigns to provide himself with a loyal skeleton bureaucracy, so Hillman drew into leadership tested Amalgamated union wheel horses who would guard the portals and protect his interests.

To get from under both Hillman's and Murray's supervision, the Communists, in a brilliant stroke, set up still another organization, this one of an elite nature, the Independent Voters Committee of the Arts and Sciences, later renamed Independent Citizens Committee of the Arts, Sciences, and Professions. Ordinarily, this would have been a subdivision of the Citizens, but as an independent organization, it enjoyed a twofold advantage for the Communists' purposes. It could rally support and raise funds as a de facto division of the CIO-led crusade; and it was free of any control. Headed by Jo Davidson, the sculptor, it was directed by Hannah Dorner, a New York theatrical agent, a Party-line organizer of exceptional ability. Employing freely the techniques and allures of the advertising and entertainment worlds, the ICC-ASP was soon graced by a board of directors ranging from Eddie Cantor, Bette Davis, and Lillian Hellman, on to Albert Einstein and Harlow Shapley. It put on spectaculars, excited the citizenry with glamor figures, and raised money. This was a recrudescence of the fellow-traveler "cultural front" on a more rewarding basis than ever before. The Writers Congresses of the thirties could not hold a candle to it; Orson Welles and Edward G. Robinson were greater drawing cards for the public than Granville Hicks or Theodore Dreiser; and the motley assemblage of "names" and "stars" took readily to the popular-front patter of progressivism and patriotism ,and, unlike a James T. Farrell or a Dwight MacDonald, did not worry about the role of artists and writers in Russia or changes in Communist partry policies.[3]

234

In the first months of 1944, compelled by the exigencies of building a mass movement, Hillman sealed his alliance with the Communists in blood. When the PAC was initiated, Hillman recognized that the American Labor Party (ALP) in New York was indispensable for the realization of his master plan. He and Dubinsky had been the god-fathers of the party launched in 1936 to corral the then Socialist vote in the state for Roosevelt. The party won a balance-of-power position in electoral contests, but was split down the middle since Stalin-Hitler-pact days. Dubinsky and his allies were in control of the governing state committee; the left wing, led by Congressman Marcantonio, and Curran and Quill of the CIO, controlled the New York metropolitan organization. In the summer of 1943 Hillman proposed to Dubinsky, and his lieutenant, Alex Rose, that the state committee be reorganized to permit a fairer representation for all unions supporting the party. He argued that cooperation between right and left factions was necessary to underwrite a Roosevelt victory in the event of a close election. Dubinsky promptly rejected Hillman's proposal. According to Dubinsky's biographer, "While innocent on its face, this plan . . . meant the swamping of the party by Communist-controlled union groups and the practical exclusion from leadership of all liberal and progressive elements unaffiliated with labor unions." Of course, the main issue between Hillman and Dubinsky was permitting or not permitting Communist participation. Complicating it was also a long history of personal rivalry between the two, as well as jurisdictional quarrels between the men's and women's clothing unions, accentuated by Dubinsky's withdrawal from the CIO and his return to the AFL.

Hillman then decided to fight it out. He initiated hostilities by making his proposal public in the form of an open letter to the newspapers. Answers were flung back in the ILG paper, *Justice* and the social-democratic *New Leader*: he was trying to take over the American Labor Party in league with the Communists, who would wreck the party when it suited their interests. Next, in January Hillman put together a Committee for a United Labor Party. In Josephson's words, "The Amalgamated's forces in New York were drawn into the fight, as was every CIO union in the city. Big rallies were held, pamphlets were circulated busily, and there was a mad ringing of doorbells throughout the city. Hillman and his aides had long been masters at stirring up powerful movements of public opinion by such measures." In the midst of the scrimmaging, he offered a compromise for an agreed-on joint slate, which would divide control between the two factions. Then he made a further concession that in the interests of harmony neither Curran nor Quill would be included on the slate. When the compromises were all summarily rejected, the campaign proceeded on its foreordained course to the primary contest in which the Hillman-Communist forces triumphed by a 3-to-2 margin. The right wing thereupon seceded and organized itself into the rival Liberal Party.

In the months preceding the primary, the battle was prominently reported in the New York press, the Red issue dominating the news. On January 14, the same day that the PAC convened a national conference in New York, right-wing ALP leaders ran a big advertisement in the *New York Times* accusing Hillman of "complete surrender to the New York Communists." The *New York Post* editorialized that "this crisis was provoked by a conspiracy hatched by the Communists and Sidney Hillman to seize the ALP." Congressman Dies tried to inject himself into the act by announcing that the PAC was under investigation and that Hillman and others would soon be called to testify before the House committee. On the eve of the primary, the Dubinsky group ran another, a full-page advertisement in the *New York Times*, branding Hillman a Communist collaborator. Hillman sailed through it all imperturbably, as Lewis had earlier waved away the Red tag. Josephson remarked breezily, "Hillman in this time of war emergency was for using everyone. . . . In 1944 it seemed politically stupid to 'wave the bloody shirt' of old left-right quarrels."

The Hillman-Communist alliance provided a textbook illustration of the fatuity of the professional anti-Communist disquisitions: that if people were only properly educated, they would never make alliances with the Communists, because they would understand that in all such alliances the Communists take the honey while the innocent ally is left with the gall. Hillman was neither fellow traveler nor innocent. He knew at least as much about the Communists as Dubinsky. He was as much a pro-Roosevelt liberal as Dubinsky. He had dealt with the Communists in the Amalgamated more ruthlessly than Dubinsky had in the ILG. He and Murray had worked to isolate them in various CIO unions. Yet in concrete circumstances of politics, when their support was desirable, he did not shrink from the alliance, nor doubt his ability to fit them into the frame of his purposes. The saying goes that politics makes strange bedfellows; which is another way of saying that the working politician is a creature of immediacy and expediency who reduces programmatic

236

propositions to tactical options. To pursue principles regardless of immediate consequences—that is for intellectuals, theologians, and eccentrics. If Hillman would forego today's tactical advantage for tomorrow's principle, so far as he could see he would not be around tomorrow to participate in the celebration of the vindicated principle. He was no less a *realpolitiker* than Dubinsky, but the two happened to be working different sides of the street that season.[4]

2

There was never any significant tension between Hillman and his Amalgamated lieutenants and Baldwin, Abt, and the others because their election aims were the same, and when it came to appointments, the Communists deferred to Hillman's wishes. The Communist policy for the campaign was securely locked into CIO policy. "The People's Program for 1944" issued by the PAC, could have been run, without editing, in either the *Daily Worker* or the *CIO News*. In May the politicos became aware of the PAC's striking power when it forced the retirement of Dies and defeated in the primaries two other members of the House Committee on Un-American Activities. As the campaign heated up, it became apparent that given a candidate and auspices that were acceptable to a broad public, CIO and Communist activists, as technicians, ran rings around the clubhouse politicians. They understood what the old-time professionals did not: how to combine doorbell-ringing with a social message. Clark Clifford testified to this later in a private memorandum to President Truman: "Those alert party machines which, beginning with 1932, turned out such huge majorities in the big cities for the Democratic ticket have all through the years of their victories been steadily deteriorating underneath—until in 1944 the Democratic organization found itself rivalled, in terms of money and workers, and exceeded in alertness and enthusiasm, by the PAC. Everywhere the professionals are in profound collapse." Communist and PAC electoral engineering, sensitive to the mass society's requirements for political packaging, became the starting point for later "New Politics" technology. The PAC left an indelible mark on the mechanics, if not on the substance, of American electoral politics.

J. David Greenstone has argued that by the 1960s, labor's alliance with the Democratic party was the partial equivalent of union alliances with the Social Democratic parties in Western Europe. Actually, in the case of the CIO, this can be pushed back to the mid-

237

1930s with the formation of Labor's Non-Partisan League. The alliance temporarily went into disarray in 1940 because of Lewis's break with Roosevelt. But this was contrary to the wishes of all other non-Communist CIO leaders; the members, including the mine workers, remained faithful to Roosevelt, and the alliance was formally reestablished with the founding of the PAC. One can extend the analogy with Western Europe by arguing that the PAC, and after the AFL-CIO unification in the mid-fifties, the Committee on Political Education (COPE), represented an American version of the Social Democratic parties of Western Europe in certain essentials though not in organization forms, that labor's political extension exercised many of the functions of labor-based parties, but as a bloc within one of the two major parties. The analogy notwithstanding, this American variation of social democratic politics gave the unions less voice in Democratic party and Democratic administration decision-making than the British unions had working through the instrumentality of Britain's Labor Party. An important part of the Democratic administration coalition, labor was never accorded representation in cabinets and departments customarily granted to coalition partners.[5]

Henry Wallace's misadventures showed that when it came to high policy, the CIO's PAC rated no differently than had Labor's Non-Partisan League. Roosevelt had imposed Wallace as the vice-presidential candidate on a hostile Democratic convention in 1940. In the intervening years, Wallace had become the darling of liberals and the CIO, a banner-bearer of advanced welfarism, and their Crown Prince in the New Deal succession. By the same token, he was considered by the party professionals and big-money contributors a wild man, an impractical dreamer, an untrustworthy and probably dangerous ideologue. As soon as it was clear toward the end of 1943 that Roosevelt was going to run for a fourth term, Edwin Pauley, the hard-driving oil millionaire who was Democratic party treasurer, set afoot an intrigue to sidetrack Wallace in favor of a safe-and-sane conservative. The main party bosses were drawn into the affair and Roosevelt was subjected to a systematic bombardment to find a replacement for the too-radical Wallace. The struggle over the vice-presidential candidate took on an unprecedented intensity and malevolence because many of the Pauley cabal assumed that Roosevelt would not live out a fourth term, that the vice-president would be the next White House occupant.

Roosevelt was facing an entrenched opposition in Congress and

238

the polarization of his own party. The last thing he intended was to run for a fourth term as the candidate of defiant liberalism under the aegis of a truncated party controlled by laborites and New Deal enthusiasts. Such a campaign would have shattered the alliance with the business community that he had fashioned with such care and at such cost; it would have upset his centrist position that required conflicting elements that could be balanced off; it would have hurled the country into the kind of struggle he was determined to avoid; and would have led, as he saw it, to the defeat of himself and the party. Hence, a running mate had to be found who would be acceptable to both camps. Although tired, harassed, and sick, the Old Fox had not lost his cunning. On the one hand, he permitted Pauley and the other party officials to persuade him at a secret meeting at the White House on July 11 of what he had decided in his own mind before, that Truman was the indicated middle-of-the-roader who "would hurt him least." On the other hand, he encouraged both Wallace and Byrnes to make the run for the nomination so that the choice of Truman would appear to the convention delegates to be an unavoidable compromise between left and right extremes that threatened to disrupt the party.

Hillman played a crucial part in this intrigue within an intrigue. Fascinated by the game of high politics, flattered by the attention he was receiving again as a national leader, Hillman permitted himself to maneuver with his own colleagues. Despite his previous dolorous experience in acting as Roosevelt's agent, he took on the role a second time. Fame was the spur, and rank and status the tempter. He had decided after matching himself against the competition during the NRA period that he needed a bigger stage than his clothing union afforded him. His union colleagues agreed with him, and, in truth, he was more capable than many administrators and functionaries who occupied impressive Washington offices. He met with the president two days after the fateful gathering of the party bosses, and was sufficiently briefed to understand that Truman was to be the nominee. He was shown both Roosevelt's lukewarm (kiss-of-death) letter endorsing Wallace, and his letter to Robert Hannegan, the party chairman, indicating that Truman and Justice Douglas would be acceptable running mates. If Roosevelt did not spell it out any further, there was no need to. Since Douglas had no support and was not an active candidate, it was obvious that his name had been thrown in as a blind. Hillman could add things up.

Hillman did not argue with Roosevelt. He did not press for the candidate his organization was pledged to support. (He did not even have a good opinion of Wallace.) He assured Roosevelt, in effect, that he would work to put Truman across with his associates. As Josephson diplomatically worded it, "Hillman reached a clear understanding with Roosevelt, according to which the PAC group was to continue to support Wallace, as it had committed itself to do; but when it became plain that Wallace could not get the nomination, then Hillman would do his best to keep the friends of the CIO at the Chicago convention from opposing the choice of Truman as an alternative."[6]

Hillman, Murray, Baldwin, and the others arrived in Chicago at the head of a large PAC-backed group of delegates, set up impressive headquarters, pressed prominent New Dealers Claude Pepper, Ellis Arnall, Oscar Chapman, and Joseph Guffy, into service as floor managers, and began to line up delegates for Wallace as if involved was a death clash between empires. Hillman was giving out interviews proclaiming undying fealty to Wallace and saying that the CIO had no second candidate. At a big Wallace rally on July 19 sponsored by the PAC, both Hillman and Murray explained that the struggle over the vice-presidency was a struggle for the New Deal against standpatters. Wallace, who in 1940 was not permitted by Harry Hopkins to make an acceptance speech because the feeling against him ran so high, was the plumed knight of the 1944 convention. Some of the demonstrations in his favor bordered on delirium. In the party at large, sentiment went the same way. According to the Gallup poll of July, he was the favorite of almost two-thirds of registered Democrats.

But while Hillman was giving out press statements for Wallace, he had already met with Truman and given him the same pledge he had given to Roosevelt. Hillman's position was in a way decisive for the labor battalions because he was Roosevelt's man in charge of the labor front. Roosevelt and the party officials dealt with him, and Murray was therefore dependent on Hillman for information about what was happening behind the scenes. Out of this role arose the myth that Hillman was a kingmaker and had veto power over candidates. The "clear it with Sidney" story, originating with Byrnes and spread by Arthur Krock, the *New York Times* conservative columnist, was repeated with suitable embellishments by Republican orators and publicists from a hundred platforms during the election campaign. It was supposed to prove that Roosevelt had become a captive of the labor bosses, or of the labor-Communist bloc. Hillman's biographer accepted the more moderate interpretation that Hillman was given veto power over the final choice for vice-president. It was not so.

According to Krock, Hannegan said Roosevelt had instructed him that on the final choice between Byrnes, Wallace, and Truman, he and the other Democratic leaders were to "clear it with Sidney." It is possible that Roosevelt used the phrase (although Hannegan later denied it), and it is a fact that Hannegan, who was pushing Truman's candidacy while pretending to be neutral, went through the motions of conferring with Hillman about Byrnes's candidacy. But it was part of Roosevelt's and Hannegan's (and Hillman's) elaborate charade. The Truman candidacy had been agreed on July 11; Hillman had given his pledge on July 13. In other words, arrangements had been concluded before Hannegan and Hillman came to Chicago. Clearing Byrnes with Hillman, in any case, was an adroit way of dropping Byrnes; one might as well clear Roosevelt with Hoover.

A spuriously reluctant Truman accepted the nomination after Roosevelt forcefully talked to him and party officials over the phone. This was on July 20, a week after Hillman's conference with Roosevelt. It was only then that Hillman burst in on Murray and the CIO staff in a hotel room to announce jubilantly, "We've stopped Byrnes!" as if he had just learned of the presidential decision. "And what are we getting?" he was asked. "Harry Truman of Missouri, it is rumored," he replied. J. Raymond Walsh turned to Murray: "Phil, what do you think about it?" and Murray's sarcastic comment was, "We stopped Byrnes, we lost Wallace, and we got Truman." By now Murray was somewhat jealous of Hillman's prominence. He had not imagined when he assigned Hillman to head the PAC that the venture would become as important as it did. Probably he would have gone along with the Truman candidacy had he been consulted from the start. Pressman had wisely observed that Murray and Hillman made a perfect team, since their political inclinations were the same. But Murray suspected that he had been strung along.[7]

Others were even further removed from decision-making than Murray. Of course, "Beanie" Baldwin was on the convention floor clutching his tally sheets and frantically directing his floor managers, who had been joined by Harold Ickes and Francis Biddle when the battle shaped up as a confrontation between New Dealers

241

and clubhouse regulars. Alas for all of them, they were misled by the White House pretense that this was to be an open convention. They did not know that their leader had already unhorsed their knight-errant. "Beanie" Baldwin, who was hearing rumors of Hannegan's arm-twisting, and of the move to line up delegates for Truman originating with FDR himself, may not have known until later that Browder, too, had decided Truman was better suited to consolidate national unity than the controversial Wallace.

Not that it would have made any difference had he known. He was committed to Wallace, and had neither the ability to change signals in the midst of the campaign, nor the inclination to evade that commitment. Starobin's suggestion that Wallace "might have succeeded Roosevelt if the Communists had been as enthusiastic about him in 1944 as they were to be in 1948" was far-fetched. If the CIO could not put across Wallace, certainly the Communists did not have the ability. The Wallace-Truman contest became public knowledge only in the last few days of the Chicago convention. Most Communist officials in unions and in the Citizens committee knew no more than "Beanie" Baldwin did of Browder's lucubrations. Following the convention, the *Daily Worker* threw out a veiled hint the significance of which was comprehensible only to the cognoscenti. Only after the election did Browder make his public pronouncement that it was fortunate Wallace had not been nominated, for his nomination would have alienated from the Roosevelt coalition the *New York Times* and Walter Lippmann. Fortunately for the Communists, this was lost in the shuffle of events along with Hillman's cloakroom wirepulling.

When the returns were in, the PAC boasted that its activity had been indispensable for Roosevelt's reelection and had succeeded in returning a more liberal Congress. Since the PAC ran no candidates of its own, there is no sure way of determining its precise strength, or validating its several claims. Of the 145 congressional candidates it endorsed, 109 were elected; of the 21 senatorial candidates it endorsed, 17 were elected. This would be a respectable achievement except that it is impossible to demonstrate how much of the credit for the victories was due to Hillman's exertions. By the general rule of thumb employed by politicos and newspapermen in evaluations of this nature, the PAC was a powerhouse, and in a number of industrial states, notably New York, Michigan, California, and Washington, a balance-of-power group. Certainly some of its feats—like retiring from public life three members of the House Committee on Un-American Activities; defeating standpatters like "Cotton Ed" Smith of South Carolina, Bennett Champ Clark of Missouri, Worth Clark of Idaho, and Hattie Carraway of Arkansas with PAC-endorsed candidates; ensuring the reelection of Senator Wagner in New York against the AFL's opposition—convinced the professionals, including Roosevelt and Truman, that a serious force had come on the scene which would have to be reckoned with. The PAC forces contributed $1½ million to the presidential campaign out of the approximately $7½ million in the Democratic party coffer, had brought into the electoral process great numbers who otherwise would not have been heard from, and had injected into the campaign an excitement and social purpose beyond the capacities of the professional clubhouse habitués.

New York State provided unique information about the new bloc since the labor forces there had separate designations on the ballot. The vote was as follows:

Dewey	2,987,647	(Republican)
Roosevelt	2,478,598	(Democratic)
Roosevelt	496,405	(ALP)
Roosevelt	329,235	(Liberal)

Thus it took the combined ALP and Liberal party vote to secure Roosevelt's victory in the Empire State. The ALP vote alone accounted for a fifth of Roosevelt's vote on the Democratic line; the combined labor-backed vote for a third of the Democratic vote. These are big figures. At the same time the data showed that the labor forces were split, and that in some contests, unlike the presidential one, AFL and CIO were backing opposing candidates. Another question was how much liberalization of Congress these activities were accomplishing. Christening opportunist politicians, who had many other commitments, as friends of labor was hazardous and often self-defeating. The 79th Congress, despite PAC boasting, was less welfare-minded than the previous one, and was to be followed by the Congress that passed the Taft-Hartley Act. All the same, Hillman's PAC—as Lewis's LNPL—blazed the trail for a more virile labor participation in politics, and the AFL, after disparaging Hillman's creation, was forced to follow his example. The 1944 campaign laid the foundation for the modern labor bloc in American politics.[8]

3

"Beanie" Baldwin directing the Wallace forces on the Democratic convention floor, and Hannah Dorner running entertainment spectaculars during the election campaign, were the meridian of the heady Communist splashing in the political mainstream, representative of the general design. It should have led to spectacular Party growth. Here was an organization reconstructed as a replica of wartime European Social Democratic parties, with a cadre of devoted, eager activists, in a period when its patriotic effusions were more or less in alignment with the outlook of liberals and laborites. Furthermore, its leaders were exerting themselves beyond the call of duty. In line with Browder's initial thrust that he was ready to meliorate social conflicts, they were sending messages to elitist circles that they were prepared to go far in their patriotic dedication, even if at times it meant irritating or provoking their allies. They had not shrunk from confrontations with certain labor and Black officials.

In the new year, they made a démarche to differentiate themselves from the entire labor officialdom, AFL, CIO, Railway Brotherhoods, in backing the military-sponsored Austin-Wadsworth "labor draft" bill, which Roosevelt endorsed in his state of the union message of January 1944. It was a proposition to unceremoniously conscript and regiment civilian labor; as advanced by army lawyers and generals, it carried pronounced authoritarian overtones, and had it been adopted and conscientiously enforced, it would have stripped unions of both seniority and security provisions. Public espousal of the bill by Bridges, Curran, and Emspak led to a crisis at the January CIO executive-board meeting, only resolved when the Communist stalwarts beat a shamefaced retreat. (The grounds for labor conscription repeatedly shifted over the period of its advocacy. At this time, it was meant by its military and dollar-a-year-men sponsors to disarm those of the Washington bureaucracy and the business community who favored a plan for reconversion. The military was strong for psychologically "toughening up" the public and cracking down on strikers.)

Communists continued of course to be pariahs in certain polite circles, and the Dies type of congressmen continued, out of habit, their prewar persecutions. But Communists were tapping new sources of respectability. One has to recreate the atmosphere of the time in which Stalin the Bloody had become benign, pipe-smoking

"Uncle Joe." An entire issue of *Life* magazine was devoted to Soviet-American cooperation. The Russians, wrote the editors, are "one hell of a people" who "look like Americans, dress like Americans and think like Americans." *Collier's* editors thought at the end of 1943 that Russia was neither Communist nor Socialist, but a country evolving "toward something resembling our own and Great Britain's democracy." Hollywood made a movie of former ambassador Joseph Davies's panegyric to Stalinist Russia, *Mission to Moscow*, later to be described as "Operation Whitewash." These propagandistic exercises naturally affected people's attitudes. In a nationwide poll of September 1944, 30 percent of the respondents answered that the Russian government had changed for the better.

If a section of the public was more complacent about Russia, it stood to reason that some of the good will should apply to native Communists. The 1943 recruiting drive for 15,000 had gone over the top, with reported increases of 100 percent in auto, 50 percent in steel, and 60 percent in shipbuilding. The recruiting drive in early 1944 swept in 24,000 new members. Outsiders as well as Communists had the impression that the Party was growing apace, well on its way to becoming a mass organization. It was an exaggerated view. Almost as many were dropping away as rapidly as new recruits were being brought in. Party registration had been 55,000 in January 1938; it was only 65,000 in January 1945. Browder gave somewhat higher figures. He estimated that before his troubles in the summer of 1945, there were 75,000 to 80,000 members. Even his figures hardly affected the growth chart since his estimate for 1938 was 74,000. Multiplying the figures threefold to account for periphery supporters similarly would leave the comparison undisturbed, since the 1938 figures would have to be increased as well.

These figures would suggest that the Party overcame the decline it suffered in the Stalin-Hitler-pact period and even improved its position somewhat from the previous high point in 1938. It did not make good the losses sustained in unions, but as against that, it could be shown that the major unions it continued to control had far larger memberships in line with the general rise of union membership. Its enhanced political position through the CIO-related organizations and the Independent Citizens Committee could be considered to outweigh in importance the setbacks it had suffered in some unions or the loss of face with leading Black spokesmen. One can argue, of course, that the new friendships it had formed were

245

beginning to qualitatively alter its status as a national political organization, putting it in line for marked advances in the postwar years—except for the destructive intervention from abroad.

But there was the rub. Communists could not claim that this was a fortuitous stroke, like the death of a leader by accident, or the change of a country's regime because a prime minister was unexpectedly caught *in flagrante delicto*. The debacle was built into the revamped Party. The Party sat on a foundation of a continued American-Russian alliance that no one had any assurance would survive wartime imperatives—and where there were many indications that it would not. Even if Browder was a less than astute student of international affairs, he knew from his own experiences that the Russian-dictated Party line could change overnight because of internal Kremlin configurations. An Americanized Party (allegedly riding on the shoulders of Washington, Jefferson, and Lincoln) whose policies could be manipulated by a Muscovite directorate was a sham that was bound to be found out. It was a case of absurdity becoming destiny, no less so because the American leaders were deceiving themselves as well as their followers. The nationalist ideology and activity had not supplied them with a new soul. The *Daily Worker*, while projecting extensive national blocs, never let up its dreary diatribes against Trotskyists, Norman Thomas Socialists, Lewisites, Reutherites, and assorted fifth-columnists. Drawn into impressive proceedings and amid far-reaching associations, the Communists continued to dwell in an esoteric, somewhat sordid, encapsulated world. They were creatures torn between their hopes for acceptance in the wider society, and their old family allegiances—and when put to the test in 1945—an article in a French magazine was sufficient to topple their Party's undisputed leader of ten years.

Foster summed up the period this way: "Opportunities for party building were exceptionally good during the war, and the party should have come into the postwar period with at least 150,000 solidly organized members. If it failed to do so, it was principally due to the opportunist Browder policies." The evidence testifies to the contrary. It was the "opportunist Browder policies" in the thirties and forties that marked out and accounted for the Party's halcyon periods of influence. Wartime Browderism did not result in the establishment of a solid party of 150,000 (before the Russian overlords again brought it low) for other, unmysterious causes: the ineradicable memory of the Stalin-Hitler-pact interlude coupled with the

246

knowledge that another somersault could occur; the cadaverous internal regime of an intellectually hollowed-out Party; the somewhat ludicrous contortions that undermined its pretentions to independence and repelled the thinking. (We do not include here the middle-class inclinations of most Americans because the talk is of a Party of 150,000; a Party of that size could have been established in the given environment.) That the Communists could assemble mass parties in France and Italy despite such handicaps was due to the special circumstances of wartime resistance, their heroic role in the resistance (and a Left tradition going back a hundred years). In the United States, in the absence of such advantages, the Party's every postule and deformity was mercilessly exposed.[9]

TEN · *Communists vs. CIO 1946-1947*

THE way the administration went about reconversion after V-J Day made inevitable the postwar strike wave and the inflationary spiral. Truman, a product of Middle America, was heavily influenced in economic matters by his old-time associate John W. Snyder, a conservative minor bank official from Missouri who took over the office of War Mobilization and Reconversion in July. Snyder, in turn, reflected the thinking of predominant business circles; and these, through the National Association of Manufacturers and other spokesmen, let it be known that they were all for a fast return to normalcy. Their cluster of dollar-a-year men at the head of the War Production Board proceeded to scrap controls so expeditiously that by November the board closed out its affairs. The precipitate reconversion undercut any possibility of an orderly peacetime wage-and-price equilibrium. Under Executive Order No. 9599 issued three days after V-J Day, unions were free to bargain, but where employers intended to seek price increases, wage raises would have to be approved by a government agency using standards that made approval unlikely.

At the same time, the major corporations were making it clear that they would not raise wages until they had assurance that they could pass on the costs. (They were able to hold out until the government met their terms. According to a Department of Commerce estimate, accumulated war profits stood at $52 billion, an additional $30 billion due in tax rebates; corporation profits after taxes would reach close to $12 billion in 1946 compared to the 1936-1939 average of close to $4 billion.)

Several government administrators had been talking with Murray and Green about continuing the no-strike pledge in return for a modest wage concession, and Davis and Taylor had what they thought were informal assurances from both of them in August that the president could obtain a temporary extension of the no-strike pledge in the postwar period. The two union heads also drew up a joint declaration that month with Eric Johnson of the U.S. Chamber of Commerce that in return for an immediate 10 percent wage increase, labor would continue its no-strike policy during the reconversion period as long as price controls continued. With personal memories of labor's crushing defeats of 1919-1920, Murray was anxious to avoid another postwar showdown. But clearly neither he, nor Green, nor the White House advisers understood the depth of the rebellion in labor ranks. Both the post-V-J Day and subsequent presidential directives and the Murray-Green conditional notes—if that is the right description—were as chaff in the wind. The time was passed when wage stabilization could be imposed by a policy of delay, supplemented by appeals to patriotism, buttressed by minor concessions. (The Communists, earlier, had gone Murray and Green several times better. In the grip of their vision of permanent Soviet-American cooperation, they had been promoting a permanent no-strike pledge to be operative after the war, as well. The proposition was only washed out when Browder was sent packing at the end of May, otherwise there would have occurred an even more bruising confrontation than the one that had taken place in connection with incentive pay.)

The tide of discontent had been rising through 1944 and 1945, and the restraining dikes were swept away when fear of peacetime insecurity was added to accumulating grievances. Plants on war work were shutting down; unemployment jumped to 3 million; long lines were forming across the country in unemployment-compensation offices; tens of millions of the employed saw their earnings drastically reduced; instead of working 48 or more hours, they were now back to the standard 40-hour week, with the majority downgraded to less-skilled, lower-paying jobs. As if they had all received the same message, the feeling swept through labor ranks that they had to take their stand on the firing line or be pushed back to the living standards of the depression decade, that the hour had to be seized while profits were high and before mass unemployment undercut their bargaining power. The result was that an almost universal cry went up for 48 hours pay for 40 hours work—meaning a 30 percent wage increase—and the stage was set for the major strike eruption.

The official historian of the Office of Price Administration (OPA) later observed that the government stabilization program was a mirage:

> In hindsight it may appear quixotic for the administration, in the transition period following V-J Day, to have depended so heavily, on the one hand, on government price control unaided

249

except for a few auxiliaries, and, on the other hand, on voluntary self-restraint among clashing interests. Looking back, it seems politically inevitable, once manufacturers were given free rein by the lifting of production controls and a financial stimulus by the repeal of the excess profits tax, that labor's no-strike pledge would end with V-J Day; that without such a pledge wage controls would be inoperative—and stabilization would therefore go out the window.[1]

Had Truman and his advisers not been sold on laissez-faire economics, however, they might have tried an updated and liberalized Little Steel formula while holding price fluctuations to their wartime tempos, and only gradually lifting production controls. How long such a policy could have been maintained in the face of a sullen Congress and an obstreperous business class is questionable. If pursued, it would have slowed and mitigated postwar inflation which was in the offing because the war had been largely financed by deficit spending and commercial borrowing; also, regressive tax laws placed enormous sums in business hands, and banks were overladen with negotiable government securities. The overheated economic plant was brought to bursting point at the end of the war by huge tax rebates, write-offs, and easy credit, all kindling to the enormous pent-up demand for consumer goods.

The UAW executive board cancelled its no-strike pledge a week after V-J Day, and the next month announced plans for strike votes at the Big Three to back the 30 percent wage demand. By this time, all CIO officials were under heavy constraint to press the wage issue to a conclusion. In September, 4,300,000 man-days were lost in strikes across the country, most in unauthorized strikes, a figure that was to double the following month. Wrote Louis Stark, labor reporter of the *New York Times*, "Among employers the 30 percent wage demand is being interpreted . . . as a move by top union leadership to bring into line a rank and file that is getting out of hand." But if the pressure was considerable on Murray and others, it was overwhelming on auto-union officials who were in danger of being engulfed by a spontaneous strike movement. The previous year a number of large wildcat strikes in Detroit and Flint took on the character of organized defiances of all international officers. The spreading rebellion of factory workers that broke out in the rubber convention, and even penetrated the tightly run steel convention, dominated the entire UAW gathering in mid-September 1944 where a newly formed Rank and File Caucus amassed 36 percent of the vote for outright repudiation of the no-strike pledge.

It was a convention in which Reuther had fared poorly. Just as Addes and Frankensteen had outsmarted themselves in 1943 on the incentive-pay-plan issue, so at Grand Rapids Reuther outsmarted himself on the no-strike pledge. Addes, Frankensteen, and the Communists argued for continued adherence on patriotic grounds of war needs; the oppositionists argued for rejection because government and management were not living up to their commitments. Reuther offered to drop the pledge on civilian work but uphold it on war work. His proposition was torn to shreds during the debate, and he was accorded the scorn for one who plays both sides. His minority report was simply shouted down in a voice vote; many of his supporters deserted him on the issue, and this time Frankensteen ran far ahead of him for the first vice-presidency.

Now, a year later, with the pledge out of the way, Reuther stepped forward to make his bid to become the John L. Lewis of the postwar wage breakthrough. It was no snap decision on his part. He had pondered the lessons of his humiliation at Grand Rapids, and had been moving toward such a leadership objective for many months. At the January executive board meeting he proposed that the CIO withdraw from the War Labor Board until it was reorganized and the Little Steel formula replaced. At the March meeting he voted against disciplining two Detroit locals for conducting wildcat strikes. In June he declared himself in favor of a resolution passed by a Detroit conference of UAW officers for a strike vote in all UAW plants to back up demands for a 30 percent wage increase. In July he proposed a new membership referendum on the no-strike pledge. Now he was convinced that the watchword had to be audacity. Strikes in a variety of industries were already under way and several million workers were milling around awaiting a clear word of direction. If the GM workers took the plunge under a fighting leader and with an appropriate set of demands, forces would be set in motion for another historic breakthrough. His reasoning was that GM, despite the huge tax rebates coming to it, would not want to let its competitors capture a bigger share of the reopened car market; and given the popular feelings, other unions would have to join the struggle. On his initiative, the executive board announced its one-at-a-time strategy in mid-September (a strategy that had been traditional in the auto union since 1937). GM—the division that he headed—was to be singled out for the union push.

251

The machine he had built in the course of five years was put to work at its ultimate capacity, all wheels and piston rods moving furiously, grinding out publicity releases and briefs, setting up supportive citizens committees, challenging the corporation spokesmen, arousing the ranks. It was a radical public campaign built around two radical slogans: "Wage increases without price increases" and "Open the books." The first was an outgrowth of Truman's directive that permitted granting wage increases where no price relief was demanded, and was intended to refute the argument that higher wages would be inflationary. The second slogan had originated with the Trotskyists. As employed by Reuther, it was meant to expose the company's protestations that they could not afford to grant the increase without a price hike: let them open their books to impartial inspection, the argument went, so that the facts can be ascertained and the union would scale its money demands accordingly. As important as the slogans was the tone of the campaign. In the month before the walkout, he conducted negotiations with the company officials in a hectoring, blustering manner that escalated the popular fever, hardened the lines of intransigence, presupposing another epochal strike battle was inevitable.

The strategy was a failure. Banking on the company's fear about losing its share of the market proved unrealistic. The strike, starting November 21, dragged on inconclusively for 113 days, exhausting the ranks and their wartime savings. It was not until the entire steel industry was shut down on January 21, a general strike was called in the electrical industry, and a strike of both CIO and AFL unions against the major meat packers had begun the week before, that the deadlock was broken—but that was nine weeks after the GM workers struck, and the deadlock was broken not on Reuther's but on the company's terms. In appearance, the strikes were regulation labor-capital disputes. In truth, the corporations were not averse to granting wage increases provided they could breach price controls. With one and three-quarter million workers on the streets and the economy nearing a state of paralysis, Truman took the decision out of OPA's hands; he and Snyder made a straight deal with the steel masters: the workers were to be granted an additional 18½ cents an hour and the price of steel was to be raised $5 a ton. This set the pattern. There was brave talk that this was only a "bulge" in the price line that would soon be smoothed out, but in reality it was the beginning of the end for price control. "From this point out," reads the OPA history, "a really firm price policy was in fact no longer possible, either administratively or politically."

Once the manufacturers got the word that they could call the tune on prices, the strikes were settled at the steel figure. Agreements were reached with Chrysler and Ford on January 26 even before the final steel contract was signed. The one-at-a-time strategy, at this juncture, at any rate, was more successful in dividing the UAW than the automobile companies. Reuther tried holding out for the extra penny to save face and his own self-respect (Truman's fact-finding board had recommended a 19½ cent increase, which Reuther with great effort convinced the GM bargaining committee to accept), but GM was adamant. It was determined to hold to the pattern and to teach the UAW leaders and ranks a lesson they would not soon forget. In his excruciating discomfiture, he lashed out at the Communist UE leaders for "unparalleled treachery" in settling for 18½ cents in the electrical division on February 9 while the main strike at GM was still on. Among the initiated this was understood to be a slap as well at Murray who had agreed to Truman's recommendation of 18½ cents just before the steel strike (not to mention the UAW directors at Ford and Chrysler who had settled for 18 and 18½ cents at the end of January, and accepted in the contracts stiff "company security" clauses into the bargain).

Neither in Ford and Chrysler, nor in steel, electrical, packing-house, rubber, was the price question injected into contract negotiations. Union officials carefully kept the two apart. In their business relations with the corporations, they demanded more wage money. On prices, they kept going nondescript, generalized propaganda assaults against inflation, unconscionable profits, and for "rollbacks," propaganda that committed them to no specific actions, and the failure of which they could blame on reactionaries and big business interests without losing face with their constituents. None of them approved Reuther's tactic of combining the two issues in contract talks. Even Reuther said little about price increases in the last stage of the GM negotiations, and he was not present at the March 15 session when the final agreement was concluded—one month after the steel settlement, six weeks after the settlements in Chrysler and Ford.

Shortly after the strike, the *Detroit News* printed a statement attributed to Reuther that his call on GM to open the books "was just a maneuver to win public support and to get the company over the barrel," with Reuther countering that he had been misquoted. Whatever he actually said, the Reuther strategists conceived the social demands as deft propaganda to throw the onus of inflation on the company's shoulders. The blow fell short of its mark. The com-

253

pany emerged remarkably unscathed despite the union's ability to quote President Truman and various other government dignitaries to the effect that auto wages could be raised without raising prices—and judging by the 1946 election returns, the country was swinging to conservatism, not to populism. At the same time, because the company, in negotiations, in press statements, and in newspaper advertisements, plucked out these demands to make the case for free enterprise, the abandonment of the issue in the final GM settlement, and the studied avoidance of similar demands in all other union negotiations made it appear as if the GM workers had been pointedly rebuked.

After the strike, Communists and other Reuther opponents started backdoor gossip that Reuther had "jumped the gun" and had thereby violated "CIO strategy." This was a blood relation of the theory of a "UAW strategy" in 1937. That he had forced the calling of the strike on the November date before receiving final approval of the board was true, but there was no CIO strategy, not even a coordination of individual union strategies. Murray had not anticipated the strike movement, was unprepared for it, and apparently—judging by his apologia to the 1946 UAW convention—he unaccountably had some faith that an arrangement might be worked out at the president's labor-management conference scheduled for November. When all his hopes were dashed, and when the steel masters proved no less obdurate than the General Motors officials, it simply took him another two months to work his way through Truman's fact-finding board and negotiations with steel company executives before calling a strike. A conference of auto, electrical, and steel union representatives, called on the initiative of UE officials, was held in Pittsburgh at the beginning of December; it accomplished nothing, and even the strike dates—January 14 and 15—that steel and UE set if no agreements resulted were broken by Murray, who at the last moment postponed the steel strike call yet another week at Truman's request.

The 1946 strike movement was more spectacular than the one in 1919, with more strikes involved (although representing a smaller percentage of the total work force), and the strikes ended with partial victories in place of the earlier defeats. Seidman noted, "Considering the magnitude of the strike wave, it was surprising how small a part the Communists played in it." Certainly, compared to the fat parts they commanded in the 1936-1937 series of strikes, they had been demoted to mere supporting roles. In part, this was due to the institutionalization of the CIO. Irregular insurgents could no longer push forward in strike situations. Once the officialdom assumed leadership of the strike movement, it necessarily moved through accepted bureaucratic channels. Then, unlike the battles of the thirties, the campaign of 1946 was one of maneuver, not of trench warfare. Employers made no effort to work their struck plants, and the combatants carried their attacks over the air waves, in the newspapers, and before government boards and committees. The members of the flying squadrons played poker or read comic strips when on picket duty.

Communist union officials did not compete with Reuther to grab leadership of the strike-and-wage movement. UE officials clung to Murray's coattails and were content to accept the steel pattern, more interested in trying to snipe at and undercut Reuther than in setting any pioneering goals of their own. In the maritime strikes in the fall of 1946, the National Maritime Union (NMU) followed the lead of Harry Lundberg's AFL Sailors Union of the Pacific; and Bridges himself became entangled in a jurisdictional strike with the AFL union. Consequently, there arose an unplanned division of labor between Communist party publicists and Communist union officials. On the one hand, the Communist press was thundering against the dread disease of Browderism; Lewis had been declared a traitor for calling strikes, now he was nailed as a capitulator for calling off a strike. On the other hand, Communist labor officials, enmeshed in the politics and alliances attendant on their wartime positions, expressed their radicalism in their union newspapers while conducting themselves like the next set of CIO officials in contract negotiations.[2]

2

Though Reuther's strike strategy failed, he achieved one major objective of his campaign: he won the presidency at the convention that met at Atlantic City a week after the GM settlement. Since he won over R. J. Thomas by 114 votes of 8,761 cast, while the Addes forces elected the other general officers and won a majority of the incoming executive board, any attempt to pinpoint the precise reasons for his victory is necessarily speculative. From the 1941 Buffalo convention on, the Reuther and Addes machines had achieved a rough parity, and R. J. Thomas could keep his presidency only at the sufferance of the two. The unsettled nature of the union at this time exaggerated the fortuitous in such a close vote. Dues-paying membership declined from a wartime peak of 1,200,000 to 540,000. Numbers of delegates cast large blocs of votes on behalf of members that were no longer there. The Addes forces were weakened by Frankensteen's withdrawal. He had announced earlier, when running for mayor of Detroit, that whatever the outcome, he would not seek another term as vice-president. He was a strong debater on the Addes side, had his own popular following, and his removing himself from the scene was a loss to the Addes coalition. Equally troublesome was the collapse of the aircraft industry, so that delegates' voting strength from aircraft locals declined by 600 votes from the previous convention. On the other hand, the Addes people had the CIO's covert support, and eventually Murray's guarded endorsement of Thomas.

These extrinsic occurrences may have aided one or the other side, but the aid was largely marginal; such advantages and disadvantages tended to cancel themselves out. It was on the plane of policy and debate that the Addes forces showed up poorly. They could have made out a strong case against Reuther, but they failed to do so. It was difficult for them to criticize the one-at-a-time strategy or the calling of the GM strike so far ahead of the steel strike, because Reuther had secured the board's formal approval for his major policy moves. There had been snide asides about Reuther's "fancy economics" and talkathons, but these had not gone beyond gossip, leaks to newspapers, and caucus horror stories. The opposition had no agreed-upon policy to counterpose to Reuther's, and Addes cut off by a parliamentary maneuver Reuther's attempt to engage Thomas in a debate for fear that Thomas was not up to such single combat.

If Reuther's aggressive leadership in the GM strike gained him the thin sliver of margin that carried him to the presidency, this has to be taken in conjunction with his general élan. He was the favorite of the liberal press and of New Deal government administrators as labor's bright new hope. Because of their own indecision and parochialism, the other officers made it possible for him to run the strike as if he were the head of the union and the fountainhead of policy, to give full scope to what one labor writer described as his "sheer genius for publicity." It was their fumbling rather than the effectiveness of his strategy that produced the aura of success. He had been prominent before; the GM strike catapulted him forward as labor's man of destiny.

The new head of the auto union, now 39, had completed the most intensive and variegated 10-year apprenticeship. "The real key to his personality," wrote Paul Webber, an old-time newspaperman who edited the *Wage Earner*, "is a kind of Boy Scout simplicity and enthusiasm which shines through everything he does. He is never disturbed by any opponent doubts of the justice of his cause or the wisdom of his course." That was one aspect of it. He was also a textbook model of Technological Man single-mindedly bent on defining and gaining the immediate objective ahead, one who naturally assumed that relations, associates, allies, would play their required subordinate roles in the pursuit of his destiny. The social phenomenon of a labor leader who yoked the vision of reforming idealism to the practicalities and limitations of business unionism, who combined Fabian social engineering with the engineering-rationalizing of industrial society, had been exemplified a generation before by Sidney Hillman.

But a cursory comparison of the two men disclosed the distance that the labor movement had traveled in the intervening years, and how much brighter Reuther's star shone at birth. Hillman was born in Lithuania, spoke English with an accent, a Jewish labor leader presiding over a union of mainly immigrant workers that until the thirties had to function outside of the AFL. Reuther was a native son, and when he flashed across the firmament, was spokesman of the CIO's major union. He appeared to many like the embodiment of the past decade's labor struggles and fulfillments, a fitting symbol of labor's augmented powers, growing ambitions, increased self-confidence. With his ear for social nuances, his ability to catch social drifts, he had made his own the prevailing doctrines and locutions of liberalism. In fact, he was at the center of its postwar mutation. It was also his good fortune to have come into the auto union, because in another union a president like R. J. Thomas might not have been displaced. Thomas was not the caliber of a Murray or a Hillman; he appeared slightly ludicrous alongside the UAW luminaries, but he compared satisfactorily with other union presidents who held on to their jobs.[3]

In Thomas's seven-year incumbency, the two factions had hardened into power-seeking and patronage-hungry machines whose survival and extension became the supreme law of their being. They resembled the two major Amerian political parties in a number of ways: each coalesced around "name" leaders; each was a multicolored coalition that flaunted now this, now that, part of its plumage;

257

each was on the hunt for "differences" to distinguish itself from, and to gain the upper hand over, its rival; each tended to move toward the center in order to attract and hold together disparate elements of its following. Even in the epochal debates over Communism, wage incentive plans, Black representation, no-strike pledge, where the reasons for the two factions presumably were made manifest, the urge was congenital to grind down sharp edges, to reduce issues to banalities, to smear the opposition, to rely heavily on machine politics of awards and reprisals. While both groups were coalitions, the dominant note was struck by the professionals for whom unionism had become a vocation and a way of life. Not only had the professionals grown excessively utilitarian and tactical minded, but as they observed the unscrupulousness with which their own and the opposing side made use of issues, and the aplomb with which individuals switched allegiances, they became somewhat contemptuous of "programs." In both camps, there was a patronizing attitude toward ideological radicals who were considered as lacking a sense of reality. Years afterward Addes could say: "Actually there were no real basic issues; the difference was about leadership and jobs"; and Frankensteen could echo the sentiment: "I cannot remember a fundamental issue that was really an issue. Oh, there were some that were made, as in the convention of 1943 on the piecework issue. Again they brought political implications to bear on what was not a political situation." Reuther never would have made such an admission to others or possibly even to himself. He clothed his ambition in the raiments of high-minded social objectives.

Professor Jack Skeels, after a close study of all the convention battles, threw up his hands in bewilderment. He came to the conclusion "that there were no fundamental differences between the factions," and that while, at the end of the war, "Communism again became an issue . . . the Communist issue does not constitute a platform, and if the various stands on controversial issues by the factions are clustered together, they give no indication of any clear 'liberal-conservative' distinction between the Reuther and Addes caucus." One is misled by trying to differentiate between the two blocs along classical Left-Right lines. Given the opportunist proclivities of power-seeking politicians of both blocs, and the capriciousness of the Communists, one has to listen not merely to the arguments of convention reporters, which are often deliberately misleading, but to the counterpoint and the cadences, if one is to understand what they are saying. The Red issue was two things. It was a demagogic device to smear the opposition. And it was something else as well. Because it had been, and was to become again, a towering fact of contemporary history, it defined and determined national attitudes and caught up all labor principals in its web.[4] For the Reuther faction the Red issue had become the transcendant proposition that defined and demarcated it in the union constellation and determined its outside alliances, the rallying point on which to marshal its troops, the axis around which the struggles for supremacy had to be waged. No matter that by this time Communist strength in both the UAW and in the Addes faction was less than threatening; the taint would not be excised until every last Communist and those who shielded him or associated with him were eliminated.

The delegates to the 1946 convention were not fully cognizant of what they had done in elevating Reuther to the presidency. By awarding the remaining offices and the majority of the executive board memberships to the other faction, they thought they were continuing the plural regime under a more effective head. They could not have been more mistaken. R. J. Thomas, for all his limitations, had been an indispensable buffer between the two factions. His presence kept the opposing gladiators from converting the joust to mortal combat. Under his regime the members had enjoyed a democracy that was legendary throughout the labor movement. And under that democracy, the mutual sniping, the factional excesses, the confusion and disorderliness inevitable in rule by rival oligarchies, did not prevent the UAW from recording far-reaching achievements in growth, shop conditions, internal vibrancy, shop-stewards representation, and general institutional effectiveness. Once they pushed the buffer aside, giving the presidency to the head of one of the power caucuses and the board majority to the other caucus, they set the stage for all-out war: Reuther was to be either the John L. Lewis or the Homer Martin of the auto union. In either case, what was, on balance, a beneficent arrangement, was carelessly and gratuitously cast aside.

3

The struggle that was to rage for twenty months until the next convention, was one in which external events determined the internal course. Although the cold war is generally dated from the promulgation of the Truman Doctrine in March 1947, and the witch hunt acquired its McCarthyism character three years later, by 1946 the campaign against Communism had become a staple of the media. Every few weeks, another sensation drove home the lesson that Communist Russia was now the enemy and that the United States might eventually have to go to war. In March, Churchill, introduced by Truman, delivered his philippic at Fulton, Missouri, calling to battle the hosts of the Lord. In June came the sensational disclosures from a defecting code-clerk in the Ottawa Soviet embassy about an atomic-espionage network. In the fall came Wallace's forced resignation from the cabinet. In between were repeated crises over Iran, Trieste, Germany, East Europe. It was a year of loud talk and saber-rattling. *Life* magazine ran newspaper ads under the headline, "Why Kid Around?" that claimed Russia and the West could never reach agreement. So the tension built up that culminated in the Truman Doctrine, and Senator Vandenberg told the president that if he wanted congressional support for his program, he had to "scare hell out of the country."

The concern over Russia's expansionist intentions affected the country's internal procedures. Through 1946 Truman sat on the requests, and did not respond to the pressures, coming both from Congress and within his own administration, for additional internal security provisions. After the Republican victory in November he abandoned caution and restraint. Now began the season of competition between moderates and primitives as to who was the best hater of Communism. Before the month was out an extraordinary commission was set up leading to the creation of a Federal Employee Loyalty Program. Truman admitted to Clifton Durr, a liberal attorney who was a member of the Federal Communications Commission, that he had issued his executive order "to take the ball away from Parnell Thomas" (the Republican chairman of the House Committee on Un-American Activities); to which Durr replied "that the order would be construed as giving presidential sanction to the fears that Thomas was trying to create." A disturbed Murray then wrote Truman a private letter asking what grave emergency had made obsolete existing laws against treason and sedition that had afforded sufficient safeguards in wartime. He expressed the fear that "the open expression of opinions on public issues may be listed by the Attorney General as subversive or disloyal."[5]

The rapid reversal in the international conjuncture and domestic atmosphere turned the liberal community into a warring camp. Particularly among the politicized intellectuals, where the tone was often set by ex-Communists turned anti-Communists, the internecine struggle took on the extremism of an apostate who turns on the old faith in which he has become disillusioned. The liberal community was thrown into a crisis because a section of it had been aligned in the thirties and in the war period with popular-front endeavors, or had approved the popular-front rationale. Now liberalism, to remain within the bounds of respectability and acceptability, had to tear itself loose from old alliances and allegiances. The tug of war between those who wanted to cling to the old faith, and those who insisted on getting into the cold war mainstream went on unrelentingly; it led at times to the breakup of lifetime friendships and even families. The ferocity of the struggle arose from the nature of the situation: there was no room for compromise, and this was not an exclusively intellectual debate; people's futures and careers were hanging in the balance.

The war of words went on throughout 1946. The popular-frontists argued that the main danger came from the side of reaction and the threat of war; that Big Three unity was still possible; that if the American government returned to Roosevelt's policy, an accommodation with Russia could be reached; that an alliance with the Communists was still in order, or at the extreme, that the hue and cry raised against Communists—obnoxious though they were— would play into the hands of reaction and hamstring the liberals. On the other side, the cold war adherents argued that Communists were totalitarians working solely in the interests of the Soviet Union; that they schemed to take over all organizations in which they gained a foothold; that the old liberal division of fascists vs. antifascists had to be discarded in favor of the new reality of totalitarians vs. antitotalitarians; that the presence of Communists discredited the liberal movement and alienated the American people from liberalism. Both sides were aware that beyond the debating points was the question whether to remain part of the Democratic coalition, or to take on the risks of opposition.

By the end of the year, the split was formalized. The popular-frontists closed ranks to form the Progressive Citizens of America (PCA), of which Wallace quickly became the spiritual leader and tribal deity. This was a merger of the National Citizens PAC and the Independent Citizens Committee of the Arts, Sciences, and Professions. Hillman, who had opposed the merger for fear that it would edge the Communists too close to the driver's seat, had died the past summer. In any case, his influence at the National Citizens had been reduced. He had been replaced as chairman by Elmer Ben-

261

son, the former Minnesota governor, in an intricate play initiated by Murray, who after the 1944 election started to cool toward his associate. Although many organizers of the merged organization were free-floaters, the PCA reliably propounded the Communist party positions of the period transposed into an appropriate liberal key: Truman had abandoned Roosevelt's liberal program, and unless the Democratic party mended its ways, it was not a vehicle for liberalism. "We cannot therefore rule out the possibility of a new political party, whose fidelity to our goals can be relied upon." It should not be thought that fellow travelers fastened the post-Browder décolletage on naive liberals against the latter's wishes. The PCA was an avowedly popular-front chautauqua at which popular-frontists foregathered. It must be recalled that in this first stage there was considerable disillusionment with Truman and fear of the cold war in liberal and labor circles; if the PCA was less than the La Follette movement of 1924, it was more than a transmission belt of fellow-travelers. Because the American climate was changing very rapidly, it took some time for many to sort out their positions, affiliations, and housekeeping arrangements. The PCA thus represented not just the Communists', but some liberals' last forlorn attempt to breathe fresh life into the fast-disintegrating wartime popular front.

A week after PCA's formation, the anti-Communist liberals assembled in Washington to regroup the liberal community on a new basis under the aegis of Americans for Democratic Action (ADA). "We reject any association with Communism in the United States as completely as we reject any association with Fascists or their sympathizers. Both are hostile to the principles of freedom and democracy" read the platform. The new organization had all the advantages. It had the blessings of Eleanor Roosevelt and a galaxy of the big names of the New Deal era. It enrolled major anti-Communist labor leaders and the spokesmen of the NAACP. It boasted the sponsorship of some of the country's most prestigious intellectuals and journalists. Above all, it was in tune with the times and trends. Despite the anguished wails coming from the *Nation* and *PM* deploring the division of the liberal community, within a year it was clear that the ADA represented the new look, the vital center of mainline liberalism. Some have pointed out that at the close of 1947, the ADA was no more than half the size of the PCA. The size of memberships in these types of organizations is not decisive for indicating influence; in any case, they should have added that the ADA was moving up and the PCA was heading for destruction.[6]

4

This was the environment in which Reuther made his supreme bid to take over the union. As in the Homer Martin civil war, the national office was split into two war camps drawing in all personnel, not excluding typists. Every difference, no matter how trifling, no matter how remote from affecting the power equation, got caught up in the desperate grapple. The fight was unlike the earlier one in that both contestants had learned that it was counterproductive to flash guns or to attempt to expel antagonists. Barring that, both camps employed every argument and device, moderate and immoderate, that seemed likely to enhance their respective fortunes. Both sides worked under the grim realization that the defeated faction would not occupy the opposition benches henceforth, but would be cast out of the assemblage.

The Addes-Thomas-Leonard coalition made several serious tactical mistakes in the course of the struggle. At the time, more importance was attributed to them in shaping the lineups than they deserved. From the historian's vantage point, it can be seen that it was the Red issue that dominated and determined the outcome. There is no other reasonable explanation for the overwhelming sweep of the Reuther forces, the crackup of the Addes caucus, and the disappearance of the neutral bloc; in other words, not a shift, but a complete overturn of the power balances that existed for seven years. For that reason, the fate of the Addes coalition was sealed unless it could rid itself of the albatross that Reuther had hung around its neck. Since Communist influence in the auto union was at this time limited, the Reuther faction belabored its opponents with the charge that was to become increasingly familiar and effective across the country in the gathering hysteria; that they were dupes of Communists, that they had Communists working for them, that they failed to repudiate and throw out the Communists. The only way the Addes crewmen could have pushed the war on to different ground was by themselves denouncing Communists and demonstratively expelling them from their faction. Even this may not have sufficed.

Under different circumstances, President Truman and Democratic liberals employed an allied strategy to take the witch hunt away from the witch hunters. It seemed to work for them in the 1948 campaign, but in the end Truman was upstaged and traduced by the rogue politicians who had sprouted in the nursery he had fostered. The Addes faction politicians, who certainly had no ideological or principled predilections that would have prevented them from throwing over their Communist supporters, were held back by organizational calculations: they were afraid that tossing the Communists to the wolves would cost them the margin that would shift the balance to the foe. They had been confronted with the Red issue in one form or another since entering union life and proceeded on the assumption that they could juggle with it as they had in the past. They did not understand until too late that their position was desperate, that the Red issue in the midst of the cold war was a time bomb that would explode in their faces at the appointed hour.

The first important test came shortly after Reuther's accession to the presidency at the Michigan state CIO convention in June. The test was the more telling because the convention was to a considerable extent an auto workers' reunion, and the Addes forces were handed a bonus with the support of the steel delegation headed by Glen Sigman. (This was a holdover from Murray's personal animosity toward Reuther, from the stage in which Murray was still trying to finesse the Red issue.) As against the 1943 Michigan convention where the entire leadership including the Communists lined up to quell strike and third-party insurgent talk, this time everything revolved around the struggle between the Reuther and Addes camps.

In their maladroitness, the Communists helped the Reuther cause along by using fast footwork to install one of their stalwarts, John Anderson, as chairman of the Sigman-Addes caucus, and to push three of their well-known reliables on to the Sigman slate. The anti-Reuther people were so terrified of the Red accusation that this almost blew up the Sigman-Addes caucus. Anti-Reuther delegates were openly cursing the Communists, announcing to all and sundry that they would not vote a straight ticket. Leonard proposed to throw the Communists out of the caucus. Addes told reporters, who were buzzing around convention lobbies, that he was against all outside groups—Communists, Socialists, Trotskyites—interfering in union affairs. What personal relations were between the Communists and their putative caucus allies can be gathered from a later report of the Michigan State Communist party that referred to "the

264

expulsion of Communists from the Addes-Thomas-Leonard caucus in June 1946."

The election results told their story: August Scholle, the Reuther candidate—a colorless functionary—won 55 percent of the vote, and the Reutherites, in addition, took all 17 vice-presidencies—the first time in the history of the Michigan CIO that one group captured all elective offices. The three Communist followers ran far behind the rest of the Sigman-Addes slate vote. Thus, in the three months between the 1946 auto convention and the Michigan CIO convention, before any of the so-called trade-union issues and embittered personal charges could appreciably sway positions, there had taken place a decided shift to Reuther, presaging his triumphal sweep at the next UAW convention.[7]

Developments in the entire CIO were no less conducive than those in Michigan for the Reuther advance. Murray had been running the national office of the CIO like an unlimited monarch in the tradition established by Lewis whose first lieutenant he had been since assuming the vice-presidency of the mine union in 1920. That machine-ridden outfit had been the model for the steel union, which he headed; the two men had the same ideas on administration, but personally, Murray was as unlike the mentor in whose shadow he had labored for two decades as Anthony Eden was unlike Churchill. Although Irish, he spoke with a soft ingratiating Scots burr, had come from Glasgow with his father to this country when he was 16, and both father and son went to work in the coal fields. His smooth-featured, open countenance, his easy, conciliatory, and courteous manner betokened the natural diplomat. His innate tact and good sense were expressions of a practical-minded man whose natural bent was to compose differences and find the common ground for agreement. This outward suavity generally hid from view the part of his personality that was intensely high-strung and prone to agonize and spill over emotionally when faced with unwanted choices. While accepting the CIO presidency at Lewis's hands, and at the travesty of a trial a year and a half later held in the basement of the United Mine Workers building when Lewis removed him as the mine union vice-president, Murray's performance resembled that of a driven character in a Graham Greene novel.

Murray had participated with Lewis in the cynical game of working with Communists, and continued to do so during the war years. Yet he could not look at Communists and Communism in the detached way that Lewis or Hillman did. He was a devout Catholic and was emotionally concerned. Lahey recalled that Murray hated Communists "because he had a genuine aversion for political unorthodoxy." His feelings surfaced at the Conference of Progressives in the fall of 1946—the last "united" gathering of liberals before the split was formalized—at which he burst out, to the consternation of the popular-frontists, that organized labor "wants no damn Communists meddling in our affairs." When Benson tried to have a private talk with Murray later to express alarm about rumors that Murray might resign as CIO head, Murray's response astounded him. As reported by MacDougall, who heard it from Benson, "Beating his breast and actually tearing at his clothing, Murray wailed, 'You don't know what I've been through. My soul has just been torn apart!' And kept repeating the same words, so that there was no use in continuing the conversation."[8]

Murray was in an acute dilemma when the cold war became the monumental political reality. His own predilection was to summarily clean out the Communists as he had done earlier in the steel union. He was under growing pressure to do so from sources that he was anxious to propitiate, not just press representatives and newscasters, and Catholic advisers like Father Rice of the ACTU to whom he was close, but also the right-wing bloc of the CIO. All the same, Communists who controlled international unions could not be expelled without causing a split. As a born fixer, he saw this as a problem that had to be manipulated. He was temporizing tactically, and he was torn emotionally. He was not straddling the issue, as he was accused of doing. He was trying to pressure, some officials into breaking with the Communist camp, so as to avoid surgical action or at least, were this impossible, minimize the loss of blood. His tacking, veering, double-tracking, which bewildered many, led Reuther, Rieve, Baldanzi, and Green of the right-wing bloc to redouble their pressure, and the Communists to cling for dear life to his coattails to save them from the hotspurs. In the overheated Communist rhetoric, this was described as an attempt to maintain the center-Left bloc against the Right. The analysis was faulty. Murray had neither a bloc nor an understanding with the Communists, and his difference with the Right was transient and secondary, centering on tempo. The men around Murray, both in the steel union and in the CIO, were staunchly conservative, heavily Catholic, all of them business-agent types decidedly opposed to all ideological unionists, prone to sneer, in their private convivial gatherings, at "pinkos" like Hillman and Reuther.

At the executive board meeting just prior to the 1946 CIO convention, he forced through the appointment of a six-man committee made up of three Communist supporters and three of the right wing, who then unanimously brought out a so-called compromise resolution. The heart of the resolution was in the declaration that the CIO delegates "resent and reject efforts of the Communist Party or other political parties and their adherents to interfere in the affairs of the CIO. This convention serves notice that we will not tolerate such interference." The board made clear that this was no mere rhetorical exercise by amending the constitution governing city and state CIO bodies. Under the altered provisions, these bodies were instructed to take no positions and issue no statements in conflict with CIO policy, or send delegates or make contributions to organizations not recognized by the CIO.

Murray read the resolution to the convention which adopted it without any debate. When two Communist officials from the maritime union broke Party discipline to vote against the resolution, they were harangued openly by their comrades, whereupon they rushed to the platform to inform Murray that they were changing their votes. Murray then primly announced to the convention that the declaration had carried unanimously. Again, as during the Stalin-Hitler-pact days, convention delegates and the public were treated to the unedifying spectacle of Communists voting to denounce themselves, while the report on tightening the screws on CP-led city and state councils was presented by none other than Reid Robinson of Mine Mill. Like overpowered captains who hoped to trade servility for time, they turned the other cheek. De Caux again came forward with his apologia: "There was some method in the meekness of the lefts. They had to retreat under conditions that threatened a rout." George Morris, the *Daily Worker* labor columnist, explained to his bewildered readers that "there can be no doubt of the correctness of the action of the Communists . . . by this agreement to vote for the statement after they succeeded in eliminating all the major damage that the right wing sought to include in it. That is how a united front works."

If that is the way a Communist united front is supposed to work, Lenin would be turning over in his grave. Disregarding the squalidness of the Communists' behavior, was it not true that had they fought the declaration they would have hastened the expulsions that took place in 1949? Possibly. And had not Lenin advised Communists to conceal their views to avoid getting expelled? Yes, he did. But he had in mind a different breed of Communists, and Communists that were not well known. Besides being public figures, Bridges, Matles, and Robinson had only yesterday flaunted their patriotism, not Leninist antiwar intransigence. It was not the last-minute tactic, it was the entire course of the Communist party over decades that was thrusting these officials into a false position where they could not admit why they switched policies.

Murray had executed a crafty maneuver: he made the Communists place the noose around their own necks. (Some of his next two years' backing and filling came, to be sure, from his perplexities and vacillations, but the direction of his movement was never in doubt.) This did not satisfy the die-hards. The Jewish Daily *Forward* accused Murray of running away from the battle. With greater perspicacity, the *New York Times* said the resolution represented a Communist defeat, and anticipated that the Communists would be swept out of the CIO.[9]

All this was in November 1946. Before the next year's convention, the Communist issue convulsed one CIO union after another, including the three strongholds of the Communist party, United Electrical, Maritime, and Mine Mill.

In the UE, Carey officially set up an anti-Communist caucus, which started to challenge the Communist administration aggressively and systematically. In a letter to the editor of *UE News*, Carey stated, "The issue between me and the present UE leadership goes solely to the proposition that our great International Union has become known as a transmission belt for the American Communist Party." Fitzgerald, the UE president, wanted to bring Carey up on charges in the CIO, but Murray ignored him. In March, the UE executive board branded the Carey caucus a "dual movement" and ordered it to disband. At the UE convention in the fall, the Communists, still riding high, ordered the opposition to dissolve or face expulsion with the executive board empowered to suspend local unions. A confident Carey, with the knowledge that he was part of the CIO majority, replied, "I am in this fight, and I will remain, in the face of any action to purge the UE. I think that ultimately we will win, and get the Communists out of this union."

268

In the NMU the passage at arms started at the same time. At the end of 1946, the *Pilot* carried the notice that Joseph Curran, the union president, had resigned from the Committee for Maritime Unity. This committee, designed to coordinate and strengthen the bargaining position of the CIO maritime unions on both coasts in relation to employers and AFL rivals, had as its main aim the enhancement of Communist control. By means of this instrumentality, Bridges and the Communists in the NMU could bring to bear their united influences. Curran, an archetype of "pork chops" unionism, had been a faithful mouthpiece for the Communist crewmen in the NMU through their various twists and turns because the Communists ran the power machine. What gave him courage to declare war on them was not just the new winds blowing through the CIO, and Murray's personal encouragement, but more important for his immediate prospects, the split among the maritime Communists themselves. In Curran's corner now stood Jack Lawrenson, a vice-president, and M. Hedley Stone, the treasurer, and the sizable following that they commanded. The skirmishing of the past months went into a war of decision. Because Lawrenson and Stone had broken with the Communist party as proponents of militant unionism, and Curran needed their support, the initial encounter took on the character of a struggle between left syndicalists and manipulable, line-changing Stalinists, although the Red issue was certainly never very far in the background. Without a change of climate in the country and in the CIO, there would have been no split of the Communist faction in the NMU, and there would have been no split between Curran and the Communists. In a disorderly 24-day convention held in September, the Curran forces trounced the Communists. And in the subsequent referendum in July 1948, the Curran slate swept the Communists out of office by 2-to-1 margins; Curran himself was reelected by a 3-to-1 vote.

In Mine Mill, the right-wing leaders, after being defeated in the referendum election, which they charged had been fraudulently conducted, organized a secession movement of eastern locals. The Communists, to disencumber themselves for the battle against the secessionists, forced the resignation of their spokesman, Reid Robinson, who had been caught soliciting a $5,000 payoff from a mine company executive, replacing him with a reliable Party man, Maurice Travis. The fight in the union was nationally reported, management publications were openly urging union members to vote against Communist candidates, Catholic priests in Connecticut were calling for support of secession officials. The CIO executive board, on Murray's proposal, set up a committee of three to investigate what was going on and to make recommendations. The committee reported back in May that the basic reason for the dissension was Communist infiltration. Copies of letters were introduced "which proved beyond question of doubt that Maurice Travis was continuously dealing with representatives of the Communist Party in shaping the policy of the union." The committee called for his resignation or removal. At the same time, it condemned secession, recommended disbanding the secessionist group, asked the Shipbuilding union to reconsider its action in issuing charters to the rebel locals, and called for the appointment of an administrator over the union. The board approved the report and recommendations, but neither Mine Mill nor Shipbuilding officials would yield. The board then voted to publish and circulate the report.

At one point, when right-wingers complained that their unions were under attack for "harboring Communists," Murray burst out, "It is high time the CIO leaders stopped apologizing for Communism. If Communism is an issue in any of your unions, throw it to hell out, and throw its advocates out along with it. When a man accepts office . . . to render service to workers, and then delivers that service to outside interests, that man is nothing but a damned traitor." This declaration was then run as a credo on the masthead of *The Real UE*, the newspaper of the Carey-Block faction. The following month, Murray threw out De Caux as CIO editor and publicity chief. Pressman was to follow eight months later.*[10]

Formally, the 1947 CIO convention meeting in Boston in October was to continue the synthetic unity of the previous convention. In reality, Murray was the impresario of a major demonstration against the Communists. The public had been deluged with press reports on how Stalin was fighting the Marshall Plan, had forced Czecho-

---

* At the same time, and on the same issue, the Communists were being pushed against the wall in the one AFL international union in which they had strength, and which they had done so much to build, the Hotel and Restaurant Workers. At the convention in April, the delegates, after an impassioned debate, voted to bar Communists from office. With the passage of the resolution, a large body of delegates carrying American flags marched to the rostrum and, with most on the convention floor joining in, sang "God Bless America."

slovakia and Poland to withdraw their support, and all because he wanted privation and disorder in Europe to further the Communist cause. Here at the CIO convention, Secretary of State George C. Marshall appeared as the major guest speaker, introduced and hailed by Murray in ecstatic superlatives. Marshall made an oblique attack against the Soviet leaders and stressed that labor had a "vital stake in the preservation of free institutions in the world," which the Marshall Plan was designed to sustain. So, while the foreign policy resolution spoke only of "sound programs for postwar rehabilitation" without mentioning the Marshall Plan by name, and was adopted unanimously, the convention action, Murray's endorsement of the "Marshall idea," as well as the thunderous demonstration for Marshall, were accepted by the delegates and the press as another calculated repudiation of the Communists—which they were. This time, on the floor, Reuther and his cothinkers, aided and abetted by Murray, lashed out at their opponents, while the Communists responded in kind—all under cover of supporting one and the same foreign policy resolution. The show of public unity was falling apart.[11]

ELEVEN · *Showdown in Auto and Electrical Unions*

As the fight went into its decisive stage in the auto union, Reuther was moving confidently in the swift-flowing CIO and national currents while his opponents were clinging to positions that the cold war was shunting aside. Their two specific mistakes, which they could have avoided, and which cost them heavily, gave comfort to a Reuther who was already on his way to victory, no longer needing the marginal votes to repeat his previous hair's-breadth election.

The first mistake revolved around another blowup at the Allis-Chalmers plant in Milwaukee. A strike was forced by the company. It withdrew the maintenance of membership that had been imposed by the War Labor Board, proposed to cut down steward representation, made a final wage offer of 13½-cent wage increase, 5 cents less than the national pattern. It was a declaration of war, and the company conceived its proposals as such. The *Wall Street Journal* reported that "The [Allis-Chalmers] companies feel they are in a good strategic position. Losses are offset to a considerable extent by tax credits." One Allis-Chalmers official was quoted as saying that the strike would end when " 'the union capitulates or when the union is broken.' " A year later, Harold Story, the architect of the company's labor policy, boasted before the National Association of Manufacturers convention that the company took advantage of the change in public opinion to crack the union.

The strike began at the end of April 1946, and mass picket lines shut the plant down. At the end of May, on the company's complaint of illegal picketing, the Wisconsin Employment Relations Board ordered the local to "stop mass picketing and interfering with anyone entering the plant." There was a lull for several months with rumors afloat that the government might take over the plant to ensure continued production of farm machinery. Secretary of Labor Schwellenbach said there might be a government seizure, and President Truman made an ambiguous remark of a similar nature in one of his press conferences. The union's hopes were dashed when Truman announced on August 12 that the strike did not constitute a national emergency.

Over the summer months federal conciliators fruitlessly tried to

272

bring the two sides together. In the fall, with members already tired out by five months of striking, the two Milwaukee newspapers launched an attack of unusual severity on the Local 248 Communist leadership. One would have to go back, in recent times, to the San Francisco press campaign against the 1934 longshore strikers for a comparative drumfire. Typical headlines in the *Milwaukee Journal* and *Milwaukee Sentinel* read: "Allis-Chalmers Union Is Bled by Red Leaders"; "Red Prober Looks at 22 More A-C Bosses"; "Communist Party Line Adhered to by Local 248." The press had no lack of ammunition. It was handed voluminous documentation by the company, which for years had been building up dossiers. Investigators of the House Committee on Un-American Activities, on the scene to collect witnesses and materials for coming hearings to discredit the strike, were not reticent in supplying reporters with lurid copy. Furthermore, the fight to wrest control of the CIO Industrial Union Council from the Communists came into the open at this time so that company officials and newspapers could quote the statements and resolutions of right-wing CIO officials as authority for their charges.

In October the company started a back-to-work movement to break the strike, and Allis-Chalmers again became a national *cause célèbre*. There were repeated clashes and outbursts of violence at the plant gates; the company again filed charges against the union for illegal picketing; and the Wisconsin board ruled at the end of the year that only two pickets were to be permitted at each gate. Thereupon, a so-called independent union appeared on the scene and petitioned the Wisconsin board for a new bargaining election, which the board scheduled for the end of January. By this time, some 4,000 workers were going through the picket lines to the daily acclaim of the newspapers. Now, the Addes-Thomas-Leonard people acted injudiciously. With their past knowledge of the obdurate character of the Allis-Chalmers company and the long history of internal dissension in Local 248, in the light of the ferocious anti-Red campaign against the union whose strike was not being supported by many anti-Communist locals in the area, they should have realized there would be no great victory that anyone could claim credit for. The strike had already dragged on for eight months, and it was no longer fully effective. Instead of binding Reuther to common decisions and ending the strike on the best terms available, they sought to portray their faction as the indomitable militant, as against Reuther, the faintheart.

At the UAW executive board meeting in December an edition of the *Milwaukee Journal* was passed around. Practically the entire front page of the paper was devoted to an attack on the strike. Also featured was a photo of Reuther at the Milwaukee airport shaking hands with Walter Cappel, the local opponent of the Local 248 strike leadership. The board majority rejected Reuther's proposal to put the local under an administrator (which the company demanded), and to proceed, in effect, to settle on the company's terms. After the local won the representation election by a vote of 4,122 to 4,091, Thomas publicly charged that Reuther had violated the constitution in personally meeting with company representatives without either Thomas (who had been appointed by the international executive board to take charge of the strike) or members of the local bargaining committee being present. Reuther, he said, had "provided the company with propaganda machinery" to mislead the workers. He sent a 39-page report to all UAW locals blaming Reuther's "peace negotiations" for swinging a sure victory in the election to a near defeat. When the company refused to permit the attendance of local officials at the negotiations, he argued, the meeting should have ended then and there. Reuther replied with a letter of his own to all locals that the board had authorized him to proceed with the meeting, and enclosed an additional letter from John Brophy, the CIO representative, in which a fine distinction was made between negotiating and exploring. He and Reuther, Brophy's letter explained, did not negotiate; they simply explored the company's proposals and reported them back to the UAW Policy Committee.

The company's offer at the second meeting was so complicated and tricky that its precise arithmetical meaning could not be readily determined. While it proceeded from a base of a 13½-cent increase, this was pegged to area averages. At the third meeting with the company, in which Thomas participated, Story reminded the union representatives that the company's offer "was conditional on cleaning up the local situation." The company's proposition was clearly unsatisfactory under ordinary circumstances, and Thomas' criticisms were amply justified by UAW standards. Whether a settlement could have been made even on those terms, in view of Story's determination to interfere in the local's internal affairs, was uncertain. But this was no ordinary situation. In effect, the UAW was trying to negotiate a settlement of a strike that was already lost, in the midst of an internal split on precisely the issue that the Allis-Chalmers management was using to its own advantage. Any settle-

274

ment at this point was bound to be less than satisfactory—if indeed a settlement was possible. In the end, because they would not and could not attempt a full-scale mobilization to save the strike, nor agree to a settlement on the best terms available (which would have meant the international taking over negotiations from the local officers and taking responsibility for a poor settlement), the situation was permitted to drag and deteriorate amidst a welter of charges and countercharges, with the Addes-faction leaders in the position of sheltering the Communist group in Milwaukee that was losing a strike.* Because the Addes-faction leaders would not force Reuther to make good on his claim that the strike could be settled, they bore the obloquy for the debacle.

The Wisconsin board announced a new runoff election for late March 1947 on the grounds that in the first election no union had won an absolute majority. This time, the Local 248 leaders did not dare face a vote. Before the election could be held, they called off the strike without a contract or any concessions. The strike had lasted eleven months, had been permitted to drift aimlessly because of the internal union paralysis. In the context of the struggle, the *Milwaukee Journal* was not far wrong in reporting, "Reuther scores victory over Thomas since the strike ended in unconditional surrender." The disintegration of their main power base brought to an end the Communists' prominence in the Milwaukee and Wisconsin CIO. In December 1946, after a three-month struggle, the right-wingers, with the help of Brophy and the national CIO, voted out all Communist officers in the Milwaukee Council. This was followed shortly with an equally resounding right-wing victory in the Wisconsin state organization.[1]

The rout in Wisconsin showed Addes that he was losing the fight. He and his lieutenants tried to reverse the tide by an organizational sleight of hand—the typical thinking of the Addes strategists. At the June 1947 executive board meeting, they sprang a surprise proposal to accept into the UAW the Farm Equipment union (FE) where its estimated 40,000 members would command some 400 votes at the next UAW convention. Since FE was Communist-controlled, it was

---

* Governor Kim Sigler of Michigan testified before the House Committee on Un-American Activities that Addes, Thomas, and Leonard were "Communist captives," testimony given prominence in the Michigan and Wisconsin press. Reuther formally disassociated himself from the governor, while the latter earned the *Wage Earner's* commendation: "He is performing a service to the people of Michigan in exposing a lot of Communist monkey-business."

foregone that these votes would be cast in favor of the Addes candidates. Addes thought to beat down challenges to the constitutionality of the board's decision by attaching a proviso that the proposed merger was to be passed on the next month in a referendum vote of all UAW locals. He was banking his hopes for a favorable outcome on the appeal of ending jurisdictional strife in this field by uniting all farm equipment workers within the UAW. For the same reason, the Reuther strategists were worried that their objections to the terms of the merger might be waved away because of the unity allure. They mobilized their top speakers, and for the next month the pitchmen on both sides determinedly hawked their wares to locals across the country.

Ostensibly, the debaters were arguing their positions on grounds of union principles. The proponents pointed out that the proposal would unite the farm equipment workers, would help fight the Taft-Hartley law, and that the merger had been favored in the past by the CIO and by Reuther himself. The opponents countered that the merger would violate industrial union principles by setting up an autonomous farm equipment division, that it would guarantee the jobs of all FE officers and staff members while saddling the union with FE's debts, that it would unconstitutionally guarantee full voting strength to FE locals. Actually, everybody understood that the merger proposition was a rigged contrivance designed to bolster the Addes faction's waning strength. Regardless of the acceptability of the proposal under normal circumstances, it was a crude strategem to introduce it in the midst of a battle in order to affect the outcome. Such gerrymandering dodges succeeded in unions in which the membership was throttled. In the auto union of 1947, it could only redound to the benefit of the opposing camp. The better than 2-to-1 Reuther triumph, 3,898 to 1,842 (the votes were computed on the basis of previous convention strength of local unions), meant that the struggle for control was settled four months before the convocation of the convention. Leaflets and brochures continued to rain down like summer squalls on union members right up to the convention date in November. It was only a response to the inertial dynamism of two geared-up and keyed-up bureaucracies. The fight to displace Reuther had been lost. All that remained was to legalize the transfer of power. (The *Wage Earner*, which had excellent sources of information, concluded that no more than 7 percent of the membership voted on the merger. Apparently, the membership was tired of the faction fight. Given the conditions, this probably further enhanced Reuther's position: he was the indicated strong man whose victory could put an end to inter-union squabbling.) The maximum strength that the Addes forces were able to muster at the convention was in the vote for secretary-treasurer, for which post Mazey defeated Addes by a vote of 4,833 to 2,599. The two Reutherite vice-presidential aspirants trounced Thomas and Leonard by even more lopsided majorities, while Reuther himself faced only nominal opposition. The Addes faction had disintegrated.[2]

Reuther's campaign has been described as the classic illustration of how to defeat the Communists democratically without resort to repression or Red-baiting. While the press generally interpreted his election as signifying the CIO's swing to the right, and the more fervent called it a victory for the "free world," numbers of anti-Communist Left writers insisted that he had fought Stalinist totalitarianism, not Left dissent or radicalism, and had done that by going to the ranks with a program of militant unionism and not by imposing administrative sanctions. Has time made it easier to ascertain the true nature of the protagonists?

The battle fire was clearly directed at a Stalinist faction that was subservient to the Kremlin. That is not controversial. But there was more to the anti-Red drive than repudiation of Stalin's tyranny and American Stalinists' unprincipledness. The drive fed on and sustained the delirium that was spreading in the wake of the cold war. It was considered by the union ranks and the media a campaign to clean up disloyal elements, a campaign for which the conservatives defined the tenets of true Americanism and of legitimate trade-unionism. Because of the uninhibited oscillations of the Stalinized Communists, the stockjobbing of the Addes caucus politicians, and the studied attempts of Reuther and his coworkers to portray themselves the expositors of progressive unionism, the older categories of Left and Right were inappropriate for describing the two contending camps. That did not gainsay the fact that cold war anti-Communism was the starting point for a generalized repudiation of political nonconformism and a strong contributory stream to the rising waters of the big second postwar Red scare.

Furthermore, the Reuther faction was not battling a Communist faction, or a Communist-led faction similar to the union leadership of Mine Mill or of the electrical union. It was battling an opposing group composed of union politicos who were like most of its own adherents. To be sure, this opposing caucus had Communist sup-

277

porters, and these depended on the caucus to maintain their position inside the union; but it was hyperbole when Reuther, in his *Collier's* article, stated: "We understood that the alternative to a finish fight was Communist control of our union." There can be argument as to the precise percentage of influence that the Communist group represented in the UAW in 1945-1947; there is no question that it was of a secondary, probably of a tertiary, order, and that it was a declining influence. As the Party criticisms of its own UAW stalwarts indicated, Communists were having to accommodate themselves to the caucus leaders, and not the other way around. (At the February 1948 plenum of the Communist party, Williamson gave the UAW as an example of "the Left becoming prisoners of its allies": "The Left Wing became so enmeshed in the Addes-Thomas-Leonard caucus—in its weaknesses, its isolation from the local unions, its job corruption, its factionalism, etc.—that the workers could not distinguish one group from the other.") The Reuther crusade against the Communists consequently had a considerable interlarding of the same flummery as that of the professional Red-hunters' crusade in the nation at large: fulminations against Communists were often designed to further political ambitions antecedent and not invariably related to the Communist issue.[3]

Regardless of the use or misuse of the issue, did Reuther embody a more militant brand of unionism than that symbolized by his opponents? That he was socially more alert than Addes does not answer the question; indeed, it is a question to which there is no conclusive answer. Both Reuther and his opponents were offspring of the same UAW tradition of labor assertiveness and self-confidence, and both had become domesticated during the war so that their outlook had undergone a sea change. They were convinced that the era of embittered agitation and massed confrontations was over, that the time of the boomer and evangel had passed, that the union had to be stabilized and businesslike relations consolidated with employers. Reuther-caucus regional directors preached a collective-bargaining and union administration that was no different than that advocated by Addes-caucus regional directors. The difference between the two factions was extraneous to employer-employee relations, or what is called bread-and-butter unionism. Reuther tried to impress the members with his superior fighting abilities in the GM strike of 1946, but that was more a matter of posturing and public relations than of substance; Addes people made similar, if less skillful, forays in the quest for factional advantage.

The fact is that Reuther's takeover spelled the end of the auto union's turbulent democracy; it triggered a rapid internal bureaucratization, and what had been a phenomenon of pluralism was snuffed out. The union went into its stage of maturity, as a postwar generation of sociologists and economists defined it, a stage in which the union became a parallel administration in the management control system. Would the union have followed a different course if the Addes caucus had triumphed? There is no difficulty in surmising that with a time lag of two years, the UAW would have evolved in the same way. The Addes officials would have disencumbered themselves of the Communist hangers-on when the CIO expelled the Communist-led unions, and union internal dispositions and bargaining with the corporations would have proceeded along lines similar to those followed by their conquerors. The speculation is hardly an arbitrary one because the Addes people were not animated by principles in their toleration of Communists; they were caught up in an association from the past that they no longer wanted but did not know how to break. Once control and patronage were not at issue, they saw eye to eye with their opponents on economic and political questions.

If Reuther publicists and admirers misinterpreted the character of the victory, they were on firmer ground when they boasted that it had all been done democratically. There was an untrammeled debate and a free and fair election. The two sides had both the opportunity and resources to get their messages to the membership, to hurl whatever accusations they saw fit at their rivals, to answer accusations in whatever fashion they thought best. But because Reuther won, and won overwhelmingly, in this democratic exchange, and by means of this democratic procedure, he did not thereby become the avatar of democracy within the UAW. He was in the long tradition of leaders who sported the democratic cockade when seeking office, and who cast it aside when they won office.

2

The surprise of the battle was not that by wielding the Red issue in the developing cold war Reuther was able to shatter the opposition, but that the leadership of the UE, which was the main Communist fortress in the labor movement, could be shaken off only by *force* *majeure* from the outside.*[4] The struggle in this third-largest union in the CIO brought into bold relief another aspect of the internal controversy, and warrants a review of this union from its beginnings.

The fundamental explanation for the Communists' ability to take over the UE in contrast to their steady decline in the UAW lies in the UE's relatively slow growth and untempestuous development. The consequences were a politically less-alert and less-demanding membership, and an inability to throw up opposition spokesmen of breadth and stature comparable to the Communist pioneers. Possibly, the greater concentration of the automobile industry compared to the electrical industry, and the continual recruitment of the young and vigorous from throughout the country, were factors, but if they were, they were two of a larger number that made Detroit and Flint, rather than Schenectady and Pittsburgh, cockpits of the CIO. So far as observers of the labor scene could tell, UAW and UE members were alike in political outlook and social behavior.

The two unions also had a similar origin. The UE came into being in March 1936 (the UAW South Bend convention was in April) after a fusion of several AFL federal radio locals and independent unions. The latter came either directly from the TUUL Metal Workers Industrial Union, or consisted of skeleton groups set up for the most part by Communists in GE, Westinghouse, and RCA-Victor. The federal locals had formed a National Council at the end of 1933, and for two years had the same frustrating experience as the auto workers in trying to obtain an industrial union charter. Negotiations were finally broken off when the AFL Executive Council ordered the radio locals to affiliate with the International Brotherhood of Electrical Workers, a building-trades union whose membership consisted largely of line craftsmen. The industrial shop workers had the

* Many impulses, personal, organizational, and economic, interacted so that it is impossible to lay out one set of rules that would account for the ranks' inability in a number of unions to dislodge Communists until the latter's expulsion from the CIO. In unions with inconsequential memberships and few bargaining arrangements, like the office-, or food and tobacco workers, the Communist machines could easily determine output. In Mine Mill, it was the shabbiness of the opposition that, in effect, handed leadership back to the defeated Communists. In the West Coast longshore union, Bridges' prestige as the Founding Father, his bending to members' sensibilities, and his close-knit relations with employers who viewed him as a force for stability and responsibility in the industry, saw him through his difficulties. In the fur union, Ben Gold and his friends, armed with a heroic record going back to the twenties, were considered by the active membership indispensable to the successful conduct of union business.

choice of paying high dues they could not afford, or accepting "Class B" memberships which gave them very few voting rights. In either case, they had no assurance that their local memberships would not be eventually divided and assigned to various craft unions claiming jurisdiction over them. The radio council, which had been in close touch with Lewis and the CIO, disregarded AFL instructions and joined with the independents to set up its own industrial organization.

Thus, the electrical union belonged to the same species as the auto union. But there was a difference in the inner spirit. There had been no Auto-Lite strike or Chevrolet strike in its formative days, no elemental upsurge of 1934 to be followed by an AFL surrender and disintegration, no face-to-face confrontations with baffled and frightened AFL hierarchs. When the auto delegates assembled in 1936, they had known smashed strikes and successful strikes, violent encounters, the clash of ideologies; they were privy to egotism, ambition, betrayal, and stupidity bred of narrowly conceived self-interest, the passions and ruthlessness of humans in conflict. The electrical contingents were tyros and provincials in comparison.

James Carey was elected president. He was from Philco in Philadelphia, the federal locals of which were an elite at the foundation convention; they were the only ones at the time that had a written agreement and a union shop. There had been a week's strike in July 1933, successfully concluded with the agreement, and the Philco group represented 40 percent of the then total membership of 16,000. Carey was 25 years old and looked like a big comer in the labor movement. He was of Irish stock, had worked his way up to the job of inspector by attending night classes at Drexel Institute, had been the spokesman of the federal locals, had purposefully and capably conducted the drawn-out negotiations with Green and the Executive Council. He was a small, wiry, terrierlike figure, quick-moving and quick-witted, boundlessly energetic and talkative. He also had a sharp tongue that he made no attempt to curb, that marked off his bantam-rooster cockiness. At 25 all this enhanced his leadership potentialities. A few years later, no longer the child prodigy, his brashness and wiseacre glibness, which sometimes bordered on the sophomoric, rubbed many the wrong way. Rather than an overflow of exuberance, they were seen as evidences of a lack of base and surface. Not that he was another Homer Martin; he was a hard worker who kept his considerable ego within reasonable bounds; but he had a touch of the ex-minister's flightiness. His

281

co-worker, Julius Emspak, the elected secretary-treasurer, came from the independent section of the fusion. He was a tool maker at the Schenectady GE plant who started as a philosophy student at Brown University. Like Carey, he had been through the ins and outs of pioneer unionism from NRA days, but in his case, as a Communist participating in the Communist operation. He made up for his lack of color or dynamism by steadiness, reliability, and dedication.

The Communists exercised far greater control at the UE founding convention than they had in auto. According to their figures, they had a 1935 membership of 1,250 in metal (excluding steel) as against 550 in auto, but these included members in miscellaneous machine shops that did not enter UE until a year later. What was decisive, in any case, was that a disproportionate number of activists outside of Carey's Philadelphia group were either Communists or allied with them, and that relations between the TUUL members and Carey were completely harmonious. In 1936 they were in auto, too, more or less, but the nonpoliticals knew who was who, and that knowledge played a big part in the apportionment of posts. In the UE executive board of twelve, at least half were either Communists or part of their group. The *People's Press*, a pseudo-independent Communist newspaper, was made the union's official organ— something no one would have dared propose at South Bend. The very obscurity and unimportance of this Buffalo convention made it possible for the Communists to fasten their grip without contest on the fledgling organization. After the convention, Carey and Emspak moved into the new national headquarters which consisted of several rooms at an office building in New York City rented at $27.50 a month and outfitted with secondhand furniture. Lee Pressman became the union's legal adviser, and Stella Abrams, a young Communist secretary who shortly married Emspak, took over the daily functioning of the office.

As if this were not sufficient, James Matles, at the head of several machinery and fabricating locals, entered UE a year later. He had come to this country as a young immigrant from Rumania, had been active in the Young Workers (Communist) League, and then, while he served a machinist apprenticeship, became a leader in the TUUL machinery field in New York City after quickly revealing unusual abilities as an organizer. In accordance with Party policy in 1935 of going into the AFL, the steel members of the Steel and Metal Workers Industrial Union joined Mike Tighe's Amalgamated Association. Matles, who headed the truncated Metal Workers Industrial Union, negotiated with President Wharton to bring the machinery shops into the AFL machinists union. These negotiations went successfully, so that when the electricals joined with Carey to form the UE, Matles and his locals went into the machinists as a body, and Matles was rewarded with an appointment as a grand-lodge representative.

A year later, when Party policy tilted heavily to the CIO, and the immense possibilities in the UE were evident, Matles marched his locals out of the machinists into the UE. The executive board created the national post of Organization Director for him, and at the September 1937 convention, the union's name was enlarged to United Electrical, Radio, and Machine Workers of America, and Matles was confirmed by convention vote. Several machinists' locals in Minneapolis, heavily influenced by Communists, also left at this time to join the UE. Thus, the Communist faction was augmented not only by additional activists, but also by a hard-driving and indefatigable fighter, in full charge of the growing staff of organizers, who had the requisite qualifications to direct a large labor organization, and was to become the dominant personality in the national leadership.[5]

Reference has been made to the UE's slow, methodical growth enabling the established Communist administration, at every stage, to absorb the newcomers without getting overwhelmed. *Mutatis mutandis*, it operated like the Lewis-Murray machine in the steel union; the apparatus was in existence and lying in wait before the mass of undifferentiated members were brought in. During Emspak's oral-history interview, the questioner remarked that UE's organizing policy had been characterized by some as "sneaky" in contrast to the UAW's which was of a "blustering type"; Emspak rejoined noncommittally, "Our approach was to use all the available government machinery for furthering organization." They assuredly did not err on the side of impetuosity. The contrast in the rate of growth between the two was conspicuous. Both the UAW and UE, let us recall, started roughly from the same membership base in the spring of 1936. Using Leo Troy's figures, the UAW membership in 1937 was 195,000, the UE's, 30,000. In 1941, at the height of war conversion, UAW stood at 460,000, UE, 133,000. In 1944, the high production point of the war, UAW went over the million mark, UE, 432,000; in 1949, a year of recession, UAW had 919,000, UE, 427,000. (There had been considerable raiding and defections of UE locals in the twelve months preceding the September 1949 convention. According to Matles, UE membership at the time of the convention was 326,000.) The smaller UE membership was not a direct reflection of a smaller potential. The three main CIO unions all went far afield in imperialistically expanding their jurisdictions, so that aside from the war years, when the auto union profited from the runaway expansion of the aircraft industry, the UE had the theoretical possibility of keeping pace.

The UE's less dramatic development is also illustrated by its slower penetration of the industry majors. Whereas the UAW signed its first exclusive national contract with General Motors in early 1937 after the sensational GM strike (followed shortly by an exclusive contract with Chrysler), and subdued the Ford holdout of the Big Three in May 1941 after another spectacular strike, UE did not sign its first national agreement with General Electric until April 1938, and that was in the nature of the initial Lewis-Taylor agreement in steel. This first GE national contract consisted of the long-established company rules and regulations, GE Q105A, "word for word," as both Matles and Emspak admitted, except for two additions: recognition in six organized plants covering about 30,000 workers, and for such other plants that the NLRB might designate as UE bargaining agents; and provisions for a grievance system. The company policy of the community gauge for wages remained in force until 1941, as well as seniority clauses where five or six "factors" were taken into consideration to determine whether an employee was to be laid off or recalled. It was in 1941, also, after a laborious plant-by-plant struggle over a period of five years that the first national contract was signed with Westinghouse wherein the community-survey method of fixing wages was abolished; and a national agreement was concluded with General Motors covering the 26,000 employees of its electrical division.

This measured pace of growth was both a product of the Communists' caution (accompanied always by a raucous verbal radicalism), and the less volatile, more compliant behavior of the members. One reinforced the other. At the time that the UE was displaying its fighting vigor by cheering on the North American strikers in the *UE News*, it was not calling any major strikes itself. This is not to say that UE did not engage in numbers of bitterly fought strikes when it had to. There was the month-long pitched battle at RCA-Victor in June 1936, with skirmishes going on until the signing of a contract fifteen months later. There was the 55-day sitdown in 1937 at Emerson Electric that established the UE as a power in the St. Louis electrical shops. There were the defensive fights in the 1938 recession: a 4-month lockout at Philco ending in a union defeat and acceptance of wage cuts, although the local managed to retain exclusive bargaining rights; and the drawn-out struggle at the Maytag Washing Machine Company in Newton, Iowa. Here, management, functioning in a company town in an agricultural state, was able to put into practice the Remington-Rand formula for breaking strikes. After 98 days the strikers returned to work, having to pass between rows of National Guardsmen. Then the union displayed resourcefulness. The company, plagued by a rash of quickie strikes, resumed contractual relations. But the UE eschewed calling national strikes like the auto union's, or the steel strike of 1937, until the 1945-1946 strike wave, and then only in consonance with steel and other unions, and when General Motors was already shut down.

Boyer and Morais, two Communist writers, later insisted that the UE was the pacesetter for the whole trade-union movement by reason of its superior contracts and wage scales. This was standard Communist propaganda for years and taken for good coin in popular-frontist circles. There was nothing to the claim. UE's contracts and wage scales were generally somewhat inferior to those in auto, steel, and rubber. This was not owing to Communist pusillanimity. An industry's traditional wage scales, its situation in the market place, its rate of profit, the aggressiveness and strategic position of its work force, all come into play in wage determination. A recitation of the Communists' patient tactics and conservative contract policy is not necessarily a criticism. These may have been justified on occasions. On balance, and on a comparative basis, the UE was an effective organization for its members in trade union terms. Still, a Fabius Cunctator should not try to pass himself off as a Julius Caesar.[6]

3

To make up for their prudence in striking and bargaining policies, they were reckless in following propagandistically the twists and turns of Communist party policies. It is unnecessary to repeat the litany of before and after the Stalin-Hitler pact, and before and after the Nazi attack on Russia. All this has been conclusively established and is well known. Neither is any new enlightenment gained from a detailed recitation of Communists' techniques of control: how they staffed the union with members and adherents, how they fixed their positions ahead of time, how they positioned their people at meetings, how they deliberately muddled embarrassing questions, how they overawed dissenters with vituperation and character assassination. These techniques have been employed by power factions since the birth of the parliamentary system three hundred years ago, and were not unknown to the ancient Romans and Greeks. Neither were they unknown to the anti-Communist managers in the CIO who also did not rely on mental telepathy to concert their moves. Just as opposing camps in war tend to develop a certain symmetry in their tactics and weapons, so the opposing factions in the CIO adopted each other's combat technologies. The Communists made no original contributions to the art of factional warfare and intrigue, except to infuse their propaganda with their own distinctive brand of bombast.

In the UE, there was no need to be original. In the five formative years they had no opposition. They were able to perfect their machine, and to do it with Carey's inestimable help. He was happy in his role of president of an important union, and in addition, from November 1938 on, as secretary of the CIO. These positions enabled him to be introduced with honors to labor and liberal gatherings, and to play the hero at Communist-front rallies. In later testimony he maintained that he had been taken in by his allies, and only woke up to the horrible truth of what was going on after the Stalin-Hitler pact. This was public-relations talk. Matles and Emspak had been attacked in the public press for Communism since 1937; and Catholic dignitaries had been sending in letters to Lewis and to Carey himself protesting Carey's speaking at the American Youth Congress and the League for Peace and Democracy. Carey was a wide-awake, knowledgable person; he did not need the Stalin-Hitler pact to make him aware of his associates' political connections. But like many others, in the thirties, he was a popular-frontist and found it particularly profitable to play that game in the UE. Ironically, the way he broke with the Communists in 1941 helped to tighten their grip on the organization. It was only in March that he brought the conflict into the open over the right of a local to bar Communists from holding office, and kept the issue alive with repeated attacks on Communists in his President's Column in the union newspaper. He knew full well that there would be a showdown at the September convention, yet he did virtually nothing in the intervening five months to organize an opposition.

After he got trounced at the convention and was replaced as president, his formal contact with the UE was limited to participation at yearly conventions as a delegate from the Philco local. For the next years, he and his allies, in their annual show of opposition, confined themselves to cursing the Communists—and with the same results. At the 1942 convention, he ignored a resolution submitted by a local to condemn Emspak for sending out a letter agreeing to the wage freeze; instead, the big fight was made opposing a resolution for a Second Front, and on the old perennial of barring Communists from office. At the 1943 convention, he went along with the resolution favoring incentive pay; the only opposition coming from a lone Trotskyite from the Ford Instrument local. Another resolution reaffirming the no-strike pledge was adopted by unanimous vote. At the 1944 convention, the no-strike pledge was reaffirmed again, with the same Trotskyite providing the sole opposition. The resolution opposing incentive pay, submitted this time by the Ford Instrument local itself, was voted down without Carey, Block, or their friends taking part in the discussion.

What faction organization went on during the war years was the responsibility of the Catholic bloc. The ACTU was a more important and a more independent entity in the UE than in the UAW. In the auto union, the anti-Communist faction was directed by an accomplished leadership commanding great resources, with the ACTU in Michigan adapting itself to the social democratic ambience, and individual ACTU members blending naturally into the Reuther faction. Since the fight was going the way the labor priests wanted it to go, they saw no need for the ACTU to emphasize its own specific contributions, particularly since they were anxious to blunt accusations that they were setting up a religious bloc within the union. In the UE, the opposition was disorganized and dispirited, and the ACTU tried to step into the breach to furnish the guidance and organization that Carey and his friends seemed incapable of providing. It is immaterial that the ACTU had a rickety national structure, that its dues-paying membership was small, that different ACTU branches did not always align their policies, that some leading labor priests working up anti-Communist groups in the UE were associated with Catholic institutions other than the ACTU, or that ACTU members, according to one specialized definition, did not work as a fraction in the labor movement. The ACTU, in this connection, is shorthand for the entire Catholic operation in the UE in which the church was a zealous participant, willing and able to supplement ACTU's endeavors.

287

Thus, Father Charles Owen Rice took the initiative in organizing the anti-Communist forces in the big East Pittsburgh Westinghouse local in early 1941. The issue around which he waged the struggle was support for the discharge by the company of one Joseph Baron (described by Father Rice as "a notorious fellow traveler"), on the ground that Baron's "activities would affect the prestige of the company." Before the matter was put to a vote of the local, Father Rice got in touch with Catholic priests who had many UE members in their congregations persuading them to read a letter from their pulpits urging workers to attend their union meetings. The response was satisfactory, workers turned out in large numbers, Father Rice carried the day, and after this victory on a dubious issue, a Catholic labor school was set up in the vicinity of the Westinghouse plant. Father Rice's intervention, however, was still exceptional (and took place during the Stalin-Hitler-pact period). ACTU wartime activities in the UE remained sporadic and localized. It was after the war, once the anti-Red drive became a national enterprise, that the ACTU seriously entered the lists to provide much of the sinew of the Carey opposition. (In the later stages of the fight for control of the UE, the steel union gave the ACTU in the Pittsburgh area a $1,000 monthly subsidy. Father Rice, located here, who had close relations with Murray, was the ACTU's major strategist on UE matters.)

Father Thomas J. Darby, an ACTU associate and teacher at the Catholic New Rochelle Labor School, was active in building a Catholic opposition in the New York area. In March 1946, at his urging, a caucus attended by members from five UE locals met after the ACTU's Communion breakfast, and adopted a program of action; they began to publish *Spotlight*, an antiadministration paper issued under the aegis of a UE Committee for Rank and File Democracy. Relations were established with other ACTU centers of opposition and a national caucus was projected. In August the ACTU entered, as an integral part, the newly formed Carey-Block faction. Yet despite the renewed activity, the covert CIO support, the flood of faction literature, the growing knowledge of the Communist character of the UE administration, opposition forces made a poorer showing than Carey had made in his initial challenge. At the 1946, 1947, and 1948 conventions, they were regularly beaten by lopsided 5-to-1 and 6-to-1 majorities. It was only at the final convention in 1949, when Fitzgerald-Emspak-Matles pushed through a resolution sealing the break with the CIO, that the Carey candidate was able to roll up a 40 percent vote against Fitzgerald for the presidency.[7]

The opposition lacked broad appeal because its program was little else besides anti-Communism. Both the ACTU and Carey-Block were aware that this was a deficiency and sought to overcome it. Father Rice, in his widely distributed pamphlet, *How to De-Control Your Union of Communists*, advised:

> Examine your local situation and find out what more the union could do than it is doing. Make up a program around this. You can always kick on wage increases, etc. as not being enough. You can always embarrass the Communists by yapping about grievances that the workers did not win, etc. Argue for more streamlined and direct grievance procedures. Better coverage on unemployment compensation cases, etc.
>
> Walter Reuther slaughtered his Communist opposition because he had a superb pro-union program and platform. You need negative issues too, but never forget the positive ones.

Animated by the same analysis, Carey-Block spokesmen tried to picture themselves as guardians of fighting unionism. In 1946, the minority on the Officers Report Committee lambasted the administration report for failing to inform the membership that piecework rates had been cut after the war and contractual clauses otherwise worsened at GE and Westinghouse. In 1947, the minority resolution on factionalism included an attack on the Communists for their wartime support of piecework and of labor conscription. None of this was successful in supplying the Carey-Block faction with the militant aura that it sought to convey. Carey, after his ouster as president, was practically an outsider to the UE ranks, three-quarters of whom had entered the union after 1941. He had been associated with the very policies he was now trying (half-heartedly) to criticize. Block was an undistinguished functionary. Most of the new spokesmen pushed forward by the ACTU had no records of accomplishment; indeed, many of them had not been active unionists until they saw in the faction struggle an opportunity to break into the officialdom. Their newly adopted militant palaver could not be taken very seriously. The credentials that so many Carey-Block people lacked could not be concocted.

The opposition bore the further onus of being hand-in-glove with

289

those who were trying to tear down, not just the leadership, but the union as well. ACTU leaders were cooperating with the House Committee on Un-American Activities to discredit UE, Father Rice was working with the FBI to nail Communist officers. Although the Carey faction deplored tendencies for secession, a number of impatient local ACTU groups broke ranks to lead locals out of UE, and the official ACTU newspaper, the *Labor Leader*, reversed its earlier opposition to splitting. Beginning with 1947, the Communists kept up a fierce attack against the ACTU, which Father Rice thought was, on the whole, successful. At the 1947 convention, too, they tried to finish off the opposition by decree and administrative threat. A constitutional amendment was pushed through empowering the executive board to suspend locals, and another resolution peremptorily ordered the Carey-Block faction to dissolve. Employing the authority of this resolution, several opposition figures were expelled, but these were isolated cases; the administration, hardpressed inside the CIO, had to restrain itself; it could not risk a civil war inside its own organization.

To most members, the opposition appeared as one manipulated by outside, hostile forces. The average UE member, consequently, was confronted with the choice of supporting an administration of experienced, dedicated, reasonably effective Communist-influenced officials, and an opposition of untested and somewhat untrustworthy aspirants to office. Whereas the UAW members had no fear that the union would disintegrate if it were entrusted to the Reuther faction, in the UE members felt no confidence that Carey and his coadjutors would do as well as the leaders they had. All of which demonstrated that workers are not completely manipulable; that even in a period of hysteria, members resisted turning their backs on economic considerations; that where anti-Communists were thought to be incompetent or irresponsible, there arose an inevitable tension between union interests and ideological loyalties, and they would cling to the proven leaders they had despite antipathy for their politics and the surrounding pressures. Where the choice was between a Reuther and an Addes, the Red issue was overwhelmingly effective. Where it was between a Carey-Block-ACTU combination and a Fitzgerald-Emspak-Matles administration, the Red issue fell short of rolling up a majority.[8] Some might even say that the ability of a combination the caliber of Carey-Block-ACTU to roll up a 40 percent vote was a high tribute in its way to the effectiveness of the Red issue.

4

The 1949 convention was the last one in which the fight was waged inside the UE. The CIO expelled the UE at its 1949 convention and chartered a competitor, the International Union of Electrical, Radio, and Machine Workers (IUE). With that, the UE was subjected to a multiple-pronged attack like few others in labor history. As soon as the new union was authorized, the CIO sent a telegram to every company under contract with UE to withdraw recognition. Most companies, including the major chains, immediately cancelled their contracts and stopped checking off union dues. Since the IUE did not have the enrolled membership to petition for new NLRB elections, both GE and Westinghouse came to Carey's rescue by putting in requests themselves, which they could do under the Taft-Hartley Act. (Carey, in his testimony before the Humphrey Senate committee, tried to make out a case that GE was helping the Communist-led UE against Carey's good American union, but he could do that only by twisting the evidence. GE was out to undermine all unionism in the industry—and succeeded.)

The national CIO office made building the IUE and crushing the UE major pieces of business in 1950. Much of Haywood's staff was assigned to the electrical campaign, and both the steel and auto unions helped in critical elections. Where it was thought advisable, Murray intervened personally with pleas and threats. In the crucial election at the Pittsburgh Westinghouse plant, in addition to asking the workers to vote for the IUE, Murray called attention to the Atomic Energy Commission's earlier ruling that UE was not to be recognized or dealt with at GE's atomic laboratory at Schenectady. He went on to say in his special letter, "If this government action is any indication of what is to come in the future, you can expect government cancellation of all UE contracts in the case of national emergency . . . this would of course apply to plants like your own where jet engines are produced."

The CIO donated over $800,000 to the IUE from November 1949 to mid-1950, as well as paying for the publication of the *CIO-IUE News,* and furnishing organizers and legal services without charge. The steel union turned over $200,000 in the first twelve months. It was a campaign almost comparable in magnitude to the Lewis-Murray effort in steel in 1936. The auto union, naturally, stopped its raids on electrical plants once the IUE was set up while redoubling them against FE agricultural implement plants. (FE had been instructed to join the UAW after the 1948 CIO convention. When it defied the instruction, and merged instead with UE, it became fair game for the CIO unions.) In addition, several AFL unions put in bids in the ensuing NLRB elections. The result was a reign of cannibalism and chaos for several years in the industries that UE and FE had heretofore claimed.

The ACTU and Catholic priests in localities where there were important electrical plants similarly took the task in hand. A priest in Newark told his parishioners that it would be a mortal sin to vote for the UE over the IUE. In Pittsfield, Massachusetts, the Reverend Eugene F. Marshall said in his sermon that the vote "represented a choice between Washington and Moscow, and ultimately between Christ and Stalin." The *Evangelist*, published by the Albany archdiocese, pronounced an anathema: "Our most reverend bishop and the priests of the Diocese of Albany declare the United Electrical, Radio and Machine Workers of America to be Communist dominated and Communist controlled. It no longer functions as a free labor union, but is merely a tool of the Communist Party and is, therefore, the enemy of God and the Catholic Church."

Government officials similarly intervened on behalf of the CIO against the UE in what was probably the most sustained barrage against a labor organization since the Wilson administration's attack on the IWW. President Truman sent a letter to the IUE for its opening convention in which he threw the prestige of his office behind the new organization. It was read to the convention by Murray to the accompaniment of cheers, and a reprint of it was distributed by the tens of thousands to plant workers. Stuart Symington, secretary of the Air Force (formerly president of Emerson Electric), and Maurice Tobin, secretary of Labor, both addressed the convention, making it clear that the government stood behind the CIO's campaign. Tobin pledged that he would be on the firing line, and as good as his word, gave speeches for the IUE at mass meetings and plant gates.

The FBI moved in with investigations of the non-Communist affidavits filed by UE officials. (The UE decided to comply with the Taft-Hartley Act requirement in 1949; it had been helpless in warding off raids on UE locals without the ability to participate in NLRB elections.) The Justice Department had to forego prosecutions since it was unable to prove actual membership or continued membership of leading officers. But UE officials were repeatedly menaced by other legal proceedings. Both Matles and Emspak were cited for contempt by a grand jury in 1951, citations that were later dismissed. Emspak was indicted and convicted of contempt of Congress but the conviction was set aside by the Supreme Court in 1955. Deportation proceedings were started against Matles in 1952. His citizenship was revoked in 1957, but again the denaturalization was reversed by the Supreme Court the following year. At the end of 1955, the UE was charged with being "Communist infiltrated" under the Communist Control Act of 1954 and hearings were held before the Subversive Activities Control Board in 1957 and 1958, but action was discontinued because key witnesses were unavailable.

Even without the hoped-for Taft-Hartley prosecutions, the House Committee on Un-American Activities, and other congressional committees, developed effective techniques of harassment. Hearings would be scheduled in the election period in the areas involved; UE local officers and members would be subpoenaed; those who pleaded the fifth amendment in refusing to answer the sixty-four-dollar question were subject to dismissal, or ostracism by fellow workers. The often reckless denunciations by anti-Communists and FBI infiltrators provided newspapers the wherewithal for a Roman festival to inflame the community and intimidate UE activists in the plants.[9]

The sustained barrage reduced the UE to a minor union in the field. The wonder is not that it lost heavily, but that it survived at all, that it was able to win as many elections and to hold the allegiance of as many members as it did. Neither was the CIO let off scot free in the war of extermination. While the IUE emerged from the ordeal as the dominant union, in the early fifties both unions combined had half the UE's early postwar membership. The remainder were not all lost to unionism; many dispersed into a multiplicity of organizations. But collective bargaining turned into a shambles for the next two decades, with wages and conditions falling far behind other major industries. Lemuel Boulware, GE vice-president in charge of labor relations, reported with satisfaction that he was dealing with more than sixty different unions. "Boulwarism"—the policy by which the company dictated the terms of settlement—reigned supreme. It was only when the IUE, the UE, and others agreed to join forces in contractual negotiations, and struck the GE empire for a hundred days in 1970, that meaningful collective bargaining was reestablished in the major electrical concerns.[10]

The crisis in the affairs of both the UE and the Communist party, rather than thickening the bonds of solidarity between the two sets of beleaguered officials, led instead to a cooling of relations. UE boycotted the CIO 1949 convention against the Party's advice, and its officers showed disdain to the Party emissaries sent over to remonstrate with them. Relations between the two chilled further when Williamson, at the September 1950 national committee plenum, accused the UE leaders of "blind factionalism" in resisting "united action of UE and IUE members," and laid down the dictum that "the main attention of the Party must be concentrated on the main body of workers and trade unions, not only on the progressive-led Internationals." He warned the UE leaders of the possibility of a Communist uprising against them: "We must yet battle through and defeat all opposition to considering work among members of the IUE of equal and necessary importance as activity among workers in UE." The controversy was brought to a climax when Matles, in a stormy session with the Party's bureau members in early 1951, told them that he rejected the policy of reentry into the so-called labor mainstream, and that he had no confidence in the CP leadership. The national UE leaders continued to consider themselves "Marxists," and remained in an adversary relationship with the CIO, but close relations with the party were at an end. Fighting for their lives against tremendous odds and against implacable opponents, Matles and his associates lost patience with the Party's prattling about united fronts from below. They had followed the directional turns in 1939 and again in 1941 without a qualm; they had accepted Browder's incentive pay without batting an eyelash; but the instruction to liquidate the union to which they had devoted their adult lives was beyond the pale of contemplation.

What induced the Party bureaucrats to push matters to a breaking point with some of their most important labor supporters? Surely, one would think, when they were under fierce attack from all sides, this was no time to split their own ranks. Nor were they carrying out instructions from Stalin or Zhdanov. It can only be explained by the functionaries' ingrained habits of resolving differences of opinion by decree. The Party was in a near-panic after the passage of the McCarran bill over Truman's veto in the summer of 1950, convinced that this presaged the Party's prosecution as a foreign agent. Preparations were underway for part of the leadership to go underground. In this overwrought atmosphere, the urge was overwhelming to find safety by losing oneself in the mass, by removing from reaction's reach all easily identifiable targets. The leaders were convinced that with the expulsion of the Communist-led unions from the CIO, the battle against the CIO right wing had been lost, that independent Communist-led unions could not survive, that the members had to get back in the shops and local committees to prepare for the long pull. "The single biggest job today," Williamson advised, "is to learn to rely upon the mass of our Party members in the trade unions and not just on a few leaders." Hence, the frantic push to dump themselves into the recognized unions on whatever terms were available, or without any terms, if need be. It was the story of the dissolution of the TUUL unions all over again, but this time several of their unions were substantial, and this time the climate was forbidding, not receptive.

In between fighting its internecine wars, the Party reiterated its new trade-union line—which Matles contemptuously ignored. Then in 1955 the Party struck. Four UE district presidents and thirty staff members announced that the UE was finished, proclaimed the necessity of finding a haven within the "mainstream," and led their followers out of the union. Two events precipitated the Party's decision. The Subversive Activities Control Board, created by the McCarran Act, was looking into the UE, preparatory, it was believed, to adjudging it "Communist-infiltrated." And the AFL and CIO were preparing for their unity convention, closing the division that had existed for almost twenty years. These events convinced the Communist leaders, for reasons best known to themselves, that the remaining avenue for independent unionism was about to be cut off, that Communist unionists had to get out of the danger zone while there was still time.

District 4 covering the New York metropolitan area went into the IUE under some agreement that part or all of its staff would be utilized. Locals in upstate New York and Ohio joined the AFL machinists, as did several farm equipment locals that had not been seized by the UAW. Members in the Michigan-Indiana area dissolved into the IUE and machinists. Some went into the AFL electrical brotherhood. There was no actual strategy in the three-way or four-way dispersal. As with a routed army, each contingent was left to fend for itself. The UE was now reduced to a small, embattled union led by a small staff of die-hard, sea-green incorruptibles. Matles said that the defectors took out 50,000 members, reducing the

295

UE to 90,000. Troy's figures show the UE had 132,000 in 1955, down to 70,000 in 1957, and down to 54,000 in 1962. So ended the saga of Communist control of a major industrial union. Like an impressive temple ruin in the desert, Matles's UE stands as a relic of what was the third-largest union in the CIO.[10]

TWELVE · *CIO Purge and Aftermath*

REUTHER'S smashing victory in November 1947 drastically altered the power balance in the Communists' disfavor inside the CIO. An aggressive, articulate leader at the head of the largest union was now deploying the augmented right-wing forces to deliver the coup de grâce. Even if Murray had other plans or timetables in mind—and he did not—he would have had to go along. The one development that might have decelerated the anti-Red campaign was an abatement of the cold war. Instead, 1948 was the year of crises: the takeover in Czechoslovakia, clashes over Berlin, unfolding of the Hiss case; war talk was so freely bandied about that Walter Lippmann thought it wise to warn that a war perspective was illusory.

What prodded the quarrel in the CIO along its foreordained course was the formation of the Wallace third party. Murray described it, in the anti-Communist hyperbole of the period, as a diabolical plot hatched in the Communist party offices for the purpose of defeating labor's choice and ensuring the election of the Republican candidate. Things were more complicated than that. There was confusion and uncertainty about what labor should do in 1948 right up to the presidential campaign. Truman had almost no support in labor and liberal circles. He was considered a bungler, a courthouse politician with little real dedication to liberal causes, a failed leader facing repudiation. When the time approached for the Democratic convention, prominent liberals like James Roosevelt and Claude Pepper, leading ADA spokesmen, party bosses in major metropolitan centers, all cheered on by CIO leaders, were trying to induce Eisenhower to accept the Democratic nomination. A few were plumping for Justice Douglas, who they felt would facilitate the reelection of congressional and local candidates and hold the demoralized party together, even if he did not win the presidency. The Roper and Gallup polls showed Truman losing to Dewey, and the delegates who gathered in Philadelphia in July did not so much pick Truman their standard bearer as become reconciled to going down to defeat with him. It was only at the end of August that the CIO executive board, with no alternative available, declared itself for Truman, to be followed by the PAC's pulling out all stops for the Democratic ticket. And even then, as the campaign warmed up and Truman pledged to work for the repeal of the Taft-Hartley law in his "give 'em hell" pseudo-populist electioneering, the bigger part of CIO and AFL efforts went into drumming up support for state and local candidates.

On the Communist party side, not everything was cut and dried either. The leaders had been toying with the proposition of a third party throughout the previous year, but they had been moving cautiously since there were disagreements between Foster and the ex-Browderites who doubted that sufficient labor support was to be had. In the beginning of 1947, Foster announced that the Communist party "must make the question of building the new party our major task and leave no stone unturned for its realization," Eugene Dennis, however, favored a third party formation as a pressure group to force Democrats to nominate a progressive "coalition candidate." By summer, an incipient third-party movement appeared to be in the making. Wallace, in his cross-country speaking tour, dumfounded professional politicians by the overflow crowds he was attracting, crowds that were even paying admission charges for the privilege of listening to his "peace" message. There appeared to be a sizable disgruntled public. The Democratic party's acting national chairman wrote to Truman "that Wallace has captured the imagination of a large segment of the population." Leading newspaper columnists and editorial writers concluded that Wallace was evoking deeply, widely felt longings for peace. Still, despite the immense, cheering crowds and despite newspapermen's freely predicting a Wallace third party in 1948, it was uncertain what Wallace would do. Some of his statements suggested that he intended to work within the Democratic party. Others pointed toward the formation of a new party. Either Wallace had not made up his mind or he was not showing his hand.

At the June 1947 Communist national committee meeting, John Gates stated in his political action report: "It is not possible at this moment to make the final decision as to the presidential ticket, nor to state definitely whether a third presidential ticket or a third Congressional ticket will be formed. . . . The decision to form such a party does not lie only in the will of the Communists. . . . Much broader forces than are now committed to a new party will have to join the movement to make it possible for it to come into existence in 1948." In August, Hugh Bryson, head of the Marine Cooks and

Stewards, with the support of California Communists, jumped the gun in breaking away from the Democratic party of California and forming a state Independent Progressive party. But Cacchione and Marcantonio of New York's American Labor Party continued readying Wallace candidates for contests in the Democratic primaries, and Communist union officials did not raise the third party issue at the September New York state CIO convention. As late as September Dennis declared in a speech at Madison Square Garden, "We Communists are not adventurers and irresponsible sectarians. We are not going to isolate ourselves. We never did and do not now favor the launching of premature and unrepresentative third parties or independent tickets." In other words, as late as September, the Communist party, while it wanted and favored a third party, and its dominated unions had been passing third-party resolutions since 1946, did not feel that it could gather sufficient backing to make the attempt. In any case, the California breakaway, possibly sponsored by local hotheads and encouraged by Foster, was a regional action to create in California an organization similar to New York's ALP. It was originally presented as something that would help those in the Democratic party favoring Wallace.[1]

A month later, the Communist party executed another of its notorious 180-degree turns. As was customary in these sweeping reversals, it was in response to a directive from abroad. In October, *Pravda* made known that a secret conference of nine European parties had been held in Poland presided over by Zhdanov and Malenkov, that a Communist Information Bureau (Cominform) had been set up, that the manifesto emanating from the conference heralded that American imperialism was leading an offensive to subjugate Europe and the world, and that it was the duty of all Communist parties to place themselves in the vanguard of the opposition. While the gravamen of the indictment was to mobilize the paladins to oppose the Marshall Plan, it was manifest that an emphatic leftism all along the line was the order of the day. Why else would the Yugoslavs be inveighing against the Italian and French leaders for not having seized power in 1944 (as if their popular-frontism had not originated from Moscow)? Whether more specific instructions concerning a third party were conveyed in private to American Communist leaders is not known, but more specific instructions were unnecessary. The American Communist leaders grabbed the bit in their teeth and began galloping. The same Dennis who in Sep-

299

tember said that the Communists were not adventurers, in February confessed, "We were much too slow in combatting the erroneous views of certain party leaders and district organizations, as well as many of our trade union cadres who, up to the announcement of Wallace's candidacy, expressed doubts as to the advisability of an independent Presidential ticket."

The Progressive Citizens of America, pushed relentlessly by "Beanie" Baldwin, made public its resolution in mid-December urging Wallace to run for the presidency on a third-party ticket. Communist-sponsored labor, youth, and women's delegations crowded around Wallace with ecstatic reports of swelling support. Wallace's offices at the *New Republic* became a "Grand Central Station." Michael Straight, the publisher, recalled, "There were steady deputations led in to see Henry. Phil Murray would criticize the third party—on the following day a 'rank and file' delegation from some painters or auto workers local in New York or New Jersey would troop in to tell Henry that Murray did not speak for the membership." It was evident by then that all but a handful of liberal and labor figures would dissociate themselves from the insurgency. Murray, Reuther, Jack Kroll, chairman of the CIO-PAC, Jacob Potofsky, president of the men's clothing union, publicly warned against a third party. Major non-Communist Wallace supporters, Frank Kingdon, Bartley Crum, to be followed by J. Raymond Walsh, A. J. Liebling, Albert Deutsch, resigned from the PCA. After Wallace formally announced his candidacy at the end of December, there was heavy press speculation that Wallace was tricked by the Communists into becoming a candidate, that he accepted their exaggerated reports, that the movement originated solely from them in response to Moscow orders. This led to a flurry of haggling over dates and meeting places in order to prove or disprove that Wallace was a Communist dupe or captive.

There is no mystery or conundrum. There were two participants in the transaction—Wallace and the Communists. The third party could not have been carried through without the consent of both. Wallace was the only available figure with the prestige to head such a movement. The Communists, given the hostility of liberals and laborites, were the only ones who could furnish the troops for Gideon's army. As was recognized, Wallace was no Communist, no fellow traveler, and certainly uninfluenced by Moscow decisions. He had been moving along his own trajectory toward a break with the Truman administration and the Democratic party. His motives were best summarized by John Morton Blum, the historian: "Many of the men in the group around him were naive; some were eager to use him to advance their own political interests; none had much political insight. Yet their pressure moved Wallace less than did his own temperament. Believing that Truman was leading the country and the world toward war, committed to the contrary view of the new century, Wallace disregarded the warnings of his family and old friends and followed his own compulsion to stand political witness to his faith." When he decided to make the run, he expected a minimum of four million votes. Communist leaders speculated that he might get as many as five million votes. Neither figure seemed outlandish in 1947. But the crowds that were applauding Wallace could not stand up under the steady pounding of recognized and respected leaders. In the end, Gideon's army was reduced to the irreconcilables and diehards.[2]

2

The documentation that the Wallace ticket was a Moscow plot, publicized by newspaper writers and reiterated by Murray and others, originated with Michael Quill, head of the Transport Workers union. Quill, a leading trade-union party-liner, demonstratively and vituperatively broke with the Party in the spring of 1948. Whether it was over the Wallace issue, as he later tried to make out, or over the Party's support of the nickel fare on New York's subways, as appeared likely, is not material in this context.* He was in the inner circle up to the first months of 1948, and went over to the Murray anti-Communist camp sometime in March—that much is certain. In a later CIO hearing, he testified that on October 18, 1947, the day after the CIO convention in Boston, he attended a meeting at the International Workers Order hall in New York City at which were present Bridges, Matles, Emspak, and many other Communist labor officials, as well as Dennis, Williamson, and Robert Thompson, the Party's New York state chairman. Dennis, according to Quill, told the gathering that a decision had been made to form a

---

* Quill renewed his alliance with Mayor O'Dwyer, and came out for the higher fare, in order to get a 24-cent hourly wage concession. On April 7, at a meeting of several thousand members at Manhattan Center, he announced that the TWU was going to remain with the CIO at all costs. "So far as 42,000 transit workers are concerned, I say, wages before Wallace." At the climax of his speech, he seized a copy of the *Daily Worker*, and raising his hands high over his head, tore it into shreds. "That's what I think of them!" he roared. So "Red Mike," reddest of Reds, bade farewell to his erstwhile comrades.

third party, that Wallace would come out in the next few weeks to announce his candidacy, and that the Party was asking all its controlled unions to line up support as soon as the announcement was made.

As reported in the most detailed of the published accounts, that of Alfred Friendly in the *Washington Post* (reprinted and distributed widely by the ADA), the discussion of the national third party did not figure at the October meeting, devoted mainly to the Marshall Plan, but at a subsequent meeting held in mid-December, and the report at that meeting was given by Thompson. According to the Friendly version, Quill attacked the decision, said that it would split the CIO, and that he would not go along. When Thompson insisted that the Communists "must pressure for an endorsement of Wallace," Quill shouted, "The hell with you and your Central Committee," and told Thompson to relay his remarks to "that crackpot Foster." At the later CIO hearing, Bridges, in his cross-examination of Quill, brought out some discrepancies in Quill's story. It is likely that Quill inadvertantly juxtaposed two meetings. Since as late as January Quill was still publicly supporting the Wallace candidacy, it is also likely that he was dressing up his own role at these meetings. There is no dispute, however, that such meetings took place, that at the December meeting the Party spokesman laid out a program to get behind the Wallace candidacy, or that at a subsequent caucus at the Hay-Adams Hotel in Washington held the night before the January 22 session of the CIO executive board, the assembled officials decided with Williamson to try to sidetrack any discussion or condemnation of the third party.[3]

The Communists understood that their decision was going to heat up the controversy inside the CIO and jeopardize their own position. Since most or all of them were aware that the groundswell for Wallace was decidedly limited, and that their stand was challenging one of the CIO's holy of holies—its alliance with the Democratic party—why did none of them (with the possible exception of Quill) put up an argument in the inner councils? Murray's tactic of pressure-and-patience, let it be noted, was not a total failure. He had won over Curran, and more recently, Quill. Numbers of second-line Communists also succumbed: Kenneth Eckert and Wesley Madill of Mine Mill who in 1948 led new secessions; James Conroy of the UE who became one of the Carey-Block leaders. At a later date after the expulsions came Livingston of New York's District 65 and Davis of hospital Local 1199 of the Wholesale and Retail union, Rubin and others of the AFL hotel union.

The other officials heading internationals, however, proved impervious to warnings and blandishments. They were in the grip of the same apocalyptic specter as the party commissars; that a war crisis was at hand, and that a stand had to be made at Armaggedon if all was not to be lost; that they could not compromise further if they were not to betray the workers' historic interests. The tension between the Party and its union officials was a real thing, and had the diverse pulls continued for another five or six years, defections would have been far heavier. But the international character of the Communist movement, and the reality of state power in the Soviet Union and the East European states—considered by the faction to be bastions of workers' rule and achievement—acted as a cement to hold together the faction under the hammer blows of the enemy and the weight of the social environment.

At the January CIO board meeting, Bridges got into an acrimonious exchange with Murray over the Marshall Plan and Murray's charge of atrocities in Eastern Europe. Murray told Bridges that if he were in Russia criticizing Stalin the way he was now criticizing Truman, he would be liquidated. To which Bridges—in a revelation of obtuseness—retorted, "I am not so sure that's so." Communist efforts to stall a discussion of the third party were unavailing; the board voted 33 to 13 to condemn the Wallace candidacy because it would split the liberal vote; it also approved a resolution to work for the implementation of the Marshall Plan. After the board sessions, Pressman was pushed to the wall to declare himself. He resigned as CIO counsel, to be replaced by Arthur Goldberg, later a Supreme Court justice. Pressman then ran for Congress in New York on the Progressive party ticket. A few weeks later, Bridges was removed as CIO regional director for Northern California.

When the CIO board endorsed Truman in August after another knock-down, drag-out debate, both sides took to the hustings to bring their respective cases before a wider public. Newspapermen who covered the campaign agreed that there was enormous CIO input in personnel, literature and money. Murray and Reuther made radio broadcasts over nationwide hookups urging labor to vote the Truman ticket. Aside from Lewis, the entire labor officialdom lined up behind the Democratic cause, including A. F. Whitney, head of the railway trainmen, who threatened after the 1946 rail

303

strike debacle to spend his entire union treasury to defeat Truman. The liberal columnists, the New Deal dignitaries, the ADA luminaries, were all similarly hitting away. After his unexpected victory, Truman said, "Labor did it." It is outside the scope of this study to review the voting blocs in 1948, but no one disputes that the CIO's exertions were essential in lining up labor support for Truman and the Democrats.

In contrast, the Communists could not deliver when put to the test. Although numbers of UE organizers were busy in the Wallace campaign, and Fitzgerald acted as chairman of the Progressive party convention, the administration dared not ask the UE convention for an endorsement. It had to be content with inviting Wallace to address the delegates, and with a declaration that the union would leave it up to the locals and individual members to make their own decisions. Similarly, Bridges did not campaign for Wallace, aside from chairing a third-party meeting in San Francisco, nor did the longshore union make an endorsement. Only Fur, Mine Mill, Food, and Marine Cooks, had the temerity to pronounce themselves for Wallace. Their belligerency did not go much beyond that. MacDougall recorded, "Most of the avowed Progressives among union officials at all levels merely sat on their hands, doing little or nothing to line up their mass memberships . . . [and in unions in which Wallace was endorsed] they could not make their members put forward vigorous efforts in the PP's behalf." Communist union officials were not leading radical constituencies, and they were torn between loyalty to the Party and loyalty to their union careers. That a consistent left-wing leadership could have built up a radical constituency in the forties is unlikely; that the Communists were not able to do so, with their Moscow-derived stop-go politics, was a certainty.[4]

3

The CIO leaders came strutting into their November 1948 convention in a jubilant, conquering mood. They chose to interpret the close victory of Truman whom they had been trying to displace in August as an unparalleled labor triumph, testimony to their own prowess and wisdom. The day of ambiguously worded resolutions that could be interpreted either way by Communists and anti-Communists was past. The officialdom nailed down its positions and dropped all restraint in flaying the opposition. It is unnecessary to dwell in detail on the arguments put forward in the major debates since these were mainly exercises in public relations. On an intellectual plane, the two camps deserved each other, both sides reducing their respective positions to caricature. The trade-union official, anti-Communist or Communist, immersed in his own enterprise, has neither time nor inclination to probe into political complexities. The mind of the trade-union official is the mind of a propagandist. In conformity with his entire training, he accepts the received wisdom and repeats it with slapdash, sloganeering abandon.

The political-action resolution reaffirmed the CIO's "nonpartisan policy" of "giving support to the progressive forces in both major parties" and rejected all proposals for a third party that would split the progressive forces in "the interests of reaction." Not for the first time, the Communist speakers labored under a difficulty of explaining why they were opposed today to what they had been fulsomely upholding for a decade. Therefore, they worked away on the theme that the CIO could not dictate political policy to the constituent organizations, that every union had the autonomous right to make its own decisions. Murray made the most of the switch in Communist policy by quoting the remarks of Reid Robinson at previous conventions that contradicted his present stand. What told most of the new stage in the proceedings was the ferocity of his repeated thrusts in the course of long, rambling, formless, emotional speeches characteristic of his oratory:

When I address myself to this convention about the reprehensible practices of the Communist Party I am addressing myself to not only the delegates here in this convention but to every saboteur who aligns himself with the Communist Party both here and abroad. I want the world to know it. My conscience is clear before my God. I am against them because they have subverted every decent movement into which they have infiltrated themselves in the course of their unholy career. There has not been an understanding delegate who has presented any degree of opposition to this resolution here today but that has supported the resolution in prior conventions. Why do they oppose it today? Why did they support it yesterday? The line has changed. Yes . . . .

Many of the leading leftists throughout the United States prior to my declaration and support of President Truman literally deluged my office with the filthiest kind of written material demanding I denounce Truman in the course of this political campaign, or that I at least remain neutral and keep out of it. I know something about the tortures to which I was subjected for some four or five months prior to the November election. I paced floors, I had an association with other men around me to think out these problems and make decisions, because it happens to be the responsibility of the president of a great organization such as this to make decisions upon important issues. I had made them before, and I intend in this instance, so help me God, to make another decision. Not in the interests of Phil Murray—no, no, no; but in the interest of these organized millions whom I was privileged to represent in my capacity as president of this great movement. . . . I thought of you. I thought of the millions whom you are privileged and honored to represent. I thought of your children and their homes, and the millions of children of your constituents. I thought of my country. I thought of my God. And I made my decision. And I submitted my recommendation to my associates, the members of my Executive Board. Now it is over, and I still believe that we saved America, we saved men, and we saved women, we saved children. And we helped save the world.

The Murray who with lamentations and tears had accepted the CIO presidency in 1940 was back on the circuit, but this time he had an easy target. The political-action resolution was adopted by a vote of 537 to 49.

This was the climax of a debate that had been going on for several days over other propositions. The Communists on the Officers Report Committee presented a minority resolution that criticized the Truman Doctrine and Marshall Plan for reinforcing fascist regimes in Greece, China, and Turkey, and rebuilding Nazi power in Western Germany. The report damned Carey for "malicious testimony" against the UE before a congressional committee; it wanted to reprimand unions who used the Taft-Hartley law to conduct raids on other unions.

The reply from the CIO camp was unceremonious and unsparing. Reuther told them, "they have a simple question to resolve in their own minds and their own hearts. It is a question of loyalty. Are they going to be loyal to the CIO or loyal to the Communist Party? Are they going to be loyal to this country or loyal to the Soviet Union?" Baldanzi informed them, "We do not have raids in the CIO. We have revolts of workers against Communist domination." Carey taunted them about answering the sixty-four-dollar question before congressional committees, and concluded with the mock plea, "Oh, please, Mr. Molotov, and Vishinsky, and Don Henderson, if you cannot help us in the way workers need help, please stay out of the way so other people can do the job." The foreign policy resolution condemned "the organized opposition to ERP [European Recovery Program] by the Soviet Union and its satellites and the method by which the economic misery of Europe is used for political advantage and to promote chaos and confusion." As summed up by Van Bittner, the resolutions committee chairman, "There is no pussyfooting in this resolution. There are no weasel words in this resolution. We say to the Soviets, 'If you want peace cooperate with the United States of America!' . . . that is what they will finally have to do."

The verbal chastisement administered to the opposition had a purpose beyond notification to the media and the public that the CIO was coming to grips with the Communists. It set the stage for isolating the small, weak, Communist-led unions preparatory to liquidating them by forced merger or raiding. Once the ax was put to the heads of these unions, it was possible that several others would take the path of Quill; in any case, oppositions could be built up to make ready for displacing the Communist officialdom by action from within or raiding from without. The Murray-Reuther majority needed extra time to prepare its forces for the denouement.

Thus Murray signaled in his opening greetings to the convention his intent to recommend that the board be empowered to review the charters of those unions which had not organized effectively in their jurisdictions. "We were created to organize the unorganized, not to issue charters to small cliques for the purpose of protecting their security as officers of certain international unions." At every opportunity thereafter he pursued the officers of these small unions. He jeered at Donald Henderson, head of the food and tobacco union, "a mighty organization of 24,000"; pronounced James Durkin, head of the office union, to be unfit and incompetent. And the convention adopted a resolution, ironically captioned "Organizing," to empower the board "to take appropriate action" with respect to affiliates who had not made "substantial progress" in organizing the unorganized. When Emspak asked whether the resolution gave the board power to revoke or suspend charters, or to set up administrators over affiliated unions, Murray's diffused reply coupled with a renewed attack on the office union leaders was less than reassuring.*

* Communist-led unions in the office, agricultural, and federal-employee fields had unsatisfactory organizing records. This could probably be blamed to some extent on their Communist officials, who were busy in outside activities, although David

The other part of the strategy, to win over leaders who would wilt once they were convinced that the showdown was at hand, seemed to be having some effect on Albert Fitzgerald, the non-Communist fellow-traveling president of UE. Murray met with him before the convention, and gave him fatherly advice on which way he ought to go. Reuther's provocative remark at the convention "to get clear in the CIO or clear out of the CIO" should also be read as an invitation as well as a threat. Fitzgerald made a pathetic speech that showed he was torn by indecision. He tried to curry favor with the convention by his avowal, "I tell you frankly I do not give a damn for Russia. I tell you frankly that I think Vishinsky and Molotov are engaging in saber rattling and war mongering," and tried to further square himself by informing the delegates that he had voted for the Marshall Plan at the CIO board meeting. But whatever was going through Fitzgerald's head, and whatever decided him, he stayed with Matles and Emspak at the convention and thereafter to the bitter end.

The Communists left the convention a routed army, but one whose shock troops were still intact. However, from the tone of the convention (*People's World*, the Communist West Coast newspaper, called it a "lynching bee"), as well as what was happening in UE, it was clear that the end was at hand. The Party itself was reconciled to the break with the revamped and unleashed Murray-Reuther leadership. It sought to stiffen the resolve of the Communist officials, many of whom were still trying to shield themselves by dodging tactics. Williamson told them they had to show greater determination:

> Left-progressive forces themselves must recognize serious weaknesses, and even capitulation of certain forces, in this fight. These weaknesses were: (a) The lack of unity of the Left, as expressed in the small vote against the lifting of the New York Council charter [UE and other representatives voted with the majority to lift its charter for opposing CIO policy on the Marshall Plan and the third party at the board meeting preceding the convention]; only a portion of the Left delegates on the Resolution

Saposs, a hard-line anti-Communist, admitted, "No other union efforts, however, were more successful in the fields covered by these jurisdictions." In any case, Murray was not proposing to launch organization campaigns among office, agricultural, or government workers, but to ease out Communist officials.

308

and Officers Report Committees signed the minority reports; the vote of such delegations as UE, longshore, and the furniture workers in support of the Officers' Report. . . . Some Left delegates exhibited timidity and fear under the impact of intimidation of hysteria. Others mistakenly thought that if they "don't stick their necks out," or if they "sit this one out," they might be forgotten or passed over. The FE delegation felt the whiplash of that mistake. That should be a lesson.

Williamson's last reference was to the action of the board at its meeting the day after the convention's close. On Reuther's insistence, the first action was not against the marginal unions, but against the farm equipment union. The board ordered it to affiliate with the auto union within sixty days or it would take steps "to implement this decision." The FE officials were defiant, and that became the signal for an unrestrained campaign of raiding. Fist fights and worse accompanied NLRB elections at contested plants on the part of "Commies" and "goons and ginks and company finks," as each side identified its opposite numbers. Pat Greathouse, a UAW vice-president, recalled later that he lost his front teeth at Peoria, where the UAW took over the International Harvester plant of 16,000 workers. An uglier confrontation took place between Mine Mill and steel union representatives over the iron-ore miners at Bessemer, Alabama. In the course of a tense struggle, Maurice Travis was slugged, making it necessary to have his right eye removed. As if the brew were not sufficiently acrid, there was the added gall of race rancor. The local whites leading the secession movement from Mine Mill held the anti-Black prejudices and associations common to the region. The Communists made the attack on Travis a national issue, part of a bill of indictment which included the charge that the steel union had cooperated with Klansmen to defeat Mine Mill and to push Blacks out of jobs. Murray had to enlist Willard Townsend, the Black president of the CIO United Transport Service union, in an attempt to refute the accusation and defuse the issue, but it was to embarrass CIO leaders for several years thereafter.[5]

The fury engendered by the raids upset the timetable of dealing with the marginal unions first—if indeed there had been a precisely thought-out strategy. In any case, events were moving to their inexorable conclusion. The 1949 CIO convention was geared up for final decision. The heated arguments on the familiar questions had all been marked out the year before. The only new element in the oratory was the louder abusiveness, and the fact that the majority was drawing the final line on the balance sheet. Reuther accurately summarized the stages: "We said at Atlantic City [1946] that they had to cease and desist in their interference. But they didn't, and we went to Portland [1948], and there we got a little bit stronger, and we said, 'Boys, you have either got to get all the way into the CIO or all the way out.' But they did neither. They stayed in the CIO and they played the Party line. At this convention, since these brothers have not been able to make up their minds for themselves, we are going to have to make up their minds for them." The major decisions on this score were (1) expulsion of FE for defying instructions to get into the auto union; (2) expulsion of UE (which had stopped paying per capita tax to the CIO, and did not bother sending delegates to the convention); (3) an enabling resolution empowering the board to expel other unions; and (4) amendments to the CIO constitution.

The CIO hierarchy faced as delicate a constitutional problem in expelling constituent unions led by Communists as the AFL had faced in expelling unions that had affiliated with Lewis's industrial committee. The CIO had been set up on the same federation principles as the AFL; constituent unions were autonomous. Thomas Kennedy, constitution committee chairman at the founding convention explained at that time that in the event of conflict between the CIO and national union constitutions, "that part of the Constitution of that particular organization as applied to its own members would govern, and not this Constitution." In practice, because the original Committee for Industrial Organization was a prime influence in organizing many of its unions, and because of the commanding stature of Lewis, the foundation leader, the CIO from the start was a more centralized establishment than the AFL had ever been. This greater centralized control was validated through the creation of CIO-sponsored and -financed organizing committees, and through calls for CIO intervention in early faction disputes. Nevertheless, even Lewis and his successor Murray exercised restraint in interfering in the several unions' internal affairs, and constitutionally, the CIO lacked sovereign powers over chartered affiliates.

On the political side, the labor tradition was murky. The AFL constitution under Gompers decreed nonpartisanship. "Party politics, whether they be Democratic, Republican, Socialistic, populistic, prohibition, or any other, should have no place in the convention of the American Federation of Labor." In fact, however, Gompers and most AFL chiefs began leaning toward the Democrats in 1906, and from the turn of the century until his death in 1924, Gompers never missed an opportunity to denounce Socialists. Things took a more pronounced turn in the first postwar period when Foster's TUEL was formally proscribed in union after union, and William F. Dunne was unseated at the 1923 AFL convention (on the motion of Philip Murray). In the late twenties, Green and the Executive Council tried, as we know, to oust regularly elected Communist officials in the fur union. Constitutionally, however, AFL affiliates' autonomous rights remained enshrined.

When the hierarchy felt threatened by Lewis in the thirties, the Executive Council had to stretch its authority by suspending the CIO-oriented unions in order to deprive them of voting rights at the coming convention. The CIO hierarchy, in contrast, was able to legally revise the constitution since it commanded a decisive majority. This it proceeded to do with the adoption of the following amendments: no member of the Communist party, or one who consistently supported its policies and activities, or of other totalitarian movements, was eligible to serve on the executive board; the board could refuse to seat or could remove any member or officer who by two-thirds vote was found to be ineligible to serve; the board by two-thirds vote could revoke the charter of, or expel, any national or international union or organizing committee that was following the policies of the Communist party or of other totalitarian movements.

These were extraordinary amendments that seemingly revamped the structure of the CIO. They provided for a political loyalty test; they demanded adherence to something called "CIO Policy," consisting of disparate pronouncements on matters of foreign affairs and electoral politics; they gave the board near-dictatorial powers to ride herd on constituent unions and expel opponents. It would appear that the CIO was decreeing a centralism and a political orthodoxy that American unionism had heretofore eschewed. Some non-Communist observers of the labor scene were worried that provisions and precedents were being set which would plague the CIO in days to come, and which could be employed to anathematize other oppositions that might arise. In reality, the consitutional changes were strictly a bill of attainder. Their proposal and adoption arose out of the peculiar constitutional conundrum posed by the Communists, not out of a desire to further centralize authority. By 1949, it was obvious that despite fervent appeals, the members of the re-

311

maining Communist-led unions either would not or could not remove their officials; that the only way to remove them from the labor scene was to lift their charters and make war on them. Since there were no grounds to bring Communist officials up on charges of malfeasance or racketeering, Murray and his associates could devise no alternative to employing a political test as the rationale for expelling affiliated organizations.

The bloodletting had serious consequences, but it did not produce a further centralization of the CIO. On the contrary, once the Communist issue was disposed of, the CIO began to lose cohesiveness. Reuther succeeded to the presidency at the end of 1952, following Murray's death, only after an embittered contest with Allan Haywood. It was on a narrow vote, and it irreparably dislocated the organization. Soon thereafter he was embroiled in a running and searing intrigue concocted by David MacDonald, the new head of the steel union, based on nothing more substantial than personal rivalry. Consequently, the CIO had to go, divided against itself, into unity negotiations with the AFL, initiated by the AFL's new president, George Meany. It was an illustration of the proposition that law expresses and regulates actual power balances and relations; it neither creates them nor supplants them.[6]

4

Aside from UE, the other Communist officials decided to follow Party advice to let the CIO take the initiative. They wanted to utilize the trials as sounding boards for what they thought was to be labor history in the making. After the CIO convention, William Steinberg, president of the American Radio Association, filed charges against nine unions; Murray designated committees made up of board members to conduct hearings and make recommendations; and in the next several months, trials were held, evidence accumulated, and the committees brought back their findings. Despite the judicial pretentions, it was all cut-and-dried. Everyone knew what the disposition would be. Paul Jacobs, a staff member of the Oil Workers union at the time, who wrote the report in the longshore case, later stated, "Bridges and everyone else knew the verdict was decided before the trial was held. The committee's decision to recommend expulsion was so certain that I began to work on the writing of it while the trial was still in progress." The CIO wanted to keep the legalities straight, and the Communists wanted the public record.

312

All the reports tabulated in some detail the changes in the Communist party line from the thirties to the time of the hearings and correlated these changes with identical zigzags in the positions of Communist officials on trial. In the case of several unions, this circumstantial proof was strengthened by direct testimony of former Communist adherents. The proposition was thus persuasively established that the designated officials followed the policies of the Communist party, and that the Party sought to promote the interests of the Soviet Union. The CIO reporters had greater difficulty in trying to distinguish honest differences of opinion from underhanded conspiracies. "Within the CIO," read the report in the longshore case, "there is the greatest freedom for differences of opinion on political and trade union matters, so long as those differences stem from an honest belief as to what constitutes good trade union policy or the best method of promoting the objectives set forth in the CIO Constitution. But there is no room for differences of opinion when those differences reflect a fundamental divergence in basic objectives such as the divergence between the CIO and the Communist Party." With slight variations, the argument was repeated in all the reports, and it constitutes a far-reaching exclusionary doctrine of conformity. If taken literally, it could be applied to any political dissident, religious pacifist, doctrinal anarchist, whose opposition likewise originated from a basic philosophical divergence from the official point of view. Could the reporters have avoided this with a more careful formulation of their position?

Their basic difficulty was not semantic. It stemmed from the contradictory character of the Communist party (described in chapter 1), an organization which they were determined to appraise as exclusively and uniformly anti-unionist to justify their punitive decree. Thus, to refute the claim that Mine Mill brought rich bread-and-butter benefits to the membership, they maintained in the Mine Mill report that "the union's blatant Communist orientation has driven more and more workers away from it and thus has deprived it of its power genuinely to serve the interests of the workers in its industry." To prove this, the report did not cite wages or working conditions, but quoted instead membership figures: where Mine Mill paid per capita on 100,000 in 1946-1947, this figure dropped to 65,000 in 1948-1949, and as of October 1949, "the figure reported to the CIO was 44,000." This was a disingenuous argument. To begin with, the figure did not accurately reflect membership. And then, Mine Mill membership losses, as the reporters knew, were due to anti-Communist secession movements and raiding expeditions on the part of other CIO unions, not because members were dropping away in disgust at the union's economic ineffectiveness. It was like a police officer taking a victim's wallet and then writing out a charge against him for having no visible means of support.

If one puts aside the subsidiary strand of propositions in what were, after all, political attacks, not judicial findings, the big question is this: given the facts of Communist domination of ten international unions, three or four of them important ones, were the expulsions necessary and wise? At the convention Reuther put the issue baldly: "The body politic has a bad case of cancer, and we have either got to save the cancer or the body. The noisy minority believes that we ought to throw away the body and save the cancer, but we have come here to cut out the cancer and save the body of the CIO." Was it true that the 1946-1948 relations could not be continued? That unless the Communists were cut out bodily, the CIO would wither away? It is irrelevant to contrast the CIO's expulsions with the different course taken by the British Trade Union Congress, or to suggest that the trade-union heavens would not have fallen had there been no expulsions, considering the subsequent evolution of the UE and longshore organizations. The regulation officialdom was convinced that the CIO could not survive in the cold-war epoch if it defied recognized public opinion as formulated by the media, by liberal dignitaries, by government authorities.

The same tropism that Gompers responded to in flailing away at antiwar advocates in the First World War, that Murray and Hillman reacted to in repudiating Lewis in the Second World War, was what Murray and Reuther yielded to in the cold war. If the labor movement of Kaiser Germany, with its putative international Marxist orientation, resolved that it could preserve itself only by a display of national loyalty, how much more compelling was the pull on an American leadership that was avowedly wedded to the system, presiding over a membership that was unreservedly nationalist. It was therefore academic to the officialdom that continued Communist leadership of a scattering of unions was not directly menacing the existence of the CIO. It could not function with its customary allies, pursue its customary folkways, with this bar sinister emblazoned on its shield. The CIO was dependent from the start on government favor, on the alliance with the Roosevelt wing of the Democratic party, on subordination to official public opinion—all of which spelled a responsible unionism and a responsbile labor leadership in terms of acceptance of welfare capitalism, and the labor official's industrial role as a disciplinarian of the work force as well as a solicitor of concessions. Only those who did not understand this dependence could be surprised that when the struggle against Communism became the consuming passion of American politics, CIO spokesmen and members would respond unhesitatingly to the bugle call.[7]

Although the constitutional changes had only ephemeral significance (and the CIO ceased existence as a separate entity with the unification in 1955), the expulsions had far-reaching sociological and political effects. They signalled that the CIO's crusading days were over, and that its constituent unions were hardening into quasi-conservative enterprises. It was not a simple cause-and-effect sequence. It was not a case of reactionaries, after tossing out militant opponents, relaxing into a Hutcheson-Tobin-Frey quietism. The Communists were not the firebrand revolutionaries that their belated antics and grimaces implied; and the Murrays and Reuthers were not throwbacks to craft-union primitives. But the CIO had been moving along the lines of a moderate, modernized, politically alert unionism since war days, and the forced surgery, like the final expiation at the end of a third act, was public notification that the curtain had fallen on the long drama of turmoil and discord. By driving out the only sizable opposition faction, the CIO was lined up for automatic approval of any action that the government declared necessary in the struggle against world Communism. It put out of bounds any fundamental debate on "CIO policy"—the name for a general set of attitudes resting on the faith that social betterment was to be achieved at home in partnership with political and industrial elites who stood at the head of an expanding imperium abroad. The process by which labor gained recognized status as part of the establishment was involuted, the product of a series of dialectical interactions. These are here pedagogically summarized as "factors."

(1) The Taft-Hartley Act, a piece of punitive legislation embodying provisions long advocated by the National Association of Manufacturers, had been drawn up with the help of corporation lawyers, its drafting paid for by the Republican National Committee. That it passed over Truman's veto by big majorities in both houses despite labor's expensive advertising and letter-writing campaigns testified to the strength of middle-class feeling that unions had to be restrained. Repeal of the Taft-Hartley Act—dubbed by the union

315

officialdom as the "slave-labor law"—was the major programmatic objective in labor's campaign for the Democrats in 1948, and a hard-pressed Truman pledged to do just that in speech after speech. In his state of the union message following his near-miraculous victory, it became clear that his proposal for repeal was not quite what it appeared to be during the electioneering. Along with repeal, he proposed certain so-called improvements in the Wagner Act, namely, prohibition of secondary boycotts and jurisdictional strikes, and limitations on strikes in vital industries. When the administration bill came on the House and Senate floors, it was further Taft-Hartleyized with amendments and then effectively bottled up. The repeal campaign was a chimera.

The unions, too weak to work their will on Congress, proved too weak also to nullify the law by ignoring and bypassing the National Labor Relations Board. They had grown dependent on NLRB election and certification procedures, had no stomach for plunging back into the organizing hazards and strife of pre-Wagner Act days. That the CIO would have defied the Act had it not been preoccupied with the internal struggle against Communists—as some left-wing writers claimed—may be doubted. The AFL unions, not entangled in such a battle, similarly moved to qualify under the Act, disregarding the thundering of John L. Lewis (in the course of which he coined another aphorism: "On this particular issue, I don't think that the Federation has a head. I think its neck has just grown up and haired over.") The passage of the Act was followed by a prodigious corporation-sponsored public-relations hubbub to shift workers' loyalty away from union officials back to employers. The comprehensive effort, though not to be compared with industry's "American Plan" of the twenties for the open shop, had the earmarks of a campaign to constrain the unions.

The first notable feature of the new landscape was the relative stagnation of unions; there was no more new major organizing. How much of this can be attributed to the new law is uncertain, since major growth had stopped at the end of the war, and membership rose again only modestly in the Korean War period. The CIO's southern organization drive fell apart, but it probably would have failed in any case, given the internal preoccupations of the CIO. There is little doubt, nonetheless, that the law's opening of federal courts to employer breach-of-contract damage suits against unions, the reintroduction of the injunction banned by the Norris-

316

LaGuardia Act, the right of government to postpone critical strikes, the attempted outlawry of the union shop (permitted again by a 1951 amendment) had chilling effect on a gamut of traditional practices. It made the labor leader doubly cautious about embarking on organization campaigns that could entangle his union in a web of costly civil and criminal litigations. It reinforced the conservative tendency. But the larger expectations of the Taft-Hartley instigators were unfulfilled. The unions devised the necessary legal formulae and facades to live with the law while continuing their round of activities. The labor structure held together, and within a very few years it became apparent that what had been forged in battle was too powerful to be decimated by legal restrictions and disabilities.[8] All the same, there were fewer dramatic clashes with employers in the absence of major organizing campaigns.

(2) Concomitant with harassment of unions, the government found that it needed the cooperation of the labor officialdom in its manifold activities around the world. The United States had emerged as the sole world power bestriding exhausted allies and defeated foes. Not only was it conducting a global struggle against Communism, but it had also to fit the different countries and economies into the structure that it had created at Bretton Woods so that the devastation of war would not lead to social disintegration or native insurrection. The importance of labor participation for shoring up the system was not in the particular expertise or trained personnel that unions could furnish American missions abroad, but in their presumed ability to elicit the support of foreign laborites and liberals. The labor officialdom did not have to be coaxed; it was ready and eager to take on such an assignment. Reuther, Carey, and Baldanzi had been calling for labor representation in the American enterprise abroad since the end of the war. It was commonplace for labor officials in their private councils to jeer at striped-pants diplomats with British accents; such types could not communicate with labor and socialist people; unionists, who understood the problems and talked the language of workers, could perfect alliances that the foreign-service mandarins could not. The CIO's own foreign-policy declaration read, "The American labor movement has channels of communication and relationships in foreign countries, the use of which is essential to the successful prosecution of a democratic foreign policy. Labor's participation in the ECA [European Cooperation Administration] has accounted for much of the popular success

of the recovery program; labor's moral appeal and experience have helped avert policies that might have weakened the understanding of ECA by the great mass of European workers."

The tradition of American labor leaders' cooperating with the government in foreign affairs went back to Gompers and the First World War. It had been reinforced under Roosevelt with the appointment of labor attachés to the State Department during the war after the massacre of Bolivian tin miners at Catavi. The original cosmetic concept behind labor representation was expressed by Senator La Follette, one among many, who made the proposal: "I do not anticipate that too much could be accomplished as a result of this action, but in any case it would be a notice to millions of workers, many of them exploited beyond description, that the President and the government of the United States are concerned and aware of the plight of these workers." Roosevelt's creation of the Office of Inter-American Affairs in 1940, under Nelson Rockefeller's leadership, was significant for the postwar entente, because Rockefeller, ahead of the business community of which he was an eminent member, stood for a sophisticated policy combining hardheaded capitalist investment with welfarist corollaries. This office (OIAA) was an important division for policy formulation in Latin American affairs, and had numbers of former labor officials and professionals on its payroll, as well as AFL and CIO representatives on its advisory committee.

Labor functionaries were dispatched to Europe immediately after the war to help reconstitute the labor movements and reestablish broken connections. At first, there was rivalry between the AFL and CIO, but that ceased after CIO and British officials broke off liaison with the Russian trade unions over the Marshall Plan and withdrew from the World Federation of Trade Unions. Eventually, both American groups joined with the British to form a new western-oriented labor body, the International Confederation of Free Trade Unions, so that by 1948, the two sets of officials were working along parallel lines. The AFL, in addition, had its own "labor CIA" headed by Jay Lovestone, the erstwhile Communist party leader (described by a newspaperman as half cloak-and-dagger and half cloak-and-suiter), whose European field marshal was Irving Brown, another Lovestoneite wheeler-and-dealer from the Communist past; this apparatus became an AFL-CIO enterprise when the two federations united.

Joseph Keenan, an official of the AFL electrical union, was labor secretary to General Lucius Clay, American proconsul in Germany, and labor representatives were bustling about to line up reviving unions in West Germany on a pro-American, anti-Communist basis. Brown nourished and financed the split in the Communist-dominated French labor federation with the formation of the minority Force Ouvrière, and engaged in similar ventures in Greece. Another cloak-and-dagger labor operative, Serafino Romualdi, set up shop in Latin America. An Italian emigré originally employed by Dubinsky's union, he was put on the payroll of Rockefeller's OIAA, and became chief AFL Latin American plenipotentiary at war's end. In half a dozen countries he intrigued, using finances and patronage as his weapons, to orient labor movements in a pro-American direction; when that could not be done, he encouraged dissident officials to set up rival movements. In the late forties the formation of the ECA to administer the Marshall Plan funds became a veritable windfall to the bureaucracy; numbers from the AFL, CIO, and Rail Brotherhoods were moved into various missions as labor advisers and specialists.

It was not long before American labor officials suffered a bad reputation for being mere creatures of the State Department, and got into a false position in their relationships with labor officials of other countries. It must be kept in mind that the fulsome rhetoric employed by high government spokesmen concerning labor's partnership in shaping foreign policy was flattery undiluted with reality. Labor representatives were exclusively consultants, technicians, leg-men, and paymaster middlemen. They had no voice in policy formulation or decision-making. They were adjuncts of the State Department, the CIA, and the ECA missions, institutions whose interest in foreign labor movements or worker uplift was limited to making use of such groups and endeavors for the struggle against Communism or insurgencies in which Communists figured, and for the stabilization of capitalist infrastructures and markets.

Since American officials gravitated toward property-holding, conservative elites, American policy was highlighted in the cold war by alliances with Catholic conservatives in Western Europe, and with military strong men on the make in Southeast Asia and Latin America. In Western Europe where there were sturdy labor movements, trained leaderships, and liberal and left democratic traditions going back a hundred years, American labor interventions and money were chiefly instrumentalities in reinforcing pro-Western Catholic and Social Democratic reform forces. Elsewhere,

where social relations were inchoate and labor traditions weak, labor emissaries found themselves embroiled in a variety of dubious enterprises; at times, in outright support of ruthless military adventurers and juntas.

As the labor operation became systematized under Meany and Lovestone, first in the AFL, then in the united labor federation, a number of unions provided "covers" and personnel for CIA projects, and the AFL-CIO initiated a three-way partnership with the State Department and major United States corporations for the purpose of setting up the American Institute for Free Labor Development (directed at Latin America), the Asian-American Free Labor Institute, and the African-American Labor Center. All these, financed by United States government agencies except for nominal and largely cosmetic contributions by the two other partners, were "an exercise in trade union colonialism" as Victor Reuther would call it later.

There is a distance of status and outlook between national labor officials and the ranks for whom they are speaking for all the reasons adduced long ago by Robert Michels. In the case of foreign policy, the distance is widened several times over, because the membership knows little what its representatives are doing, does not view the union as an instrument of foreign policy, and has no ready mechanism to control these activities. In the absence of significant internal opposition groups, the labor officialdom, in this sphere, operates as a virtually sovereign power responsible to itself alone. Where it both articulated and exploited memberships' true sentiments in the anti-Communist campaigns within unions, it went far afield in translating these campaigns into generalized espionage and counterrevolutionary activities in far corners of the globe. Meany and his staff imposed on the labor movement commitments, attitudes, and associations that were to alienate organized labor from sections of the population from which it traditionally drew strength when the political climate altered again in the sixties. In these later years Reuther became concerned with the excesses of "Lovestone diplomacy." But when he tried to introduce quite modest modifications and a note of sobriety, he was rebuffed; the forces he had been so prominent in starting had become too powerful to contain.[9]

(3) These and related political activities enhanced labor leaders' standing as solid citizens with whom one could do business. Labor officials were permitted to associate with policy makers and opinion molders, they were invited to serve on government and foundation

panels, their proposals were respectfully reported by commentators. At this time in the fifties, there was a palpable mellowing in leading managements' attitudes. It is impossible to refer to a specific year or month, or to point to a specific dramatic occurrence. If one confined oneself to reading the declarations of the National Association of Manufacturers or listening to trade association orators, one might conclude that nothing had changed in basic postures over the past decades. Since the thirties, the industrialist has been a schizophrenic personality; his stage declarations are unrelated to his industrial practices. So far as recognizing, dealing, and bargaining with unions, major corporations had been doing that since the CIO breakthrough. In the next few years, they also agreed to checkoffs and modified union shops, so that unions were relieved of the work that used to take up three-quarters of their energies; in consequence, officials were discouraged from condoning wildcat or irregular job actions or resisting industrial discipline; the labor professional had a stake in the maintenance of amicable relations with management. Nevertheless, for over a decade there had been strong reservations in industry circles about the permanence or reliability of these arrangements; now these reservations were attenuated.

That the attitudinal changes were neither uniformly adopted nor avowedly articulated can be deduced from the difficulty that most labor experts had in trying to pinpoint them. Yet most agree that there was a pronounced shift in the fifties to accepting unionism as a durable feature of the industrial scene. The position enunciated in the Rockefeller Brothers 1958 reports indicates the new approach:

> Since labor's role in economic growth is so vital, it is important to establish and maintain an environment which will call for the most honorable, responsible, and imaginative trade union leadership. . . . Cooperation with responsible labor leadership should serve to stimulate the full contribution labor can make to growth and eliminate the forces which might take root in a strained and troubled labor movement.

It became clear in actions of steel and auto managements that this was not just relegated to the realms of discourse, that it expressed itself vividly in employer-union relations. In the 1956 industry-wide steel strike, the United States Steel Corporation set up mobile toilets for pickets at a number of plants, and at South Chicago ran a power line and water pipes to the union's six trailers. In the 1967

321

strike at Ford that went on for two months, Reuther learned when he visited the picket line that the company was delivering coal and oil drums to the pickets in accordance with an understanding with the local. "Karl Marx would never believe this," he exclaimed in astonishment. Most telling of all was the action of the General Motors management in the 1970 strike—another two-month marathon. The union was in a financial squeeze. Its strike fund was going down fast—$14 million a week paid out for strike benefits and $23 million a month due to the corporation for employees' health and insurance payments. So a special arrangement was worked out. GM agreed to pay the $23 million insurance costs and to hold off billing the union. After the strike was over, the UAW repaid the $46-million-due bill at 5 percent interest. "We have to live together," stated Earl Bramblett, the GM chief negotiator, in explaining the corporation decision.

All this was certainly a far cry from April 1948 when Walter Reuther was shot at by hired killers, when there was a similar attempt to murder Victor Reuther a year later, and when earlier, a number of active unionists of the Briggs local were brutally beaten by professional hirelings—the evidence pointing to collusion between some elements of industry and the underworld. When Victor Reuther was admitted to the Henry Ford Hospital, the private nurse was informed at the nursing registry that the injured person was Reuther "the union man"; she was then asked whether she would be willing to take care of him—a revealing incident.

Strikes were not eliminated in the new labor-management orchestration, but as in feudal warfare, they were played out as stylized, limited engagements, at least in well-organized industries. These more benign management attitudes were related to the unusual economic position of American industry in the entire decade of the 1950s. Despite its being punctuated with three short recessions, it was a decade of headlong boom, phenomenal growth, increase of the labor force, and steady inflation. An ideologically loyal and industrially moderate labor movement, which bargained for concessions without challenging basic dispositions of a business society, was more or less accepted as a constructive addition to the team in a period of cold war confrontations and economic expansion.[10]

5

The concentration in this study on the Communists and the controversies that they provoked can give the impression that the CIO was a machine primarily devoted to grinding out foreign policy declarations and triggering ideological debates. Nothing could be further from the truth. Despite their increasing attention to political campaigns, and subsidiary dabbling in international intrigue, labor unions remain essentially economic organizations whose claim on members' loyalty rests on their ability to safeguard and improve wages and conditions in the workshops. That is the overwhelming interest, and often the sole interest, of the ranks. The daily life of the union local revolves around what is happening in the workshop, not around what is happening in the State Department, the CIA, or at meetings of the Democratic National Committee. The consequent grievances, demands, projects, and aspirations of workers may have far-reaching consequences for the social order, but the work place is the hub that holds the enterprise together. The aggregate of locals and shop subdivisions in a given industry make up a national union, which is no sooner created than it both represents and dominates the membership for which it speaks. Consequently, the union's decision-making structure, on-job practices, and wage-and-bargaining standards are of more vital interest to the dues-payers than are many other features on which outside well-wishers center their attention; for the same reason, changes in the inner mechanism of national organizations affect them more immediately than palace politics in the composite federation. The following examples illustrate the structural evolution of two industrial unions after the Communist smashup.

In the National Maritime Union, Curran interpreted his victory over the Communists in the July 1948 referendum as a mandate to drum out any and all opponents and to fasten a personal regime on the union. He put former officials on trial before administration-dominated committees on general charges of working to create chaos in the union and had them expelled. His attempt to amend the constitution to bar Communists from membership led to a split with his ally, Jack Lawrenson, who put together a new opposition made up of a coalition of nonpolitical militants and non-Communist radicals. After the National Council approved a resolution for submission to the coming convention barring Communists from membership, Curran summarily removed David Drummond, the agent of the Port of New York for opposing "union policy." When 14 patrolmen refused to accept instructions from his appointed replacement, they were suspended for insubordination. Thereupon, in November the NMU experienced a crisis resembling the one in the

UAW in Homer Martin's day. A contingent of 400 oppositionists physically took over the national offices, fights broke out, and a number of national staff people suffered injuries and had to be escorted from the headquarters by police. Curran regained control of the situation by ruthlessly utilizing the leverage afforded through control of the union's finances and staff. He brought supporters from other ports into New York, and at an extralegal mass meeting held in December secured the ratification of his removal of Drummond and the 14 patrolmen.

After he buried the new opposition by sweeping majorities in the referendum elections of 1950, he expelled the main supporters of Drummond and Lawrenson. Then Vice-President Hulbert Warner and National Secretary Neal Hanley, who supported Warner against Lawrenson, had to walk the plank, as did M. Hedley Stone later, a key figure in ensuring Curran's original victory, and who remained a Curran lieutenant in the fight with the new opposition. At one point in the uproarious struggle, the Socialist leader Norman Thomas, at the head of a citizens committee, urged the observance of minimal democratic procedures in the dispute, but his suggestions were brushed aside by the administration. By the fifties, with all major critics expelled from the union, and others properly intimidated, the NMU settled into the familiar pattern of pure-and-simple unionism. Some labor writers thought it represented the triumph of a "stable unionism" that had finally settled accounts with the nondescript revolutionism of its past. It was that. It was also unionism directed by a one-party regime, presided over by a putatively infallible and increasingly domineering (and according to information coming to light in the seventies, increasingly avaricious) leader. A high-handed pseudo-populist Communist management had been replaced by a despotic business management.

The second case history furnishes possibly the most revealing insight into the mechanics of labor bureaucratization, since it concerns the auto union. Reuther's conclusive victory over a disintegrating opposition guaranteed him an initial honeymoon period. This was facilitated by his major adversaries' reading the handwriting on the wall and leaving the union; R. J. Thomas took a staff job with the CIO; Leonard followed suit after an interval; Addes opened a tavern; later it was reported that he got a job as a purchasing agent with the Auto-Lite Corporation. Reuther lost no time in replacing all opponent national staff and department functionaries with his own loyalists. The few opposition executive board members who managed to survive the convention either switched over to the victors' side, or in the case of several, agreed not to run at the next convention in return for staff appointments. All this was to be expected. It was in strict accordance with Jacksonian principles and union practices.

At first Reuther permitted his caucus machinery to stand idle, since there was no opposition to organize against and the caucus machinery seemed a purposeless duplication of the official administration machinery. However, at the 1949 convention, held twenty months after he had taken power, Reuther found that the rebellious spirit had not been entirely extinguished. The administration proposal for biennial conventions was defeated; the requested dues increase was met with widespread opposition so that it had to be withdrawn; the motion to divide the Illinois region barely passed. Moreover, a lot of the criticism was coming from Reuther supporters. This would not do, and after the convention, Reuther refurbished and converted the caucus into a steel hoop to bind and restrain the entire officialdom and membership.

Even to the present, the national caucus meets only during conventions; it is a virtual mass meeting and serves the sole purpose of giving delegates the reassuring comfort of being part of the "in" group, privy to the leaders' plans before these are formally offered to the convention. The important body is the steering committee composed of some 200 local officials. These are handpicked by the international officers and regional directors. The steering committee endorses policy positions and candidates for international offices on the recommendations made by the top leadership, and these decisions are binding on caucus members. The national caucus has its counterparts in regional administration caucuses. These pick the administration candidate for the board, so that nomination by the caucus is equivalent to election. With the passage of years, as remaining opposition was quashed, the administration had less need of this extralegal apparatus, but it is there to be used when the occasion requires.

Any attempt to break through this network is met with sure, swift, and deadly reprisal. It is a cardinal sin against "leadership ethics" to run against a caucus nominee in open convention. Those guilty place themselves outside of the caucus to become enemies of the administration. What happened to Panfilo Ciampa, an international representative on the staff of Thomas Starling, director of the southeastern region, was both an object lesson and a warning. In 1953, Starling was renamed the nominee for director at a regional caucus. Ciampa broke the unwritten law when he put himself up as a candidate and was elected by the delegates of the region. He then discovered that it was impossible for him to function. Staff men outside the region were sent in to plague, harass, and smear him; he was ostracized and deprived of the support of the international office. At the next convention he gave up, declining to run for reelection. His remarks to the convention explained his dilemma: "I cannot say that I would do a service to you, the members, in another two years . . . under the same circumstances. . . . The principle [involved here] is true democracy versus controlled democracy. I hope that you, the delegates, in sober thought . . . will elect people who against any obstacle will represent the members rather than being the controlled individuals." A scattered membership thus found itself confronted by a solid phalanx of a disciplined and drilled officialdom of some 700 labor professionals commanding the services of a variety of experts, and in full control of the levers of power.

Reuther introduced several more-stringent constitutional rules governing convention procedures, but these by themselves were less important than the fact of the one-party regime that converted conventions into plebiscitary proceedings to approve or disapprove leadership decisions; and the caucus mechanism reduced much of this right to a formality. In the first Reuther years, as incidental oppositions still had the temerity to rear their heads, they were efficiently cut down. In 1949, the convention adopted the Grievance Committee report to expel Tracy Doll and Sam Sage for printing and distributing a report on alleged racketeering in the UAW. The report found its way into the hands of FE officials who used it to defeat the UAW in a contested NLRB election in Iowa. Reuther made a long impassioned speech in support of the Grievance Committee's recommendation in which he affirmed his determination "to protect the millions of kids in their homes," drawing a sharp distinction between "honest opposition" and "treason." Since the action of the convention went beyond the written constitution, the convention proceeded to amend the constitution to give the international executive board the right to prefer charges against members "in case of extreme emergency."

The next convention in 1951 broadened the power of the board to proceed against members who allegedly engaged in a conspiracy against the union. This amendment was made retroactive to 1949, and under it, the board expelled six and suspended seven members of Local 205—an amalgamated local in Detroit that had been Communist-influenced. The expellees took their case to the courts and were reinstated after the decision was handed down that the union had violated its own constitution. By the time the courts intervened, the international executive board was constitutionally armed with greater authority, and the expulsions had served their purpose of intimidating would-be dissenters.

The same convention gave its approval to the crackdown on local newspapers, so that within a few years the entire UAW press spoke with one voice. The international office had sent out a letter to every local editor advising that an international publications board would review local newspapers printed in conjunction with the *United Automobile Worker* for possible libel and to ensure conformity with international policy. Chevrolet Local 659 of Flint appealed to the convention an order of the board to stop printing in the local newspaper, *The Searchlight*, materials "detrimental" to policies of the international union. The convention rejected the appeal. In 1954 an administrator was placed over the local for violations of the 1951 mandate. Subsequently, a representative of the international public-relations department was appointed to pass on all articles prior to publication. By 1958 the local leaders had been successfully reeducated, for *The Searchlight* was running editorials lauding Reuther and the international union's policies.

"Controlled democracy" became unchallengeable when the regime wore down and beat down the last stronghold of significant opposition, Local 600 under the presidency of Carl Stellato. Local 600 had jurisdiction over the huge Ford River Rouge plant. At one time River Rouge employed 60,000 workers. Even in the period under discussion, when the plant declined in importance in the Ford empire, its work force was not much under 30,000. Stellato was a colorful and astute union figure. He had come to the local presidency in 1950 as a Reuther-backed candidate, but shortly went into opposition in response to local sentiments and pressures. There had been a Communist faction in the local since its foundation; by 1950 it was a minor element in the local's councils. But the local atmosphere was heavily charged with rank-and-file assertiveness and suspicion of international "pork-choppers" and "piecards." After the local repeatedly clashed with the international, Reuther put the local under receivership in the spring of 1952, which was extended for six months by stretching the constitution. He also approved the appearance of international staff members before the House Committee on Un-American Activities that was holding hearings in Detroit, who identified several past and present Communist party members in Local 600. The appeals of five local council members who had been removed by the administrator and declared ineligible to run for office led to a further constitutional extension of the powers of the board at the 1953 convention. Trial procedure was amended to permit the board to set aside an acquittal verdict of a local union trial committee, and to order a new trial by an international trial committee. While Stellato and his associates managed to get reelected after the receivership was lifted, he was emphatically contained by the now irresistible power of Solidarity House. He tried to work his way out of the impasse by taking the Frankensteen road, but with equally poor results. In 1958 and 1960 he was narrowly defeated in the Democratic primaries for congressman. In 1961, he returned by the back door to the Reuther camp when he ran for reelection to the local presidency.

Just as in American industry all initiatives and creativity have been pulled out of the workshops and centered in the engineering departments and managerial offices, so in the UAW, planning and decision-making was withdrawn from the locals and concentrated in the international office. Many of the formal democratic rights of members remained written into the constitution as before, but once the ability to formulate competing programs and plans was nullified by prohibiting, in effect, opposition organizations, they atrophied like limbs in disuse. Conventions became lifeless when they were no longer sovereign decision-makers, but now ratification conclaves. Local unions were dominated by regional directors and their staffs when the vital functions of collective bargaining and contract enforcement that they had performed in the past were taken over, in the basic sections of the industry, by the chain and systems negotiating committees. These, in turn, became dependent upon, and fell under the sway of, the international officers who were the repositories of statistics, relevant facts, conceptual plans, and bargaining strategies. The top leaders were in a position to cow and eliminate any occasional recalcitrant or maverick delegate who had found his way into the negotiating body. The members of these committees were thus described by William Serrin, the Pulitzer Prize-winning reporter from Detroit: "They are ancillary figures at best,

328

sounding boards for the union leadership. . . . Union leaders may bounce proposals off them to gain readings on how the proposals might fare with the rank and file. . . . But mostly they provide the image to give the negotiations the smell of democracy." Emil Mazey, the secretary-treasurer, confessed in a moment of indiscretion, "The basic decisions are not made by the committee; we make decisions, the top leaders of the union. And the decisions are conveyed to the committee and they agree."

This centralization, with the consequent drying up of local sources of power, did not start with Reuther's ascendancy. It had been going on throughout the war years under the pluralistic leadership. It took on a systematic and finished character under Reuther because he was the most formidable exponent of bureaucratic edifice-building to occupy the presidency, and because he was in sole charge of the national office. The tendency of all bureaucracy is toward centralization, and the tendency in centralization within a bureaucratic framework is to entrust final power to a super-arbiter who can manage and rationalize the bureaucracy. Other things being propitious, the super-arbiter becomes the director of the bureaucracy as well as its spokesman. This became the hallmark in the UAW with other top officials becoming privy counsellors to the president. Most union constitutions grant kingly powers to presidents, and in the UAW the regal regime was the more unassailable because Reuther's prestige outshone any luster radiated by his lieutenants.

Of course, all this has to be placed in context. Reuther's UAW was of a different world from the one uncovered by the McClellan Senate Committee before whom, week after week, witnesses laid out a sordid story of thievery, grafting, strong-arm "gorilla" rule, mayhem in both national and local unions. It represented in the postwar constellation what Hillman's then "new unionism" stood for in the twenties: harnessing of a membership to shape a socially acceptable reform power structure; the tradeoff of shop discipline and industrial rationalization for economic concessions. Reuther's bureaucracy was cast in its master's image. It was high-minded; it was social-minded; it was honest; it applied itself, according to its own definitions of labor relations realism, to the task at hand of lifting the status of its constituency; it was the defender and expositor of a paternalistic and autocratic regime.

David Dubinsky, in his address to the UAW convention in 1957, said, "I am informed that Reuther was elected unanimously. Well,

329

Walter, you have joined my class." That was correct. Over the years he became a law unto himself, as witnessed by his building of the union's education center. To quote Serrin again:

> In the last year of his life [1970], Reuther devoted much time to what was to be a memorial to himself, the UAW's sumptuous recreation and education center at Black Lake. . . . The project, originally budgeted at 5 million dollars, spreads for 850 acres along the shore of a beautiful, 10,000-acre lake. . . . Reuther demanded that the project be perfect. He would sit up late at night, poring over plans for the center. He charged about the grounds in a green velour Alpine hat, personally marking the trees he wanted kept, touring the facilities with one of the construction men. . . . Without approval from the executive board—not to mention the membership—Reuther poured a constant stream of money into the project until it cost more than 23 million dollars and placed the union in grave financial difficulties. By that time, it was hard to find a union official who had approved of the project. It was Walter's doing, they said.

In the course of a few years the UAW was transformed from an insurgent, membership-participatory, bellicose union into a progressive, efficiently run, machine-controlled union that traded off long-term contracts, management prerogatives, and stable relations for economic benefits like an annual improvement factor, a cost-of-living escalator clause (actually proposed initially by General Motors management), supplemental unemployment benefits, and pension benefits. The period was put on the UAW as crusade, and the page was turned to a new chapter on the modern industrial union as an independent, parallel welfare component of the industrial corporation.[11]

6

Few Communist-led unions were able to survive as independent organizations. Once out in the cold, they were fair game for attacks on all sides. What happened to UE (and FE) has been told in chapter 11. But the longshore union held its own. Bridges bent before the political winds, and the organization settled into the mold of a business union. Today, it officially claims a membership of 60,000, larger than at the time of its expulsion, and remains a power in West Coast shipping and in the economy of Hawaii. Curran's National Maritime Union tried to take over the Marine Cooks and Stewards, but its raid fell flat. Black workers who formed a large part of the membership were fiercely loyal to the only West Coast union on the ships that strongly protected their job rights. Bridges took the MCS under the longshore wing, but it could not survive in the face of hostile NLRB rulings, and its membership was eventually absorbed by the AFL Seafarers International Union. The Fishermen's union did become part of the longshore organization.

The American Communication Association lost members to the anti-Communist American Radio Association, which seceded the year before from the ACA and was chartered by the CIO. What remained of the ACA then joined the Communications Division of the AFL Teamsters. The Fur union which probably could have maintained itself as an independent union, negotiated a merger with the AFL Amalgamated Meat Cutters on onerous terms. Gold was barred from holding any office, and the Meat Cutters executive board reserved the right to expel without trial or hearing at any time within five years anyone held guilty of Communist activity. Even so, the AFL Executive Council tried to hold up the merger, but it was finally consummated in February 1955. The marginal unions, Office and Professional Workers, and Food and Tobacco, through intermediate merger and raiding, were eventually absorbed by the CIO Retail, Wholesale and Department Store union. The United Public Workers, another marginal union, was dissolved. The expulsion order against the Furniture Workers was withdrawn when an anti-Communist leadership took over the union.

Mine Mill was able for a number of years to successfully beat back Steel union raiding attacks. But the continued state of siege under repeated NLRB representation elections, hearings before Congressional committees, trials of leading officials for falsely signing Taft-Hartley non-Communist affidavits, the ruling of the Subversive Activities Control Board that the union was "Communist infiltrated," took a heavy toll. With new faces in its leadership, Mine Mill negotiated a merger agreement with the Steel union in 1967, with the understanding that Mine Mill staff servicing non-ferrous locals would be retained.

Since both UE and the longshore union were out of the Communist orbit by the late fifties, party strength in the unions was reduced to scattered local and shop influences.[12]

THIRTEEN · *Postscript: Concepts of Labor Development*

SOME years ago, in an essay, "The Impact of the Political Left," Bernard Karsh and Phillips Garman wrote that "left wingers . . . contributed a somewhat lasting tone to organizations in which they were most active." What they meant by this elliptical allusion was that under left-wingers' influence, unions began to accept social and service functions beyond the narrow confines of earlier AFL bread-and-butter shop unionism, that they set in motion political action programs drawing in broad ranks, and pushed for adoption of non-discriminatory regulations involving Blacks and other minorities.

Actually, this thought can be fleshed out and elaborated more than Karsh and Garman ventured to do. The concept of industrial unionism was promulgated and pioneered by political radicals and, until the advent of the CIO made it conventionally acceptable, was associated with Debs and the American Railway Union, IWW's, Socialists, left progressives, and in the post-World War I days, Communists. To left idealists, industrial unionism meant not just a more logical and efficient structure of organization, but an organizational realization of labor solidarity and militancy that would transcend craft, ethnic, racial, political divisions, and timidities to wring concessions from the minions of entrenched corporate privilege in the march to a more radiant future. Once the proposition was taken over by a host of functionaries, committeemen, lawyers, and statisticians, and the incandescent idea was transformed into a mundane institution, the vision of the prophets and pathfinders underwent a change. Industrial unionism did spell greater labor solidarity, but not for anticapitalist assaults; mass political activities, but not for Socialist or Labor party candidates; the conversion of unions into more socially purposeful, less discriminatory mechanisms, but for social service, not radical, purposes. Though industrial unionism was not the left-wing enterprise that so many of the pioneers thought or hoped it was going to be, it was nevertheless a far cry from Gompers' parochial federation. True, George Meany, as a personality, would have fitted neatly in Gompers' intimate circle, but

332

that assemblage of business agents and walking delegates would have been shocked by some of the practices of the quasi-social-democratized organization over which he presides.

Over the years, it was the radicals who initiated and popularized the governing ideas for the labor changeover, and in the thirties, when radicals meant Communists in the first instance, supplied front-line assault troops in a number of crucial campaigns and battles that brought the new unionism into existence. Unfortunately for them, for all their prominence in the CIO's formative history, and their central position in the left milieu for thirty years, the Communists could not create a compelling myth nor bequeath a romantic tradition, as did the IWW or Debs Socialists before them; this was not only, and not primarily, because they were disgraced and repudiated in the cold war years—that might conceivably enhance their standing for another generation of rebels—but because, with their repeated changes of front and profession at the behest of a tyranny abroad, they fashioned for themselves a Jesuitical and chameleonlike image, leaving a legacy both ambiguous and shady.

If radicals had an impact on the unions, unions had as great an impact on the radicals. Once the initial struggles were over and the smoke cleared from the battlefields, the trade-union environment acted as a dissolvent of labor radicalism. Legally underwritten unionism, the ability to make meaningful gains in an expanding economy, the stabilization of amply financed union institutions as a usufruct of collective bargaining, the elevation of labor officials to positions of importance—this combination of lures was difficult to resist; a carrot-and-stick system that drained leaders of the will to oppose. The Socialists in the CIO became indistinguishable in their attitudes and behavior from other union officials; they made the transition from socialism to liberalism, from left-wing unionism to no-nonsense unionism, in a bare few years, whereas Socialist unionists of the previous generations, whose paths of advancement were rockier and thornier, adapted more slowly. And irony of ironies, the Communists could not remain impervious to these societal imperatives. For all their conditioning, zealotry, revolutionary past, they were moving in the same direction. Their movement was uneven, anguish- and guilt-laden; there was backtracking, but that was the direction. Disregarding the conflicting loyalties and the compulsion to self-caricature, wasn't that what Browderism meant? Had history favored them with an altered time table, and

333

had the cold war come a decade later than it did, Communist officials in the CIO would have tried to join with their labor opponents
as the Italian and French Communists are clamoring to do today.

This brings us to the next proposition. The bureaucratization of
the maritime and auto, as of the rest of the CIO, has been considered by labor analysts to be an example of a general law of union
development. In this reading, figures like Reuther, Curran, and
their friends, for all their flamboyance and will to power, were instruments of an impersonal, inexorable spirit, who similarly presided over earlier transformations of the machinists, carpenters, and
other AFL unions, which also started as militant organizations led
by political radicals. As Richard Lester saw it, unions pass through a
natural evolution:

> In their early stages such organizations will be militant and tur-
> bulent, with internal factionalism and vigorous external opposi-
> tion. At first they must fight for existence as well as for goals that
> generally are considered radical. Under the circumstances mem-
> bership participation is likely to be high and leadership positions
> in the organization are apt to be won by the agitators and table-
> pounders. Later on, as the organization gains acceptance and se-
> curity and succeeds in establishing new rights and other aims, a
> transformation tends to occur not only in the organization's goals,
> but also in the nature of its leadership . . . oratorical agitators are
> superseded by skillful managers.

Dubinsky enunciated the same thought in 1958 to a graduating
class at an ILG institute:

> Thirty years ago the important thing was for a union leader to
> know how to organize economic strength. Organize! Strike! Set-
> tle! That was labor-management relations. But today, with laws
> and labor boards, almost all of our problems are settled at the con-
> ference table through negotiations. This requires new skills, a dif-
> ferent kind of intelligence. Now it is diplomacy instead of the big
> stick.

There is an assumption behind this sociology of industrial relations, sometimes articulated, more often accepted as an article of
faith, that there has been a secular trend—disregarding subsidiary
oscillations and breaks—from opposition to acceptance (of
unionism), from ideology to pragmatism, from conflict to coopera-

334

tion; that we can anticipate progressively more stable, institutionalized industrial relations in which conflict is muffled and regulated by legal stipulations and orderly procedures. That is the prevalent view. Others have insisted, however, that the future of industrial relations is undetermined, that recent trends toward stability do not prefigure an indefinite era of peace; they are only a phase in the recurrent cycle of conflict and stabilization. Forces within both industry and society create new strains, set up new tensions, which are then liable to erupt into new controversies and hostilities. Social malfunctions and disaffections accumulate to become a critical mass that can generate a chain reaction of deepened labor unrest and assertion. Writing in the complacent fifties, William Kornhauser offered this alternative interpretation in an almost apologetic manner, too well aware of its being out of favor and out of intellectual fashion. "In many labor as well as management circles," he set forth, "it is unpopular to point to divergent group interests, problems of changing power relations, and the importance of political action in industrial affairs. Such emphasis smacks of class consciousness and foreign labor movements."

One hardly need point out that since the course of labor-management relations is dependent on the course of the larger society, the great corporations are no less capable, under the stress of circumstances, of altering their labor policies than their investment modalities. The underlying tendency toward orderly, businesslike relations between employers and unions in our advanced capitalist society can be intermittently thwarted by countervailing currents arising from systemic failures or cyclical seesawing. In other words, "mature unionism" and the "civilized relationship" on which it depends, has to be viewed in the context of a dynamic, potentially unstable arrangement whose major impulses come from the greater society. The trade-union official who, generally speaking, lives for the day, has a sublimal glimmering about this. While a loquacious expositor of the theory on the identity of labor and capital's interests, he is forever nervously looking over his shoulder to ward off possible blows. Wrote Leiserson, after several decades of experience with labor officials, "Among unions the sense of insecurity is pervasive; they seem to live in constant fear for the safety of the organizations." The sense of insecurity, the sense that harmonious labor-management relations are subject to sudden reversals, is not an unreasoning primordial fear resting on ancient folk memories of

335

broken strikes, punitive laws, crippling court rulings, and economic slumps. It is a conviction kept alive by constant pinpricks and jolting reminders that what happened before can happen again.

A dynamic approach is all the more called for when we see what happened to an older organic theory of the labor movement, Selig Perlman's job consciousness. Perlman's was the most ambitious attempt to ground the thinking of the Commons school in a comprehensive concept based on the experiences of labor unionism both here and abroad. Despite his cautionary reservations and prudential asides, it was an apotheosis of Gomper's pure-and-simple unionism. At the time he wrote his thesis in 1927—a period of labor stagnation—it appeared to many to express the hard-headed realism of union leaders whose strategy was a distillation of a half century of hard lessons. Eight years later, with the formation of the CIO, Gompers' heirs were fighting for their lives, and the elaborate intellectual structure fell apart. Perlman and his disciples tried to refurbish the thesis to encompass the new unionism, but it was like trying to revamp a garment that had been fashioned for a different physique. This is not to deny that Perlman's theory was an acute analysis of the unionism of his day, or that the business-unionist archetype lurked in the insurgent of the thirties. But the new industrial unionism, with its aggressive political tactics and confident reliance on liberal government, its disposition to social-democratic initiatives and bombast, and the wider solidarity induced by the irrelevancy of restricting labor in the mass-production environment, was an extreme mutant of the old species. It could not be co-opted, as spirit or genre, to Gompers' voluntarism or Perlman's job consciousness. *Autre temps, autre moeurs*.[1]

The elders of the labor theorists of maturity are Weber and Michels. The stages from turbulence to routine are a pertinent realization of the tendencies in industrial society toward bureaucratism and the working out of the "iron law of oligarchy," concepts that Seymour Lipset systematized in attempting to trace a pattern of trade union behavior. In a free rendition and reformulation of his major propositions, it can be stated that unions are constrained to centralize and bureaucratize their structures because of internal and external imperatives. Internally, there are the intrinsic demands of large-scale organization. The increased size and complexity of operations require the subdivision of responsibilities among a specialized staff under the control of the top officialdom; to ensure organization dis-

336

cipline, cohesiveness, and incentive, the bureaucracy is set up hierarchically according to a fixed pecking order. For external purposes, the union needs a centralized apparatus that parallels the apparatus of industry in order to cope effectively in bargaining pugilism. In the event of strikes, the union has to confront a centrally directed and bureaucratically coordinated national mechanism with its own symmetrical counterforce; in negotiations, the union has to control its own camp so that locals do not undercut each other's positions; in contract-keeping, the union has to be in a position to vouch, in return for security grants, that it can and will discipline its ranks to guarantee uninterrupted production. The union's dependence in recent decades on government, and the proliferation of administrative and mediation boards and personnel, as adjuncts of the two principals in collective bargaining, has reinforced an already prevalent tendency. It has meant more professional experts in the proceedings. It has forced local unions to yield powers that they once exercised as the locus of decision shifted from local to national levels, and raw encounters were transmuted into polemics between opposing lawyers and accountants.

Bureaucratization, however, has a price: overwhelming power at the top and very little power in the ranks. The administration controls all effective means of communication, has a monopoly of the press, is able, in practice, to define and promulgate union programs, opposition to which from subordinate units and members can be construed as disloyalty to the union and punished accordingly. The administration is in a position to prevent the formation of those preliminary associations, to forestall those discussions and exchanges of opinion, without which the exercise of democracy is reduced to individual and ineffectual protest. Even when there is widespread discontent, it may be impossible for dissenters to come together for the purpose of drawing up their grievances before the administration cracks down on outspoken critics and intimidates and disperses the rest. When this power of executives is considered in conjunction with their almost complete monopoly of political skills, and with the fact that except in periods of special stress, only a small minority usually participates in union activities, it is evident that the membership can displace an entrenched officialdom only by a virtual upheaval.

Just as the entrepreneur struggles without letup to eliminate the uncertainties and risks of competition by fixing and administering prices, so the union leader battles unceasingly to establish security

337

of tenure by eliminating the democracy that for him spells permanent insecurity. His determination to eliminate the risks of displacement are the more uncompromising since the special skills of a union leader are not readily marketable elsewhere in our society. There is a big difference between the defeated union official and the defeated holders of public office. The latter are generally drawn from the ranks of lawyers, journalists, business executives. Not only can they return to their former occupations without loss of status; but more often they are also able to capitalize on the connections built up while in office to enhance their influence. It is an entirely different story for the union leader. For him to return to the blue-collar job he worked at before rising to high office, or to take a secondary appointive job with another union, would be tantamount to an admission of failure. It would place him in a demeaning position. He who had been a person of influence and affairs, would find his pumpkin coach vanished and himself back in the kitchen. It is not a fate that he can accept with equanimity. The sociological pressures for bureaucratization are therefore strengthened by the grim resolve of labor politicians to hold fast to their favored status.*

We thus arrive at a paradox. The labor union is as dependent on democracy in society for its existence as a green plant is for sunlight and oxygen; without legal toleration, it could not survive for a day. The labor movement puts democracy at the center of its ideology and propaganda; its major raison d'être is to extend democracy to the industrial cosmos. It heatedly proclaims devotion to the holy cause, and without a doubt constitutes a sustaining force for democracy in the body politic. Its alliances are usually with the most liberal sections of the political establishment, and, as Clark Kerr has written, by creating a separate power center, the unions are a force for pluralism. Yet, with very few exceptions, this noisy advocate of democracy on the outside practices a kind of Caesarian populism on the inside. To justify this glaring inconsistency, one of the main explanations—offered unabashedly by Lewis—was that democracy had to be subordinated to efficiency. Over the years, two-thirds of the mine union districts were placed under administrators, and Lewis fiercely beat down all attempts to restore self-government to them. At the 1936 convention he argued:

* In the last several years, because of growing acceptability of union leaders, top-ranking officials may find it easier, here and there, to obtain a suitable appointment in government or industry. The situation has not changed all that much, however; the displaced labor leader's job opportunities remain limited.

It is not a fundamental principle that the Convention is discussing. It is a question of business expediency and administrative policy as affecting certain geographical areas of the organization. It is a question of whether you desire your organization to be the most effective instrumentality . . . or whether you prefer to sacrifice the efficiency of your organization in some respects for a little more academic freedom.

In an equally startling display of candor at the longshore union's 1947 convention, Bridges defended his union's one-party regime on the ground that it resembled Stalin's or vice versa:

What is totalitarianism? A country that has a totalitarian government operates like our union operates. There are no political parties. People are elected to govern the country based upon their records. . . . That is totalitarianism . . . if we started to divide up and run a Republican set of officers, a Democratic set, a Communist set and something else, we would have one hell of a time.

Dave Beck, then president of the Teamsters and a member of the Board of Regents at the University of Washington, also expatiated on the topic. "Unions," he said, "are big business. Why should truck drivers and bottle washers be allowed to make big decisions affecting union policy? Would any corporation allow it?"

The concept that the expert knows best has considerable acceptance at certain times in a technocracy-avid society. It was not for nothing that this country originated "nonpolitical," technocratic city-manager government schemes. The concept is generally not formulated as crudely as in these outpourings because these fly in the face of our society's operative rhetoric and ideological pieties. The more common defense consists of Orwellian word-juggling. Union democracy is equated with a one-party regime by bald pronouncement, as in Dubinsky's inimitable remark to Victor Reuther during the tumultuous 1937 UAW convention: "In my union we have democracy too—but they know who is boss!" Some labor writers, in a more sophisticated vein, seek to redefine democracy as if they thought it the same thing as Rousseau's "general will." Others, without doing violence to terms or actualities, maintain that unions, even when dictatorship-ridden, represent their members' interests in a general socio-economic sense; oligarchical cliques that do not advance the needs of their ranks will find their organizations falling into a state of desuetude to the point that they are unable to exact concessions from employers. Sumner Slichter put it this way:

If one asks whether unions give their members what they want, the proper answer is that for most unions the question is irrelevant. The great majority of the members do not have much opportunity or desire to consider and discuss alternative policies. Hence they are not to be regarded as making a choice. The proper question to ask is: "Do the members like what they get?" The answer to that question is usually, "yes."

It is probably correct sociology that over the long stretch unions must respond, to one or another degree, to the economic needs of their members, but it should not be forgotten that members sometimes have to stage a revolt to throw out corrupt or petrified officials in order to forcibly push their organizations back on the path of responsiveness. This brings us to the proposition that for members, democracy is often necessary to keep their leaders on the mark, all the more true in modern unions that inevitably extrude a caste of professionals with its own subculture and interests. Members need to be free to voice opposition to leaders and policies without fear of reprisal; and the theoretical freedom is made instrumental only by the corollary right to organize opposition factions. The problem is not disposed of by pointing out that a lot of manipulation goes on in democratic societies as well; that the presence of different parties does not necessarily protect a populace from being offered the choice of individuals, not of policies; that the trend toward bureaucracy and oligarchy is as pronounced in society as in the labor union. Willy nilly, by nature and function, unions are populist forces aiming at a more equitable distribution of wealth and a larger democracy in the work places. When officials forget this—as they often do—they open the door to stagnation, regression and corruption.[2]

2

While the story of American unionism would seem to furnish textbook illustrations of oligarchy and bureaucracy, the thesis has the shortcoming that is characteristic of merely descriptive sociology: by implication or affirmation, its authors tend to freeze the evolutionary process, in this case, with the consolidation of the bureaucracy. This is especially inapplicable for unions that, because of their function, cannot gain the stability, or receive the assured legal guarantees, of the business corporation in a business society. Even in a boom period, when business unionism appears to vindicate most successfully its ideological assumptions, the subterranean tussle goes on between managements intent on maximizing profits, and workers intent on maximizing their shares. That this tussle is generally transposed into the realm of orderly presentations across negotiation tables and to routine political lobbying, and that most strikes are carried on in symbolic fashion, does not negate the tension nor the fact that conflict, though channelized, continues to disturb the equable tenor of the industrial nexus. When, however, boom is supplanted by bust, when a particular firm or industry comes on hard times, or when an industry's technology or mode of operation is revolutionized, and the union official faces his ranks as the apologist for a lack of improvements or even for losses, the strongest bureaucratic machine can begin to show cracks. John L. Lewis's heirs in the mine union can testify to that.

Basically, the unionist is dependent on the system's growth for winning higher real wages and significant workshop improvements. Far from conducting themselves as monopolies, exploiting mercilessly their strictly economic possibilities, most of the time unions act more like political brokerage firms reconciling members' demands with managements' capabilities within existing social arrangements. This was evident during the war when Lewis, by ignoring government regulations, was able to win larger benefits than all other union leaders. Furthermore, according to authoritative surveys, wages in unorganized areas went up more than in such highly organized areas as Seattle and San Francisco. Again, between 1960 and 1967 hourly earnings in largely unorganized service and retail trades went up far more than in highly organized manufacturing industries (although other factors were admittedly at work besides unionization). "Experience in other democratic capitalistic nations," wrote Clark Kerr, "also indicates that a high level of institutional controls has not been associated with abnormal wage advances but rather the opposite." The conclusion appears to be substantiated by the stability in the distribution of national incomes in this country: recent studies reestablish that wage earners' shares have not changed materially since 1929.

The explanation for this, going counter to received opinion, is that the wage complex has legal and social, as well as economic dimensions. Unions, particularly big unions in basic industries, cannot most of the time fully exploit with impunity their position in a rising market. Had all or most labor officials emulated Lewis, they would have brought on a social crisis, and very likely a showdown, between the corporations and government on one side, and the

341

unions on the other. In other situations justified purely by market considerations, pressing of demands that would seriously disturb, or seek to alter, income and power structures, would lead to exhausting strikes and probably violent employer counteroffensives. Practical unionists, as a rule, eschew such notions and confrontations; they attune themselves to the going milieu, determined to maintain good relations with their opposite numbers, for on those good relations rest the union apparatuses as well as their own power. Not that the ranks ordinarily have more far-reaching social ambitions than their leaders. Often, in general political outlook, the progressive professional is more radical-minded than most of his members. But the wage earner, on the receiving end of industry's insatiable dynamism, is more prone to resist inequities than is his spokesman.

Hence, the tension. On the one hand, industrial centralization coupled with demands for a responsible labor leadership that can discipline its ranks in return for beneficial contractual relations calls forth union centralization, union bureaucratization, and a corresponding officialdom that is ready to fit the labor structure into the existing social topography. On the other hand, this adaptation to, and acceptance of, ongoing relations and realities, leads to estrangement from groups of dissatisfied workers, and in the event of a crisis brought on by economic depression, the decline of an industry, or the revised pattern of geographical location and work-force requirements, the possible emergence of an insurgent faction calling for changes. Because there is no tradition of multi-party parliamentarianism, and a tendency to ruthlessness in the conduct of faction fights, any serious programmatic conflict becomes necessarily enlarged into a power conflict for control of the union's job-awarding as well as decision-making apparatus. (This should not be taken to mean that every election contest is an event of deep social significance. Many insurgent factions in the more volatile unions do little more than exploit grievances for careerist ends, and their taking over of administrations represents a circulation of elites rather than a movement of authentic reform. As with other political devices, democracy can be used for small as well as large purposes.)

Conflicts between business unionists and radicals go back to the last century. Gompers and his early circle of associates, all of whom began as Marxists of one or another variety and then passed over to what their opponents derisively called pure-and-simple unionism, fought bitterly over the years against De Leonists, Socialists, and

IWW's. In the course of hostilities, they built up a centerpiece of counterposition between outside ideologists and indigenous pragmatists. According to the exegesis, the trade-union official, coming out of the workshops, his feet firmly planted on the ground, naturally sets his thinking to the actual problems and possibilities inherent in the worker's existence in a business society. The intellectual, coming from the outside, his head stuffed with fanciful theories of saving humanity, impatient with piecemeal solutions, tries to impose on trade unions alien ideas and programs that would divert them from their true paths of measured and gradual advances. In the drawn-out struggle with the Communists, the later representatives of the ideological tribe, the item of national loyalty, rather than absence of practicality, was brought to the fore, although this too had been foreshadowed in the previous period after the Socialist party voted in 1917 to oppose the war. This counterposition and imagery, employed countless times by, among others, intellectuals in sympathy with conservative unionism, has become a cliché and stereotype. Whatever the adequacy of the scholarship in such an evaluation of the two contestants and the nature of the contest, it leaves an important question unanswered: why have sizable groups of union workers, all accredited natives of workshops, who should have scorned false gods, succumbed periodically to their wiles and allurements? Clearly, sizable groups, in certain periods, found the explanations and achievements of regulation officials less than acceptable. Why?

On this score, a previous generation of writers, influenced by Social Gospel and Wisconsin School teachings, had more to say than present-day academics, many of whom so took for granted the immutability of recent arrangements that they often treated labor unionism as another branch of market economics. In contrast, John R. Commons, founder of the Wisconsin School, who had to struggle at first to convince colleagues that the subject of unionism even had a place in the college curriculum, could better envision the union in transition when it was still struggling for existence. Proceeding from a somewhat extreme economic determinism, he tried to account for the oscillations in workers' temper by correlating radicalism with the business cycle, first putting the stress on reform panaceas displacing strikes during depressions; then in the early thirties, influenced by Communist activities, theorizing that quasi-revolutionary strikes would replace the " 'business' strikes of unionism" during depressions. Although his generalizations have long since been outdated, Commons showed an awareness of alterations in mass moods, an interest in labor dynamics, and the need to provide a theory to account for them that contrasts favorably with later ahistorical attitudes. Not that unions will again face anything resembling the Communist invasion. The Communist Party was *sui generis*. It is now reduced to a minor sect never likely to reappear on the American scene as a significant current. But that does not rule out new conflicts between expediency-oriented and freshly radicalized officials. The now dormant urges that brought past radical movements into being can become active again under the goad of new dislocations. Kornhauser's proposition remains valid, though the long-term trend in industrial countries has been—contrary to the hopes of radical pioneers and contrary to the fears of business foes—to make labor unions both accepted institutions and stabilization instrumentalities of a more modern, more complex, more resilient capitalism.[3]

Appendix I

IT has been pointed out that the Communist heads hesitated for a year before committing themselves to the CIO. The accusation originated with Benjamin Stolberg (*The Story of the CIO*, Viking Press, 1938, pp. 147-148), who said that "although the Communist press gave lip service to industrial unionism, the Stalinists actually did most of their organization work for the A.F. of L. until May 1937." Howe-Coser made a similar point "about the slowness of the party in recognizing the significance of the CIO," but credited Communist ranks with ignoring "the cautious signals of the party leadership" (pp. 369-370).

At the time that Stolberg was writing, the left-liberal public idolized the CIO and scorned the AFL, so the charge was meant to convey Communist duplicity as well as lack of acumen. Today, the Communist leaders' caution, or as some might have it, unwarranted timidity (a reaction from the debacle of red unionism), can be appraised dispassionately. The initial statements of Communist leaders emphasized the conditional nature of their support for the CIO for understandable reasons: they did not know how far and how determinedly Lewis, Hillman, and Dubinsky intended to proceed, and they were afraid of getting the party out on a limb. Thus Foster writing in early 1936 made clear that the Communists supported the CIO struggle, leveled his main attack on the AFL hierarchy, but made a number of "constructive criticisms" of the CIO position (*Industrial Unionism*, Workers Library Publishers, April 1936). This was the public stance of a party keeping its options open in a highly fluid situation. From an occasional stray remark of Browder's and the holding back of Bridges, Gold, and Mike Quill, it can be inferred that even toward the end of the year there was hesitation in the inner councils. It must be recalled that the CIO was maneuvering with the AFL Executive Council all through these months, that Dubinsky and others were far more conciliatory than Lewis and anxious to avoid a split, that it was only in September 1936 that the unions adhering to the CIO were suspended from the AFL, and it was only in March 1937 that the CIO authorized the issuance of certificates of affiliation to national, state, city, and local bodies. (*AFL*

Executive Council Proceedings on charges filed by Metal Trades Department, 1936, pp. 134-136; *Union News Service*, March 15, 1937.) The Communist party's caution is reflected in Foster's *History*: "Lewis, apparently taking it for granted that the organizational work had to be done outside of direct contact with the Green reactionaries, made no determined fight to maintain affiliation with the A.F. of L. On this tactical question the Communists disagreed with him. The Communists believed that inasmuch as Lewis had 40 percent of the A.F. of L. unions behind him and a vast following among the rest of the labor movement, it would have been possible for him to beat the Green machine by a resolute fight. . . . The Party opposed the split" (pp. 306-307).

All this while, however, the Communists were not passing up opportunities to penetrate the new movement. The newly formed United Electrical and Radio Workers union, while dickering *pro forma* with Green for an AFL charter, invited Lewis to participate in the RCA negotiations in June 1936, and CIO representatives were on hand to direct the strike. This could not have occurred without Communist approval since Julius Emspak was running the UE national office. (Galenson, p. 244; James B. Carey, Oral History, p. 81, and Julius Emspak, Oral History, p. 86, both at Columbia University.) Similarly, the auto union was for all practical purposes in the CIO column at the time of the South Bend convention held in April 1936. This represented Communist decision or concurrence since the Communists were the dominant force at the convention, and Communist delegates were being directed by John Williamson and Willliam Weinstone. (Williamson, *Dangerous Scot* (New York: International Publishers, 1969), p. 103; Sidney Fine, *Sitdown*, University of Michigan Press, 1969, p. 90.) Nevertheless, the convention made a big to-do about the union not leaving the AFL. In his maiden speech, Walter Reuther swung a haymaker at Hearst because the Chicago *Herald-Examiner* had run a headline: "Forty Thousand Auto Workers Quit Labor Federation." This, he shouted, was "vile slander," demanded nothing less than a boycott, and concluded on this spirited note: "let us destroy Hearst." Homer Martin added this eloquent best to the matter, and the convention duly passed a resolution declaring itself in no uncertain terms. (*Proceedings*, 1936, pp. 64, 69.) Everybody understood this was tactical mumbo-jumbo. Two months later, the UAW formally adhered to the CIO. When the steel drive was started in the summer of 1936,

Communists were very resourceful in getting a strong representation on the payroll. And so on.

Two Communist-dominated unions that might have adhered to the CIO in 1936 rather than in 1937 were Bridges' West Coast longshoremen and Gold's fur workers. Changing affiliation is no routine matter: it can create awkward problems—materializing for Bridges' union after it adhered to the CIO. Shipowners maintained that their contract was with the AFL affiliate and expressed doubts that the new union represented a majority of the employees. Another NLRB election had to be held, and although the longshore union was recertified as bargaining agent, it lost, after a prolonged wrangle, three AFL locals in Tacoma, Anacortes and Port Angeles. In the case of the fur union, its biennial convention was not due until May 1937, and regulation officials on the union's executive board opposed leaving the AFL. After the convention voted to affiliate with the CIO, one of the old-line officials tried unsuccessfully to take the Twin Cities locals out of the union. Possibly, considerations of internal difficulties were not the determinant for the year's delay, but from the Communist party point of view, nothing was lost by waiting until the CIO split with the AFL was formalized.

Appendix II

FINE is mistaken in questioning the spontaneous nature of the Cleveland strike (*Sitdown*, p. 142). Of course, strike fever was in the air, Atlanta and Kansas City were already out, GM had refused to bargain nationally, the sit-down wave was enveloping Detroit, and some union activists wanted to close down the plant at the first opportunity. What does Fine think "spontaneity" means in human affairs? Some individuals do make some decisions, otherwise nothing could happen. But the actions of decision-makers are not in response to a central concept, they are not carrying out assignments coming to them through appropriate organization channels. The statement of Paul Miley—upon which Fine relies—that he coordinated his activities with Travis in Flint cannot be correct. Miley may have been in touch with Travis, and there may have been loose strike talk. But that he acted on a signal is fanciful. If the Communist caucus in Flint had been set on calling a strike, they would have started with Flint Fisher No. 2 where the union had forces, not with Fisher in Cleveland where it had very little.

According to both Kraus and Mortimer, the first that Travis knew of the Cleveland strike was when Mortimer received a telephone call at his hotel room in Flint from Louis Spisak, the Cleveland local president. Both Kraus's and Mortimer's accounts have to be accepted on this point because if Travis had been coordinating strike action with Miley, Kraus would not have been reticent in telling about it. On the contrary, he would have proclaimed it. Instead he wrote,"These [Cleveland] workers took strategy into their own hands when on December 28 a surprise sitdown in one department swiftly spread through the entire factory" (p. 82). Charles Beckman, either a Party member or in its supporting circle, and later president of the Cleveland Fisher local, said the same thing, that the stoppage was "a spontaneous movement" (Oral History, Wayne State, pp. 6, 8). The author, stationed in Cleveland at the time, discussed the strike in early 1937 with several workers who had taken part in the sit-down. Everyone was excited by the national events, they said, and the sit-down just spread from one department to

348

another when word came through that a strike was on, even though most workers were not members of the union.

The one instance that can authentically be called a decision took place on December 30, two days later, when Travis called on the union stewards to close down Fisher No. 1. It is immaterial whether he was actually frightened by a report that the company was loading dies on freight cars to ship them to other centers, or whether that was just the cover story—as Bud Simons later maintained—to justify closing down the plant. (Travis had no authority to order the strike.) Earlier that day, the smaller Fisher No. 2 plant, employing about 1,000, had been closed by a spontaneous sitdown. And according to Mortimer, he had called Travis from Cleveland on the evening of the twenty-eighth and told him to close down Fisher No. 1 as soon as possible. (Mortimer also had no authority to issue that kind of order.) Why Travis did not act on the twenty-ninth and waited until the second-shift evening lunch hour of the thirtieth is a question. At any rate, given the overwrought mood, Fisher No. 1 would have been shut down by shop militants within the next day or two, with or without Travis's intervention.

Both the "spontaneity" and the shop workers' intervention in decision-making are further attested to by a talk that William Weinstone had with Walter Moore during Moore's lunch-hour break after the Cleveland sit-down had started. When Moore told Weinstone that strikes in the Flint Fisher plants were imminent, Weinstone was aghast. "You're not prepared for a sitdown strike," Weinstone warned. "You haven't got Flint organized. What are you talking about?" Moore replied, "We can't stop it. The sentiment's too great." Weinstone then reluctantly accepted the situation. "If you can't stop it, you can't stop it." (Interview with Weinstone, November 27, 1971, quoted in Roger Roy Keeran, "Communists and Auto Workers: The Struggle for a Union, 1919-1941," Dissertation, University of Wisconsin, 1974, p. 242.)

349

Notes

ONE · *The Communist Party—Structure and Evolution*

[1] Allen J. Matusow, ed., *Joseph R. McCarthy* (Englewood Cliffs, N. J.: Prentice-Hall, 1970), p. 81; Sherman Adams, *Firsthand Report* (New York: Harper, 1961), pp. 139-140; Earl Latham, *The Communist Controversy in Washington* (Cambridge, Mass.: Harvard University Press, 1966), pp. 369-371.

[2] U.S., Supreme Court, Decision on Constitutionality of 9(h) of the Labor-Management Relations Act of 1947, October Term, 1949. Chief Justice Vinson delivered opinion of the Court, May 8, 1950. Reprinted in U.S., Congress, Senate, subcommittee of Committee on Labor and Public Welfare, Hearings on *Communist Domination of Unions*, 82nd Cong., 2nd sess., pp. 70-78. Jackson's paper, delivered as a separate opinion, was authoritative. His credentials as a high-minded and committed liberal were impeccable and accepted as such by the liberal community. Even in concurring with the majority decision, he dissented for that part of the affidavit which called on a union officer to swear that "he does not believe in . . . the overthrow of the United States Government by force or by any illegal or unconstitutional methods." The Communists, for reasons he explained, were in a special category; otherwise, he denied that "Congress has the power to proscribe any opinion or belief which has not manifested itself in any overt act."

[3] The essay appeared originally in the *New York Times Magazine*, July 9, 1950, and was reprinted in the book of the same title (New York: John Day, 1953).

[4] *Communist Domination of Unions*, pp. 74-76; Hook, *Heresy, Yes*, pp. 22-24.

[5] Arthur M. Schlesinger, Jr., *The Vital Center* (Boston: Houghton Mifflin, 1949), pp. 103-130, 201-218.

[6] *Correspondence between the Central Committee of the Communist Party of Jugoslavia and the Central Committee of the All-Union Communist Party (Bolsheviks)* (Belgrade: Jugoslovenska Knjiga, 1948); *Statement of the Central Committee of the Communist Party of Jugoslavia* (Belgrade: Jugoslovenska Knjiga, 1948); *Yugoslavia's Struggle for Proper Relations Between Socialist Countries* (London: Cosmo Publications, 1949), pp. 9-15.

[7] New York State Legislative Committee Investigating Seditious Activities, *Revolutionary Radicalism, Its History, Purpose, and Tactics*, April 24, 1920 (Albany: J. B. Lyons Co., 1920), vol. 1, pp. 618-626, 706-738; Theodore Draper, *The Roots of American Communism* (New York: Viking, 1957), p. 105 (hereafter cited as Draper I); David A. Shannon, *The Socialist Party of America* (New York: Macmillan, 1955), pp. 126-149.

[8] *Writings and Speeches of Eugene V. Debs* (New York: Hermitage Press, 1948), p. 442; *Autobiography of Lincoln Steffens* (1931; rpt. New York: Grosset and Dunlap, n.d.), p. 799.

[9] Nathan Glazer, *The Social Basis of American Communism* (New York: Harcourt, Brace, 1961), p. 86; *The Second Congress of the Communist International* (Washington, D. C.: GPO, 1920), p. 154; John R. Commons et al., *History of Labor*

in the United States (New York: Macmillan, 1935), vol. 3, p. 41; Glazer, pp. 28-29: "The IWW was certainly a more 'American' organization in terms of ideology and organization, than the Marxist-influenced parties. Its tactics arose out of the struggles of Western miners and migratory workers against their employers, and it owed almost nothing to European ideas. However, its membership was, if anything, more heavily foreign-born than that of the Socialist Party."

[10] Many students argue that Communists do not want to improve conditions of workers on the theory that if conditions improve, workers will lose interest in Communist or revolutionary solutions. This is an old problem that left-wingers grappled with even before the Communist movement: whether the struggle for "bourgeois reforms," "immediate demands," etc., sidetracks or advances the struggle for socialism. Some left-wingers of the pre-World War I Socialist party insisted that revolutionists were more successful in winning reforms than reformers because they more effectively frightened capitalists into making concessions; that reforms, rightfully viewed, were a byproduct of resolutely pursued revolutionary activities. Others, like De Leon, flatly opposed "immediate demands" as an invitation to corruption. Leninism never accepted the "impossibilist" position in theory or in practice. The ongoing Communist conception was that small-scale victories and achievements would enlarge the worker's outlook, increase his self-confidence, and thus ready him for a higher stage of confrontations. Of course, this is a murky area. In their concrete decisions, Communist leaders sought at times to sacrifice "immediate" interests in favor of "historic" interests, which meant to manipulate a given contest to conform to their party objectives of that moment. In its bald form, however, the proposition that Communists did not or do not want to improve the conditions of the working class (Gabriel A. Almond, *The Appeals of Communism* [Princeton, N. J.: Princeton University Press, 1954], p. 386) is false, or at least, simplistic. It cuts across much of the conduct of Communist parties and members. Communists think they are connecting immediate struggles with labor's historic mission to reconstruct society. That does not mean that they are indifferent to improvements of workers' conditions on the job or through welfare legislation.

[11] Theodore Draper, *American Communism and Soviet Russia* (New York: Viking, 1960), pp. 211-214 (hereafter cited as Draper II); Latham, *Communist Controversy*, pp. 80-86, 106; U.S., Congress, House Committee on Un-American Activities, *Hearings Regarding Communist Espionage in United States Government*, 80th Cong., 2nd sess., pp. 565-575.

[12] Almond, p. 231; Richmond, past editor of *People's World*, the Party's West Coast newspaper, joined when he was fourteen. Forty-five years later, while still a member of the Party (he resigned the following year), he wrote that his generation was "the most vital" in the country "because it was comprised of men and women purposefully committed . . . to the attainment of a just, rational, human social order" (Al Richmond, *A Long View From the Left* [Boston: Houghton Mifflin, 1972], p. viii). Starobin, for years foreign editor of the *Daily Worker*, wrote after he left the Communist movement that Communists tried to build "a political party which they tried to make into a fraternity of comrades, animated by the great ideal of human brotherhood" (Joseph R. Starobin, *American Communism In Crisis, 1943-1957* [Cambridge, Mass.: Harvard University Press, 1972], p. ix).

[13] Draper II, p. 189; David A. Shannon, *The Decline of American Communism* (New York: Harcourt, Brace, 1959), p. 92; Irving Howe and Lewis Coser, *The American Communist Party* (Boston: Beacon, 1957), pp. 225, 528-529. Draper estimated

that in the first decade 1919-1929, about 100,000 entered the Party of whom only 10,000 stayed long enough to represent a basic membership, and that 250,000 to 350,000 passed through the Party in the three decades. Ernst and Loth gave a much higher figure. They concluded that some 700,000 left the Communist party in "the last thirty years," but offered no specific breakdown for their estimate or guess (Morris L. Ernst and David Loth, *Report on the American Communist* [New York: Henry Holt, 1952], p. 14).

[14] For some, leaving the Party held special terrors: breaking with one's lifelong friends, going into a cold world without credentials or connections, blurring one's sense of identity. The whip of excommunication that the leaders held over the heads of dissidents was a very short one, however. Communism was never more than a small, abhorrent sect—even in the halcyon days of the popular front—membership in which compromised rather than enhanced an individual's position in the larger society. A few defectors at congressional hearings gave testimony that they were threatened, or heard that others were threatened, lest they testify against their erstwhile associates. Much of this was either exaggerated or garbled. There was one authenticated case of terrorism against John Lautner, who had been a state official of the Communist party. When suspected of being an informer, he was lured to a cellar by Party hatchet men, stripped naked, threatened with a revolver, and brutally interrogated. Then, without trial or formal conviction, he was publicly charged with treachery, ostracized by his former comrades, and abandoned by his wife. According to Lautner, it was only after the inquisition and expulsion that he contacted the FBI and became a star witness in at least two dozen trials and proceedings (Herbert L. Packer, *Ex-Communist Witnesses* [Stanford: Stanford University Press, 1962], pp. 182-183). In the twenties and thirties, the Communists were guilty of hoodlum attacks on Trotskyists and others who distributed literature at Communist meetings, and they forcibly broke up meetings of opponents. They had their final fling against "social fascists" while the united front policy was already germinating. In February 1934, several thousand Communist stalwarts stormed a rally at Madison Square Garden sponsored by Socialists and trade unionists to protest the killing of Socialists in Vienna by the Dolfuss regime, and turned an orderly meeting into a bloody riot. Nevertheless, these were peripheral forays. The Communist party leaders did not methodically transfer Stalin's police-state methods into the American movement, not because they did not have the propensity, but because they lacked the power.

[15] Almond, pp. 100, 101, 103, 106, 109, 113, 117, 383.

[16] The author, when a young trade union official, was acquainted with numbers of Communists in the unions, both officials and foot soldiers. He was able to come to an opinion about their perception of themselves and their party based on observation over a period of time.

[17] Melech Epstein, *The Jew and Communism* (New York: Trade Union Sponsoring Committee, n.d.), pp. 371-381.

[18] A relentless opponent like Eugene Lyons acknowledged that "in the larger sense the phenomenon of Russia-worship had in it more of religious ecstasy than political chicanery. The Russia they worshipped was in their own minds" (*The Red Decade* [Indianapolis: Bobbs-Merrill, 1941], p. 93; Richmond, p. 135). Morris Hillquit, the foremost intellectual leader of the old Socialist party, considered himself a representative of the tendency spoken for by Karl Kautsky, the authoritative theoretician of the German party and of the Socialist International. In the debate at the 1912 convention over the adoption of an antisabotage clause in the party's con-

353

stitution, Hillquit and others who favored adopting the clause invoked the authority or example of the German party. Richmond's comparison of the two has the cogency of likening a dreadnought to a rowboat since both travel on water. Bertolt Brecht, the German playwright, foresaw as early as 1931, with an artist's intuition, what the bureaucratization of communism would lead to. In his play, the director of one of the Party houses instructs four Party agitators that they must divest themselves of their personalities before they can be ready to take on their assignments: "You are without name or mother, blank leaflets on which the revolution writes its orders" (*Die Massnahme*, quoted in Ruth Fischer, *Stalin and German Communism* [Cambridge, Mass.: Harvard University Press, 1948], pp. 615-625).

[19] William Z. Foster, *History of the Communist Party of the United States* (New York: International Publishers, 1952), p. 431.

[20] Foster, p. 436.

[21] Judge Harold R. Medina, at the initial trial—*U.S.* v. *Dennis et al.*—elaborated and obfuscated the customarily accepted judicial interpretation of the First Amendment to the Constitution (no limitations on free speech or free press unless those present a "clear and present danger") by instructing the jury that the Communist leaders could be convicted if they intended to forcibly overthrow the government "as speedily as circumstances permit." All the defendants in the *Dennis* trial were convicted, a decision that was affirmed by the U.S. Supreme Court in 1951 upholding the constitutionality of the Smith Act (over the dissent of Justices Black and Douglas). Six years later, Smith Act indictments were brought to a halt by a de facto Supreme Court reversal in the case of *Yates* v. *U.S.* On review of the conviction of a group of secondary leaders of California, the court held that the trial, which had followed the prevalent pattern of the Smith Act proceedings, had not made a sufficient distinction between "abstract advocacy" of revolutionary doctrines that were constitutionally protected, and actual incitement to revolution.

[22] Interviews with John Gates, September 20, 1973, and George Blake Charney, September 18, 1973; Glazer, p. 93; *Party Voice*, July 1956, p. 4; Shannon, p. 231.

[23] Starobin, pp. 219-223; Eugene Dennis, the post-Browder general secretary, told the National Committee in February that the party was "in a race with time" in connection with the oncoming war. In July, Foster reiterated that the war danger was "acute," because reactionaries wanted to use the atom bomb before Russia had produced it too. This war excitation was deflated several months later because Stalin, in an interview with Alexander Werth, dismissed war talk as a species of blackmail related to America's and Britain's internal politics. This led to a new round of self-criticism: Dennis referred darkly to "tendencies which did exist to regard World War III as imminent . . . were not sufficiently combatted." The thermometer shot up again with alarms over the Berlin blockade. Then in early 1949, Communist fears raced to a climacteric when the Togliatti and Thorez declarations were broadcast—in response to the creation of NATO—that the peoples of Italy and France would not resist the Soviet armies in the event of war between Russia and the United States. This was followed by a provocative Foster-Dennis declaration in the first week of March that the American Communists would be opponents in a new war, that they would work "to defeat the predatory war aims of American imperialism and bring such a war to a speedy conclusion," a declaration repeated by Dennis on the eve of his going to jail in May 1950 (Dennis, *What America Faces* [New York: New Century, 1946], p. 32; Foster, *Political Affairs*, August 1946, p. 691; January 1947, p. 15; April 1949, pp. 1-2; July 1950, p. 17; Starobin, p. 219).

354

[24] Starobin, p. 312; Shannon, pp. 79-80; Whittaker Chambers, *Witness* (New York: Random House, 1952), pp. 275, 279-280; Elizabeth Bentley, *Out of Bondage* (New York: Devin-Adair, 1951), pp. 90, 97; Gates interview.

[25] Hook, p. 34: "Free and independent trade unions, which are essential to a democracy, cannot be liberated from the organizational stranglehold of the Communist Party by government intervention. Only an aroused membership . . . can do the job." See also Walter P. Reuther, "How To Beat the Communists," *Collier's*, February 28, 1948; Arthur J. Goldberg, *AFL-CIO Labor United* (New York: McGraw-Hill, 1956), p. 183.

TWO · *Decade of Failure*

[1] New York State Legislative Committee Investigating Seditious Activities, *Revolutionary Radicalism*, vol. 2, pp. 1899-1901; *The Communist*, May 1, 1920, p. 8.

[2] Draper I, p. 321.

[3] *The Worker*, February 24, 1923.

[4] Leon Trotsky, *The First Five Years of the Communist International* (New York: Pioneer Publishers, 1945), vol. 1, pp. 84-86.

[5] Ypsilon, *Pattern for World Revolution* (Chicago: Ziff-Davis, 1947), pp. 41, 44.

[6] Earl Browder, *Trade Unions in America* (Chicago: TUEL, 1924), p. 26; Browder, Oral History, Columbia University, p. 151; Philip Taft, *The AFL in the Time of Gompers* (New York: Harper, 1957), p. 454; Draper II, pp. 71-72; David J. Saposs, *Left Wing Unionism* (New York: International Publishers, 1926), pp. 79-80.

[7] Arne Swabeck, a member of the Communist delegation conferring with Fitzpatrick, quoted in Draper II, p. 41; Max Shachtman, "The Problem of the Labor Party," *New International*, March 1935, pp. 33-37.

[8] Foster, *History of Communist Party*, p. 208; Foster, *From Bryan to Stalin* (New York: International Publishers, 1937), p. 195.

[9] Browder, Oral History, p. 154; Trotsky, *First Five Years*, pp. 12-14. Eight days after the secret Comintern decision, La Follette made his letter to the attorney general of Wisconsin public in which he read the Communists out of his camp as "the mortal enemies of the progressive movement and democratic ideals" (*New York Times*, May 29, 1924); Belle and Fola La Follette, *Robert M. La Follette* (New York: Macmillan, 1953), vol. 2, pp. 1098-1105. Browder claimed that La Follette did this only because he learned of the secret Comintern decision (Oral History, p. 163).

[10] *Daily Worker*, August 29, 1925 supplement.

[11] Foster denounced Debs for "complete capitulation" when the veteran Socialist supported La Follette. Debs retorted that the Communists had also supported La Follette until the "Vatican in Moscow" decreed otherwise (*Daily Worker*, July 31, 1924).

[12] Arthur Naftalin, "A History of the Farmer-Labor Party of Minnesota," Dissertation, University of Minnesota, 1948, p. 116.

[13] *Bolshevizing the Communist International* (London, 1925), pp. 185-191; *Daily Worker*, May 19, 1925; Georg Von Rauch, *A History of Soviet Russia* (New York: Praeger, 1972), pp. 172-173. (The decision was made at the Fifth Plenum, March 21-April 6, 1925.)

[14] Swabeck quoted in Draper II, p. 41.

[15] Philip Taft and Philip Ross, "American Labor Violence," in Hugh Davis Graham and Ted Robert Gurr, *Violence in America: A Report to the National Commission on*

the Causes and Prevention of Violence (New York: New American Library, 1969), p. 270; also Graham and Gurr, "The Commonality of Collective Violence in the Western Tradition," op. cit., pp. 774, 783.

[16] Ted Robert Gurr, *Why Men Rebel* (Princeton: Princeton University Press, 1970), pp. 4-5; Neil J. Smelser, *Theory of Collective Behavior* (New York: Free Press, 1963), pp. 247-269; Charles Tilly and James Rule, *Measuring Political Upheaval*, Center of International Studies, Princeton University, Research Monograph No. 19, 1965.

[17] Draper I, p. 394; Shannon, *Socialist Party*, pp. 178, 193, 218; Foster, *History of Communist Party*, pp. 333-334, 391; Roy V. Peel and Thomas C. Donnelly, *The 1928 Campaign* (New York: Smith, 1931), p. 171.

[18] *The Labor Herald*, July 1924, pp. 151-154; *Daily Worker*, August 14, 1925.

[19] Perlman and Taft, vol. 4 of Commons, *History of Labor*, p. 557; Mary Heaton Vorse, *The Passaic Textile Strike* (Passaic: General Relief Committee, 1927); Morton Siegel, "The Passaic Strike of 1926," Dissertation, Columbia University, 1953; Albert Weisbord, "Lessons from Passaic," *Workers Monthly*, December 1926.

[20] Fischer, *Stalin and German Communism*, pp. 432-455; Browder, Oral History, p. 167; *International Press Correspondence*, April 22, May 13, 1926 (Sixth Plenum resolution); Robert R. R. Brooks, "The United Textile Workers of America," Dissertation, Yale University, 1935, p. 114: "The union appeared to consist almost entirely of a suite of offices, a complement of officers, and a splendid array of filing cabinets."

[21] *The Communist*, December 1931, p. 1015.

[22] Perlman and Taft, *History of Labor*, pp. 557-558.

[23] *Fortune*, December 1933.

[24] Robert W. Dunn and Jack Hardy, *Labor and Textiles* (New York: International Publishers, 1931), pp. 206-207.

[25] Liston Pope, *Millhands and Preachers* (New Haven: Yale University Press, 1942); Fred E. Beal, *Proletarian Journey* (New York: Hillman-Curl, 1937); Samuel Yellen, *American Labor Struggles* (New York: Harcourt, Brace, 1956), pp. 308-316; Irving Bernstein, *The Lean Years* (Boston: Houghton Mifflin, 1966), pp. 1-43 (hereafter cited as Bernstein I).

[26] Paul Blanshard, "Communism in Southern Mills," *The Nation*, April 24, 1929.

[27] Tom Tippett, *When Southern Labor Stirs* (New York: Cape and Smith, 1931), pp. 109-115, 140-155; Bernstein I, pp. 13-20, 29-32; Yellen, *Labor Struggles*, pp. 301-303; Benjamin Stolberg, "Madness in Marion," *The Nation*, October 23, 1929.

[28] Epstein, *Jew and Communism*, p. 132; Dwight E. Robinson, *Collective Bargaining and Market Control in New York Cloak and Suit Industry* (New York: Columbia University Press, 1949), pp. 43-48; William F. Dunne, "The ILGWU Convention," *Workers Monthly*, February 1926; ILG convention *Proceedings*, 1925, pp. 45, 53; ILG *Proceedings*, 1928, pp. 61, 97-99, 105; Benjamin Stolberg, *Tailor's Progress* (Garden City: Doubleday, 1944), pp. 126, 129.

[29] The passions aroused by the Communist-Socialist tug of war in the needle trades are reflected in the literature. Most accounts show a pronounced bias toward the right-wing administration, and repeat the not always valid right wing's accusations against its opponents. A judicious critique can be found in a short, unsigned memorandum written by a strike participant, apparently a left-winger at the time, who was also opposed to the Communists. See Daniel Bell Papers, Box 10, Tamiment Library, New York University. Accounts of the controversy and strike are included in Melech Epstein, *Jewish Labor in U.S.A., 1914-1952* (New York: Trade

Union Sponsoring Committee, 1953); Max D. Danish, *The World of David Dubinsky* (Cleveland: World, 1957); Joel Seidman, *The Needle Trades* (New York: Farrar and Rinehart, 1942); Louis Levine, *The Women's Garment Workers* (New York: Huebsch, 1924); Benjamin Gitlow, *I Confess* (New York: Dutton, 1939); David M. Schneider, *The Workers (Communist) Party and American Trade Unions* (Baltimore: Johns Hopkins, 1928); Perlman and Taft, *History of Labor*. See also letter of Norman Thomas to Hillquit, June 14, 1926, Morris Hillquit Papers, State Historical Society of Wisconsin, copy in Catherwood Library, Cornell University; Will Herberg, "The Jewish Labor Movement in the United States," *American Jewish Year Book*, 1952; Hillquit's remarks in ILGWU convention *Proceedings*, 1928, p. 108. For the Communist side, see Jack Hardy, *The Clothing Workers* (New York: International Publishers, 1935); for later union evolution, see "David Dubinsky, the ILGWU, and the American Labor Movement," *Labor History*, Special Supplement, Spring 1968; Samuel Lubell, "Dictator in Sheep's Clothing," *Saturday Evening Post*, November 19, 1949.

[30] Epstein, *Jewish Labor*, pp. 168-177; Hardy, *Clothing Workers*, pp. 120-134; Perlman and Taft, *History of Labor*, pp. 543-546; Philip S. Foner, *The Fur and Leather Workers Union* (Newark: Nordan Press, 1950), pp. 179-312.

THREE · *Red Unionism*

[1] For Ninth Plenum: *International Press Correspondence*, March 15, 1928, pp. 311-320. For new trade-union modification: A Losovsky, *Communist International*, March 15, 1928, p. 146. For Profintern Congress: *International Press Correspondence*, March 22-April 12, 1928; *Protokoll über den Vierten Kongress der Roten Gewerkschafts Internationale*; Gitlow, *I Confess*, pp. 453-463. On American resolution adopted at Profintern Congress: attached to "Communist Party Political Committee Minutes #35," May 16, 1928, Bell Papers, Box 1. On Comintern: Ypsilon, *Pattern for World Revolution*, p. 120.

[2] *The Trade Union Unity League: Its Program, Structure, Methods and History* (New York, n.d.). The program made clear that the AFL and the Socialist party "are vital parts of the expanding fascist organization of the capitalists," and that both the Socialist party and Muste group are "social fascists." The TUUL stood for "the mass political strike" and pointed to Gastonia as a shining example of "revolutionary strike strategy" where workers "defended themselves with guns in their hands." The TUUL membership was listed as 125,000 (the high point) by Foster in the year before its dissolution. Foster's breakdown was as follows: needle trades, 25,000; metal, 21,000; agricultural, 20,000; coal, 10,000; food, 10,000; shoe, 9,000; furniture, 8,000; marine, 7,000; textile, 7,000; auto, 5,000; lumber, 3,500; fishery, 2,000; tobacco, 1,400. These figures, largely fictitious, do not even tally with figures provided by party officials in theoretical publications and formal reports. Foster credited needle trades with 25,000. J. Peters gave the fur union 10,000 and the party fur fraction 100, and Jack Stachel gave the entire party needle-trades membership as about 2,200, which probably means that the needle-trades union should be credited with a maximum of 13,000. Foster credited textiles with 7,000. Browder reported that its membership was 1,000—"the same as in 1929." Foster credited auto with 5,000. Kutnik gave the auto union "only a few hundred." Foster credited coal with 10,000. Kutnik gave the miners union only 1,000. Foster credited maritime with 7,000. Kutnik gave the marine union 3,000 to 3,500. Harry Bridges in his 1939 deportation

hearing gave the marine union "some 2,000." Not that these other figures are impeccable, either. Foster, *History of Communist Party*, p. 298; Kutnik, *The Communist International*, September 20, 1934, pp. 601-602; Browder in *The Communist*, August 1933, p. 719; Peters, *The Communist*, September 1933, p. 949; Jack Stachel, *The Communist*, July 1935, p. 626; Bridges quoted in Charles P. Larrowe, *Harry Bridges: The Rise and Fall of Radical Labor in the U.S.* (Westport: Lawrence Hill, 1972), p. 35.

[3] U.S. Temporary National Economic Committee, *Economic Prologue* (Washington, D. C.: GPO, 1939), pp. 61, 197.

[4] Edmund Wilson, *Shores of Light* (New York: Farrar, Strauss and Young, 1952), p. 524; Alfred Kazin, *On Native Grounds* (New York: Doubleday-Anchor, n.d.), p. 285.

[5] Edwin A. Lahey, Oral History, Columbia University, pp. 48, 50; *Culture and Crisis* (New York: Workers Library Publishers, 1932).

[6] Studs Terkel, *Hard Times* (New York: Avon, 1971), p. 149. In one survey of unemployed, a quarter felt that a revolution might be a very good thing. Dixon Wecter, *The Age of the Great Depression* (New York: Macmillan, 1948), p. 36; William E. Leuchtenburg, *Franklin D. Roosevelt and the New Deal* (New York: Harper and Row, 1963), pp. 26-27; Theodore Dreiser in Bernstein I, p. 435; Louis Adamic, *My America* (New York: Harper, 1938), pp. 298-302.

[7] Glazer, *Social Basis of American Communism*, pp. 92, 101, 207-210; *The Communist*, October 1934, p. 1005.

[8] *The Communist*, November 1932, p. 1044.

[9] Bernstein I, pp. 128-136; McAlister Coleman, *Men and Coal* (New York: Farrar and Rinehart, 1943), pp. 105-114, 135; James O. Morris, *Conflict Within the AFL* (Ithaca: N. Y. State School of Industrial and Labor Relations, Cornell University, 1958), p. 120; Saul D. Alinsky, *John L. Lewis* (New York: Vintage edition, 1970), p. 51; John Brophy in J. B. S. Hardman, ed., *American Labor Dynamics* (New York: Harcourt, Brace, 1928), pp. 186-191; United Mine Workers, *Attempts of Communists to Seize American Labor Movement* (Indianapolis, 1923); Perlman and Taft, *History of Labor*, pp. 564-566; Edmund Wilson, *The American Earthquake* (Garden City: Doubleday, 1958), p. 327.

[10] John Brophy, Oral History, Columbia University, p. 467.

[11] *Ibid.*, p. 483.

[12] Coleman, *Men and Coal*, pp. 139-143; Harriet Hudson, *The Progressive Mine Workers of America* (Urbana: University of Illinois, 1952), pp. 12-41. Statisticians for the Illinois District gave out figures in 1929 that out of over half a million soft-coal miners, only 84,395 were UMW dues-paying members, with 53,088 of these in Illinois. The International office blustered, but never issued an opposing set of figures. If we generously assume that there were another 40,000 members in anthracite, the total membership, which was about 425,000 when Lewis took over in 1920, was well under a third of that at the end of the decade.

[13] Bernstein I, pp. 386-388; *Party Organizer*, August 1931 (an issue consisting of articles by different party and union leaders all on the mine strike); in *Daily Worker*, 1931: Carl Price, July 6; Browder, July 14; Politburo resolution, August 15; Foster, September 7; ECCI resolution, *The Communist*, May 1932, pp. 402-410; Foster, *From Bryan to Stalin*, p. 231.

[14] Edmund Wilson, *The American Earthquake* (Garden City: Doubleday, 1958), pp. 310-327; *New York Times*, July 7, August 18, 1931; Helen G. Norton, "Feudalism in West Virginia," *The Nation*, August 12, 1931.

[15] U.S., Congress, Senate Subcomm. on Manufactures, *Conditions in Coal Fields of Harlan and Bell Counties, Kentucky, 1932*, Hearings on S. Res. 178, 72nd Cong., 1st sess.; Bernstein I, pp. 377-381; Theodore Dreiser et al., *Harlan Miners Speak* (New York: Da Capo Press reprint, 1970); *New York Times*, September 28-October 3, 1931; Homer Lawrence Morris, *The Plight of the Bituminous Coal Miner* (Phila.: University of Pennsylvania Press, 1934), pp. 135-137; Malcolm Ross, *Machine Age in the Hills* (New York: Macmillan, 1933), pp. 171-185; Herbert Abel, "Gun Rule inKentucky," *The Nation*, September 23, 1931; John Dos Passos, "Harlan: Working Under the Gun," *The New Republic*, December 2, 1931; *Daily Worker*, December 15, 17, 1931; Arthur Garfield Hays, "The Right to be Shot," *The Nation*, June 1, 1932; Jack Stachel, "Lessons of Two Recent Strikes," *The Communist*, June 1932, pp. 527-542; Theodore Draper, "Communists and Miners," *Dissent*, Spring 1972, pp. 371-392.

[16] *New York Times*, May 9, 1929; Morris A. Horowitz, *The New York Hotel Industry* (Cambridge: Harvard University Press, 1960), pp. 210-243; David J. Saposs, *Communism in American Unions* (New York: McGraw Hill, 1959), pp. 82-93; Irving Bernstein, *Turbulent Years* (Boston: Houghton Mifflin, 1969), pp. 116-123 (hereafter cited as Bernstein II); Jay Rubin and Michael J. Obermeier, *Growth of a Union* (New York: Historical Union Association, 1943), pp. 225-250; Matthew Josephson, *Union House, Union Bar* (New York: Random House, 1956), pp. 173-180; Herbert Solow, "The New York Hotel Strike," *The Nation*, February 28, 1934; James P. Cannon, *History of American Trotskyism* (New York: Pioneer Publishers, 1944), pp. 126-132.

[17] Joseph P. Goldberg, *The Maritime Story: A Study in Labor Management Relations* (Cambridge, Mass.: Harvard University Press, 1958), pp. 110-111, 117; Leo Wolman, *Ebb and Flow of Trade Unions* (New York: National Bureau of Economic Research, 1936), pp. 186-187; *Fortune*, September 1937, pp. 123-128; Cannon, *American Trotskyism*, p. 21.

[18] For Seamen's Church Institute battles and Mink quote, see Richmond, *A Long View from the Left*, pp. 167-180. On Mink see U.S., Congress, House Committee on Un-American Activities, *On Methods of Communist Infiltration* in re H. Res. 282, 82nd Cong., 2nd sess., Valtin testimony, p. 8498; N. Sparks, *The Struggle of the Marine Workers* (New York: International Pamphlets, 1930), pp. 60-62; Marine Workers Industrial Union, *Four Fighting Years* (New York, 1933); *Marine Workers' Voice*, November 1932 to April 1933; Murray Kempton, *Part of Our Time* (New York: Simon and Schuster, 1955), p. 91; Al Richmond to author, September 20, 1975; Goldberg, *Maritime Story*, pp. 127-129; Sam Darcy in *The Communist*, July 1934, pp. 665, 682; Larrowe, *Harry Bridges*, pp. 12-14, 19; Richmond, pp. 215-216; Bernstein II, pp. 259-260.

[19] William H. McPherson, *Labor Relations in the Automobile Industry* (Washington, D. C.: Brookings Institution, 1940), pp. 76-77; Bureau of Census, *Historical Studies* (Washington, D. C., 1960), p. 92. In 1922 average hourly rates in auto and parts industries were 65.7 cents compared to 48.7 cents in manufacturing as a whole; in 1928, 75 cents compared to 56.2 cents. Sidney Fine, *The Automobile Under the Blue Eagle* (Ann Arbor: University of Michigan Press, 1963), pp. 17, 19.

[20] Phil Raymond, Oral History, Michigan Historical Collections, Ann Arbor, pp. 1-5; Robert W. Dunn, *Labor and Automobiles* (New York: International Publishers, 1929), pp. 186-195; on Communist party in Detroit, Homer Martin Papers, and Josephine Gomon, Oral History, p. 7, both in Wayne State University Labor History Archives; *The Communist*, April 1929, p. 182, and January 1932, p. 114; Wolman, *Ebb and Flow*, pp. 174-175; Morris, *Conflict Within AFL*, pp. 23-24; Alex Baskin,

"The Ford Hunger March—1932," *Labor History*, Summer 1972; *New York Times*, March 8, 1932; Philip Bonofsky, *Brother Bill McKie* (New York: International Publishers, 1953), pp. 39, 53, 75; Keith Sward, *The Legend of Henry Ford* (New York: Rinehart, 1948), pp. 231-242; Frank Marquart, Oral History, Wayne State, pp. 2, 10; Marquart, *An Auto Worker's Journal* (University Park: The Pennsylvania State University Press, 1975), pp. 34, 38.

21 Early NRA strikes in Brown Collection and Kraus Papers, Wayne State; Samuel Romer, "That Detroit Strike," *The Nation*, February 15, 1933; Bonofsky, *Brother Bill McKie*, pp. 88-103; John W. Anderson, Oral History, Michigan Historical Collections, pp. 6-12, 20-21; Fine, *Automobile Under Blue Eagle*, pp. 28-29, 176-178; *Business Week* in Sward, *Legend of Henry Ford*, p. 222; "Report of Mayor's Committee on Briggs Strike," February 21, 1933, Mayor's Papers, Burton Historical Collection, Detroit Public Library; Stachel, "Some Lessons of Recent Strike Struggles," *The Communist*, August 1933; "Developing Shop Work in Detroit," *Party Organizer*, July 1933; Fred Thompson, *The IWW: Its First Fifty Years* (Chicago: IWW, 1955), pp. 165-167.

22 Philip Taft, *The AFL from the Death of Gompers to the Merger* (New York: Harper, 1959), pp. 59-60; UAW convention *Proceedings*, 1936, p. 13; *Industrial Unionism* (CIO pamphlet, 1935), p. 16; AFL correspondence in Fine, *Automobile Under Blue Eagle*, p. 150; *AFL Weekly News Letter*, August 25, 1934; William Green to McWheeney and Lehman, August 21, 1934, and William Green to Paul Smith, January 9, 12, 1935, AFL Papers, Wisconsin Historical Society, Madison.

23 Wyndham Mortimer, *Organize! My Life as a Union Man* (Boston: Beacon Press, 1971), pp. 58-59, 63, 65-66. I had a nodding acquaintance with Mortimer in the auto union. I considered him a dyed-in-the-wool Stalinist factionalist, all the more effective since his clean-cut, Anglo-Saxon appearance and easy manner gave the impression of sincerity and honesty (which, according to his lights, he unquestionably was). He wrote his memoir when he was in his mid-eighties, but could not shake the habits of a lifetime even then. In relating the incident of how he and his friends resolved to join the AFL, he tells of his conversation with Joe Zack, at that time the trade union organizer of the Communist party in Ohio.

> When I told Zack that our TUUL union was joining the AFL and the Metal Trades Council, he argued vociferously against it. Finally I got tired and told him we were joining the AFL and there was no point in arguing the matter further. Seeing that I was determined, he quickly changed. "All right," he told me, "go ahead. . . . But don't forget, you are joining the AFL only to smash it!" I told him flatly that was not my intention. . . . I wanted to build, not destroy. . . . Zack was expelled from the Communist party about a year later. It was eventually revealed that he was an informer and stool pigeon for the FBI. . . . Zack's real name, it turned out, was Joseph Kornfeder. He was an Austrian. (P. 60.)

This is disingenuous to the point of fakery. It misrepresents by insinuation rather than fabrication.

Mortimer was not making a personal decision; the Party line (as will be shown) was changing at this time. Zack wanted to stay with the TUUL policy. He had been an advocate of independent revolutionary unions as far back as 1927, as everybody in the Party leadership knew, and it was his recalcitrance on this score that led subsequently to his expulsion. Mortimer's self-righteous declaration that he wanted to build, not destroy, covered over the proposition that in the Third Period, it was the Communist party—not just Joe Zack—that considered the AFL to be fascist.

360

As to Joe Zack's real name being Kornfeder, that too had been common knowledge for years (see Draper II, p. 558), and the practice of using assumed names was not exactly unusual in the Communist party. This could not have been unknown to Mortimer since he himself used the name of Baker inside the Party. One would have thought that he would heed the maxim that one does not talk of rope in the house of the hanged. Finally, there is the insinuation that Zack's proposal to smash the AFL was connected with his being an FBI informer. Zack had been a Party functionary since 1920, and no one believed that he was anything but a Communist revolutionary in all that period. In later years, like a number of ex-Communists, he became a testifier against the Communists at many government hearings. At one of them he said that he had recruited Mortimer into the Party (U.S., Congress, House, *Investigation of Un-American Propaganda, 1944*, H.R. 1311, 78th Cong., 2nd sess). That had nothing to do with Zack's anti-AFL position or his discussion with Mortimer.

²⁴ Harry Dahlheimer, *A History of the Mechanics Educational Society of America* (Detroit: Wayne State University Press, 1941), pp. 1-4, 20-26, 36-37; *Detroit News*, October 13-15, 23-31, 1933; Brown Collection, MESA file; Elizabeth McCracken, Oral History, Michigan Historical Collections, pp. 11-12; *Daily Worker*, October 11, 18, 1933; Fine, *Automobile Under Blue Eagle*, p. 427; John Brophy, *A Miner's Life* (Madison: University of Wisconsin Press, 1964), pp. 102, 259; author's conversations with Matthew Smith in late 1930s.

²⁵ *The Communist*, January 1933, pp. 27, 31.

²⁶ "Comintern Documents on United Front," *The Communist*, May 1935, pp. 471-473.

²⁷ Franz Borkenau, *World Communism* (Ann Arbor: University of Michigan Press, 1962), p. 377; Fritz Heckert in *The Communist International*, April 15, 1933, pp. 211-219; June 1, 1933, pp. 327-338; *Thesis, Reports, Speeches of Thirteenth Plenum ECCI* (New York: Workers Library Publishers, 1934); *Stalin Reports*, Seventeenth Congress of CPSU (New York: International Publishers, 1934), pp. 25-26.

²⁸ *The Communist*, August 1933, pp. 707-725; November 1933, pp. 1163, 1167; May 1934, pp. 446-447; October 1934, p. 983; February 1935, p. 107; *International Press Correspondence*, January 12, 1934, p. 52.

²⁹ *The Communist International*, September 5, 1934, pp. 555-558; March 5, 1935, pp. 183-194; April 5, 1935, pp. 333-343; *International Press Correspondence*, March 23, 1934, pp. 481-482; July 27, 1934, p. 1055; October 12, 1934, pp. 1403-1404; October 5, 1935, pp. 1264-1265; November 2, 1935, pp. 1424-1425.

³⁰ Bonosfky, *Brother Bill McKie*, pp. 56, 59; Anna Rochester, *Labor and Coal* (New York: International Publishers, 1931), p. 227; *The Communist*, May 1930, p. 419; June 1930, pp. 500-501.

³¹ *The Communist*, June 1930, p. 528; October 1931, pp. 838-850; February 1932, p. 112; September 1933, p. 950; October 1934, p. 1005; July 1935, pp. 625-627; October 1936, pp. 968-969; March 1938, pp. 220-221.

³² Arthur M. Schlesinger, Jr., *The Politics of Upheaval* (Boston: Houghton Mifflin, 1960), pp. 199-201; Bell in Donald Drew Egbert and Stow Pearsons, *Socialism and American Life* (Princeton: Princeton University Press, 1952), I, p. 398.

FOUR · *Who Gets The Bird?*

¹ Report of Executive Council of American Federation of Labor, 1934, p. 15; Coleman, *Men and Coal*, p. 148; *United Mine Workers Journal*, June 15, 1933; Kentucky leaflet in Roosevelt Papers, quoted in Schlesinger, *The Coming of the New*

Deal (Boston: Houghton Mifflin, 1959), pp. 139, 402-403; Wieck, quoted in Fine, *Automobile Under Blue Eagle*, p. 230; Gellhorn in Hopkins Papers, quoted in Bernstein II, p. 171.

² Broadus Mitchell, *Depression Decade* (New York: Rinehart, 1947), p. 283, 446; *Survey of Current Business*, March 1934.

³ John V. Spielmans, *Journal of Political Economy*, December 1944, p. 323; U.S. Bureau of the Census, *Historical Statistics* (Washington, D. C.: GPO, 1960), p. 99.

⁴ *Automotive Industries*, September 2, 1933, p. 267; Alfred M. Bingham and Selden Rodman, eds., *Challenge to the New Deal* (New York: Falcon, 1934), pp. 113-115; *New York Times*, August 29, 1933, March 14, 18-21, 23, 1934; *Detroit News*, March 19-21, 23, 1934.

⁵ Irving Bernstein, *New Deal Collective Bargaining* (Berkeley: University of California Press, 1950), pp. 76-83; Franklin D. Roosevelt, *Public Papers and Addresses*, 1934, ed. Samuel I. Rosenman (New York: Random House, 1938), p. 301; Robert R. R. Brooks, *As Steel Goes* (New Haven: Yale University Press, 1940), pp. 46-74; Carroll R. Daugherty et al, *Economics of Iron and Steel Industry* (New York: McGraw-Hill, 1937), II, pp. 942-977; Harvey O'Connor, *Steel—Dictator* (New York: John Day, 1935), pp. 298-310.

⁶ Bernstein II, pp. 298-315; Maurice Goldbloom et al, *Strikes Under the New Deal* (New York: League for Industrial Democracy, n.d.), pp. 56-63; Robert R. R. Brooks, "The United Textile Workers of America," chapter 10; the *New York Times*, September 3-17, 1934; Margaret Marshall, "Textiles: An NRA Strike," *The Nation*, September 19, 1934, pp. 326-329; Jonathan Mitchell, "Here Comes Gorman!" *The New Republic*, October 3, 1934, pp. 203-204; Alfred M. Bingham, "Industrial War and Peace," *Common Sense*, October 1934, p. 19; William Haskett, "Ideological Radicals, the American Federation of Labor and Federal Labor Policy in the Strikes of 1934," Diss. University of California, L. A., 1957, pp. 310-330.

⁷ According to David J. McDonald, the UMW treasury stood at $150,000 that year (*Union Man*, Dutton, 1969, p. 72).

⁸ Coleman, *Men and Coal*, pp. 148-152; Alinsky, *John L. Lewis*, p. 71; Max D. Danish, *World of David Dubinsky*, pp. 75-82; Matthew Josephson, *Sidney Hillman* (Garden City: Doubleday, 1952), pp. 363-366.

⁹ "Electric Auto-Lite," *Fortune*, October 1936, pp. 99-104; Fine, *Automobile Under Blue Eagle*, pp. 274-283; A. J. Muste, "The Battle of Toledo," *The Nation*, June 6, 1934, pp. 639-640; Louis F. Budenz in Bingham and Rodman, *Challenge to New Deal*, pp. 100-106; William Haskett, "Ideological Radicals" pp. 166-192; Bernstein II, pp. 218-229 (Auto-Lite strike), and 229-252 (Minneapolis truckers); Charles R. Walker, *American City* (New York: Farrar and Rinehart, 1937); "Revolt in the Northwest," *Fortune*, April 1936, pp. 112-119; Walter Galenson, *CIO Challenge to the AFL* (Cambridge: Harvard University Press, 1960), pp. 478-486 [hereafter cited as Galenson]; Cannon, *History of American Trotskyism*, pp. 139-168; Herbert Solow, "War in Minneapolis," *The Nation*, August 8, 1934, pp. 160-161; Meridel Le Sueur, *North Star Country* (New York: Buell, Sloan, 1945), pp. 289-297; Bruce Minton and John Stuart, *Men Who Lead Labor* (New York: Modern Age, 1937), pp. 172-202; Paul Eliel, *The Waterfront and General Strikes* (San Francisco: Industrial Association, 1934); Frances Perkins, *The Roosevelt I Knew* (New York: Viking, 1946), pp. 315-319; Larrowe, *Harry Bridges*, pp. 32-137; Goldberg, *Maritime Story*, pp. 134-141; Yellen, *Strike Struggles*, pp. 327-358; Louis Howe to Roosevelt, July 15-16; Frances Perkins to Roosevelt, July 14-17, Roosevelt Papers, Hyde Park, New York; Bernstein

II, pp. 259-298; Sam Darcy on maritime strike, *The Communist*, July 1934, October 1934; *New York Times*, July 17-21, 1934.

¹⁰ Quote in Brooks, *As Steel Goes*, p. 55; Larrowe, *Harry Bridges*, p. 12.

¹¹ Foster, *History of Communist Party*, pp. 274-275; Draper II, pp. 430-432; Browder, Oral History, p. 226. Foster and Browder's accounts are almost laughable in their tendentiousness; valuable, though, for what they leave out as well as for what they put in.

¹² Quotation in Draper II, p. 433; see also pp. 234, 267; Draper I, pp. 307-314; Epstein, *Jew and Communism*, pp. 405-407; Cannon on Foster and Browder: *Fourth International*, Fall 1955, pp. 127-131; on Foster's activities during Browder regime: Gates interview; Browder, Oral History, pp. 381, 386, and *passim*; Bertram Wolfe on Browder, in Starobin, *American Communism in Crisis*, pp. 262, 264; M. J. Olgin, *That Man Browder* (New York: Workers Library Publishers, 1936); Foster, *From Bryan to Stalin*; also Foster, *Pages From a Worker's Life* (New York: International Publishers, 1939); Elizabeth Gurley Flynn, *Labor's Own: William Z. Foster* (New York: New Century, 1949); Paul F. Douglass, *Six Upon the World* (Boston: Little Brown, 1954), pp. 57-123; David Brody, *Steelworkers in America: The Nonunion Era* (Cambridge, Mass.: Harvard University Press, 1960), pp. 245-246.

¹³ Schlesinger, *Politics of Upheaval*, chapters 10 and 11; *The Nation*, editorial, July 3, 1945.

¹⁴ De Caux, *Labor Radical*, p. 219; Bernstein, II, p. 452; Lahey, Oral History, p. 99; Brophy, Oral History, p. 677; Murray Kempton, *Part of Our Time*, p. 78; U.S., Congress, House Committee on Un-American Activities, *Hearings Regarding Communism in the United States Government*, 81st Cong., 2nd sess., 1950, II, pp. 2853-2854.

¹⁵ Foster, *History of Communist Party*, pp. 349-350; Williamson, *Dangerous Scot*, pp. 125-126; Galenson, p. 86; U.S., Congress, Senate, subcommittee of Committee on the Judiciary, *Subversive Influence of Certain Labor Organizations*, hearings to investigate administration of Internal Security Act, 83rd Cong., testimony of Arthur G. McDowell, December 21, 1953.

¹⁶ Alinsky, *John L. Lewis*, pp. 152-153.

¹⁷ Danish, *World of David Dubinsky*, p. 137; "We've Got the Reds on the Run," *The American magazine*, September 1948.

¹⁸ An undated official tabulation of Socialist party members in auto (probably referring to mid-1937) read as follows: "Detroit 85, Flint 13, Hamtramck 3, Milwaukee 4" (Bell Papers, Box 30). The author affirms, of his own knowledge, that these are optimum figures. The Communist membership was ten times as large. Stachel estimated that the CP had 1,500 members in auto in 1938 (*The Communist*, March 1938, p. 225). Aside from the small number of Socialists available for organizational pioneering was the character of their activities. They operated not in party factions, but as supreme individualists. When they got immersed in union activities, their connections with the party became ephemeral, often merely ceremonial. Marquart later lamented this absorptive process; when Socialists got active in unions, he said, "they forgot about their socialist orientation" (Marquart, Oral History, p. 15). So far as Lewis or other union heads were concerned, there were not too many Socialists available, and those that were available were of a different status than Communists. When the official put a Socialist on the payroll, he had no political problems with him, but he was securing the services of an individual, not of a network.

¹⁹ Quotation: Bernstein I, p. 123. When John Owens addressed the Goodyear

rubber strikers in February 1936, when Ora Gasaway tried to instruct the auto workers on constitution-making at the Milwaukee convention in 1937—they were barely tolerated, and then only because they were Lewis's emissaries. Mine-official directorship was also one of the big reasons for the Little Steel strike debacle. Running a strike against the determined resistance of a Eugene Grace and a Tom Girdler was something for which Lewis spear-carriers had little training and less aptitude. (See Stolberg, *Story of the CIO*, p. 87; Williamson, *Dangerous Scot*, p. 130; Alinsky, *John L. Lewis*, p. 256.)

[20] *Steel Labor*, July 28, 1939; Lloyd Ulman, *The Government of the Steel Workers Union* (New York: John Wiley, 1962), pp. 6, 15-21; John Brophy, *A Miner's Life* (Madison: University of Wisconsin Press, 1964), pp. 259, 289.

[21] In the November 1940 executive board meeting preceding the CIO convention at which Lewis stepped down, there were bitter exchanges between right-wing representatives and Lewis. At one point Lewis turned on Emil Rieve, president of the United Textile Workers, with the accusation that the textile organization campaign, to which the mine union had contributed $200,000, was "the only great [CIO] campaign that failed" (*CIO Executive Board Minutes*, November 15-23, 1940, p. 49). It should be noted that the Textile Workers Organizing Committee, headed by Hillman, was the one major campaign from which Communists were excluded. That was not the reason for its failure. There were major obstacles and difficulties. Hillman's refusal to let the Communists in, however, was symptomatic of his attempt to subdue the open-shop South without risking a social conflict.

FIVE · *From Akron to Flint*

[1] *Industrial Unionism* (CIO pamphlet), p. 24: a reprint of minority report and speeches of Lewis and Howard at AFL 55th convention. *Union News Service*, January 20, February 23, April 13, April 20, June 15, 1936; Galenson, pp. 85-86.

[2] John L. Lewis, *Industrial Democracy in Steel*, CIO pamphlet No. 7, n.d., *passim*.

[3] This was all very clear to labor analysts in the heat of the events. (See J. Raymond Walsh, *CIO*, Norton, 1937, p. 112; Frank N. Trager, "Autos: The Battle for Industrial Unionism," January 11, 1937, MS in Norman Thomas Papers, New York Public Library.) Fine (*Sitdown*, p. 147) unnecessarily mystified the issue by quoting Lewis's general remarks made in a different context at a CIO board meeting in December 1935 to support organizational efforts in rubber and auto "as our first thrust," or by adducing the evidence of a conference between UAW and CIO officials in December 1936 on the developing crisis in GM plants. Lewis proved flexible enough to adapt his conduct to the changing situation. This does not negate the proposition that the CIO had a battle strategy and tried to adhere to it. The amount of money that Lewis funneled to the rubber strikers in the first months of 1936, and to the GM strikers a year later, was quite small compared to the amounts placed at Murray's disposal for the steel drive.

[4] Bernstein II, pp. 580-582, 589-602, 608-609; *Historical Statistics*, pp. 73, 409; Broadus Mitchell, *Depression Decade*, pp. 447, 451; Goldberg, *Maritime Story*, pp. 150-162; Galenson, pp. 245-246, 269-273, 433-437; Harold S. Roberts, *The Rubber Workers* (New York: Harper 1944), pp. 147-150; Rose Pesotta, *Bread Upon the Waters* (New York: Dodd, Mead, 1945), pp. 195-227; footnote: John Newton Thurber, *Rubber Workers' History 1933-1955* (United Rubber, Cork, Linoleum and

Plastic Workers, 1955), pp. 33-34; B. J. Widick to author; Harry A. Millis et al, *How Collective Bargaining Works* (New York: Twentieth Century Fund, 1942), pp. 245-246, 269-273, 793-796; Carey, Oral History, pp. 36-42; Brophy, *A Miner's Life*, pp. 274-275; Edward Levinson, *Labor on the March* (New York: Harper, 1938), pp. 143-146; Leuchtenburg, *Roosevelt and New Deal*, pp. 188-189; for opposition to sit-down: United Rubber Workers Convention, *Proceedings*, September 1936, p. 429; Schlesinger, *Politics of Upheaval*, pp. 592-595; James M. Burns, *Roosevelt: The Lion and the Fox* (New York: Harcourt, Brace, 1956), pp. 286-287.

[5] Edward Levinson, *Rise of the Auto Workers* (UAW pamphlet No. 28, November 1946); *Daily Worker*, June 26, 28-30, 1934; *UAW Weekly News Letter*, June 27, 1934; the *New York Times*, June 25, 1934; Fine, *Automobile Under Blue Eagle*, pp. 296-298; *Proceedings* of first constitutional convention, UAW-AFL, Detroit, August 26-31, 1935, pp. 71, 79; Mortimer, *Organize!*, p. 87.

[6] Fine, *Automobile Under Blue Eagle*, pp. 425-426; UAW convention *Proceedings*, 1936, pp. 71-77, 135-143, 159-160; Galenson, pp. 130-132; *New Militant* (Trotskyite weekly), May 9, 1936; Jack Skeels, "Background of UAW Factionalism," *Labor History*, Spring 1961, pp. 170-171; George D. Blackwood, "The United Automobile Workers of America, 1935-1951," Dissertation, University of Chicago, 1951, pp. 50-52.

[7] The rapidly evolving Communist party line was reflected in Communist uncertainties at the convention. The majority passed a resolution for a farmer-labor party; voted down a resolution to back Roosevelt; then after Germer's private warning to Homer Martin, adopted a pro-Roosevelt motion. The delegates, on Mortimer's prompting, defeated the proposal to "expel from membership all known Communists," then passed without any opposition another resolution opposing Fascism, Nazism, and Communism. There were only a handful of Socialists at the convention, and they did not act in concert. UAW convention *Proceedings*, 1936, pp. 29, 39, 124, 160-162, 232, 265; *United Automobile Worker*, May 1936; Frank Cormier and William J. Eaton, *Reuther* (Englewood Cliffs, N. J.: Prentice-Hall, 1970), pp. 60-62, 64; Jean Gould and Lorena Hickok, *Walter Reuther* (New York: Dodd, Mead, 1972), pp. 105-106; Fine, *Sitdown*, pp. 90-91; Blackwood, "United Automobile Workers," p. 54; Irving Howe and B. J. Widick, *The UAW and Walter Reuther* (New York: Random House, 1949), p. 53; Adolph Germer Diary, April 30, May 2, 1936, Wisconsin State Historical Society, Madison; Foster, *History of Communist Party*, p. 333; Starobin, *American Communism in Crisis*, pp. 54, 263; *Sunday Worker*, May 2, 1936; *Daily Worker*, May 4, 5, 8, 1936.

[8] U.S., Congress, Senate, subcommittee of Committee of Judiciary, *Communism in Labor Unions*, hearings in Internal Security, 83rd Cong., 2nd sess., Jan.-Feb. 1954, p. 27; Cormier and Eaton, *Reuther*, p. 67; Fred J. Cook, *Walter Reuther* (New York: Encyclopedia Britannica, 1963), p. 83; Fine, *Sitdown*, pp. 111, 114; Blackwood, "United Automobile Workers," p. 357; Nat Ganley, Oral History, Wayne State, pp. 1-8; Mortimer, *Organize!*, pp. 78, 98, 118.

[9] Marquart, *Auto Worker's Journal*, p. 81; quoted in Galenson, pp. 150-151.

[10] Philip Taft, *Organized Labor in American History* (New York: Harper and Row, 1964), p. 493; Midland edition, *United Automobile Worker*, December 10, 1936; *Detroit News*, November 18-26, December 11-24, 1936; Fine, *Sitdown*, pp. 98, 130; Henry Kraus Papers, Box 7, Wayne State; Merlin D. Bishop, "The Kelsey-Hayes Sit-In Strike," Michigan Historical Collections, Ann Arbor; Richard Frankensteen, Oral History, Wayne State, pp. 32-36; U.S., Congress, House Committee on Un-

American Activities, *Un-American Propaganda Activities*, H. Res. 282, 75th Cong., 3rd sess., 1938, ii, p. 1494.

[11] George F. Addes, Oral History, Wayne State, pp. 14-15. Chaotic condition of UAW: Germer to Brophy, Germer Papers, November 30, 1936.

[12] Pieper letter and replies, Kraus Papers, Boxes 7 and 8; *United Automobile Worker*, November 1936.

[13] Galenson, pp. 152-153. Winn did not quote the telegram accurately, but apparently this is the telegram he was referring to.

[14] *Detroit News*, December 18, 20, 1936; Brophy to Germer, Germer Papers, December 19, 1936. For a different contribution to the hagiology of the strike, in which Lewis is the fountainhead, see Lewis's speech in UAW convention *Proceedings*, 1940, p. 104.

[15] *United Automobile Worker*, November 1936; Germer to Brophy, March 30, 1936, Germer Papers; Fine, *Sitdown*, pp. 117-118.

[16] Henry Kraus, *The Many and the Few*, (Los Angeles: Planten Press, 1947), pp. 78-79; Mortimer, *Organize!* pp. 103-104, 121; Mortimer, Oral History, p. 36; Robert C. Travis, Oral History, pp. 13-15, Michigan Historical Collections.

[17] Cleveland Fisher membership: Williamson, *Dangerous Scot*, p. 108; (see also Fine, *Sitdown*, pp. 368-369. The per capita figures are probably not reliable as to dates in this instance); the *New York Times*, December 29-30, 1936; Mortimer, *Organize!* pp. 125-126.

[18] Roy Reuther, Oral History, p. 15, Wayne State; Carl Haessler, for years head of the Communist-run Federated Press and editor of the Local 174 *West Side Conveyor* during the Reuther-Communist alliance, told Blackwood that William Weinstone, the CP Michigan District Organizer, advised Travis during the 1937 strike ("United Automobile Workers," p. 84n). Simons' letter to his wife in Simons Papers, Wayne State. Browder (Oral History, p. 215) claimed that Hapgood "was a sort of fellow traveler of the Communists" from early days. Gitlow in *I Confess* claimed he was a secret Party member (p. 383). He was generally considered an authentic popular-frontist. Probably the difference between one and the other is sometimes more theoretical than practical. There were other radicals, very important in the strike, who kept their distance from the Communists. Among them were Kermit Johnson, chairman of Chevrolet No. 4, and Genora Johnson head of the Women's Emergency Brigade—both Socialists who later became Trotskyites. There was Ted La Duke who either was, or became after the strike, a Lovestoneite. The inter-radical struggles remained muted, however; they blazed only after the strike. Kraus, who settled many old scores in his book on the strike, took revenge on Kermit Johnson by cutting him out of his leadership role—in the process confusing some labor writers on the point—in the seizure of Chevrolet No. 4. This was a turning-point of the strike. Kermit Johnson gave a full account in an anniversary issue of the Chevrolet local paper, *The Searchlight*, February 11, 1959. His article was reprinted in another anniversary issue on February 5, 1976, and for good measure, the local set aside February 10 as Kermit Johnson Day to commemorate him.

[19] Mortimer, *Organize!* pp. 106-107, 118-120. During the faction fight that followed the strike, Martin tried to compromise Mortimer and Travis by claiming that they looted the account. The charge that Communists diverted funds from union treasuries to various Communist enterprises was made repeatedly, often without any documentation. In one House hearing it was specifically anchored. James Conroy, who had been a United Electrical (UE) union field organizer, as well as a Communist

party member, stated that the UE contributed $1,000 to the Civil Rights Committee in early 1947, and that the minutes of the International Executive Board showed that substantial contributions had been voted to the Joint Anti-Fascist Refugees Committee, the *Daily Worker* and to the support of Communist party candidates running for public office. He also charged that the UE acted as an "employment agency" for displaced Communists: Carl Marzani was taken on as a film consultant after he was fired from his job in the State Department; Herbert Morais was employed after quitting his teaching job, etc. (U.S., Congress, House, *Communist Infiltration of UERMWA*, Committee on Education and Labor, 80th Cong., 2nd sess., pp. 84-87). All acquainted with activities in Communist-dominated unions know that such examples can be duplicated many times over. The question is: to what extent can such contributions be considered unethical or improper when openly voted on by union bodies? Most unions make contributions to organizations like the Red Cross, Community Funds, to liberal candidates running for office, and the like. Sometimes such contributions are of a more esoteric nature as when a leading officer has a strong attachment to a particular eleemosynary cause. Conservative or Social Democratic union officers also give employment to personal or political friends, to relatives, etc. What is the difference in principle between the two sets of contributions or actions? It reduces itself to this: An honest poll of the membership would probably show that more often the great majority favored a contribution to a Community Fund, etc., than a contribution to a Communist front organization.

[20] House Committee on Un-American Activities, 75th Cong., 3rd sess., II, pp. 1454-1689 *passim*.

[21] Brophy, *A Miner's Life*, pp. 269-270.

[22] Glazer, *Social Basis of American Communism*, pp. 92, 115; Gitlow, *I Confess*, p. 228; Epstein, *Jew and Communism*, p. 251; Epstein, *Jewish Labor in U.S.A.*, p. 234; *International Press Correspondence*, February 19, 1938, p. 139; Earl Browder testimony, House Special Committee on Un-American Activities, 76th Cong., 1st sess., VII, p. 4284; ownership statement, *Daily Worker*, December 5-6, 1949.

[23] Philip Selznick, *The Organizational Weapon* (New York: McGraw-Hill, 1952), p. 6.

SIX · *Factionalism and Anti-Communism*

[1] Galenson, pp. 32, 650 (note 78); Levinson, *Labor on the March*, p. 315; Addes report to executive board, September 1937, Addes Collection, Wayne State; UAW convention *Proceedings*, 1937, p. 61.

[2] Stolberg, *Story of CIO*, pp. 170-186; Galenson, pp. 150-175; Blackwood, "United Automobile Workers," pp. 85-136; Jack Skeels, "The Development of Political Stability Within the United Auto Workers Union," Dissertation, University of Wisconsin, 1957, pp. 31-99; Fountain, *Union Guy*, pp. 67-106.

[3] *New York Times*, April 3, June 18, 1937; *United Automobile Worker*, March 20, 1937; Edward A. Wieck Papers, MS on sit-down strikes, Box 5, pp. 55-57; and Roy Reuther, Oral History, pp. 10-12, and William Genske, Oral History, p. 9, all at Wayne State; Blackwood, p. 82.

[4] *United Automobile Worker*, May 22, June 19, 1937; Homer Martin letter, June 11, 1937 (Local 121 UAW-CIO Labor Collection), Wisconsin State Historical Society, Madison; *West Side Conveyor*, November 16, 1937.

[5] Brophy, *A Miner's Life*, pp. 268-269; Bernstein II, p. 509.

[6] Galenson, p. 153; Haessler in Stolberg, *Story of CIO*, p. 173; Mortimer, *Organize!* p. 114; Fine, *Sitdown*, p. 111.

[7] Joseph C. Goulden, *Meany* (New York: Atheneum, 1972), p. 121; Galenson, pp. 151-153; Bernstein II, pp. 555-559; *Workers Age*, 1937, *passim*.

[8] Stolberg, *Story of CIO*, p. 161; *United Automobile Worker*, January 22, February 12, 1938; *Workers Age*, January 22, 1938; *Daily Worker*, February 5, 1938.

[9] *Daily Worker*, August 4-6, 1938; *Workers Age*, August 6, 13, 1938; correspondence between Lovestone, his Detroit supporters, and Martin later reproduced in *United Automobile Worker*, February 11 and 18, 1939; Browder materials in Bell Collection, Tamiment Library.

[10] *United Automobile Worker*, September 18, November 27, December 18, 1937; *West Side Conveyor*, November 16, 1937; C. Wright Mills, *The New Men of Power* (New York: Harcourt, Brace 1948), p. 198. Mills wrote, "Once in the earlier days of the UAW, when President Martin refused to name Communists' candidates to central office positions, they called some 200 wildcat strikes to make him look too weak and irresponsible to handle the union."

[11] Williamson, *Dangerous Scot*, p. 104; Addes, Oral History, p. 31.

[12] Quote by Earl Browder, *The Peoples' Front in the United States* (New York: International Publishers, 1938), pp. 176-177; Foster, *The Communist*, September 1939, p. 814; Fountain, *Union Guy*, pp. 69, 85; Williamson, *The Communist*, July 1943, p. 627; Glazer, *Social Basis of American Communism*, p. 219; Williamson in U.S., Congress, House, *Colonization of America's Basic Industries*, report of House Committee on Un-American Activities, September 3, 1954, p. 5; Starobin, *American Communism In Crisis*, pp. 97-98; Foster, *American Trade Unionism* (New York: International Publishers, 1947), p. 282.

[13] Galenson, p. 158; *United Automobile Worker*, March 12, 1938; *West Side Conveyor*, March 15, 1938; Borchardt to GM Locals, Local 121 UAW-CIO Labor Collection.

[14] UAW convention *Proceedings*, 1939, p. 14; Edward Levinson, *Rise of Auto Workers*, p. 16; R. J. Thomas, *Automobile Unionism* (UAW pamphlet No. 28), p. 2.

[15] Fountain, *Union Guy*, pp. 84-85; Galenson, pp. 159-160; *Socialist Appeal*, May 7, 1938; *United Automobile Worker*, April 30, 1938; *Daily Worker*, April 30, 1938; *New York Times*, June 14, July 23, 1938; Frankensteen proposal to UAW officers and board members, April 21, 1938, Kraus Papers. A 20-point program was adopted unanimously by the executive board at its mid-May 1938 meeting that, for the moment, put Martin in a commanding position. The idea and most of the contents for the program originated with a number of Trotskyists and dissident Socialists who had been in the Unity faction. Now, concerned with the Communist threat after the intrigue at the Michigan State CIO convention, and mindful that Martin's positions on national questions coincided approximately with their own (though no one who knew Martin took his political commitments very seriously), they tried to find some means of cooperating with him against the Communists and their allies. Cooperating with Martin, however, was like trying to catch a wraith in a hailstorm. A month after the adoption of the program, Martin was again in a panic that he was about to lose his majority on the executive board. He decided to cut the Gordian knot by suspending and putting on trial the other officers. That was the end of the 20-point program, the end of the Left try at cooperation, and the beginning of the end of Homer Martin. (See *United Automobile Worker*, May 14, 1938 for program; declaration of suspended officers and letters of Addes and Martin-Garst to local financial secretaries, Local 121

UAW-CIO Labor Collection.) National Socialist Party leaders (outside of Michigan) also wanted to support Martin to forestall further Communist encroachments. After the expulsions, many changed their minds. (See Socialist correspondence in Bell Collection; also confidential report of Ben Fischer, June 7, 1938, in Kraus Papers.)

[16] De Caux, *Labor Radical*, pp. 315-316; Williamson, *Dangerous Scot*, p. 104.

[17] Blackwood, "United Automobile Workers," p. 127n; *Daily Worker*, April 7, 1939; UAW convention *Proceedings*, 1939, p. 322; Murray-Hillman letter, February 8, 1939, Frankensteen Collection, Box 5, Wayne State. Before the Cleveland convention, Murray and Hillman sent a signed circular letter to all UAW locals denouncing evenhandedly both Stalinite and Lovestoneite Communists for interfering in the affairs of the union.

[18] UAW convention *Proceedings*, 1939, p. 87.

[19] Ibid., pp. 249, 362-363.

[20] Howe and Coser, *American Communist Party*, p. 395.

[21] *New York Times*, January 25, October 26, 1940; Galenson, pp. 218, 637; CIO convention *Proceedings*, Atlantic City, 1940, pp. 24-26, 44, 218-236; De Caux, *Labor Radical*, pp. 347, 361; *Daily Worker*, October 11, 1939; Richmond, *Long View from Left*, p. 243; Josephson, *Sidney Hillman*, pp. 473, 485; David J. Saposs, *Communism in American Politics* (Washington, D. C.: Public Affairs Press, 1960), p. 73; Seidman, *Needle Trades*, pp. 216-217.

[22] Browder, Oral History, p. 376; *The Communist*, August 1940; Foster, *History of Communist Party*, pp. 391-393.

[23] Vernon H. Jensen, *Lumber and Labor* (New York: Farrar and Rinehart, 1945), ch. 12; Galenson, pp. 394, 396; IWA convention *Proceedings*, Aberdeen, October 7-12, 1940, *passim* in pp. 58-116.

[24] Vernon H. Jensen, *Collective Bargaining in the Nonferrous Metals Industry* (Berkeley: Institute of Industrial Relations, University of California, 1955) pp. 6-7.

[25] Mine Mill edition, *CIO News*, February 3, March 17, July 21, 1941; MM convention *Proceedings*, 1941, pp. 404-406, 556-560; Vernon H. Jensen, *Nonferrous Metals Industry Unionism* (Ithaca: New York State School of Industrial and Labor Relations, Cornell University, 1954), chs. 6 and 7.

[26] *UE News*, July 27, 1940; March 22, July 12, 1941; UE convention *Proceedings*, 1940, p. 215, and UE *Proceedings*, 1941, pp. 77-88, 103-113.

[27] UAW convention *Proceedings*, 1939, pp. 105-108; Sward, *Legend of Henry Ford*, pp. 400-429.

[28] UAW convention *Proceedings*, 1940, pp. 293, 301, 425-440, 499; Ganley, Oral History, p. 23.

[29] Mills, *New Men of Power*, pp. 102-106, 111-121, 190-192; R. R. Brooks, *When Labor Organizes*, pp. 260-262; Alvin W. Gouldner, *American Journal of Sociology*, March 1947, pp. 389-392; Ely Chinoy, *Automobile Workers and the American Dream* (Boston: Beacon edition, 1965), pp. 96-109.

SEVEN · *Political Strikes in Defense Period*

[1] Mitchell, *Depression Decade*, pp. 382-385; Tugwell, *Democratic Roosevelt*, pp. 610-611; John H. Ohly Memo, quoted in P. A. C. Koistinen, "The Hammer and the Sword: Labor, the Military, and Industrial Mobilization," Dissertation, University of California, Berkeley, 1964, p. 125; Roosevelt, *Public Papers and Addresses*, 1936, ed. Rosenman (New York: Random House, 1938), pp. 568-569; press conference in

Roosevelt, *Public Papers and Addresses*, 1943, ed. Rosenman (New York: Harper, 1950), p. 569; Burns, *Lion and Fox*, pp. 375, 445.

[2] W. S. Woytinsky, *Employment and Wages in the United States* (New York: Twentieth Century Fund, 1953), p. 655; U.S. Dept. of Labor, *BLS Handbook of Labor Statistics* (Wash., D. C.: GPO, 1950), p. 155; Josephson, *Sidney Hillman*, pp. 504, 520, 523-524; "Strikes in Defense Industries During 1940," *Monthly Labor Review*, April 1941; Joel Seidman, *American Labor from Defense to Reconversion* (Chicago: University of Chicago Press, 1953), pp. 42-43; Arthur P. Allen and Betty V. H. Schneider, *Industrial Relations in the California Aircraft Industry* (Berkeley: Institute of Industrial Relations, University of California, 1956), pp. 11-18; Jack Barbash, *Labor Unions in Action* (New York: Harper, 1948), p. 214; Mortimer, *Organize!*, p. 173.

[3] Seidman, *American Labor*, p. 55; Taft, *The AFL from Death of Gompers*, p. 215; *CIO News*, March 10, 1941; Josephson, *Sidney Hillman*, p. 542; U.S. Dept. of Labor, BLS, *Report on Work of National Defense Mediation Board, March 19, 1941-January 12, 1942*, bulletin No. 714 (Wash., D. C.: GPO, 1942), pp. 19, 39, 53; BLS, *Cost of Living in 1941*, bulletin No. 710 (GPO, 1942), p. 1; BLS, *Strikes in 1941 and Strikes Affecting Defense Production*, bulletin No. 711 (GPO, 1942), pp. 1, 4; BLS, *Work Stoppages Caused by Labor-Management Disputes in 1945*, bulletin No. 878 (GPO, 1946), p. 6; U.S. Civilian Production Administration, Demobilization Bureau, Historical Reports No. 23, pp. 172-173; Galenson, *CIO Challenge to AFL*, pp. 116, 181, 219; Koistinen, "Hammer and Sword," pp. 96, 107; William F. Ogburn, ed., *American Society in Wartime* (Chicago: Univ. of Chicago Press, 1943), pp. 45-50; Byron Fairchild and Jonathan Grossman, *The Army and Industrial Manpower* (Wash., D. C.: Office of Chief of Military History, 1959), pp. 59-60.

[4] Quotes cited in Seidman, *American Labor*, pp. 25, 48 (Tobin), 64 (Pearl), 71 (Murray and AFL Executive Council); Rep. Sumners in *New York Times*, March 28, 1941; Koistinen, "Hammer and Sword," pp. 82-85.

[5] *We Work in a Great Tradition at Allis-Chalmers* (company booklet), p. 14; Thomas W. Gavett, *Development of the Labor Movement in Milwaukee* (Madison: University of Wisconsin Press, 1965), pp. 155, 163, 178; Robert W. Ozanne, "The Effects of Communist Leadership on American Trade Unions," Dissertation, University of Wisconsin, 1954, pp. 197, 203; National Labor Relations Board, 12th region, case No. XII R-40, July 12, 1937 (government and union documentary material in *UAW Local 248 Papers*, Wayne State; U.S., Congress, Senate, Subcomm. of Committee on Judiciary, *Subversive Influence in Certain Labor Organizations*, 83rd Cong., McDowell testimony, December 21, 1953.

[6] 1939 and 1940 agreements in *UAW Local 248 Papers*; *Wisconsin CIO News* (also at Wayne State), April 24, July 3, 1939, May 6, 1940.

[7] Gavett, *Labor Movement in Milwaukee*, p. 181; Industrial Union Council, July 20, November 23, 1938, *UAW Local 248 Papers; Wisconsin CIO News*, May 7, August 9, 1938; Josephson, *Sidney Hillman*, p. 539; Allis-Chalmers' statement before House Committee on Education and Labor, February 24, 1947 (in publication issued by company), p. 11; Ozanne, "Effects of Communist Leadership," p. 291.

[8] Ozanne, pp. 277-281; *Wisconsin CIO News*, all issues, September and October 1938, February 12, 1940, February 17, 1941, July 3, 1941; Donald A. Schwarz, "The 1941 Strike at Allis Chalmers," paper for Master's degree, University of Wisconsin, 1943, pp. 35-36.

[9] *Wisconsin CIO News*, May 22, August 20, September 3, October 8, October 15,

1938; testimony of Farrell Schnering, ex-Communist Local 248 member, quoted in Ozanne, pp. 295-296.

[10] *Wisconsin CIO News*, December 30, 1940, January 6, January 27, 1941; *Milwaukee Journal*, March 1, March 4, March 6, 1941; Josephson, *Sidney Hillman*, p. 540; National War Labor Board, Panel Report, quoted in Ozanne, pp. 260-269.

[11] *Washington Post*, March 27, 1941; *Milwaukee Journal*, March 28-April 2, 1941; Koistinen, "Hammer and Sword," p. 113; BLS Bulletin No. 714, pp. 98-100.

[12] Congressional report, quoted in Seidman, *American Labor*, p. 44; Lyons, *Red Decade*, pp. 395-396; Kampelman, *Communist Party vs CIO*, p. 26; Davis in *Milwaukee Journal*, April 8, 1941; Josephson, *Sidney Hillman*, p. 540; Budenz, quoted in Gavett, *Labor Movement in Milwaukee*, p. 182, and *Milwaukee Journal*, February 16, 1947.

[13] Ozanne, p. 220.

[14] Allen and Schneider, *Industrial Relations in California*, pp. 14, 27-28; UAW convention *Proceedings*, 1941, pp. 422-438; Mortimer, *Organize!* pp. 180-181; William H. Davis, Oral History, Columbia University, pp. 116-117; Henry L. Stimson Diary, Yale University Library, June 11, 1941; Louis and Richard Perry, *A History of the Los Angeles Labor Movement* (Berkeley: University of California Press, 1963), pp. 421, 424, 514; *New York Times*, June 5, June 10, 1941; *Los Angeles Times*, May 30, June 8, June 10, 1941; Josephson, *Sidney Hillman*, pp. 544-546; Freitag and Michener, Oral Histories, Wayne State; Koistinen, "Hammer and Sword," pp. 114-116; Michener testimony: Cormier and Eaton, *Reuther*, p. 180; *Dear Brother* (Local 683 pamphlet issued by North American Communist leaders); BLS Bulletin No. 714; National War Labor Board #202, North American, Memoranda from Bradshaw and Patterson, Box 13; National Defense Mediation Board, North American Proceedings, June 18-20, 1941, National Archives, Washington, D. C.; Albert A. Blum, *Drafted or Deferred* (Ann Arbor: Bureau of Industrial Relations, Univerity of Michigan, 1967), pp. 199-201; John H. Ohly, *History of Plant Seizures During World War II* (Washington, D. C.: Office of Chief of Military History, n.d.), 1, pp. 14-34.

[15] *Seattle Post-Intelligencer*, May 27, June 6, 1941; Jensen, *Lumber and Labor*, pp. 264-266.

[16] Michener, Oral History, p. 27; UAW Convention *Proceedings*, 1941, p. 423; letter from Dorothy Healey to author, February 4, 1974.

[17] Hook, *Heresy, Yes*, p. 33; Deutscher, *Stalin*, p. 447.

[18] *Daily Worker*, June 17, 1941; Coleman, *Men and Coal*, p. 201; Pressman, Oral History, p. 320; *CIO News*, June 16, 1941; CIO Convention *Proceedings*, 1941, pp. 108-110; *Labor* quoted in Seidman, *American Labor*, p. 49.

[19] Cormier and Eaton, *Reuther*, p. 177; *New York Times*, August 6, 8, 14, 1941; *Michigan Labor Leader*, September 8, 1939, May 23, August 1, 1941.

[20] Allis-Chalmers: *New York Times*, August 14, 1941; UAW convention *Proceedings*, 1941, pp. 53-58, 78-99, 108-117, 303-332, 573-574; Skeels, "Political Stability Within UAW," pp. 141-144; *Fortune*, "The Gas-Engine Union," November 1941.

[21] Reuther Personality: Eli Ginzberg, *The Labor Leader* (New York: Macmillan, 1948), pp. 7-8, 11-12; Jean Gould and Lorena Hickok, *Walter Reuther* (New York: Dodd, Mead, 1972), p. 158; Bell Collection, Box 30, Tamiment Library; Egbert and Persons, *Socialism and American Life*, I, p. 391; Cormier and Eaton, pp. 132-140, 183; anti-Reuther handbill in Brown collection, 1941 convention, Wayne State.

[22] North American: Frankensteen, Oral History, Wayne State, p. 56; UAW convention *Proceedings*, 1941, pp. 243-268, 400-446, 457, 772; Skeels, pp. 136-138.

[23] Anti-Communist debate: UAW convention *Proceedings*, 1941, pp. 688-710, 712-714, 724, 772; Skeels, pp. 139-141; Victor Reuther letter: Walter Reuther was quoted earlier that year in an interview printed in the *Detroit News* as saying that Victor had written the letter in a burst of adolescent enthusiasm, and that he did not agree with the letter now or at the time it had been written. This led to a quarrel between the brothers; the letter had been signed "Vic and Wal." Victor Reuther, in his memoirs, rested his claim on the letter ending simply with "Carry on the fight," while "for a Soviet America" had been gratuitously inserted. Even if this is so, it does not negate the nature of the letter as a panagyric to Soviet Russia building the great socialist society and genuine proletarian democracy. (See Victor G. Reuther, *The Brothers Reuther and the Story of the UAW* [Boston: Houghton Mifflin, 1976], pp. 216-219); ACTU: Richard Ward, "The Role of the Association of Catholic Trade Unionists in the American Labor Movement," Dissertation, University of Michigan, 1958, pp. 34-35, 58, 91, 233, 245; Michael Harrington, "Catholics in the Labor Movement," *Labor History,* Fall 1960; *Fortune,* "The Labor Priests," January 1949; UAW convention *Proceedings*, 1941, pp. 85, 690.

[24] CIO Intervention and UAW Neutrals: *New York Times*, August 8, 1941; Cormier and Eaton, p. 178; *Socialist Call,* August 17, 1941; UAW convention *Proceedings,* 1941, pp. 711-712; *United Automobile Worker,* August 15, 1941.

EIGHT · *War Years—I*

[1] National unity: Seidman, *American Labor,* p. 131; Frederick Lewis Allen, *The Big Change* (New York: Bantam edition, 1946), p. 143; In Seidman: Frank P. Graham quote, p. 99; Little Steel formula, pp. 115-120; labor freeze, pp. 160-164; coal settlement, pp. 122-123, 140-141; Lewis Pearl Harbor statement in Alinsky, *John L. Lewis,* p. 247; Daniel J. Tobin to Roosevelt, March 30, 1942, Roosevelt Papers, PPF 1180; coal strike: Colston E. Warne, *Yearbook of American Labor* (New York: Philosophical Library, 1945) I, pp. 278-303; James Wechsler, *Labor Baron* (New York: Morrow, 1944), pp. 214-224; William Davis to Roosevelt, April 28, 1943; Ickes to Roosevelt, July 9, 1943, Roosevelt Papers, OF 407-B; Michigan State CIO *Proceedings,* June 28-July 1, 1943, pp. 136-146; *Detroit News,* July 1, 1943; Truman Committee quotes in Alinsky, pp. 291-295; Smith-Connally Act: *New York Times,* June 26, 1943; *Congressional Record,* June 25, 1943, p. 6489; *Daily Worker,* April 29-May 4, 1943; Emspak to Roosevelt, June 1, 1943, CIO Sec.-Treas. file, Wayne State; National War Labor Board Transcripts, June 2, 1943, p. 262; July 31, 1943, p. 940; Roosevelt Order: *New York Times,* August 17, 19, 1943; CIO convention *Proceedings,* 1943, pp. 105, 153, 157; CIO executive board minutes, October-November 1943, p. 322; Stimson Diary, April 29, 1943.

[2] U.S. Dept. of Labor, Termination Report of War Labor Board, vol. 1, 1947, pp. 443-467; Allen Richards, *War Labor Boards in the Field* (Chapel Hill: University of North Carolina Press, 1953), p. 151; *Monthly Labor Review,* May 1944, p. 927, 935; May 1945, pp. 957, 965; May 1946, pp. 718, 729; CIO executive board minutes, June 1944, p. 167; November 1944, p. 49; March 1945, pp. 8, 89; George W. Taylor in Warne, *American Labor Yearbook,* p. 138; Bureau of Labor Statistics, "Union Membership as a Proportion of Labor Force 1930-1956," Division of Wages and Industrial Relations, January 1958. (Figures projected by Irving Bernstein from Leo Wolman's series, *American Economic Review,* June 1954, pp. 303-304, are lower and probably more accurate. The differences in the two tabulations do not affect the argument of

my study. I used BLS figures because the BLS runs a series that excludes Canadian membership, and gives American membership as a percentage of nonfarm employment. Leo Troy's National Bureau of Economic Research figures do alter my proportions. They give a distorted picture for the 1936-1939 period, however, because Troy bases his data on dues payments. This seriously underrates de facto CIO membership in this period because the auto union was going through an internal crisis, and the steel and other unions had not yet stabilized their dues-collection apparatuses.) Wages and national income: Seidman, *American Labor*, pp. 270-271; H. M. Douty, "A Review of Basic American Labor Conditions," pp. 109-136, and Lenore A. Epstein and Eleanor M. Snyder, "Urban Price Trends," pp. 137-176—both in E. Colston Warne, *Labor in Postwar America* (New York: Remsen Press, 1949); Woytinsky, *Employment and Wages*, table 60, p. 655.

³ Green quoted in Seidman, p. 174; Murray report, CIO convention *Proceedings*, 1942, pp. 43-45; labor representation in Seidman, pp. 176, 178; William J. Schuck, Industry and Advisory Committees of the War Production Board, National Archives, Washington, D. C., pp. 20-23, 42-44, 62-65; George C. Clark, "The strange Story of the Reuther Plan," *Harper's*, May 1942; Walter P. Reuther, *Selected Papers* (New York: Macmillan, 1962), pp. 1-12; Aaron Levenstein, *Labor: Today and Tomorrow* (New York: Knopf, 1945), p. 145; Frances Perkins, *The Roosevelt I Knew* (New York: Viking, 1946), pp. 126-127; Clark Kerr, "Employer Policies in Industrial Relations" in Warne, pp. 43-76.

⁴ John Gates, *The Story of an American Communist* (New York: Thomas Nelson, 1958), pp. 80-81; *Daily Worker*, June 30, July 21, 1941; Foster in *The Communist*, September 1941, p. 799, and October 1941, pp. 851-852; Joel Seidman, "Labor Policy of the Communist Party During World War II," *Industrial and Labor Relations Review*, October 1950.

⁵ Foster in *Daily Worker*, December 8, 1941; Browder, *Communism and National Unity* (Workers Library pamphlet, 1944); Joseph P. Lash, *Eleanor and Franklin* (New York: Signet edition, 1973), pp. 906-907; Jaffe in *Survey*, Spring 1972, p. 40.

⁶ Foster in *Daily Worker*, December 9, 1941; Browder, *Communism and National Unity*; Glazer, *Social Basis of American Communism*, pp. 123, 209; Troy, *Trade Union Membership*, pp. 8, A20-A23.

⁷ *Daily Worker*, March 3, 1942; *The Communist*, July 1942, p. 499, and August 1942, p. 595; *Communists and National Unity* (PM interview with Earl Browder); UAW convention *Proceedings*, 1942, pp. 60-68, 253; Julius Emspak, Oral History, Columbia University, II, p. 293; Browder, *Victory and After* (New York: International Publishers, 1942), pp. 14, 228; Bureau of the Budget, *The United States at War* (Washington, D. C., 1946), p. 51; Browder to 1942 national conference, *The Communist*, January 1943, pp. 20-21, 29; Browder, *Wage Policy in War Production* (Workers Library pamphlet), p. 5; Browder to UE conference, February 23, 1943, Browder Papers in Bell Collection, Tamiment Library; Albert Ramond, *Advanced Management*, October-December 1942, p. 159.

⁸ *UE News*, January 16, July 10, September 11, November 13, 1943; *UE Guide to Wage Payment Plans*, 1943, pp. 4-5; *10 Years of Communist Control of UE* (IUE pamphlet No. 5), pp. 12, 14; CIO convention *Proceedings*, 1943, pp. 152-172; CIO executive board minutes, February 1943, pp. 222-308; Bridges quoted in *10 Years of Communist Control* and in Art Preis, *Labor's Giant Step* (New York: Pathfinder Press, 1972), p. 185.

⁹ Union unrest: *Wage Earner*, March 5, June 11, July 23, 1943; the *New York*

Times, April 10, 1943; UAW convention *Proceedings*, 1943, pp. 132-133, 179-181, 183-186, 207, 225, 231, 467; article from *Detroit Times* quoted in Fountain, *Union Guy*, p. 161; Paul Ste., Marie, in *Detroit News*, March 3, 1943 (see also May 20, 1943); GM Council vote in *United Automobile Worker*, April 15, 1943 (see also May 15, 1943); *How Collective Bargaining Works*, pp. 551-552; J. Frederick Dewhurst and Associates, *America's Needs and Resources* (New York: Twentieth Century Fund, 1947), pp. 13-15, 560-562; UAW executive board minutes, March 10, April 19, 1943; Walter P. Reuther, "Labor's Place in the War Pattern," *New York Times Magazine*, December 13, 1942; Hudson in *The Communist*, November 1943, p. 1011; Ganley, Oral History, p. 40; Murray letter to CIO affiliates, April 13, Murray interview, April 14, 1943, quoted in Nelson N. Lichtenstein, "Industrial Unionism Under the No-Strike Pledge," Dissertation, University of California, Berkeley, 1974, pp. 408-409.

[10] *Monthly Labor Review*, November 1943, p. 957; *Wage Earner*, October 15, 1943; *Socialist Call*, October 22, 1943; Robert Shogan and Tom Craig, *The Detroit Race Riot* (Philadelphia: Chilton, 1964), pp. 70-87; Roi Ottley, *New World A-Coming* (Boston: Houghton Mifflin, 1943), pp. 266-269; Alfred M. Lee and Norman D. Humphrey, *Race Riot* (New York: Dryden, 1943), pp. 46-63; John M. Blum, *V Was for Victory* (New York: Harcourt Brace, 1976), pp. 200-204; Polenberg, *War and Society*, pp. 126-130; Reuther on race riot quoted in Howe and Widick, *UAW and Reuther*, p. 222; *Detroit News*, April 12-15, June 22-23, 1943; UAW convention *Proceedings*, 1943, pp. 370-388, 414-419; Fountain, *Union Guy*, p. 165.

[11] *The Communist*, September, 1941, p. 806; October 1941, p. 889; July 1943, p. 643; Robert E. Kanet, "The Comintern and the 'Negro Question,' " *Survey*, Autumn 1973, pp. 118-122; Wilson Record, *Race and Radicalism* (Ithaca: Cornell University Press, 1964), pp. 120-126; Gunnar Myrdal, *An American Dilemma* (New York: Harper, 1962) I, pp. 409-425; Louis Ruchames, *Race, Jobs and Politics* (New York: Columbia University Press, 1953), pp. 3-21, 91-95; A. Philip Randolph, "Why I Would Not Stand for Reelection," *American Federationist*, July 1940; Herbert Hill, "The Communist Party: Enemy of Negro Equality," *Crisis*, June 1951; Glazer, *Social Basis of American Communism*, p. 175; Ray Marshall, *Industrial and Labor Relations Review*, January 1964, p. 185; Philip S. Foner, *Organized Labor and the Black Worker* (New York: Praeger, 1974), pp. 278-279; Julius Jacobsen, ed., *The Negro and the American Labor Movement* (Garden City: Anchor-Doubleday, 1968), pp. 189-190; Herbert Garfinkel, *When Negroes March* (New York: Atheneum, 1959), chaps. 1 and 2; Jervis Anderson, *A Philip Randolph* (New York: Harcourt Brace, 1973), pp. 229-259.

NINE · *War Years—II*

[1] Browder, *Victory and After*, pp. 83, 112-113; Browder in *The Communist*, January 1944, pp. 3-8; Browder, *Teheran* (New York: International Publishers, 1944), pp. 47, 66, 72-74, 79, 87, 117; on party branches: Williamson, *The Communist*, September 1942, p. 701; party changeover: *The Communist*, February 1944, p. 101; June 1944, p. 506; Starobin, pp. 74-76. The Duclos article printed in the April 1945 issue of *Cahiers du Communisme* has been pointed to as proof that Stalin took the initiative in breaking off the friendly wartime relations with the West. It is not a persuasive argument. The foreign Communist parties were for Stalin auxiliary detachments to exert pressure on their respective governments; neither they nor the (nominally dis-

banded) Comintern were initiators of policy. Had Stalin wanted to signal such a momentous change as a break in friendly relations with the United States government, or to issue a warning that such a step might be taken, it would necessarily have assumed a less Aesopian form. The early date of the Duclos article, before VE Day, before the Potsdam conference, necessarily written before Roosevelt's death, suggests that this masked directive had a limited and preventive purpose: to nip in the bud any possibility that the American Communist movement might break out of its Comintern harness. It should not be forgotten that the French and Italian Communist parties, the two most important parties in the West, continued to cling to the popular front until their expulsions from coalition cabinets after the promulgation of the Truman Doctrine two years later.

[2] CIO convention *Proceedings*, 1943, pp. 82-85, 239-251; CIO executive board minutes, July 1943, pp. 145-150, and October-November 1943, pp. 150-168; *Daily Worker*, August 15, 1943; *Detroit News*, July 1, 1943; Josephson, *Sidney Hillman*, pp. 594-637; Delbert D. Arnold, "The CIO's Role in American Politics, 1936-1948," Dissertation, University of Maryland, 1952, pp. 134-140; MacDonald, *Union Man*, p. 169.

[3] *UE Guide to Political Action* (1944); Joseph Gaer, *The First Round: The Story of the Political Action Committee* (New York: Duell, Sloan and Pearce, 1944), pp. 213, 247; Philip Murray Papers, PAC folders, Catholic University, Washington, D. C.; La Follette Civil Liberties Committee: Robert Wohlforth, Oral History, p. 26; Will W. Alexander, Oral History, pp. 474-487; Gardner Jackson, Oral History, pp. 352-353, Columbia University; Clark Foreman, "Statement of National Citizens PAC," *Antioch Review*, Fall 1944, pp. 473-475.

[4] Josephson, pp. 602, 604; Danish, *World of David Dubinsky*, pp. 140-142, 290-292; Saposs, *Communism in American Politics* (Washington, D. C.: Public Affairs Press, 1960), pp. 75-79; Report of House Committee on Un-American Activities, 78th Cong., 2nd sess., March 29, 1944, pp. 77-79; *New York Times*, September 4, 1943, January 14, 1944; *The Communist*, July 1944, pp. 620-631.

[5] Confidential Memorandum to President by Clark Clifford, November 18, 1947, Clifford Papers, Political File, Box 21, Truman Library; Richard Rovere, "Labor's Political Machine," *Harper's Magazine*, June 1945; Joseph Rosenfarb, "Labor's Role in Election," *Public Opinion Quarterly*, Fall 1944, p. 378; James C. Foster, *The Union Politic, The CIO Political Action Committee* (Columbia, Mo.: University of Missouri Press, 1975), pp. 40-48; J. David Greenstone, *Labor in American Politics* (New York: Vintage edition, 1970), p. 361.

[6] Memorandum from Edwin S. Pauley on Events Leading Up to Election of Harry S Truman as Vice-President, in Jonathan Daniels, Oral History folder, Truman Library; Edward J. Flynn, *You're the Boss* (New York: Viking Press, 1947), p. 179; Flynn Memorandum, May 1944, Rosenman to Roosevelt, March 15, 1944, and Roosevelt to Byrnes, April 8, 1944, Roosevelt Papers, OF 1113, Roosevelt Library; Roosevelt to Hannegan, Roosevelt, *Public Papers and Addresses*, 1944-1945, ed. Rosenman (Harper, 1950), p. 197; Samuel I. Rosenman, *Working with Roosevelt* (New York: Harper, 1952), p. 438; James F. Byrnes, *All in One Lifetime* (New York: Harper, 1958), pp. 223-226; George E. Allen, *Presidents Who Have Known Me* (New York: Simon and Schuster, 1960), pp. 121-136; Josephson, *Sidney Hillman*, pp. 617-618; John M. Blum, *The Price of Vision: Diary of Henry A. Wallace* (Boston: Houghton Mifflin, 1973), pp. 304-305, 317, 365, 371.

[7] Arthur Krock, *New York Times*, July 25, 1944; Krock, Oral History, Columbia

University, p. 90; Harry S Truman, *Memoirs* (Garden City: Doubleday, 1955) I, p. 191; Jonathan Daniels, *The Man from Independence* (Philadelphia: Lippincott, 1950), p. 245; John Morton Blum, *From the Morgenthau Diaries* (Boston: Houghton Mifflin, 1967) III, pp. 280-281; Alben W. Barkley, *That Reminds Me* (Garden City: Doubleday, 1954), pp. 188-191; Grace Tully, *FDR My Boss* (New York: Scribner's, 1949), pp. 275-277; De Caux, *Labor Radical*, p. 442.

8 Curtis D. MacDougall, *Gideon's Army* (New York: Marzani & Munsell, 1965) I, pp. 20-21; De Caux, p. 444; Pressman, Oral History, Columbia University, I, p. 93; *Daily Worker*, July 23-24, 1944; "Browder Questions and Answers," *New Masses*, January 2, 1945; Arnold, "CIO's Role in American Politics," pp. 193-194, 211.

9 CIO executive board, January 27, 1944; Koistinen, "Hammer and Sword," pp. 483-490; *Daily Worker*, January 22, 1944; Bruce Catton, *The War Lords in Washington* (New York: Harcourt, Brace, 1948), pp. 211-225; Roosevelt, *Public Papers and Addresses*, 1944-1945, pp. 36-39, 517-518; Howe and Coser, *American Communist Party*, pp. 431-434; membership: *The Communist*, June 1943, pp. 539-543; *Political Affairs*, January 1945, p. 49; Glazer, pp. 92, 108; Foster, *History of Communist Party*, pp. 421, 437.

TEN · *Communists vs. CIO, 1946-1947*

1 John T. Dunlop, "The Decontrol of Wages and Prices," in Warne, *Labor in Postwar America*, pp. 4-12; Barton J. Bernstein, "The Removal of War Production Controls on Business 1944-1946," *Business History Review*, Summer 1965, pp. 243-260; *NAM News*, September 1, 1945; *Why Wages Must Be Raised* (CIO pamphlet, 1946); *CIO News*, January 21, 1946; U.S., Congress, House, Hearings on *Causes of Labor Disputes*, Committee on Labor, 79th Cong., 2nd sess., 1946, pt. II, pp. 111-112, 223-226, 230-234; "Work Stoppages," *Monthly Labor Review*, May 1947, p. 789; Harvey C. Mansfield, *A Short History of the OPA*, pp. 85, 89; John T. Dunlop, "A Review of Wage-Price Policy," *Review of Economic Statistics*, August 1947, pp. 154-160; NMU *Pilot*, June 9, 1944; *San Francisco Chronicle*, May 26, 1944; *Daily Worker*, April 8, 1945; Robert Lekachman, *The Age of Keynes* (New York: Random House, 1966), pp. 150-151.

2 UAW executive board minutes, January 26, March 5, July 16, August 23, September 10, 1945; United Steel Workers convention *Proceedings*, 1944, pp. 129-139; United Rubber Workers convention *Proceedings*, 1944, pp. 72-79, 137-138; UAW convention *Proceedings*, 1944, pp. 147-225, 235, 247, 468; Addes, Oral History, p. 35; Jack Conway, Oral History, pp. 14-16; *Wage Earner*, June 22, 1945; Reuther, "How to Raise Wages Without Increasing Prices," *Ammunition*, October 1945, also *Selected Papers*, pp. 13-21; House Hearings on *Causes of Labor Disputes*, pt. II, p. 223; Seidman, *American Labor*, p. 230; *ILWU Dispatcher*, June 2, July 28, 1944; *Political Affairs*, April 1945, pp. 692, 697; January 1947, pp. 20-21; *CIO News*, November 19, 1945, May 20, 1946; *United Automobile Worker*, September 1945-May 1946; Warne, *Labor in Postwar America*, pp. 388-391, 502-506; *Detroit News*, February 9, 11, 15, 16, March 26, 1946; *New York Times*, March 15, September 13, 21, 22, October 27, 1946; Barton J. Bernstein, "Walter Reuther and the GM Strike of 1945-46," *Michigan History*, September 1965, pp. 262-263; Transcript of UAW-GM Negotiations 1945-46, UAW-GM Collection, Wayne State; *Daily Worker*, March 15, April 23, 1946; Schwellenbach to Truman, August 12, 1945, Truman Files, OF 1353, Truman Library; Barton J. Bernstein, "The Truman Administration and its Recon-

version Wage Policy," *Labor History*, Fall 1965, p. 223; NMU *Pilot*, September 6, 1946; *Marine Fireman*, November 21, 1946; Murray's explanation of his role, UAW convention *Proceedings*, 1946, pp. 91-101.

³ *Wage Earner*, February 15, March 29 (Webber quote), 1946; James Wechsler, "Labor's Bright Young Man," *Harper's*, March 1948; Murray Kempton, *Part of Our Time*, pp. 295-298; Howe and Widick, *UAW and Reuther*, pp. 187-204; Lahey, *The New Republic*, April 8, 1946; "F. O. B. Detroit," *Fortune*, December 1945; *New York Times*, March 11, 22-28, 1946; UAW convention *Proceedings*, 1946, pp. 91-147, 212-224; Skeels, p. 266.

⁴ Addes, Oral History, p. 34; Frankensteen, Oral History, p. 50; Skeels, pp. 259-260.

⁵ *Public Papers of the Presidents of the United States: Harry S Truman*, 1947 (Wash., D. C.: GPO, 1963), pp. 178-179; Josep M. Jones, *The Fifteen Weeks* (New York: Viking, 1955), pp. 8, 146; Dean Acheson, *Present at the Creation* (New York: Norton, 1969), p. 219; Vandenberg quoted in Eric F. Goldman, *The Crucial Decade* (New York: Knopf, 1956), p. 64; Murray letter, *Truman Papers*, OF 252-I, Truman Library.

⁶ Alonzo Hamby, *Beyond the New Deal* (New York: Columbia University Press, 1973), pp. 151-154, 164-168; Schlesinger in *Life*, July 15, 1946; *New Republic*, May 13, May 20, May 27, June 10, July 1, July 15, 1946; *The Nation*, September 14, 1946; Karl M. Schmidt, *Wallace: Quixotic Crusade* (Syracuse: Syracuse University Press, 1960), pp. 25-29, 261-276; MacDougall, *Gideon's Army*, I, pp. 38, 52, 100, 105, 107, 113, 120-122; Norman D. Markowitz, *The Rise and Fall of the Peoples' Century* (New York: Free Press, 1973), pp. 244-250; Loeb Reports to ADA National Board, September 20, December 3, 1947, ADA Manuscript Collection, Wisconsin State Historical Society; *ADA World*, March 29, May 15, 30, 1947; *Daily Worker*, December 30, 1946; New York *Herald Tribune*, December 30, 1946; Shannon, *Decline of American Communism*, pp. 145-146; Wechsler, *Age of Suspicion* (New York: Random House, 1953), pp. 211-217; Wechsler in *The Progressive*, January 13, 1947; Bendiner in *The Nation*, January 18, 1947; Magil in *New Masses*, January 28, 1947; *PM*, January 6, 9, 1947; *New York Times*, January 5, 1947.

⁷ *Wage Earner*, June 14, 1946; *Detroit News*, June 13, 1946; Addes column, *United Automobile Worker*, July 1946; *Sunday Worker*, sec. 3, June 27, 1948; Michigan CIO council *Proceedings*, 1946.

⁸ Charles A. Madison, *American Labor Leaders* (New York: Ungar, 1950), pp. 295-334; Bernstein, *Turbulent Years*, pp. 441-447; Brophy, *A Miner's Life*, pp. 137, 288; De Caux, *Labor Radical*, p. 474; Alinsky, *John L. Lewis*, p. 222, 266-272; Lahey, Oral History, pp. 100-102, 108; MacDougall, *Gideon's Army*, pp. 106-107.

⁹ CIO convention *Proceedings*, 1946, pp. 111-117; De Caux, p. 475; *New York Times*, November 17, 24, 1946, January 9, 1947; *Wage Earner*, November 22, 1946; *Ternstedt Flash*, June 1946; *Forward* quoted in Shannon, p. 50; *Daily Worker*, November 29, 1946; Dennis to CP June Plenum, *Political Affairs*, August 1947, p. 693.

¹⁰ Kampelman, *Communist Party vs. CIO*, pp. 66, 130-131; *UE News*, January 8, 1947; *New York Times*, February 23, 1947; UE convention *Proceedings*, 1947, pp. 129, 147; NMU *Pilot*, July 5, December 27, 1946; January 14, February 4, 1947; July 30, 1948; NMU convention *Proceedings*, 1947, pp. 292-295, 468-492, 725-765; Jensen, *Nonferrous Metals Industry Unionism*, pp. 173-192, 208; Report to Philip Murray by Committee appointed to investigate the breach within Mine Mill, May 16-17,

1947; Mine Mill convention *Proceedings*, 1947, pp. 206, 218, 277-287; De Caux, p. 470; Hotel and Restaurant and Bartenders convention *Proceedings*, 1947, p. 188.

[11] Jones, *Fifteen Weeks*, pp. 233, 253; Acheson, *Present at Creation*, p. 231; Department of State Bulletin, June 15, 1947, p. 1160; CIO convention *Proceedings*, 1947, pp. 197-204, 258-263, 274-293; Williamson in *Political Affairs*, December 1947, p. 1085.

ELEVEN · *Showdown in Auto and Electrical Unions*

[1] *Wall Street Journal*, September 21, 1946; Harold W. Story, speech at NAM, New York City, December 4, 1947, Allis-Chalmers Company (pamphlet); R. J. Thomas, Hearings before House Committee on Education and Labor, 80th Cong., 1st sess., IV, pp. 2053, 2069; Gavett, *Development of Labor Movement in Milwaukee*, pp. 185-191; *Milwaukee Sentinel*, June 7, October 18, 21, 1946; *Milwaukee Journal*, September 23, 1946; *Wisconsin CIO News*, Loc. 248 ed., September 20, October 4, 18, 25, November 8, 30, 1946; Milwaukee Industrial Union Council, 1946-1947, Wisconsin State Historical Society; Conciliation transcripts, Local 248 Papers, Box 6, Wayne State; UAW executive board minutes, August, October, December 1946, March 1947, Addes Collection; UAW executive board meeting, December 1946, Thomas to author; Thomas letter to locals, February 1947, Thomas Papers; Reuther letter to locals, February 1947, Joe Brown Collection; *Wage Earner*, January 31, February 14, 21, 1947; U.S., Congress, House Committee on Un-American Activities, *Hearings Regarding Communism in Labor Unions*, 80th Cong., 1st sess., February 27, 1947, and *Hearings to Curb or Outlaw the Communist Party*, 80th Cong., 1st sess., March 1947, Sigler testimony, pp. 309-326; *Detroit News*, March 29, 1947; U.S., Congress, House Committee on Education and Labor, *Hearings on Amendments to NLRA*, 80th Cong., 1st sess., III, p. 1394; *Milwaukee Journal*, March 23, 24, 1947; *New York Times*, January 22-25, 28-29, March 24, 1947; Brophy, *A Miner's Life*, p. 290.

[2] UAW *Competitive Shop Organizer*, July 1947; "Defend Your Union," Reuther leaflet opposing FE merger, author's collection; *Wage Earner*, June 27, July 4, July 18, 1947; *United Automobile Worker*, September, October 1947; numerous handbills and brochures between July and November 1947, in author's file; Fountain, *Union Guy*, pp. 205-208; UAW executive board minutes, June 11, 1947; UAW convention *Proceedings*, 1947, pp. 284-285; Skeels, pp. 282-284; FE merger statement, July 16, 1947, Thomas Papers; *New York Times*, June 14, 22, 1947.

[3] Reuther, "How to Beat the Communists," *Collier's*, February 28, 1948; Philip Taft, *Organized Labor in American History* (New York: Harper, 1964), p. 571; Wechsler, "Labor's Bright Young Man," *Harper's*, March 1948; Howe and Widick, *UAW and Walter Reuther*, p. 171; Howe and Coser, *American Communist Party*, pp. 458-459; Williamson in *Political Affairs*, March 1948, pp. 234-235.

[4] Mine Mill references in previous chapters; Robert D. Leiter, "The Fur Workers Union," *Industrial and Labor Relations Review*, January 1950, p. 174; Larrowe, *Harry Bridges*, pp. 351-371; Pressman, Oral History, p. 259.

[5] William Goldsmith, unpublished MS on early electrical unionism, Bell Papers; James M. Matles and James Higgins, *Them and Us* (Englewood Cliffs, N. J.: Prentice-Hall, 1974), pp. 34-37, 44-50; James Carey testimony, Special Subcommittee of House Committee on Education and Labor, *Communist Infiltration of UE*, 80th Cong., 2nd sess., September-October 1948, pp. 15-21; Communist mem-

bership in Glazer, *Social Basis of American Communism*, p. 115; Epstein, *Jew and Communism*, p. 207; Carey, Oral History, pp. 36-42, 69-75; Emspak, Oral History, pp. 61-86, Columbia University.

[6] Troy, *Trade Union Membership*, A-20, A-21; Matles and Higgings, pp. 56-59, 85-99, 194; *How Collective Bargaining Works*, pp. 573, 745; National Recovery Administration, Research and Planning Division, "Henderson Report," p. 23; Emspak, Oral History, pp. 219, 222; *UE News*, April 5, May 3, June 14, 1941; Matles testimony, U.S. Senate Subcommittee on *Communist Domination of Unions*, 82nd Cong., 2nd sess., pp. 490-492; UE convention *Proceedings*, 1938, pp. 117-130; Richard O. Boyer and Herbert M. Morais, *Labor's Untold Story* (New York: Cameron, 1955), p. 161; General Electric Company, *National GE-UE Agreement and Wage Agreement*; Westinghouse Electric Corporation, *Agreement between Westinghouse and UE*; for comparative wages: Woytinsky, *Employment and Wages*, pp. 459-461, and also Saposs, *Communism in American Unions*, pp. 184-185; Jules Backman, *The Economics of the Electrical Machinery Industry* (New York: New York University Press, 1962), p. 250 and *passim*.

Communist publicists, and those more or less sympathetic to their point of view, have insisted that they not only signed the best contracts, but that they ran the most democratic unions. That was the thesis of De Caux (*Labor Radical*, p. 240); and also of James R. Prickett, a young historian who accepted many Communist claims at face value. (*Science and Society*, Summer-Fall 1969, p. 319 and *Industrial Relations*, October 1974, p. 219. Prickett develops his argument at greater length in his doctoral dissertation, "Communists and the Communist Issue in the American Labor Movement," University of California, L.A., 1975.) On the anti-Communist side, many allegations were similarly simplistic. Thus, Arthur J. Goldberg maintained that the Communist union official, "unable to give articulation to the revolutionary hard core of Marxist theory . . . more often than not became a far weaker, more vacillating, more opportunistic leader of labor than the tough-minded nontheoretical, non-Communist labor leader" (*AFL-CIO Labor United*, p. 7). More judiciously, Cyrus Ching, past Federal Mediation Service director, reported that Mine Mill officials accepted during the Korean War Ching's recommendation for a settlement at the Kennecott Copper Company which other negotiators would probably have rejected because the Communists were afraid of being raided at the time by the steel union (Oral History, Columbia University, p. 568). Certainly they made easier settlements when their unions were under fire and their authority was insecure than they would have held out for when their positions were strong. But in similar circumstances, other labor officials have also made weaker bargains. If one were to generalize over the entire period from 1936 to 1950 when Communists were important negotiators in important industries, one would say that their overall performance compared to that of other CIO officials (aside from their démarche in the war period—and they were saved from the worst effects of that because basic wage guidelines were set by government fiat) was merely average.

On their vaunted democracy, Prickett made a misjudgment because he tried to build his thesis, not from direct knowledge of how Communists conducted themselves in unions, but by deductive reasoning: since both the maritime and auto unions were less democratic after the Communists were expelled than they were before, the Communists must have been a force for democracy. (See chap. 12, sec. 5.) The reasoning is faulty and the conclusion is wide of the mark. Anyone acquainted with their conduct when they were in authority was aware of their high-handedness,

379

their campaigns to bury gainsayers under an avalanche of denunciations and slander, the dictatorial regimes they fastened on those unions in which resistance was slight or could be eliminated. Nevertheless, there was a lot of democracy in the woodworkers union when they were in control, a lot of democracy in the UE from 1946 to 1949, and at certain times in other national and local unions whose administrations were in their grip. In all these instances there were opposition factions too strong to be intimidated, too large to be expelled; or, as in the case of the maritime union, an unusually turbulent membership and a competitive AFL union in the field. The pluralism of forces made for democracy. That the maritime and auto unions were less democratic after the Communists were expelled is proof of the efficacy of pluralism, not a testimonial for the democratic practices of the Communists.

[7] *Communist Infiltration of UE*, House subcomm. hearing, p. 35; Carey, *American Magazine*, September 1948; letters from Catholic officials quoted in Matles, *The Members Run this Union*, UE publication No. 94, pp. 34-36; *UE News*, March 22, July 12, July 26, August 2, 1941; UE convention *Proceedings*, 1942, pp. 121-135, 194, 208-230; 1943, pp. 122, 166, 181; 1944, pp. 65, 237; Michael Harrington, "Catholics in the Labor Movement," *Labor History*, fall 1960; Philip Taft, "The ACTU," *Industrial and Labor Relations Review*, January 1949; Joseph Baron incident in Harrington, p. 240; Richard Ward, "Role of the ACTU in American Labor Movement," Dissertation, University of Michigan, 1958, pp. 133-139; *UE News*, August 22, 1949; *Proceedings*, 1946, pp. 101, 157; 1947, pp. 170-171; 1948, pp. 65, 115; 1949, pp. 133, 140; Father Rice, Oral History, quoted in Ronald L. Fillipelli, "The United Electrical, Radio and Machine Workers of America, 1933-1949," Dissertation, Pennsylvania State University, 1970, p. 182; see also pp. 175, 183.

[8] On secession: Block to Murray, October 15, 1948, Carey Papers, Wayne State; on repression: UE convention *Proceedings*, 1947, pp. 129-141, 312-333; on administration competence: Herbert R. Northrup, *Boulwarism* (Ann Arbor: University of Michigan), p. 41.

According to Block's faction report, delegates from 17 locals ignored their instructions to vote for the right wing. Had their 503 votes been reversed, Kelly, the right-wing candidate for president, would have defeated Fitzgerald by a vote of 2,022 to 1,877. His report failed to mention, however, that on the other side, 81 delegates from 26 Canadian locals were barred from entering the country to attend the convention. Had these Fitzgerald supporters been able to cast their 190 votes for him, he would have won by 2,067 to 2,022, even were Block's claims granted. Of course, calculations of this sort are little more than propaganda exercises. Participants on both sides, knowing that the union was on the verge of a split, were disposed to brush aside legal niceties, and were not disposed to pay any attention to instructions from their opponents. Father Rice, for example, in a letter to all ACTU members, advised delegates to disregard any contrary instructions and vote the right-wing ticket. Rice letter and Block report, quoted in Fillipelli, pp. 214, 217-220; see also UE convention *Proceedings*, 1949, pp. 133, 140; Kampelman, p. 138.

[9] Father Rice letter, *UE Organizers Bulletin*, May 1949; *New York Times*, May 9, 1949; Connan to Murray, September 1949, Carey to Murray, September 1949, Philip Murray Papers; CIO convention *Proceedings*, 1949, pp. 301-328; Matles and Higgins, p. 199; GE to Murray, February 1950, Murray Papers; Senate Subcommittee, *Communist Domination of Unions*, pp. 434-435; also Appendix A, pp. 511-513; Westinghouse press release of Gwilyn A. Price speech, November 25, 1955; IUE

convention *Proceedings*, 1950, p. 32; McDonald et al. to Murray, February 22, 1950, and Murray to Westinghouse employees, May 18, 1950, Murray Papers; Newark priest quoted in Harrington, p. 255; *New York Times*, November 22, 1949; *Evangelist* quoted in Carey testimony, *Communist Domination of Unions*, p. 222; IUE convention *Proceedings*, 1950, pp. 135, 145; on T-H affidavits, *New York Times*, October 25, 1949; House Committee on Un-American Activities, 81st Cong., 2nd sess., *Annual Report for 1949*; Hearings in Cincinnati, Ohio Area; Hearings on *Communist Infiltration in Labor Unions*, 81st Cong., 1st and 2nd sess., part i on UE Local 601, part ii on Security Measures Relating to UE Officials; Melvyn Dubofsky, *We Shall Be All: A History of the IWW* (Chicago: Quadrangle, 1969), chaps. 16 and 17.

[10] Troy's figures for the 1950s are not reliable. For 1953, he credits 265,000 for the IUE and 202,000 for UE. According to Ernest De Maio, a UE vice-president, the combined membership of both unions in 1971 (when both had grown) was less than 60 percent of the UE's high membership, which was probably about 425,000-450,000 in 1948. Thus, when the IUE listed its membership as 300,000 and UE as 163,000 in 1971, their combined membership was probably closer to two-thirds of that figure, if that high. De Maio quoted in Frank Emspak, "Breakup of the CIO," p. 355; L. R. Boulware, *What To Do about Communism in Unions* (General Electric Company, 1952), p. 5; Matles and Higgins, Chapter 17.

[11] Starobin, *American Communism in Crisis*, pp. 202-203; Williamson in *Political Affairs*, November 1950, pp. 42-43, 52-53, 57; on Matles break, John Gates interview; John Swift [Gil Green] in *Political Affairs*, April, May 1952, February 1953; Matles and Higgins, pp. 230-231; James McLeish (UE District 4 head), *Questions and Answers on Unification* (in author's file).

TWELVE · *CIO Purge and Aftermath*

[1] Brophy, *A Miner's Life*, p. 294; CIO convention *Proceedings*, 1948, p. 301; *CIO News*, September 6, 1948; *Christian Century*, June 4, 1947; *New York Times*, May 20, 22, June 10, 1947, September 1, October 25, 1948; Sullivan to Truman, June 2, 1947, Clifford Papers, Wallace File, Truman Library; "How Labor Campaigned," *Business Week*, November 13, 1948; *Political Affairs*, January, February 1947; MacDougall, *Gideon's Army*, i, pp. 147-172; Shannon, *Decline of American Communism*, pp. 142-147; Gates in *Political Affairs*, August 1947; *Daily Worker*, August 25-27, September 25-28, 1947; Starobin, *American Communism In Crisis*, pp. 288-289.

[2] *Political Affairs*, December 1947; Jaffe, "Rise and Fall of Browder," *Survey*, Spring 1972, pp. 54-55; *Political Affairs*, March 1948, p. 217; Straight quoted in Shannon, p. 147; MacDougall, pp. 248-249; John Morton Blum, ed., *Price of Vision* (Boston: Houghton Mifflin, 1973), pp. 47-48; Wallace interview quoted in Shannon, p. 147; George Blake Charney to author, September 18, 1973.

[3] CIO Hearings before Committee to Investigate Charges Against the International Longshoremen's and Warehousemen's Union, May 17, 1950, pp. 66-74, 99-101; L. H. Whittemore, *The Man Who Ran the Subways* (New York: Holt, Rinehart, 1968), p. 143; *Washington Post* article reprinted in Arthur M. Schlesinger, ed., *History of American Presidential Elections* (New York: Chelsea House, 1971) iv, pp. 3177-3181; Starobin, pp. 174-177, 292-293.

[4] *New York Times*, January 23, 24, September 1, November 4, 1948; *CIO News*, January 28, August 23, September 6, 1948; *United Automobile Worker*, September

1948; CIO convention *Proceedings*, 1948, p. 276; Arnold, "CIO's Role in American Politics," pp. 305-306; Morton H. Leeds, "The AFL in National Politics," Dissertation, New School for Social Research, 1950, p. 150; Irwin Ross, *The Loneliest Campaign* (New York: New American Library, 1968), pp. 222-224; UE convention *Proceedings*, 1948, pp. 24, 65; MacDougall, *Gideon's Army*, III, pp. 612-613; Starobin, p. 295.

⁵ CIO convention *Proceedings*, 1948, pp. 157-158, 218, 228-250, 263-303; on weak unions: pp. 18, 164, 175, 336, 341-344; on Reuther and Fitzgerald: pp. 171, 181-182; Saposs, *Communism in American Unions*, p. 184; executive board on FE, CIO *Proceedings*, 1949, pp. 334, 347; pre-convention executive board: *New York Times*, November 21, 1948; Williamson in *Political Affairs*, January 1949, p. 35; "Labor Violence—New Style," *Fortune*, July 1949, pp. 151-152; Pat Greathouse, Oral History, p. 25, Wayne State; Jensen, *Nonferrous Metals Industry*, pp. 236-243; *CIO News*, May 23, 1949; Resolution on Duties and Obligations of Members of the Executive Board of the CIO, May 1949 (mimeographed); De Caux, pp. 531-532.

⁶ CIO *Proceedings*, 1949, pp. 269; FE expulsion and enabling resolution: pp. 334-336; Kennedy in CIO *Proceedings*, 1938, p. 133; Marc Karson, *American Labor Unions and Politics* (Carbondale: Southern Illinois University Press, 1958), pp. 48, 305; Perlman and Taft, *History of Labor*, IV, p. 542; Dunne's speech at AFL convention, TUEL Labor Herald pamphlet No. 9; *Proceedings*, 1949, pp. 240, 288; *New York Times*, December 5, 1952; CIO *Proceedings*, 1952, p. 472; Arthur J. Goldberg, *AFL-CIO Labor United* (New York: McGraw-Hill, 1956), p. 73.

⁷ Williamson in *Daily Worker*, December 6-9, 1949; Paul Jacobs, *State of the Unions* (New York: Atheneum, 1963), p. 90; Reports of CIO executive board committees in cases of nine unions, reprinted in U.S. Senate, *Communist Domination of Certain Unions*, 82nd Cong., 1st sess., Doc. 89, 1951; on differences of opinion: *Communist Domination of Certain Unions*, pp. 15, 83, 99; Troy, *Trade Union Membership*, A-22; CIO convention *Proceedings*, 1949, pp. 266-267; for explanations favorable to Communist view, see James R. Prickett, "Some Aspects of the Communist Controversy in the CIO," *Science and Society*, Summer-Fall 1969, pp. 320-321; Emspak, "Breakup of CIO," pp. 388-390; De Caux, *Labor Radical*, p. 547.

⁸ E. Wright Bakke and Clark Kerr, eds., *Unions, Management and the Public* (New York: Harcourt, Brace, 1948), pp. 207-208; Gallup polls quoted in Arthur Kornhauser et al., *Industrial Conflict* (New York: McGraw-Hill, 1954), p. 248; Harry S Truman Public Papers, 1948, pp. 284, 297, 307; *Congressional Record*, 81st Cong., 1st sess., 1949, pp. 8717, 8808; Lewis quoted in Alinsky, p. 338; R. Alton Lee, *Truman and Taft-Hartley* (Lexington: University Press of Kentucky, 1966), chap. 7; Daniel Bell in *Industrial Conflict*, p. 254; Irving Bernstein, "Growth of American Unions," *Labor History*, Spring 1961, p. 135; Ray Marshall, *Labor in the South* (Cambridge: Harvard University Press, 1967), p. 251.

⁹ CIO convention *Proceedings*, 1950, p. 293; La Follette quoted in Henry W. Berger, "American Labor's Foreign Policy in Latin America," Dissertation, University of Wisconsin, 1966, pp. 195-197, 228, 234-267, 300-302, 352, 360, 384; John P. Windmuller, *American Labor and the International Labor Movement 1940 to 1953* (Ithaca: School of Industrial and Labor Relations, Cornell University, 1954), pp. 134-150, 167-170; "European Trade Unions," Brophy Papers, Catholic University; AFL International Labor Relations and Irving Brown reports, 1947-1948, Florence Thorne Papers, Wisconsin State Historical Society; Lens in *The Nation*, July 5, 1965; Berger in *The Nation*, January 16, 1967; Serafino Romualdi, *Presidents and Peons* (New

York: Funk and Wagnalls, 1967); Murray report to 1948 CIO convention, *Proceedings*, pp. 119-121; John P. Windmuller, "The Foreign Policy Conflict in American Labor," *Political Science Quarterly*, June 1967, pp. 205-218; Cormier and Eaton, *Reuther*, pp. 405-419; Joseph C. Goulden, *Meany* (New York: Atheneum, 1972), p. 397; Victor Reuther, *Brothers Reuther*, pp. 412-427, 488-490.

[10] *Proceedings*, Industrial Relations Research Association (IRRA), December 1956, pp. 90-99; Rockefeller Brothers Fund, *The Challenge to America: Its Economic and Social Aspects* (New York: Doubleday, 1958), p. 31; William Serrin, *The Company and the Union* (New York: Knopf, 1973), pp. 153, 202; Statistical Supplement to U.S. Dept. of Commerce, *Survey of Current Business*, vol. 53 (December 1973), pp. 1, 40, 81; "Steel's Strangest Strike," *Fortune*, September 1956; Victor Reuther, p. 302.

[11] *New York Times*, December 2, 1949; NMU *Pilot*, May 6, 20, 1949, July 27, 1950; Goldberg, *Maritime Story*, p. 259; Philip Taft, *Structure and Government of Labor Unions* (Cambridge: Harvard University Press, 1954), pp. 202-205; H. W. Benson in *Labor History*, Spring 1960, pp. 210-215; Dorian J. Fliegel, "Curran's NMU," *The Nation*, January 30, 1967; *Wage Earner*, November 21, December 5, 1947; *United Automobile Worker*, December 1947; Skeels, pp. 303-338; Jack Stieber, *Governing the UAW* (New York: Wiley, 1962), pp. 14-166; *Labor Action* (newspaper of a Trotskyist group that supported Reuther, well informed about union's internal politics), April 18, 1955; UAW convention *Proceedings*, 1949, pp. 149-152, 220; Doll-Sage case: *Proceedings*, 1949, pp. 278-289; *Proceedings*, 1951, pp. 341-356; *Proceedings*, 1955, p. 193; *Searchlight* described in Stieber, p. 143; *Ford Facts*, February 23, March 15, 22, 1952; *Proceedings*, 1953, pp. 119-128; UAW administrative letter in Stieber, p. 146; Frank Marquart, Oral History, p. 38, Wayne State; Brooks in IRRA *Proceedings*, 1956, p. 39; Serrin, pp. 145, 212; Stieber on democracy, pp. 167-170; Leonard Sayles and George Strauss, *The Local Union* (New York: Harper, 1953), pp. 24, 42; Alfred P. Sloan, *My Years with General Motors* (New York: McFadden Books, 1965), pp. 390-396.

[12] Larrowe, *Harry Bridges*, pp. 345-371; June C. Record, "Rise and Fall of a Maritime Union," *Industrial and Labor Relations Review*, October 1956, pp. 81-92; Kampelman, *Communist Party vs. CIO*, pp. 187-188, 198, 214-215, 221-222; CIO convention *Proceedings*, 1950, pp. 103-104, 277-279; *New York Times*, January 3, 1955; Jensen, *Nonferrous Metals Industry Unionism*, pp. 270, 303-304; Robert S. Keitel, "Merger of Mine Mill and Steel," *Labor History*, Spring 1974, pp. 36-43; F. S. O'Brien, "Communist-Dominated Unions in U.S. Since 1950." *Labor History*, Spring 1968, pp. 191-204.

THIRTEEN • *Postscript: Concepts of Labor Development*

[1] Karsh and Garman in Milton Derber and Edwin Young, eds., *Labor and the New Deal* (Madison: University of Wisconsin Press, 1957), pp. 114-115; Richard A. Lester, *As Unions Mature* (Princeton: Princeton University Press, 1958), pp. 21-22; Dubinsky in *Justice*, June 15, 1958; Clinton S. Golden and Harold J. Ruttenberg, *The Dynamics of Industrial Democracy* (New York: Harper, 1942), p. 58; David Brody in Stephen E. Ambrose, *Institutions in Modern America* (Baltimore: Johns Hopkins University Press, 1967), pp. 11-36; Harry A. Millis and Emily C. Brown, *From the Wagner Act to Taft-Hartley* (Chicago: University of Chicago Press, 1950), pp. 3-29; Kornhauser in *Industrial Conflict*, pp. 519-526; William M. Leiserson,

American Trade Union Democracy (New York: Columbia University Press, 1959), p. 68; Selig Perlman, *A Theory of the Labor Movement* (New York: Kelley, 1949), pp. 162, 169; Robert Michels, *Political Parties* (Glencoe, Ill.: Free Press, 1958); Max Weber, "Politics as a Vocation," in Hans Gerth and C. Wright Mills, *From Max Weber* (New York: Oxford University Press, 1946); Alvin W. Gouldner, *American Political Science Review*, No. 2, 1955, p. 506.

[2] Seymour Martin Lipset et al., *Union Democracy* (Glencoe, Ill.: Free Press, 1956), pp. 3-16, 400-418; Lipset, *Political Man* (Garden City: Doubleday-Anchor, 1963), pp. 387-436; Lewis quoted in Joel Seidman, *Democracy in the Labor Movement* (Ithaca: School of Industrial and Labor Relations, Cornell University, 1969), pp. 11-12; and in Leiserson, p. 244; Bridges quoted in Sidney Lens, *The Crisis of American Labor* (New York: Sagamore Press, 1959), p. 69; Sumner H. Schlichter, *Challenge of Industrial Relations* (Ithaca: Cornell University Press, 1947), p. 114; Robert F. Hoxie, *Trade Unionism in the United States* (New York: Appleton, 1924), p. 183; George Strauss, "Control by the Membership in Building Trades Unions," in Richard A. Lester, *Labor: Readings on Major Issues* (New York: Random House, 1969), pp. 170-184; Seidman in Proceedings of Industrial Relations Research Association, 1952, p. 154; V. L. Allen quoted in *Union Democracy*, p. 408; *American Journal of Sociology*, May 1956 special issue on labor unions; Franz L. Neumann, "Approaches to the Study of Political Power," *Political Science Quarterly*, June 1950, pp. 161-180.

There is no necessary juxtaposition between bureaucratization and union officials' venality, extortion, bribe-taking, alliances with the underworld, terrorization of opponents, big salaries, looting of union treasuries, "sweetheart" agreements and other forms of corrupt collusion with employers. The two phenomena are often yoked together in journalistic writing and indeed, are often intertwined. They are nonetheless distinct, discrete phenomena. The auto union under Reuther has been offered as a classic study in the development of bureaucracy and authoritarianism; yet the auto union is clinically free of the kind of malfeasances disclosed by the Senate McClellan Committee. In the one important instance, when there were reports that Richard Grosser, the regional director in Toledo, was engaged in shady business ventures, he was painlessly eased out of the officialdom. Moreover, racketeering is a unique American contribution to western labor unionism, a mimicking of the turpitude of an untempered business society. In none of the European unions, which also exhibit bureaucratic and oligarchical traits, are officials guilty of these gross corruptions, nor are they paid the overgenerous salaries that are de rigueur in America.

Some have argued that business unionism, in accepting the mores of a business society, makes inevitable the union official's aping the business man with whom he is dealing, up to and including personal enrichment, as well as adoption of questionable methods and allies to achieve that end. It goes without saying that the one can spill over into the other, and sometimes does. But in many activities and pursuits, humanity saves itself from its worst impulses because individuals do not push to their outer limits the logic of their philosophic positions. Most business unionists do not borrow money from employers or join with them in business speculations, not because anything in their system of thought precludes such ventures in free enterprise, but because they know that such undertakings could discredit them with their members and peers. On the other hand, high salaries, high living standards, fraternization with business executives, breed a subtler and formally acceptable form of corruption. Bonds of sentiment and sympathy, strands of common orientation and outlook are fabricated, which is accepted as a complement of business unionism, particularly in the American climate of prevailing middle-class opinion.

³ *Seidman*, p. 5; on Commons theory: article on labor movement in *Encyclopedia of Social Sciences*, and *History of Labor*, I, p. 11; Clark Kerr, "Labor Markets: Their Character and Consequences," *American Economic Review*, May 1950, pp. 278-291; Arthur M. Ross, "The Trade Union as a Wage-Fixing Institution," *American Economic Review*, September 1947, pp. 566-588; Lloyd G. Reynolds, *The Evolution of Wage Structure* (New Haven: Yale University Press, 1956), p. 190; Kerr in G. W. Taylor and F. C. Pierson, eds., *New Concepts in Wage Determination* (New York: McGraw-Hill, 1957), pp. 260-298; Derek C. Bok and John T. Dunlop, *Labor and the American Community* (New York: Simon and Schuster, 1970), p. 285; Selma F. Goldsmith, *Studies in Income and Wealth* (National Bureau of Economic Research), Nos. 13 and 23.

Index

Abt, John, 232, 233
Addes, George F., 110, 135, 141, 192,
    195, 219, 220, 324; no plans for GM,
    116; supports Lewis, 152; attacks
    ACTU, 186; incentive pay, 214ff; no-
    strike pledge, 251; errors of last coali-
    tion, 263; against all radicals, 264;
    Farm Equipment union maneuver,
    276; faction disintegrates, 277
Addes-Thomas-Leonard coalition, 263,
    273. See also Addes, George F.
Alien Registration (Smith) Act, 8; trials
    of Communists under, 15, 354
Allis-Chalmers local, 166; 1941 strike,
    163; hostile management, 168; local
    administrator appointed, 168; Wiscon-
    sin CIO News, 170; In Fact, 170;
    flying squadron, 170; stuffed ballot
    box, 174n; 1946 strike, 272. See also
    Christoffel, Harold, political strikes
Almond, Gabriel, study, 12
Amalgamated Association of Iron, Steel
    and Tin Workers, 75; rank and file
    movement, 84, 89
Amalgamated Clothing Workers, 87, 89.
    See also Hillman, Sidney
Amalgamated Food Workers, 58
American Federation of Labor, 21, 37,
    38, 83, 84, 163; Perlman and Taft on,
    33; and Fur union, 42; 1933 auto cam-
    paign, 66; federal locals, 66; NRA
    strikes, 84; dual unionsim, 89; mem-
    bership figures, 203; relation to elec-
    trical unionists, 280; proscribed
    TUEL, 311. See also Green, William
American Labor Party, 17, 235
American Peace Mobilization, 149-151
Americans for Democratic Action, 145,
    262; some for Eisenhower in 1948,
    297
Anderson, John, 70, 113, 142, 192, 264

anti-Communist resolutions, CIO
    executive board (1939), 145; Wood-
    workers (1941), 148; defeated at UE
    (1941), 151; UAW (1940), 152; ra-
    tionale of anti-Communism, 153, 154,
    277; UAW (1941), 192; CIO (1946),
    267
Association of Catholic Trade Unionists,
    152, 193-194
Auto Workers Union, 63, 67, 70, 75;
    Briggs strike, 64

Baldwin, C. B. (Béanie), 233, 241, 244,
    300
Bass, George, see United Rubber Work-
    ers
Beal, Fred, 35, 38
Bedacht, Max, 91, 137
Bell, Daniel, 80
Benson, Elmer, 234, 261f
Bittelman, Alexander, 25
Bittner, Van, 97, 200, 307
Bridges, Harry, 90, 145, 181, 214, 255,
    280n, 301, 304, 330, 339; 1934
    maritime strike, 61, 88; deportation
    attempts, 89n; incentive pay, 214;
    labor draft, 244; argument on Mar-
    shall Plan, 303; initial affiliation with
    CIO, 347
Brookwood Labor College, 33, 36, 37,
    48, 50n, 53, 110
Brophy, John, 48, 49, 95, 99, 103, 117,
    129; Save the Union Committee, 48;
    GM strike, 123f; Allis-Chalmers
    strike, 274
Browder, Earl, 15, 24, 77, 146, 206;
    biography, 91f; scores Chrysler left
    wingers, 136; jailed in 1940, 145; indi-
    rect correspondence to Roosevelt,
    207; jail sentence commuted, 209;
    production czar proposal, 210; incen-

Browder, Earl (*cont.*)
tive pay, 210; attack on Reuther and
Lewis, 217; Teheran thesis, 230; dis-
bandment of CP, 230; ouster on Mos-
cow's signal, 230n, 231n; Wallace can-
didacy, 242
Brown, Irving, 318, 319
Buckmaster, L. S., *see* United Rubber
Workers
Budenz, Louis, 175, 200
Byrnes, James F., 197, 198, 239, 240

Cannon, James P., 21, 24, 27, 28, 59, 90;
Foster-Cannon bloc, 91
Carey, James B., 98, 317; forced out of
UE presidency, 151; sets up caucus,
268; sketch of, 281; as popular frontist,
286
Chicago Federation of Labor, *see*
Fitzpatrick, John
Christoffel, Harold, 166, 173, 175; jailed
for perjury, 167; at UAW convention,
188ff. *See also* Allis-Chalmers local
Clifford, Clark, 237
Cominform, 9, 299
Comintern, 9, 23; 1928 Congress, 43;
1932 plenum, 71; 1933 plenum, 76
Committee for Industrial Organization
(CIO), 71, 95, 364
Committee on Political Education, 238
Communist party (of France), New
Model Communism, 76; popular
front, 77
Communist party (U.S.), cold war, 3;
conspiracy thesis, 4; origin of, 6;
ethnic composition, 7; leaders and
Stalin, 9; Soviet espionage, 9; membership turnover, 10, 79, 353; 1957
split, 11; members' perceptions, 13;
dissolution in 1944, 14; reconstitution
in 1945, 15; underground organization, 16; membership statistics, 16,
46, 124, 208, 245; witch hunts inside,
17; barred from Minnesota Farm-
Labor Federation, 26; Russian Revolution, 30; 1926 cloakmakers' strike,
40, *see also* Lovestone, Jay and Foster, William Z.; Detroit hunger
march, 63; 1933 Briggs strike, 65;

Communists in first auto locals, 67,
see also Green, William; working
within AFL, 74; Unemployed Councils, 79; "front" organizations, 80f;
1934 maritime strike, 88, *see also*
Bridges, Harry; Stalinization of, 90;
Communists in steel union, 96, 101n;
Communists in rubber union, 107n;
1937 GM strike, 122; seek union
posts, 128; wildcat strikes, 135; back
Roosevelt in 1936, 135; relations with
Communist union officials, 136; maneuver at 1938 Michigan CIO convention, 140; during Stalin-Hitler pact,
143; loss of prominent fellow-
travelers, 146f; wartime *union sacrée*,
206; incentive pay, 212; wartime position on Blacks, 226; for labor draft,
244; permanent no-strike pledge, 249;
and Addes caucus, 278; fate of CP-led
unions, 330f; and social myth, 333;
Communists in Hotel and Restaurant
union, 270n; in CIO, 333; at 1936
UAW convention, 365; initial position
on CIO, 345-346; on immediate demands, 352; hoodlum activities, 353;
on war danger, 354
concepts of labor development, Karsh
and Garman, left influences, 332; Lester, Dubinsky, union maturity, 334;
Kornhauser, cycles of conflict and
stabilization, 335; Leiserson, unions'
lack of security, 335; Perlman, job
consciousness, 336; Weber, Michels,
Lipset, bureaucratization, 336-337;
Kerr, pluralism and wage stabilization, 338, 341-342; Lewis, Bridges,
Beck, Dubinsky, union democracy,
338; Slichter, member satisfaction,
340; business and ideological
unionists, 342-343; Commons school,
336, 343; racketeering and bureaucratism, 384
Congress of Industrial Organization
(CIO), 147, 163, membership figures,
203; fought race discrimination, 222n;
decision to oust Communists, 310;
constitution amended, 311; trials of
Communists, 312; expulsion of CP-led

unions, 314; failure of southern campaign, 316; foreign policy, 317

Connelly, Philip, 177, 180

Curran, Joseph, 235, 236, 244; alliance with ex-Communists, 269; trounces Communists, 269; expels erstwhile allies, 323-324

Daily Worker, 36, 121, 146, 246; circulation, 125

Davies, William H., 175, 179, 203, 248

De Caux, Len, 95, 100, 145, 267, 270, 379

Debs, Eugene V., 5, 7, 93, 332

Dennis, Eugene, 175, 301; on third party, 298ff

Dies, Martin, 121, 236, 237. *See also* House Committee on Un-American Activities

Dillon, Francis, J., 108, 109, 131

Dimitrov, George, 95

Dorner, Hannah, 234, 244

Dreiser, Theodore, 46; Harlan strike, 56

dual unionism, 89. *See also* American Federation of Labor

Dubinsky, David, 95, 131, 133, 235, 330, 334, 339; 1934 campaign, 87; on Communists, 98. *See also* International Ladies Garment Workers

Duclos, Jacques, 15

Emspak, Julius, 200, 209, 213, 244, 283, 286, 301, 307, 346; court convictions of, 293; reversal by Supreme Court, 293

Fair Employment Practices Committee, 227, 228

Farm Equipment union, 275-276, 326; defy CIO order, 309. *See also* Addes, George F., United Automobile Workers

Fitzgerald, Albert, 213, 268, 304, 308

Fitzpatrick, John, 24, 33, 41

Food Workers Industrial Union, 57, 75

Ford Motor Company, 253; 1967 strike, 321f

Foster, William Z., 15, 24, 33, 44, 51, 206, 299, 345, 346; TUEL, 21; 1926

cloakmakers' strike, 40; Foster-Cannon bloc, 91; alliance with Fitzpatrick, 92; 1919 steel strike, 93; North American strike, 183; criticizes Teheran thesis, 231n; third party, 298

Fountain, Clayton, 137, 225

Frankensteen, Richard, 111, 128, 140, 152, 194, 220; at North American strike, 177ff; understanding with Reuther, 184; incentive pay, 214ff; no-strike pledge, 251; withdrawal from leadership, 256

Freiheit, 39

Freitag, Elmer, 177, 178, 180

Fur Workers union, 39, 41, 280n, 331

Ganley, Nat, 111, 114, 152, 220; claim that Reuther was secret Communist, 112n

Gastonia strike (1929), 34, 35; murder of Higgins, 36; trial of strikers, 36. *See also* Beal, Fred

Gates, John, on third party, 298

General Motors Corporation, 1937 strike, 120, 349; Kraus-Mortimer thesis, 118-119; contract with UAW, 134, 139; loan to UAW during 1970 strike, 322; Beckman on 1937 strike, 349; author on 1937 strike, 349-350. *See also* Miley, Paul, and Weinstone, William

Germer, Adolph, 99, 111, 120, 130, 148

Gold, Ben, 41, 280n; initial CIO affiliation, 347

Goldberg, Arthur J., 303, 379

Gompers, Samuel, 24, 157, 203, 310, 314, 342

Green, William, 37, 248; calls for expulsions of Communists, 67; auto board, 84, steel board, 85

Hall, Gus, 96

Hannegan, Robert, 239, 241

Hapgood, Powers, 99, 120, 366

Harding, Gamaliel, 6; Harding-Coolidge era, 26, 31

Haywood, Allan, 190, 312

Haywood, William D., 93, 149

Hillman, Sidney, 95, 135, 144, 241, 314;

Hillman, Sidney (*cont.*)
1934 campaign, 87; 1938 UAW convention, 141; split in New York State CIO, 146; government representative, 158; 1941 Allis-Chalmers strike, 173; North American, 179; PAC, 231; worked with Communists, 232, 236; Roosevelt's agent (1944), 239. *See also* Amalgamated Clothing Workers
Hillquit, Morris, 14, 23, 41, 353
Hoffman, Alfred, 36ff
Hook, Sidney, 3, 182-183
Hotel and Restaurant union, 57, 75
House Committee on Un-American Activities, 121, 260, 328
Howat, Alexander, 24, 50

Ickes, Harold L., 198, 199, 200
incentive pay, 209, 210; War Labor Board on, 210; and productivity, 217. *See also* Browder, Earl
Independent Citizens Committee of the Arts, Sciences, and Professions, 234, 245
Industrial Workers of the World, 7, 20, 33, 352; maritime, 59; Murray strike, 65
International Association of Machinists, 24, 75; contest with UAW, 159
International Confederation of Free Trade Unions, 318
International Labor Defense, 36, 54, 80
International Ladies Garment Workers, 75; Sigman-Dubinsky administration, 39; 1926 cloakmakers' strike, 39; 1934 campaign, 87
International Seamen's Union, 59, 75; Curran rebellion, 108
International Union of Electrical Workers, formed by CIO, 291; ACTU backing, 292; government officials' aid, 292
International Woodworkers union, 147-148

Jackson, Robert H., 3, 159, 179, 351
Jewish Daily Forward, 38, 42, 268
Johnson, Genora, 366
Johnson, Kermit, 366

Keeney, Frank, 48, 52, 53

Khrushchev, Nikita, 11, 14, 18
Knox, Frank, 156, 174
Knudsen, William S., 123
Kraus, Henry, 112, 115, 118f, 120, 131, 177, 366
Krzycki, Leo, 99, 111, 130

Labor's Non-Partisan League, 107, 238
La Follette, Robert M., 25, 26, 28, 31
Lenin, V. I., 5, 12; internationalism, 22; "21 conditions," 23
Leonard, Richard, 140, 186, 191, 194, 220, 264, 324
Lewis, John L., 47, 51, 95, 103, 117, 198, 339; Jacksonville agreement, 49; Illinois revolt against, 50; 1934 campaign, 83; and Communists, 97; challenges steel industry, 104; GM strike, 123; breaks with Roosevelt, 144; warns Communists, 145; 1941 mine strikes, 161; denounced, 163; lashes Hillman on North American strike, 183; Taft-Hartley affidavit, 316; criticizes textile campaign, 364. *See also* United Mine Workers
Liberal party, 236
Little Steel formula, 197, 213
Losovsky, A., 43
Lovestone, Jay, 24, 90, 94, 320; 1926 Passaic strike, 31; 1926 cloakmakers' strike, 40; adviser to Martin, 131; his group's history, 132; support of Bukharin, 132; headed AFL's "CIA," 318
Lovestoneites, 64, 132-133
Lowery, Worth, 148, 153

McCarran Act, 17; board investigation of UE, 295; Mine Mill condemned, 331
McClellan Senate committee, 329
McDonald, David, 101, 312
McGrady, Edward F., 37, 106
Marcantonio, Vito, 228, 235, 299
March-on-Washington, 226
Marine Workers Industrial Union, 60, 61, 75, 90
Marquart, Frank, 63, 112
Marshall, George C., 271
Marshall Plan, 271, 299

Marshall, Ray, 228

Martin, Homer, 116, 117, 123, 128, 129, 130, 168, 346; wildcat strikes, 134, 138; secession from CIO, 140; 20-point program, 368. *See also* Communist party (U.S.)

Marx, Karl, 322; concept of working class, 20

Matles, James, 286, 301; incentive pay, 213; biography of, 282-283; enters IAM, 283; UE organization director, 283; indictments of, 293; denaturalization reversed, 293; break with Communist party, 294

Mazey, Emil, 187, 277

Meany, George, 133, 312, 320, 332

Mechanics Educational Society of America, 68-69, 111

Michener, Lew, 142, 182, 191

Miley, Paul, 186, 349

Mills, C. Wright, 135

Mine, Mill and Smelter Workers, 149, 280n, 313; conflict with steel union, 309; absorbed by steel union, 331

Mink, George, 60

Mortimer, Wyndham, 67, 109, 111, 115, 118-121, 131, 139, 141, 192; Vultee strike, 158; North American strike, 177, 179, 182; exchange with Zack, 360

Murphy, Frank, 64, 113

Murray, Philip, 15, 96, 135, 158, 174, 191, 200, 201, 241, 248, 260, 291, 314; and Communists, 97, 266; Little Steel strike, 101; steel organizing financing, 105; at 1938 UAW convention, 141; scores Orton, 181; demands end of Little Steel formula, 213; incentive pay, 215n, 216; PAC, 231; surprised by postwar strike wave, 254; 1946 support of Thomas, 256; one-man rule, 265; character of, 266-267; removal from UMW vice-presidency, 265; opposes Wallace, 300; speech for Truman, 303; decisive attack on Communists (1948), 305ff

Muste, A. J., 50, 50n; Unemployed Leagues, 78; supporters in 1934

Auto-Lite strike, 88

Myrdal, Gunnar, 222n, 226

National Association of Manufacturers, 248, 321

National Citizens Political Action Committee, 233. *See also* Political Action Committee

National Defense Advisory Commission, 158

National Defense Mediation Board, 160; North American settlement, 181

National Industrial Recovery Act, 66, 82; strike wave, 83; in rubber, 106

National Labor Relations (Wagner) Act, 106, 162, 316

National Maritime Union, 255; Communist faction splits, 269; expulsions following Communist defeat, 323-324. *See also* Curran, Joseph

National Miners Union, 50; Pennsylvania-Ohio strike, 51-52; Harlan strike, 54-55; dissolution of, 75

National Textile Workers, 34ff, 38, 47, 75

Needle Trades Industrial Union, 75

Niebuhr, Reinhold, 3, 145

no-strike pledge, 196, 199, 201, 202, 203

Office of Inter-American Affairs, 318, 319

Office of Price Administration, 249; end of price control, 252

Orton, O. M., 147, 148, 180; lumber strike, 181

Palmer, A. Mitchell, 26

Passaic strike (1926), 31f

Patterson, Robert, 179, 180

Perkins, Frances, 123,199

Perlman, Selig, 33, 336

Pesotta, Rose, 99-100

Political Action Committee, 231, 236, 237; 1944 electoral results, 242; financial contribution, 243; support of Truman, 298

political strikes, 173, 184; Budenz on Allis-Chalmers, 175

Pressman, Lee, 95, 100, 120, 145, 303

Prickett, James R., 379
Pritchett, Harold, 147, 148
Profintern, 21, 43
Progressive Citizens of America, 261;
  urges Wallace presidential run, 300
Progressive Miners of America, 50. *See
  also* Muste, A. J.
Proletarian party, 64, 119

Quill, Michael, 235, 236; joins anti-
  Communists, 301, 301n

race riots, 221, 222
Randolph, A. Philip, resigns from National Negro Congress, 147, 227;
  March-on-Washington, 226
Raymond, Phil, *see* Auto Workers Union
Reed, John, 7
Reuther, Roy, 110, 120, 122, 131
Reuther, Victor, 110, 131, 140, 224, 272,
  322; letter from Russia, 193, 372; incentive pay, 219; "trade union colonialism," 320
Reuther, Walter, 15, 110, 128, 139, 144,
  186, 213, 220, 306, 314, 317, 322, 324,
  346; allied with Communists in 1936-
  1937, 112, 113; Ganley claim, 112n;
  1936 Kelsey-Hayes strike, 114; iden-
  tifies with Hillman, 152; faction in
  1940, 153; understanding with Frankensteen, 184; personality, 190, 257;
  letter from Russia, 193, 372; incentive
  pay, 218; special Black representation, 224; no-strike pledge, 251; radical campaign preceding 1945 GM
  strike, 252; attack on UE leaders, 253;
  wins presidency, 255; nature of red issue, 258-259; 1946 Allis-Chalmers
  strike, 272; wins vote rejecting Farm
  Equipment merger, 276; victory in
  1947, 297; against Wallace candidacy,
  300; speech for Truman, 303; CIO
  president, 312
Rice, Father Charles Owen, 266, 289,
  380; close to Murray, 288; subsidy
  from steel union, 288
Richmond, Al, 14
Rieve, Emil, 202
Robinson, Reid, 149, 150, 213, 267; replaced by Maurice Travis, 269

Rockefeller, Nelson, 318; and Office of
  Inter-American Affairs, 319; Rockefeller Brothers Report, 321
Romualdi, Sarafino, 319
Roosevelt, Franklin D., 67; first New
  Deal, 82; auto labor board, 84; steel
  labor board, 85; textile labor board,
  87; GM strike, 123; new political
  course, 156; Dr. Win-the-War, 157;
  takeover of North American, 179;
  mine strikes, 198; defense czar proposal, 210; "hold the line" order, 216;
  1944 election figures, 243
Rubin, Jay, 57
Russian Revolution, 6, 7, 23

Sailors Union of the Pacific, 59, 255
Seidman, Joel, 196
Selznick, Philip, 125
Serrin, William, 328f, 330
Sigman, Morris, 39, 41
Simons, Bud, 118, 120, 121, 350
sit-down strike, 105, 114
Skeels, Jack, 258
Smith, Matthew, 70, 71
Smith-Connally anti-strike law, 199, 233
Snyder, John W., 248, 252
Socialist (Second) International, 22, 72
Socialist party, 5, 99, 110, 112f, 125,
  193; language federations, 7; relations
  with unionists, 137
Socialists, 29, 30, 368; in Workers Al-
  liance, 78; in 1912 AFL, 125; in CIO,
  333
Soviet espionage, 18
Stachel, Jack, 55, 74, 94
Stalin, Joseph, 5, 10, 24; Zinoviev-
  Kamenev-Stalin bloc, 25, 32; Stalin-
  Bukharin bloc, 27; break with Bukha-
  rin, 43; Third Period and social fas-
  cism, 44; and Hitler, 73; and Laval, 76
Starobin, Joseph, 16, 242
Steel and Metal Workers Industrial
  Union, 75, 89
Steel Workers Organizing Committee,
  95, 100, 101n, 103; Little Steel strike,
  101, 364; became United Steel Work-
  ers, 100-101; accord with Little Steel
  162. *See also* Communist party
Steffens, Lincoln, 7

Stimson, Henry L., 156, 159; on Allis-Chalmers, 174; on North American, 179; 1941 mine strikes, 198; 1945 seizure of Goodyear and Firestone, 202

Stolberg, Benjamin, 39, 127, 135, 345

strike statistics, 84, 157, 161, 164, 201; postwar strike wave, 254

Sugar, Maurice, 120

Taft-Hartley Act, 243, 276, 315

Taylor, George W., 248

Thomas, Norman, 31, 144, 324

Thomas, R. J., 135, 141, 159, 174, 186, 213, 221, 255, 257, 259, 324; 1946 Allis-Chalmers strike, 274

Tighe, Michael, 84, 103

Tito, 5

Tobin, Daniel, 163, 197

Trade Union Educational League, 21, 24, 27, 45; branded a dual union, 25; in coal, 47-48; in auto, 62

Trade Union Unity League, 44, 47, 51, 57, 74; dissolution of, 75; membership figures, 357-358

Travis, Maurice, 270, 309

Travis, Robert C., 112, 118, 119, 120, 121, 122, 131

Trotsky, Leon, 5, 25; bloc with Zinoviev, 43

Trotskyists, 64; in 1934 Minneapolis truck strikes, 88; "open the books," 252; 20-point program in UAW, 368

Truman, Harry S, 239, 240, 241, 248, 262, 272, 297; steel price increase, 252; Truman Doctrine, 260; federal loyalty program, 260; red issue, 263-264; supports IUE, 292; promise to repeal Taft-Hartley, 298; endorsed by CIO, 303; credits labor for victory, 304

Unemployed Councils, 63, 70, 77

United Automobile Workers, 71, 108, 127; factions in, 131, 134, 138, 257ff; flying squadrons, 140; Vultee strike, 158-159; Ford strike, 161; 1941 Allis-Chalmers strike, 163; debate on Allis-Chalmers, 185ff; North American Aviation local, 176; debate on North American, 189ff; neutrals, 195, 220; Black representation, 221, 223; cancellation of no-strike pledge, 250; rank and file caucus, 251; 1946 Ford and Chrysler settlements, 253; price issue in GM negotiations, 253; Farm Equipment union, 275-276; Reuther administration caucus, 325; Ciampa case, 325-326; expulsion of Doll and Sage, 326; *Searchlight* censored, 327; conflict with Stellato, 327; staff members before Dies Committee, 328; bureaucratization, 329; education center, 330

United Electrical Workers, 108; incentive pay, 211-212; 1946 strikes, 255; Carey ordered to disband caucus, 268; history of, 280ff; Communists in, 282; membership figures and industry penetration, 283ff; major strikes, 284-285; Association of Catholic Trade Unionists in, 287; Father Rice, 288; Carey-Block faction, 288; opposition vote in 1949, 289; ACTU paper endorses secession attempts, 290; formation of rival union by CIO, 291; FBI harassment; 292; indictments of officials, 293; reduced to minor union, 293; Williamson attacks UE leaders, 294; Matles's break with Communist party, 294; Communist revolt against UE leaders, 295; membership 1955-1962, 295f; initial invitation to CIO, 346; dispute over 1949 convention vote, 380. *See also* Matles, James and Emspak, Julius

United Mine Workers, 24, 51; 1931 Harlan strike, 53; 1934 campaign, 87; 1941 strikes, 161, 198; 1929 membership, 358. *See also* Lewis, John L.

United Rubber Workers, start of sitdown strike, 105; 1936 Goodyear strike, 105; NRA upsurge, 106; 1948 power struggle in, 107n; Communist influence in, 107n-108n; Bass opposition, 107n-108n; revolt against Dalrymple and no-strike pledge, 202; army takeover of Goodyear and Firestone, 202

United States Steel Corporation, 284; 1956 strike, 322

United Textile Workers, 32, 34, 36, 37; 1934 general strike, 86. *See also* Roosevelt, Franklin D.

Vinson, Fred, 202

Wage Earner (originally, *Michigan Labor Leader*), 152. *See also* Association of Catholic Trade Unionists, 184, 275n, 276
Wallace, Henry, 15, 238, 239; favored by ranks in 1944, 240; resignation from Truman cabinet, 260; third party, 297; cross-country speaking tour, 298; Blum on Wallace, 301; movement cut down, 301
Walsh, J. Raymond, 233, 241, 300
War Labor Board, 196, 197, 199, 201, 214, 272
War Production Board, 248
Weinstone, William, 137, 138, 346; 1937 GM strike, 350

Weisbord, Albert, 31
Western Federation of Miners, 44, 149
West Virginia Miners union, 53
Wharton, A. O., 66, 103
Widman, Michael, 151
Williamson, John, 96, 137, 230, 278, 294, 295, 301, 308, 346
Willkie, Wendell, 102, 144
Wilson, Edmund, 45, 48
Winn, Frank, 113, 117
Woodcock, Leonard, 194
Workers Alliance, 78f
Workers International Relief, 36, 51, 54, 80
World Federation of Trade Unions, 318

Young Communist League, 36, 63; National Student League, American Youth Congress, 81

Zack, Josesph, 74, 360
Zimmerman, Charles S., 39, 132

Books Published for the Research Institute on International Change, Columbia University*

Diversity in International Communism, Alexander Dallin, ed., in collaboration with the Russian Institute, Columbia University Press, 1963.

Political Succession in the U.S.S.R., Myron Rush, published jointly with the RAND Corporation, Columbia University Press, 1965.

Marxism in Modern France, George Lichtheim, Columbia University Press, 1966.

Power in the Kremlin, Michel Tatu, Viking Press, 1969, was first published in 1967, by Bernard Grasset under the title *Le Pouvoir en U.R.S.S.*, and also in England by William Collins Sons and Co., Ltd. in 1968.

The Soviet Bloc: Unity and Conflict, Zbigniew Brzezinski, revised and enlarged edition, Harvard University Press, 1967.

Vietnam Triangle, Donald Zagoria, Pegasus Press, 1968.

Communism in Malaysia and Singapore, Justus van der Kroef, Nijhoff Publishers, The Hague, 1968.

Radicalismo Cattolico Brasiliano, Ulisse A. Floridi, Istituto Editoriale Del Mediterraneo, 1968.

Stalin and His Generals, Seweryn Bialer, ed., Pegasus Press, 1969.

Marxism and Ethics, Eugene Kamenka, Macmillan and St. Martin's Press, 1969.

Dilemmas of Change in Soviet Politics, Zbigniew Brzezinski, ed. and contributor, Columbia University Press, 1969.

The U.S.S.R. Arms the Third World: Case Studies in Soviet Foreign Policy, Uri Ra'anan, The M. I. T. Press, 1969.

Communists and Their Law, John N. Hazard, University of Chicago Press, 1969.

Fulcrum of Asia, Bhabani Sen Gupta, Pegasus Press, 1970. (Sponsored jointly with the East Asian Institute.)

Le Conflict Sino-Sovietique et l'Europe de l'Est, Jacques Levesque, Les Presses de l'Universite de Montreal, 1970.

Between Two Ages, Zbigniew Brzezinski, Viking Press, 1970.

The Czechoslovak Experiment, Ivan Svitak, Columbia University Press, 1970.

Communist China and Latin America, 1959-1967, Cecil Johnson, Columbia University Press, 1970. (Sponsored jointly with the East Asian Institute.)

Communism and Nationalism in India: M. N. Roy and Comintern Policy in Asia, 1920-1939, John P. Haithcox, Princeton University Press, 1971.

* Formerly the Research Institute on Communist Affairs.

Les Regimes politiques de l'U.R.S.S. et de l'Europe de l'Est, Michel Lesage, Presses Universitaires de France, 1971.

The Bulgarian Communist Party, 1934-1944, Nissan Oren, Columbia University Press, 1971. (Sponsored jointly with the Institute on East Central Europe.)

American Communism in Crisis, 1943-1957, Joseph Starobin, Harvard University Press, 1972.

Sila i Interesi: Vanjska Politika SAD, Radovan Vukadinovic, Centar za Kulturnu Djelatnost Omladine, Zagreb, 1972.

The Changing Party Elite in East Germany, Peter C. Ludz, The M. I. T. Press, 1972.

Jewish Nationality and Soviet Politics, Zvi Gitelman, Princeton University Press, 1972.

Mao Tse-tung and Gandhi, Jayantanuja Bandyopadhyaya, Allied Publisher, 1973.

The U.S.S.R. and the Arabs, the Ideological Dimension, Jaan Pennar, Crane, Russak, and Co. (New York) and Christopher Hurst (London), 1973.

Moskau und die Neue Linke, Klaus Mehnert, Deutsche Verlags-Anstalt, 1973.

Bukharin and the Bolshevik Revolution: A Political Biography, 1888-1938, Stephen F. Cohen, A. Knopf, 1973.

The Soviet Volunteers: Modernization and Bureaucracy in a Public Mass Organization, William E. Odom, Princeton University Press, 1973.

The Origins of the Cultural Revolution. I: Contradictions Among the People 1956-1957, Roderick MacFarquhar, Columbia University Press, 1974.

French Communism, 1920-1972, Ronald Tiersky, Columbia University Press, New York, 1974.

The Last Days of United Pakistan, G. W. Choudhury, Indiana University Press, 1974.

Divided Korea: The Politics of Development 1945-1972, Youngwon A. Kim, Harvard University Press, 1975.

Dissent in the U.S.S.R.: Politics, Ideology, and People, edited by Rudolf L. Tokes, The Johns Hopkins University Press, 1975.

Beyond Marx and Tito: Theory and Practice in Yugoslav Socialism, Sharon Zukin, Cambridge University Press, 1975.

Library of Congress Cataloging in Publication Data

Cochran, Bert, 1916-
  Labor and communism.

  Published for the Research Institute on Inter-
national Change, Columbia University.
  Includes bibliographical references and index.
  1. Trade-unions and communism—United States—History.
I. Columbia University. Research Institute on
International Change.   II. Title.
HX544-C56   331.88'0973   77-071975
ISBN 0-691-04644-1